THE MYSTERY OF FAITH

Edited by James McEvoy and Maurice Hogan SSC

The Mystery of Faith

REFLECTIONS ON THE ENCYCLICAL
ECCLESIA DE EUCHARISTIA

the columba press

First published in 2005 by
the columba press
55A Spruce Avenue, Stillorgan Industrial Park,
Blackrock, Co Dublin
in association with
Irish Centre for Faith and Culture
St Patrick's College, Maynooth

Cover by Bill Bolger
The image on the back cover is a monogram of the name of Jesus ,
acopper engraving from Hieronymus Natalis, *Adnotationes et
meditationes in Evangelia quae in Sacrosancto Missae sacrificio toto anno
leguntur* (Antverpiae: Martinus Nutius, 1595)
in the Russell Library, St Patrick's College, Maynooth.
Origination by The Columba Press
Printed in Ireland by ColourBooks Ltd, Dublin

ISBN 1 85607 487 0

Table of Contents

List of Contributors

Desmond Connell is Archbishop Emeritus of Dublin. He studied Philosophy at the Catholic University of Louvain and was Professor of Philosophy at UCD, where he specialised in Metaphysics. He is the author of a number of publications, among them *Christ Our Life, Pastoral Letters 1988-95* (Four Courts, 1995). He was created a Cardinal in 2001.

Godfried Danneels was ordained for the Diocese of West Flanders and was Professor of Liturgy and Sacraments at the Katholieke Universiteit of Leuven, Belgium. He is Archbishop of Malines-Brussels. He was created a Cardinal in 1983.

Michael Duffy is a Capuchin friar. He studied at UCC and Trier and was active in his Order's formation team from the early 1970s. He taught Liturgy at All Hallows, has conducted retreats for religious and clergy throughout the world and spent three years attached to the Capuchin Delegation in South Korea. Currently he works in the Capuchin Retreat Centre, Ard Mhuire, Co Donegal.

Caroline Farey is a graduate in Philosophy from UCD. She also holds qualifications in theology and catechetics and is a lecturer and course organiser at the Maryvale Institute, Archdiocese of Birmingham. Her pedagogical speciality lies in distance learning in relation to theology and catechetics. She is the author of several publications.

Patrick Gorevan is a priest of the Opus Dei Prelature. He studied in Dublin and Rome and has written a doctoral thesis on the philosophical influences upon the young Karol Wojtyla, especially that of Max Scheler. He is chaplain and teacher of religion in Rosemount school. In recent years he lectured in the Faculty of Philosophy, NUIM, and St Patrick's College, Maynooth. He is the author of a number of publications on philosophical and religious topics.

Edward Holden is a graduate in music from NUI, Maynooth and a composer of church music. He is currently attached to the Department of Music, NUIM.

Maurice Hogan is a member of the Society of St Columban and Professor of Sacred Scripture (Old Testament) at the Pontifical University, Maynooth. He is author of *Seeking Jesus of Nazareth: An Introduction to the Christology of the Four Gospels* (Columba, 2001) and is a member of the Pontifical Biblical Commission.

Thomas Kelly is a Doctor of Philosophy of the Université de Fribourg and a Senior Lecturer in Philosophy at NUI, Maynooth. He is author of a number of books on metaphysics and contemporary philosophy, among them *Language, World and Being* (Columba, 1996).

James McEvoy is a priest of the Diocese of Down and Connor. He has been a Professor of Philosophy at Queen's University, Belfast, the Université Catholique de Louvain, the Pontifical University, Maynooth, and NUIM. He was Director of ICFC from its foundation in 1997-2004. He is currently Professor of Scholastic Philosophy at Queen's University and is the author of numerous publications.

Paul McPartlan is a priest of the Archdiocese of Westminster and lecturer in systematic theology at Heythrop College in the University of London. He is a member of the international Catholic-Methodist ecumenical dialogue and a consultor to the International Anglican-Roman Catholic Commission for Unity and Mission (IARCCUM). He is also a member of the International Theological Commission.

Raymond Moloney is a priest of the Irish Province of the Society of Jesus. He lectures in Systematic Theology at the Milltown Institute, Dublin. His most recent publication on the Mass and the Eucharist is called *Our Splendid Eucharist* (Veritas, 2003).

Michael Mullins is a priest of the Diocese of Waterford and lectures in Scripture at the Pontifical University, Maynooth and the National Centre for Liturgy (Ireland). He was formerly President of St John's College, Waterford, where he was Professor of Sacred Scripture. Among his recent publications is *The Gospel of John: A Commentary* (Columba, 2003).

Francesca Aran Murphy is Reader in Systematic Theology in the Department of Divinity, University of Aberdeen, UK, where she runs an M.Th. in Catholic Studies. Her most recent books are *Art and Intellect in the Philosophy of Etienne Gilson* (Missouri University Press, 2004) and *A Companion to Religious Studies and Theology* (Edinburgh University Press, 2002).

Thomas Norris is a priest of the Diocese of Ossory and a graduate of the Gregorian University, Rome. An expert on John Henry Newman, he lectures in Systematic Theology at the Pontifical University, Maynooth and is a member of the International Theological Commission.

Breda O'Brien writes a weekly column for *The Irish Times*. She is a graduate of the Mater Dei Institute, and recently completed a research Masters in communication at DCU. She is a teacher of Religious

Education and English. She has worked as a researcher in RTÉ, as a video producer and a communications consultant. She is married to Brendan Conroy, and they have four children.

Paul Poupard is a former President of the Institut Catholique de Paris. He is the author of numerous books on Faith and Culture issues and is currently President of the Pontifical Council for Faith and Culture, Rome. He was created a Cardinal in 1985.

Philipp Wolfram Rosemann received his education in Paderborn, Hamburg, London, Belfast and Louvain-la-Neuve. He is author of philosophical works in German, French and English. He is currently Professor of Philosophy at the University of Dallas, Texas.

Michael Spence is a priest of the Diocese of Down and Connor. He was educated at Queen's University, Belfast and at St Patrick's College, Maynooth. He holds an STL from the Pontifical University. He is currently Head of Religion at St Malachy's College, Belfast and Director of Formation in the diocesan seminary.

Liam Walsh is a member of the Irish Province of the Dominicans, a Professor Emeritus of Sacramental Theology of the University of Fribourg, Switzerland. He has published research on the theology of the liturgy and played a part in the Dominican translation of the *Summa* of St Thomas. For some years he held the educational brief of the Dominican Order, visiting each one of its provinces. He is currently Regent of Studies in the Irish Province.

Penelope Woods is Librarian at the Russell Library, St Patrick's College, Maynooth, and Bibliographer. She teaches the History of the Book at under- and post-graduate levels, has published *Maynooth Library Treasures* (1995) and has contributed to the Oxford *DNB*. She gives public lectures on the Library's theological and historical collections.

Introduction

James McEvoy and Maurice Hogan SSC

The Encyclical Letter Ecclesia de Eucharistia

The present collective work has grown out of a conference which was held at St Patrick's College, Maynooth on 'The Church and the Eucharist' (6-8 May, 2004). The event was organised by the Irish Centre for Faith and Culture, which carries out its work chiefly on the Maynooth campus, as an agency for the interrelation of Christian, and especially Catholic, faith with the heritage and culture of present-day Ireland.[1] The conference was conceived as a theological and pastoral follow-up to the encyclical letter, *Ecclesia de Eucharistia*, which was promulgated on Holy Thursday (17 April) 2003.[2] The same event was intended to mark the twenty-fifth year of the Pontificate of Pope John Paul II. From the beginning it was intended to produce a book featuring the lectures delivered at the event.[3] To further their aim of producing a rounded and fully up to date statement of the Catholic doctrine of the Eucharist, the editors of the present work planned the amplification of the lectures through commissioned articles by a number of seasoned writers. Contributors to this volume were requested to pitch their writing for an educated public that would include laypeople and students of theology as well as priests and members of religious communities. It is hoped that numerous readers will find the result useful to their own efforts to penetrate with understanding the church's eucharistic faith – as far as that is possible within the limitations of human insight.

The message of Ecclesia de Eucharistia

The centrality of the Eucharist in the life of God's people is the leading idea of the encyclical, which focuses on the sacrament in its relationship to the church (#7; #31). Rich in doctrinal and pastoral content, it aims to help the faithful deepen their awareness of this great gift and to live it more intensely. The encyclical

builds upon the themes addressed early on in the present pontificate through the apostolic letter *Dominicae Cenae* of 1980, which
was written with priests especially in mind. Some points of doctrine and practice are clarified, while some reductionist tendencies regarding eucharistic faith and the sacramental presence are
criticised (#10): these include the understanding of the Eucharist
as a meal without any sacrificial dimension; the playing down of
the ministerial priesthood, grounded though it is in the apostolic
succession; and the breaching of the link between visible ecclesi-
ial communion and the reception of the sacrament.

The two aspects of sacrifice and nourishment are inseparable
in the Eucharist because they are inherent in its very nature; it is
at one and the same time 'the sacrificial memorial in which the
sacrifice of the cross is perpetuated, and the sacred banquet of
communion with the Lord's body and blood' (#12; cf *Catechism
of the Catholic Church*, #1382). The Mass is a ritual meal, com-
memorating the Last Supper which took place entirely in the
context of Jesus Christ's self-sacrifice, so that the meaning of sacrifice pervades the memorial sacrament.

The Eucharist makes the church and unifies it, building up
the Body of Christ (Jn 6:56; 1 Cor 10:17). To be a communicant in
the Catholic Church presupposes faith and full ecclesial communion. The Eucharist should not be regarded as a means of restor-
ing fractured Christian unity, for to look on it by analogy with
table hospitality would be to create in fact an obstacle to full communion in the truth, and to suggest, misleadingly, that full communion among Christians is closer than it really is at the present
time (#44).

Faithful to the commandment, 'Do this in memory of me' (1
Cor 11:25-6), the church continues to celebrate the Eucharist
through the ages 'until he comes again', and is presently called
to live its eucharistic faith with renewed dedication in the new
millennium. The Eucharist gives an impetus to the journey of
Christians through history and nourishes their hope of eternal
life. For the Eucharist has an essentially eschatological dimension, one that is strongly emphasised in the encyclical.

To help us live the eucharistic mystery with ever greater depth and intensity, Pope John Paul II invites us to take our place 'at the school of the saints, who are the great interpreters of true eucharistic piety', and above all to listen to Mary 'in whom the mystery of the Eucharist appears as a mystery of light … In her we see the world renewed in love' (#62).

Instruction: Sacramentum Redemptionis
The publication of the encyclical was followed up in 2004 by that of an instruction, *Sacramentum Redemptionis*, seeking to promote the reverent celebration of the Mass, and devotion to the Eucharist in accordance with the church's liturgical norms.[4] This document follows (in every sense of the word) the encyclical, as a liturgical interpretation and as an application of its doctrine. To consider the instruction outside of the context of the major document (as has sometimes been the case, rather unfortunately) would be to do violence to its essential meaning, and to make it appear unduly ritualistic and legalistic, thus betraying its true character.

The Year of the Eucharist …
The editors also hope that the publication of this collective volume may prove to be timely and valuable in the 'The Year of the Eucharist'. The Holy Father has proclaimed that the period of time between the World Eucharistic Congress held at Guadalajara, Mexico (10-17 October, 2004) and the Synod of Bishops in October 2005 should be a year of special devotion to the Eucharist and of promotion of its doctrine and catechesis. The theme of the Synod of Bishops will be, 'The Eucharist: source and summit of the life and the mission of the church: celebrating with those of different ethnic background and languages.'

… and the Apostolic Letter Mane Nobiscum Domine
The inauguration of the Year of the Eucharist has been marked by the publication (October, 2004) of an apostolic letter (taking its title from Luke 24:29, 'Stay with us, Lord').[5] The document is

intended to give practical encouragement to parishes and religious communities to renew their eucharistic practice. It is in
that sense another follow-up to *Ecclesia de Eucharistia*. While it
cannot be adequately summarised here, the following points
may be noted.

Evaluation by communities of their progress in the celebration of the Litury of the Word should emphasise careful preparation of the readings, devout attention, and meditative silence
enabling the Word of God to touch people's minds and hearts.
Renewed commitment should be made to eucharistic adoration
outside of Mass, in reparation for acts of carelessness and neglect of the presence of Jesus Christ in the Eucharist. The Feast of
Corpus Christi should be celebrated with particular attention
during this year. Communities should also build upon the impulse which the Eucharist gives to the community for a practical
commitment to building a more just and fraternal society:

> 'Can we not make this Year of the Eucharist an occasion for
> diocesan and parish communities to commit themselves in a
> particular way to responding with fraternal solicitude to one
> of the many forms of poverty present in our world? I think,
> for example, of the tragedy of hunger which plagues hun-
> dreds of millions of human beings, the diseases which afflict
> developing countries, the loneliness of the elderly, the hard-
> ships faced by the unemployed, the struggles of immigrants'
> (#28).

The Holy Father's hope and prayer for this Year of the
Eucharist is for deepened interiority and for a revival every-
where of the celebration of Sunday Mass, accompanied by an increase in eucharistic worship outside of Mass. He concludes
with an appeal to priests:

> 'Be challenged by the grace of this special Year; celebrate
> Holy Mass each day with the same joy and fervour with
> which you celebrated your first Mass, and willingly spend
> time in prayer before the tabernacle' (#30).

Acknowledgements

The organisers of the conference on the encyclical had the great privilege of welcoming as the principal speaker Cardinal Godfried Danneels, Archbishop of the Diocese of Malines-Brussels and Primate of Belgium. A multi-linguist, he may be said to have his finger on the pulse of Western European society and culture, and his intuitions regarding the latter are original and telling. He is at the very forefront of contemporary Catholic reflection on Faith and Culture issues.[6] Cardinal Danneels has also given his permission for the translation, and the publication in the present volume, of one of his Easter pastoral letters, *The Night He was Betrayed*. The editors acknowledge this permission with gratitude, and return their sincere thanks to the translator, Fr Peter Forde, the Parish Priest of Ballymoney, Co Antrim.[7]

His Eminence, Cardinal Desmond Connell was very supportive of the project and offered every encouragement from the beginning. He deserves the particular thanks of the editors of the present volume for writing the preface to it.

His Eminence, Cardinal Paul Poupard, President of the Pontifical Council for Culture (Rome) graciously agreed to contribute a chapter to this book. It is very rewarding to be able to print his contribution, in which he gives the reader the benefit of his own faith-experience. Cardinal Poupard has been generous in lending his active support to the work of the ICFC at Maynooth, during the years since its foundation in 1997. The editors of the present volume wish to express to him our gratitude and our sense of indebtedness.

The conference organisers felt privileged that His Excellency, Dr Giuseppe Lazzarotto, the Papal Nuncio to Ireland, accepted their invitation to attend the opening session and concelebrate the Mass thereat. Through his presence the participants were enabled to experience the visible and worldwide communion of the Catholic Church.

Thanks are hereby expressed to all the speakers at the conference on The Church and the Eucharist. Their papers made up the substance of the event, and each author was good enough to rework the spoken text as a chapter for the present book. In order to ensure a wider coverage of the encyclical's themes than the colloquium at Maynooth could by itself deliver, a number of writers were commissioned to address aspects of Catholic doctrine regarding the Mass and the Eucharist. The editors are very grateful to these authors, who have made it possible to include biblical, doctrinal, historical, devotional, ecumenical and catechetical perspectives in the book. We likewise wish to express our indebtedness to several expert referees who advised the editors regarding the content and length of papers selected for publication. Our consultants prefer to remain anonymous, but they should rest assured that their contribution is deeply appreciated.

The young Irish composer, Mr Edward Holden, responded to a commission given him by the ICFC with a specially-composed setting of *O Sacrum Convivium* in an English version: 'O Sacred Feast'. The composer has graciously given permission for his piece to be printed as an appendix. The hymn was premiered at one of the conference Masses by the Saint Patrick's College Seminary Choir under the direction of Mr John O'Keeffe.

The Russell Library for Research at Maynooth has a rich heritage of Latin and Irish manuscripts and of books printed between 1468 and 1850. The librarian, Mrs Penelope Woods, graciously offered to place on exhibit some rare items of particular interest in connection with the conference themes, and to conduct a tour of the exhibition and of the Library. Her bibliographical notes on the books exhibited make very interesting reading and we are happy to publish them in this volume.

The editors wish to express cordial thanks to the publisher for making the path towards publication an unusually easy one. They are in the debt of Mr Hugh O'Neill for his expert help at the stage of proofreading.

Preface

Cardinal Desmond Connell

We would all wish to express our gratitude to the Irish Centre for Faith and Culture under its Director, Father James McEvoy, for arranging a conference on the Holy Father's encyclical letter, *Ecclesia de Eucharistia*. The contributions of His Eminence, Cardinal Danneels, likewise of His Eminence, Cardinal Poupard and of the other distinguished participants contained in this publication will be greatly appreciated by the wider public to which they are now made available.

The intention and significance of the encyclical are briefly stated in #5 of the Introduction. The manner in which the Pope develops his theme can be presented in commentaries ranging from the profoundly theological to easily accessible catechetical presentations. The very concrete allusions the Pope makes to the historical influence of the Eucharist in the life of the church direct the attention of the church to its historical memory. And so I would like to respond to the Pope's implicit invitation to us to recall that memory as the church in Ireland preserves it.

When the Holy Father came to visit us in Ireland twenty-five years ago he celebrated Mass in the Phoenix Park in the midst of the greatest gathering of the church ever to have assembled in our land. For the first time in our history the church in all the variety of its membership was visibly present: the bishops in communion with the Successor of Peter, surrounded by the clergy and united with the vast concourse of the laity – all together manifesting the unity of charity in the diversity of the gifts of the Holy Spirit, and realising the liturgical vision of the Second Vatican Council.

In his homily the Pope recalled the history of the Eucharist in Ireland:

'I have come to you as Bishop of Rome and pastor of the whole church in order to celebrate this union with you in the sacrifice of the Eucharist, here in Ireland's capital city of

17

Dublin, for the first time in Irish history. As I stand at this moment, a pilgrim for Christ to the land from which so many pilgrims for Christ, *peregrini pro Christo,* went out over Europe, the Americas, Australia, Africa, Asia, I am living a moment of intense emotion. As I stand here in the company of so many hundreds of thousands of Irish men and women, I am thinking of how many times, across how many centuries, the Eucharist has been celebrated in this land. How many and how varied the places where Mass has been offered – in stately medieval and in splendid modern cathedrals; in early monastic and in modern churches; at Mass rocks in the glens and forests by "hunted priests" and in poor thatch-covered chapels, for a people poor in worldly goods but rich in the things of the spirit; in "wake-houses" or "station houses", or at great open-air hostings of the faithful – on the top of Croagh Patrick and at Lough Derg. Small matter where the Mass was offered. For the Irish, it was always the Mass that mattered' *(Homily of Pope John Paul II during the Mass at the Phoenix Park, Dublin, 29 September, 1979).*

The encyclical begins with the words 'The church draws her life from the Eucharist.' Historically, as the Pope's homily reminds us, the church in Ireland has drawn her life from the Eucharist. 'For the Irish it was always the Mass that mattered.' The influence of the Eucharist on the whole history of our people has been incalculable. When the state attempted to impose a new liturgy which priests and people found to be incompatible with their Catholic eucharistic faith, a centuries-long conflict between state and people ensued. Rather than abandon the Mass, succeeding generations accepted social exclusion as the price of their fidelity. The history of the Eucharist formed the history of the church itself in Ireland.

Two central aspects of the eucharistic mystery are given special prominence in the encyclical. The first is the relation between the Eucharist and the paschal mystery of Christ's death and resurrection; the second concerns the sacramental identity between the ministerial priest and Christ in the offering of Mass.

Both need to be reasserted clearly following confusions that have arisen in recent times.

Because the Eucharist is the sacramental representation of the paschal mystery, that mystery is rendered present by the very act which constitutes the sacrament, namely, the act of consecration of the bread and wine. The presence of the paschal mystery is emphasised by the Pope:

> 'When the church celebrates the Eucharist, the memorial of her Lord's death and resurrection, this central event of salvation becomes really present and "the work of our redemption is carried out" (*Lumen Gentium,* #3). This sacrifice is so decisive for the salvation of the human race that Jesus Christ offered it and returned to the Father only after he had left us a means of sharing in it as if we had been present there'(*EdE,* #11).

St Thomas Aquinas, the great Doctor of the Eucharist, considers theologically the significance of the consecration: he tells us that the sacrament of the Eucharist is fully accomplished *(perficitur)* in the very consecration of the bread and wine. While the other sacraments are fully accomplished in the application of the matter to the person to be sanctified (*ST,* 73, 1 ad 3), the Eucharist does not have to await sacramental communion to be present in its fullness. Sacramental communion draws upon the inexhaustible wealth of the sacrifice already offered in the act of consecration. This is the presence of the paschal mystery. This is the reality about which the Pope expresses the amazement which he would wish to share with us (*EdE,* #5). Like the sacrifice of the cross, the Eucharist is, in the first place and in an order of absolute priority, the worship of God offered by Christ on the cross with which we are privileged to unite the total offering of our hearts and lives. One would see this as a devaluation of communion only if one were to fail to realise what the act of consecration accomplishes as the source of the amazing gift of communion.

As I make these comments, my mind travels back to an earlier time when a hush descended upon the congregation at the

sound of the Sanctus bell. That silent worship of the congregation was rendered all the more perceptible by the outbreak of
coughing that followed immediately after the consecration. Are
we beginning to lose something of our realisation of this radical
truth of the Eucharist? Is the moment of consecration still for us
what it was for our forebears? Is it still the focus of our eucharistic faith? I sometimes wonder when I see the congregation sitting through the consecration. Should we not be on our knees in
the awesome presence of Christ in his paschal mystery? Should
we not be ready to humble ourselves in imitation of him who
humbled himself as far as death on the cross so as to be raised
with him in the consummation of the paschal mystery which reveals the staggering reality of divine love?

There are some practical points that follow from what I have
said. Although our full participation in the Eucharist is accomplished in sacramental communion, and although one would
wish to see as many as possible of our congregations united with
Christ and with one another in sacramental communion, it
would be wrong to say that those who are prevented from receiving communion do not participate in the Eucharist. At the
time when the discipline of the eucharistic fast made it impracti-
cal for those who came to the later Masses to receive communion, no one doubted that they participated in Mass. Today one
sees whole congregations coming automatically to communion,
almost as if this were simply one of the things one does when
one comes to Mass. Catechesis is needed to enable people to understand that coming to communion is a matter of no small importance, and that in coming to communion one ought to be
properly disposed and prepared.

The second aspect of the Eucharist emphasised by the encyclical to which I would like to refer is revealed in the expression
chosen by the Pope when he speaks about the union of the
ministerial priest with Christ in the eucharistic celebration. It is a
truly striking expression: 'sacramental identification' (EdE, #29).

In order to appreciate the truly powerful significance of this
expression it is helpful to turn once again to St Thomas. There

the objection is made that whereas on Calvary the gift which was offered and the priest making the gift were identical, namely Christ himself, the same cannot be said of the Mass, where Christ is the gift but the priest making the offering is a different person, namely the ministerial priest. How then can the Mass be identical with the sacrifice offered on Calvary? St Thomas replies: 'In the same line of thought, the priest also is the image of Christ in whose person and by whose power he pronounces the words of consecration. And so in a certain way the priest and the victim are the same' (*ST*, 83, art. I ad 3). By the sacrament of Holy Orders the priest is configured to Christ as head and shepherd of the church. In virtue of that sacramental configuration the priest is enabled to act in sacramental identification with Christ. To deny this identification would be to posit a sacrifice no longer identical with the sacrifice of the cross.

'Know what you are doing, and imitate the mystery you celebrate: model your life on the mystery of the Lord's Cross.' These words addressed to the newly-ordained priest in the ordination rite, invite him to constantly renewed reflection on the dignity and call to holiness of his sacramental identity with Christ. But it is necessary too that our people be helped to rediscover the surpassing dignity of the priestly office. May that renewal to which the Pope's encyclical invites us bring forth abundant fruit in the increase of priestly vocations.

CHAPTER ONE

Liturgy Forty Years after the Second Vatican Council: High Point or Recession

Godfried Cardinal Danneels

1. A Major Turnabout

For those who have not experienced it for themselves, it must be difficult to imagine just how much liturgical praxis has changed in less than half a century. The evolution which has taken place in the last thirty years is barely perceptible nowadays since the new liturgical model is considered evident practically every-where. Such a situation is certainly gratifying but does it mean that the profound intentions of *Sacrosanctum Concilium* have thereby been realised? Perhaps now is the appropriate moment for an evaluation.

It is evident that the last half-century has brought about a major change in the relationship between the minister and the people in the liturgy. This change, however, was not without consequence for our understanding of the relationship between the sacred and the profane, and even the church and the world. The situation might be roughly stated as follows: prior to the liturgical reforms the distance between the minister and the people was clearly designated. This was even given material expression in the ordering of church buildings: the distinct choir area reserved to the priest, the altar oriented to the east, priest and people separated by a communion rail. Even more questionable than the features of church architecture was the parallel configuration of the celebration; it was frequently the case that the priest celebrated the official liturgy while at one and the same time the people set about their personal devotions. The use of Latin, of course, had a significant role to play in this parallel configuration. The consequence of all this was the fact that the liturgy came to be considered untouchable, an entity regulated by rubrics to be performed with great obedience and respect. Liturgy was simply a given, and a good liturgist was seen for the most part as an observant performer. The people assisted, of course, but took little or no part in the liturgy itself.

2. Active Participation

From its very beginnings, the aim of the liturgical movement, which originated in Belgium in 1909, was to close the gap between the official liturgy of the priest and that of the people. The term 'active participation' was born out of this movement and has since become part of our common usage. It became a key term in the liturgical constitution of Vatican II. Active participation was first promoted through the circulation of the People's Missals which contained the Sunday liturgy: the faithful were at least able to follow along. Before long, however, a desire for more than just following in the book emerged: people wanted to participate and join in. Vatican II satisfied this desire by introducing the use of the vernacular, by simplifying liturgical symbolism to make it more transparent, by returning to the praxis of the early church and dropping elements which had later come to overshadow the essentials, and by a correct distribution of roles in the service of the liturgy. The result was a far greater involvement of the people, even to the very heart of the liturgy.

3. From Rubricism to Manipulation

The active involvement of the people in the liturgy is, of course, an unparalleled gift from the Council to the People of God. As with every worthy reform, however, there is a shadow side. Active participation in the liturgy, preparing together, concern to get as close as possible to the culture and sensitivity of the faithful, can lead imperceptibly to a sort of taking possession of the liturgy. Participation and mutual celebration can lead to a subtle form of manipulation. In such an event the liturgy is not only set free of its untouchable quality – which in itself is not a bad thing – but it becomes in a sense the property of those who celebrate, a terrain given over to their 'creativity'. Those who serve – the priests and laity – become its 'owners'. In some cases this can even lead to a sort of liturgical 'coup' in which the sacred is eliminated, the language trivialised and the cult turned into a social event. In a word, the real subject of the liturgy is no longer the Christ who through the Spirit worships the Father and sanctifies the people in a symbolic act. The real subject is the human person or the celebrating community. The exaggerated emphasis from before the 1950s on discipline, obedience, fidelity to the rubrics, the reception and entering of a pre-existent entity, is replaced by self-will and by the elimination of every sense of mystery in the liturgy. In this case the liturgy is no longer '*leitourgia*': the work of the people and for the people with respect to their relationship with God; it becomes a purely human activity. Fortunately, the trend we have outlined is not universal. Nevertheless, any attempt to evaluate liturgical praxis in our time would be wrong to ignore it.

4. *The Liturgy is Beyond Us*

There is a liturgical ground rule which runs as follows: the liturgy is first 'God's work on us' before being our work on God. Liturgy is *datum* or prior given in its very essence: it is beyond us and has already existed for a long time, long before we could participate in it. The acting subject of the liturgy is the risen Christ: he is the first and only High Priest, the only one who is competent to bring worship to God and to sanctify the people. This is not only an abstract theological truth: it must become evident and visible in the liturgy. The core of the liturgy is already given in the Lord's acts of institution. This does not mean that the individual and the celebrating community are neither capable nor permitted to make a creative contribution. The community is creative, but it is not an 'instance of creation'. Otherwise the liturgy would no longer be the epiphany of the Christian mysteries through the service of the church, the continuation of his incarnation, crucifixion and resurrection, the 'incarnation' of a divine project in history and in the world of human persons via sacred symbols. In such a situation the liturgy would become nothing more than the community celebrating itself.

The liturgy 'pre-exists'. The celebrating community enters into it as into a pre-established, divine and spiritual architecture. To a certain degree this is also determined by the historical location of Christ and his sacred mysteries. The Eucharist as such is not a 'religious meal' but rather the making present of a particular meal, that of Christ with his disciples on the night before he suffered. In this sense the liturgy can never be a self-fashioned concoction of the celebrating community; we are not creators, we are servants and guardians of the mysteries. We do not own them nor did we author them.

5. The Fundamental Attitude of the 'Homo Liturgicus'

This entails that the fundamental attitude of the 'homo liturgicus' – both individually and collectively – is one of receptivity, readiness to listen, self-giving and self-relativising. It is the attitude of faith and of faithful obedience. It is not because a particular caricature of this attitude of obedience led at one time to slavish and nonsensical dressage and rubricism that the sense of 'entering in to what transcends us' has been so diminished. The 'homo liturgicus' does not manipulate, nor is his or her action restricted to self-expression or auto-realisation. It is an attitude of orientation towards God, readiness to listen, obedience, grateful reception, wonder, adoration and praise. It is an attitude of listening and seeing, of what Guardini called 'contemplating', an attitude so alien to the 'homo faber' in many of us. In short, the fundamental attitude of the 'homo liturgicus' is none other than an attitude of prayer, of handing ourselves over to God and letting his will be done in us.

It should not surprise us, then, that in a period of history like our own, with its active intervention in everyday reality and its submission of that reality to our scientific thinking and our technological expertise, it will be particularly difficult to be genuinely liturgically-minded. The 'contemplative' dimension of the human person is no longer evident these days. This being the case, the core of the liturgy is even less evident. Active participation, therefore, has to be situated within this 'contemplative' attitude, in which case it must also bear the particular characteristics of such an attitude.

6. The Incomprehensibility of the Liturgy

One of the primary concerns of Vatican II and of the church is that the liturgy be understood by the celebrating community. Every reform proposed by the Constitution is rooted in that concern. 'Understand what you do' is a basic demand of everything we do, including what we do in the liturgy. The incomprehensibility of the liturgy was blamed, in the first place, on language. Immediately after the introduction of the vernacular, however, it became apparent that it had to do with more than just language usage; the content of the liturgy itself was equally unfamiliar.

The liturgy, of course, is almost entirely structured on the Bible. It is said that the Hebrew Bible or Old Testament is particularly unfamiliar to us. Everything takes place in an agrarian context which barely applies nowadays in many parts of the world. At the same time, the biblical texts are rooted in a rural culture, and a peculiarly Mediterranean one at that. Many images, such as shepherds, flocks or water wells, are no longer part of the day-to-day vista of the modern city-dweller. In other words, the Bible uses a language from a bygone era.

The non-biblical texts in the liturgy are also a little strange, however. The Latin collects with their succinct and metrical structure are untranslatable, not so much because the words cannot be transposed into a modern language but because the mentality from which they stem has disappeared. A great many texts, when detached from their musical setting, end up seeming extremely archaic. Think, for example, of the *Salve Regina* and the *Dies Irae* or even the ordinary sung Gregorian Introits and Communion Antiphons and the archaic image of God which such texts maintain (the God who sleeps, the God of wrath, etc.).

Certain symbols – although secondary – no longer seem to function: the drop of water in the chalice, mixing a particle of the host with the wine, the *lavabo*, the washing of the feet. One frequently hears reproaches such as 'old-fashioned', 'passé', 'medieval' and 'monastic'.

7. Abbreviate or Eliminate?

People often opt for a short-term solution which barely touches on the real problem. In the case of the liturgy certain terms were replaced with other more understandable terms. There are biblical terms, however, which cannot be replaced. What do we do, for example, with words like 'resurrection', 'Easter', 'Eucharist', *'metanoia'*, 'sin'? They are part of a sort of biblical and liturgical 'mother tongue' which simply cannot be replaced. They have to be learned. It is hard to imagine a Jew using a different term for *'shabbat'* or *'pesach'*.

Certain biblical images are, indeed, barely perceptible in our modern urban culture. The sight of shepherds and flocks is no longer an everyday occurrence. Does this mean, however, that such images are no longer comprehensible in themselves? Is it because no one has ever met a seraph that the metaphorical power of this angelic messenger no longer speaks to us? Half of the poetry ever written makes use of images and terms which are not part of the daily life and environment of the reader. A great many symbols from medieval German culture were taken up in the Roman Pontifical. People sometimes opt for alternative poetic texts, especially for weddings and baptisms. Leaving aside the fact that there is a profound theological distinction to be made between an aesthetically valuable text and a biblical text, it is also true that many such texts belong to an even more limited culture than the Bible which, it would appear, possesses a much greater universality.

The remedy employed in most cases often does not help. Most of the time it is limited to questions such as: 'What can we drop?' – 'How an we abbreviate?' – 'What would function better to express what is going on in our lives as individuals and as a community?' Is the latter question justified, however? What precisely do we have to say in the first instance? What is going on in our lives? Or what is God saying to us? In a manner, of course, which we can understand.

There appears to be only one solution: if the liturgy is not simply a structuring of common human religiosity, but rather

the epiphany of God in human history (from Abraham to
Christ), then we cannot avoid the need for catechesis and initiation. Liturgy demands schooling because it is both proclamation
and celebration of mysteries, mysteries which have occurred in
the history of Judaism and Christianity.

8. What Is Understanding?

What exactly is understanding? It is evident that if the liturgy is
the epiphany of God's dealings with his church then the deepest
core or heart of the liturgy will never be open to our grasp. There
is indeed a hard core in the liturgy – the mystery – which is un-
graspable. One can only enter into it in faith.

There is more to say about understanding, however. Our
contemporaries often conceive understanding as the ability to
grasp at first hearing. Something is understandable if we can
grasp it immediately. Such an approach is valid for the ordinary
objects of our knowledge which can only be grasped at a purely
cognitive level, but this is more a question of registering than
understanding. Where the depths of human – and divine – reality
are concerned this approach does not work. Love, death, joy,
solidarity, knowledge of God, can never be grasped at once and
on first inspection. In these cases, understanding is more a question of the biblical notion of 'knowing-penetrating'. It is a
lengthy and progressive process of becoming familiar with a
particular reality. The same is true for the liturgy. It is not an
object of knowledge in the commonplace sense of the word. It is
not an object of knowledge at all, rather it is a source of knowledge, a source of understanding. This is why analysis is out of
place here; only a prolonged listening and familiarisation is appropriate. This implies that the liturgy will only be open to
understanding from a perspective of 'empathy'. The liturgy lets
itself be understood only by those who have faith in and who
love it. For this reason it remains inaccessible and incomprehensible outside of the faith.

Moreover, the liturgy is only understandable through its
repetitiveness. Profound realities only gradually yield their full

significance. This is why we have the phenomenon of 'ritual' in the liturgy; and whoever speaks of 'ritual' speaks of repetition. Many changes in the liturgy in order to make it understandable have been inefficient because they focused on the immediate, cognitive, informative aspect of understanding. They wanted to explain everything, to provide commentary, to analyse. They never lead to familiarity with the liturgy.

They are surgical and medical interventions (abbreviating, replacing, scrapping, describing) on a dying reality, a sort of palliative care which can never heal the sick individual. The only approach is the 'dialogical' approach: allowing the liturgy time to say what it has to say; listening attentively to its harmonics and allowing its deeper meaning to unfold; not looking for an alternative but letting the liturgy speak for itself and expose its own virtualities.

9. Our Disrupted Relationship with the Liturgy

The incomprehensibility of the liturgy is not so much due to the unintelligibility of its major symbols. Indeed, all of us are well able to grasp the deep fascination which flows forth from symbols such as fire, light, water, bread, wine, laying on of hands, anointing. These major (natural) symbols speak to us all in our archetypal imagination. Secondary symbols can, of course, be more problematic. At the same time, however, they are of lesser importance and Vatican II correctly discarded a number of them.

A more significant contributor to the problem of understanding is the fact that the symbolic universe within which such symbols functioned has been lost. Removed from its proper context, a liturgical symbol is like a fish out of water, and is left bereft of much of its vitality. Proof of this fact can best be found in what one might call 'contrary' situations, where the symbolic universe continues to thrive even today. Why is it so that short Latin phrases and Gregorian refrains continue to function in Taizé but not in the parishes? Because they are in their proper place within the religious community of Taizé and its monastic liturgical life.

Why is it that the symbols we have been discussing continue to function in the abbeys, the monastery churches and the charismatic communities? For the same reason! Why does a Gregorian requiem function well at a funeral? Liturgical comprehensibility also depends on a number of non-liturgical surrounding elements. It is our entire relationship with the liturgy – even outside the cultic celebration – that makes so much possible.

The incomprehensibility of the liturgy is not only due to the liturgy itself but in part to us. Our own attitude needs to be worked on. We examine our global relationship with God, our faith, our lifestyle, etc. Does the liturgy give meaning to these dimensions of our life or does it turn them into a *'corpus extraneum'*? We need to be aware of the fact that understanding the liturgy is far more than a cognitive exercise; it is a loving 'entering in'. At the same time our contemplative gaze is weak. Since the Renaissance we have lost our disinterested contemplative ability; it was pushed aside to make way for analytic observation.

10. What Should We Do? What Can We Do?

10.1 Theme and Variations

It is quite clear that 'entering into the already existing' structure of the liturgy does not mean that we must exclude any kind of flexibility in our liturgical style. Far from being ruled out, creativity is actually called for. If the problem does not lie with creativity then where does it lie?

The problem lies with the boundaries of our intervention. One cannot simply transform and rearrange the whole thing. Changes have to be made with intelligence. The liturgy contains certain given themes which, while they cannot be changed, do remain open to possible variation. Some of those clearly delineated and unchangeable liturgical paths were determined by Christ himself. In classical terms they are referred to as the 'substance' of the sacraments, over which even the church itself has no power. The liturgy remains Christ's liturgy.

There are also more historically derived elements of the liturgy which one cannot change. Certain forms of prayer and certain

words and ways of speaking, like the Bible texts, remain unchangeable. Perhaps even the liturgical order of scripture reading, lyrical response (psalm) and prayer fall into this category. It
is more than just a liturgical vagary, it is a deep theological truth:
God speaks first and our response follows.

In order to be able to establish the boundaries between theme
and variations a thorough liturgical training is indispensable.
Liturgy demands knowledge of tradition and history, in short,
documentary knowledge. In order to take one's place in the
liturgical enterprise one has to know one's craft; liturgy requires
instruction and insight together with a good helping of spirituality and pastoral awareness. Perhaps the reason for the evident
liturgical poverty in so many places throughout the world can
be found here. There is no lack of engagement or dedication or
imagination: there is simply a lack of competence. There is no
point in setting up liturgical work groups if they are not trained
for their job.

10.2 The Duration of the Celebration

It might come across as strange in the ears of many, but our liturgical celebrations are for the most part too short. The liturgy
needs time to deliver its riches. It has nothing to do with physical time or 'clock' time but with the spiritual time of the soul.
Since liturgy does not belong to the world of information but to
the domain of the heart, it does not work with 'clock' time but
with *kairos.* Many of our liturgies do not provide enough time or
space to enter into the event. In this regard Eastern liturgy provides a worthy example, taking its time and inviting those who
participate to 'leave all worldly cares behind' (hymn of the
cherubim). It is not enough that people have heard the liturgy or
that it has been spoken. Has it been 'proclaimed to them'? Have
they been given the opportunity to integrate it? It is not enough
for us to have heard the liturgy, we need to have grasped and
appropriated it as well.

A major factor in all of this is silence and the time to interiorise. The liturgy of Vatican II provides time for silence but in

practice it is not given much of a chance. Lack of silence turns the liturgy into an unstoppable succession of words which leaves no time for interiorisation. Here, too, is a reason for the liturgy's 'incomprehensibility'.

10.3 The Articulation of Word and Gesture

A major handicap of the liturgy as it is practised *de facto* in the West is its 'verbosity'. In essence, liturgy has become a matter of language and speaking. The word that was once ignored and neglected has made a comeback. How many presiding priests consider the homily to be the climax of the liturgy and the barometer of the celebration? How many have the feeling that the celebration is more or less over after the liturgy of the Word? Indeed, there is clearly an imbalance in duration between the liturgy of the Word and the liturgy of the Eucharist. At the same time too much attention is given to the 'intellectual' approach to the liturgy. There is not enough room for imagination, affect, emotion and properly understood aesthetics. This leads in turn to the consequence that the liturgy begins to function in an extremely intellectual fashion and fails thereby to reach many of those who participate in it, either because they are of a non-intellectual cast of mind or because they do not consider such stuff to be nourishing for their lives.

A liturgy which is almost exclusively oriented to the intellect is also not likely to involve the human body in the celebration to any great extent. It is small wonder that people end up sitting down for almost the entire celebration: sitting being the typical attitude of the listener. There is a serious imbalance in the articulation of word and gesture. Without introducing rhetorical gesticulations and building in theatricality one can still argue, nevertheless, that the tongue and the ear are frequently the only human organs in use during the liturgy. Liturgy then ends up lapsing from celebration into mere instruction and address.

11. The Instrumentalisation of the Liturgy

One of the consequences of the verbosity we have been discussing is the danger that the liturgy will be instrumentalised and used for ends which lie outside it. Liturgy, however, is a global, symbolic activity which belongs to the order of the 'playful'. The uniqueness of 'play' is the fact that one 'plays in order to play', one plays for the sake of playing. The death of play lies in competition and financial interest.

Liturgy will also die if it is subordinated to ends beyond itself. Liturgy is neither the time nor the place for catechesis. Of course, it has excellent catechetical value but it is not there to replace the various catechetical moments in the life of the Christian woman or man. Such moments require their own time. Nor should liturgy be used as a means for disseminating information, no matter how essential that information might be. It should not be forced to serve as an easy way to notify the participants about this, that and the other unless such things are themselves entirely subordinate to the liturgy itself. One does not attend the liturgy on Mission Sunday in order to learn something about this or that mission territory: one comes to the liturgy to reflect on and integrate one's mission from Christ to 'go out to all nations'. The establishment of all sorts of thematic Sundays and thematic celebrations has little or no future, except in the death of the liturgy as such. Liturgy ought certainly not to serve as a sort of 'warm-up' for another activity, even a church activity. It is not a meeting but a celebration. It can indeed follow from the liturgy that one departs from it with a greater sense of engagement, faith and love informing and inspiring one's actions. Liturgy is a free activity: its end is in itself. Although it is the 'source and summit' of all ecclesial activities, liturgy does not replace them nor does it coincide with them.

12. The 'Sensorial' Pedagogy of the Liturgy

The uniqueness of the liturgy is that it gives pride of place to 'experience'. Experience comes first, and while reflection, analysis, explanation and systematisation might be necessary, they must follow after experience. 'Celebrate first, then understand' might seem a strange proposition to some and perhaps even come across as obscuranist and anti-intellectual. Does it imply a call for irrationality or an abandonment of the massive catechetical effort the church makes in order to prepare people to receive the sacraments? Think, for example, of the creed and confirmation. The church fathers adhered to the principle that mystagogical catechesis (in which the deepest core of the sacred mysteries was laid bare) should only come after the sacraments of initiation. Prior to baptism they limited themselves to moral instruction and teaching on the Christian 'way of life'. Immediately after baptism – during Easter week – they spoke about the deep meaning of baptism, chrismation and Eucharist. Their pedagogical approach remained 'sensorial': participate first and experience things at an existential level in the heart of the community, and only then explain. Their entire method of instruction was structured around a framework of question and answer such as: 'Did you notice that ...?' – 'Well, what this means is ...'

Perhaps we do not have to adhere to the letter of such a pedagogical approach – the *disciplina arcani* also had a hand in things – but it certainly provides a hint in the right direction. One can only understand the liturgy if one enters into it with faith and love. In this sense no catechetical method will succeed if it is unable to depend on good community celebrations of the liturgy. In the same way catechesis as such will be of little use if it is not accompanied by a liturgical praxis during the period of catechesis. Where the liturgy is concerned, the following rule applies: first experience, first 'live' the liturgy, then reflect and explain it. The eyes of the heart must be open before the mind, because one can only truly understand the liturgy with the intelligence of the heart.

This has consequences for liturgical work groups; those who desire to work with the liturgy and, as we already noted, 'vary the given theme', will first have to listen attentively to that theme and participate in the celebration of the liturgy as it is. If they do not, then their entire liturgical endeavour will turn out to be nothing more than 'self-expression' and not the shaping of a pre-given entity which has its roots in the liturgical tradition of both the Old and New Testaments and in the living tradition of the church. What would we think of a composer who refused to listen to his predecessors or a painter who refused to visit a museum? Every musician listens to music and every poet reads poetry. This is simple human wisdom but it applies in full to the liturgy which is primarily God's work with his people. The worthy liturgist listens first, meditates, prays and interiorises. Only then can he or she 'modulate'.

13. Ritual and Boredom

The very terms 'rite' and 'ritual' summon up the idea of boredom and monotony. 'It's always the same ...', we hear day in day out. Ritual is synonymous with rigidity and sclerosis. Is that really so, however? It is true that an exaggerated attachment to particular forms does exist, but that is ritualism, unsound ritual. We have to admit that every good thing has its pathology. Ritual, however, is something other than ritualism. Ritual is priceless and irreplaceable. It has its place in every human activity. Every human being has a morning and evening ritual just as every society has its regular festivities which are celebrate in the same way each year. Ritual is an unavoidably anthropological *datum*. Every significant human reality is surrounded and protected by ritual: birth, marriage, love, death. Every transition is adorned and embellished with ritual. Every time we encounter something that transcends the human person we 'humanise' it with ritual.

The unique characteristic of every ritual is its repetitiveness and stereotyped nature. In order for us to interiorise profound matters, we need identical stereotypes, the reassuring ceremonial wordings we call ritual. This kind of repetition, however, does not necessarily imply monotony or the stifling of any kind of personal element. Every marriage rite, for example, is stereotyped: everyone marries in the same manner and with the same words and gestures. Yet in so doing those involved are not left depersonalised, a mere number in the line. Every marriage remains unique even though it took place in just the same way as any other. As a matter of fact it is essential for every couple that they are able to take their place in line with every other marriage in and through the fixed marriage rite. In this way the fragility of their personal engagement is socialised and, in their eyes, protected and guaranteed. The same is true for the language of love. It remains endlessly unvarying yet it is experienced as fresh and new each time it spoken.

Repetitive ritual provides, in addition, the opportunity for in-depth reflection and interiorisation. Serious matters (such as the liturgy) cannot be grasped all at once: they need time, and time means repetition. Only pure information, such as an order or computer language, does not require repetition since it can be understood immediately. More profound matters only let their real significance emerge over time.

Ritual, finally, provides a protection against direct, unmediated religious experience. Only the great religious geniuses (such as Moses before the burning bush) are able to negotiate such direct experiences of the numinous; the rest of us need the protective mediation of ritual and the 'decelerating', 'delaying' role of repetition. Indeed, there will a certain monotony and perhaps boredom associated with ritual. Perhaps we simply have to be aware of it and reconcile ourselves to it, as long as we continue to bear in mind how necessary this aspect of ritual can be.

Further reflections might also be useful. If we constantly emphasise the 'tiresome' aspect of ritual we reveal just how individualistic our experience of the liturgy has become. Ritual, however, is necessary in order to bring a community together and allow it to celebrate. If we turn the liturgy into the most individual expression of individual emotion then we wipe out any possibility of communal celebration. If, however, we enter into the eucharistic celebration with its fixed *ratio agendi* it is because we want to make it possible for many to celebrate in the same rhythm. There can be no community without ritual. We need to bear in mind, furthermore, that we attend the liturgy at God's invitation. The liturgy is not a feast we laid out for ourselves, according to our own personal preferences. It is God's feast. We attend by invitation and not simply to satisfy our own needs.

A great deal depends, to be sure, on the person of the presiding priest. He is someone who must lead a community event on God's behalf. He is the living vehicle of something that goes beyond him. He is, therefore, neither robot nor actor; he is a servant.

14. *The Cosmic Grounding of the Liturgy*

One important fact about the liturgy is its relatedness to the cosmos. Many of its symbols are borrowed from cosmic realities such as fire, light, water, food, bodily gestures. Times and seasons, the position of sun and moon, night and day, summer and winter are also related to the liturgy. In the liturgical event all the major human archetypes have their place. What is important, however, is that the cosmic realities in question are given their chance to appear in their full reality as created things. The liturgy must work with 'real' things. Although everything is to a certain degree transformed by culture, it should never be overshadowed by cultural accretions. Fire needs to be real fire, light real light, linen real linen, wood real wood. Time must also be respected, such as the hour for the Easter vigil celebration. Thus liturgy often becomes the true repository of the authenticity of the objects around us. To serve God we use only the best things as he created them. Expediency and comfort need to make way here for authenticity.

We should be aware, however, that all our Jewish and Christian symbols are no longer purely cosmic or natural. They have all been determined and conditioned by the history of God with his people. Although all our Jewish-Christian feasts have an agrarian origin, they have all been conditioned by the events of salvation which are historically situated and no longer natural; they are fact-historical. The Passover feast is no longer purely agricultural, it is also the celebration of the exodus from Egypt. *Shebuoth* is no longer a celebration of the first harvest but of the giving of the law on Mount Sinai. With Christian feasts which are entirely determined by the historicity of the Christian mysteries it is even clearer. There are no more purely cosmic, natural feasts. The Christian festal calendar is no longer a purely natural calendar, it consists rather of a series of memorial days which celebrate historical events between God and his people.

15. The Liturgy and the Senses

Liturgy is closely related to the body and the senses. As a matter of fact there is only one fundamental symbolism: that of the human body as an expression of the human soul and thus the primary location of all symbols. All other symbolic gestures can be situated in the extension of the human body.

The eye is the most active of the senses. In the liturgy nowadays, however, it tends to be somewhat undervalued. There is a lot to hear but little to see. At one time the situation was reversed. At a time when the verbal dimension was not understood the visual dimension was pushed to the fore. Certain secondary liturgical gestures, such as the elevation of the bread and wine at the consecration, are a consequence of this fact. Even eucharistic worship outside of Mass has its roots here. We can certainly re-evaluate the visual side of our liturgy but that does not always mean that we have to supply additional visual effects. It is always best to let the great symbols function. How, for example, can baptism symbolise 'reception into the church' if it takes place in an almost empty church building? How can it be understood as a water bath if it turns out to be little more than a sprinkling with water? How can we speak of 'hearing the message' if everyone is sitting with their heads bent reading the texts in their missalettes at the moment when they should be listening? The three great focal points of the celebration: the presidential chair, the ambo and the altar, also have a strong visual significance.

The assembly has the most important place in the Christian liturgy, and rightly so. Liturgy is a celebration of the faith and the 'faith comes from the congregation'. As a matter of fact, if the Christian mysteries being celebrated are all rooted in historical facts and are thus memorial celebrations, then it is equally true that this should be spoken about. History is impossible without the element of 'narrative'. It is of great importance that the different text genres should be respected: a reading is not a prayer, a hymn is not a psalm, a song is not a *monitio* nor is a homily a set of announcements. Each of these genres requires its own *auditive* treatment. Furthermore, it is clear that neither rhetoric nor theatricality nor pathos have a part in the liturgy. Reading is not acting; it is allowing oneself to be the humble instrument of a word that comes from beyond. The exaggerated impact of the personal individuality of the man or woman who reads can kill the liturgy and eliminate its harmonics. Even the place from which the scriptures are read has some significance. It is better not to read from the middle of the community because the word comes to us from elsewhere. It is proclaimed; it does not simply arise out of the community. It is also best to read from the Book of the Gospels and from an ambo surrounded by symbols suggestive of respect (light, incense, altar servers).

The sense of touch finds its most profound expression in the laying on of hands and in anointing. These are among the most physical gestures of the liturgy and they can have an enormous impact on the human person. The significance of praying in the presence of a sick person takes on quite a different character if one places one's hands on that person or anoints them.

The sense of smell, to conclude, is almost completely unused in the liturgy. It is not to our advantage that the use of incense has been pushed aside into the domain of superfluity and hindrance. The Eastern Church is much better off than we are in this regard. One rather absurd case is the scentlessness of the chrism which we use to suggest the 'good odour of Christ' to our newly confirmed. Here, too, the Eastern Church is ahead of us (perhaps too generously!) in their use of tens of different scents and spices in the manufacture of their chrism.

16. 'Inculturation'
The problem of 'inculturation' is a recent phenomenon. It was

treated in a remarkable document produced by the Sacred
Congregation for the Sacraments and Divine Worship in 1994.
We cannot discuss every aspect of the problem at this juncture.
The principle, however, is clear: if the liturgy is an 'incarnational'
fact then it is an inherent requirement that it be inculturated in
the various cultures of humanity. Such is evident. Liturgy must
be inculturated; or rather, liturgy will inculturate itself if it is
lived with faith and love of Christ by people of all cultures.

There are also limits, however. The liturgy is not only a structuring of human religiosity, it gives form to the Christian mysteries. These mysteries took place in history, in a particular place
and time and using particular rites and symbols. The Last
Supper is not just a common, human, religious meal, it is the
meal the Lord ate with his disciples the night before he suffered.
This implies that all eucharistic celebrations need to be recognisable as such, which includes even formal connection and references. No cultural religious meal is equivalent to the Christ
meal. In this sense the Eucharist can never be completely 'inculturated'. The liturgy is not only an incarnational *datum*, it also belongs to the order of salvation. As such it has a salvific impact on
the cultures of humankind.

Not every religious practice or popular 'liturgy' can be used
as a 'vehicle' for Christian liturgy. There are levels of incompati-
bility and there are prayers and practices which are not appropriate for use in the Christian liturgy. 'Discernment' here will
not always be so simple. Inculturation does not take place so
much on the liturgist's desk as in the praxis of liturgy itself. It is
not an act of bureaucratic sophistication but rather a faithful,
loyal discernment which takes place in the celebration itself.
Only after long and deep immersion in the real liturgy, accompanied by a great desire for Christ and his mysteries, for church
tradition and for the historicising of the 'natural' liturgy through
the coming of Christ, will we see the slow but steady emergence
of inculturated liturgy. This is how the Jewish liturgy transformed into the Greek and the Greek liturgy into the Roman,
and the Roman liturgy was supplemented and augmented by

the German and Anglo-Saxon liturgy and so forth. Such work of inculturation has always been the fruit of the thoughts and deeds of a few significant church figures and of the patient sensitivity and faith-filled discernment of the many peoples of the world.

It remains an open question whether we should consider inclusive language to be a question of inculturation. The discussion is still in full swing and would demand a separate and more thorough treatment than is possible here. In fact the question remains if we are being faced with a radical cultural change and if this has religious implications. It appears to me to be more of an anthropological problem which is significant not only for biblical and liturgical texts but for the use of language as such and for the whole dimension of conviviality between men and women.

17. Liturgy and Life

There has been a great deal of discussion in recent years concerning the exotic character of the liturgy and its distance from the everyday life of Christians. It is true indeed that a liturgy which has no impact on or consequences for the way Christians live their lives is off the mark. If, according to Pope Leo the Great, the Christian mysteries have crossed over into the liturgy then it is equally true that liturgy must cross over into the moral and spiritual life of Christians. *Imitamini quod tractatis* – 'Do in practice what you do in the liturgy' – resounds the ancient text from the liturgy of ordination.

Some have endeavoured to draw the conclusion from this axiom that the liturgy is not important when compared with our day-to-day lives or that it is a sort of preparation or 'warm-up' for life itself, an option for those who need it but redundant for those who don't. Others have suggested that liturgy and life coincide and that true service to God takes place outside the church in one's daily life. Liturgy does not coincide with life, rather it has a dialectic relationship with life. Sunday is not Monday nor vice versa.

Aside from the liturgy's profound and significant content as an indispensable source of grace and power for life, we must also bear in mind that the Sunday ritual interrupts monotony and differentiates and articulates human time. The liturgy is not life and life is not liturgy. Both are irreducible and both are necessary. They do not coincide. It is sometimes said that the liturgy gives shape to life, that it symbolises life. This is not entirely incorrect. What we do throughout the week in a varied and diluted way we also do in the liturgy, but in a more concentrated and purified fashion: we live for God and for others. Liturgy, however, is not only a symbolisation of human life. Liturgy symbolises and makes present: firstly the mysteries of salvation, the words and deeds of Christ, but also our deeds in so far as they are reflected, purified and redeemed in Christ. His mysteries – made present to us in the liturgy – are our archetypes. This Christological determination of our lives in the liturgy is of the essence.

On the other hand, it is a fact that the liturgy finds its field of application in daily life. It flows over it and nourishes it but never coincides with it nor complies with it. Life and liturgy are in a dialectical relationship: the life of the Christian is built on two things: *cultus* and *caritas*.

PART I

Scripture

CHAPTER TWO

'Make me a sanctuary…'
Worship in the Old Testament

Maurice Hogan SSC

A People Set Apart

In the story of the liberation of God's people recounted in the book of Exodus, Moses is commanded to go to the Pharaoh and say: 'The Lord, the God of the Hebrews, sent me to you to say: "Let my people go, so that they may serve me in the wilderness"' (Ex 7:16). This request is repeated with slight variations (cf. 8:1; 9:1, 13; 10:3) that the Pharaoh understands as the offering of sacrifice (cf. 8:25). In the subsequent negotiations it becomes increasingly clear that the worship must take place at the location and in the manner that God demands and is not subject to any bargaining or compromise. In time, Israel was able to depart from Egypt to worship its God in the wilderness before it took possession of the land promised to Abraham. Israel received the gift of the land so that worship of the true God could take place there, so something more than just possession was involved: 'You brought them in and planted them on the mountain of your own possession, the place, O Lord, that you made your abode, the sanctuary, O Lord, that your hands have established. The Lord will reign forever and ever' (15:17-18). The land of Israel becomes the fulfilment of the promise to Abraham only when it becomes the place where God abides and reigns, i.e. where God's will is done and the proper kind of existence befitting God's people is lived out.

The land is given to the people to be a place for the worship of the true God. Mere possession of the land, mere national autonomy, would reduce Israel to the level of all the other nations. The pursuit of such a goal would be a misunderstanding of what is distinctive about Israel's election.[1]

In the course of its wanderings through the desert, Israel discovered what kind of worship God had in mind. At Sinai, God appeared to Moses and a covenant[2] relationship was established between God and his people. The charter, or constitution, of this new people, incorporating God's will for them, was the Decalogue (20:1-17), and the covenant was sealed with a proper sacrificial ritual (24:1-11). Israel learned to worship in the way God desired and liturgy or cult became part of that worship together with a rule of life that expressed God's will for them. The cult enabled them to live in such a way that God is properly honoured and thus Israel became the people of God. In the covenant at Sinai, worship, law and ethical living belong together and an intimate connection exists between them. Morality and law not grounded in God sooner or later become a new kind of slavery. Where there is no recognition of God, human beings are diminished because they are deprived of that relationship with God for which humans by their very constitution are made (cf. Gen 1:26-27). Law and morality need a connection with God that is anchored in the cult and inspired by it. It is only when the human relationship with God is rightly ordered that all other relationships – with others, with creation – will be in order. It follows then that a right relationship with God is essential for a proper human existence. Accordingly, what took place at Sinai gave meaning to the possession of the Promised Land where the Israelites were free to live the truth of their humanity. They are now able to reach beyond the everyday to pursue an ever more perfect human existence. The function of the cult then was to facilitate and deepen that relationship with God without which life would be meaningless, because it would be bereft of its proper goal. However, if God had not revealed himself and indicated how he wishes to be worshipped, human beings would be left groping in the dark. When he does reveal himself, worship is no longer seeking the unknown God in the hope of finding him, but it now becomes God bending down in grace to draw human beings to himself.

For Worship

After the ratification of the covenant, Moses was instructed to build the tabernacle: 'Have them make me a sanctuary, so that I may dwell among them. In accordance with all that I show you concerning the pattern of the tabernacle and all of its furniture, so you shall make it' (25:8-9). The tabernacle is then described in the dimensions of the later Temple. At its completion, it is mentioned seven times that Moses did everything 'as the Lord commanded him' (40:16 ff). Then the cloud covered the tent and 'the glory of the Lord filled the tabernacle' (40:34). God now dwells in the midst of his people to accompany them on their journey to the Promised Land. The holy object symbolising the divine presence was the Ark that contained the Decalogue and was housed in the tabernacle. After gaining possession of the land, Israel worshipped at different shrines (Gilgal, Shiloh, Bethel, Ramah, etc.). The people gathered at them on important occasions to offer sacrifices to their God (Josh 14:16; 1 Sam 7:16; 11:14 ff; 13:4; 15:2; Am 4:4; 5:5) until David brought the Ark to Jerusalem and it was permanently installed in Solomon's temple. It was there Yahweh dwelt in the midst of his people enthroned upon the cherubim. However, after the division of the kingdom, royal temples were erected at Bethel and Dan, but the Israelites still continued to worship at the local shrines in towns and villages until the centralisation of worship in the Jerusalem Temple during Josiah's time.

The essential work of Moses, then, after he had led his people out of Egypt and sealed the covenant, was the construction of the tabernacle and the ordering of worship that was also at the heart of the law and moral instruction. In Israel, worship from the very beginning was linked to social and ethical responsibility. Its social consciousness was directly rooted in its religion and was nourished by worship. In time, the most important bearer of the Israelite tradition became the cult. It functioned as a means of renewal and purification that directly contributed to the formation and deepening of Israel's religious experience. Aware of the precariousness of their situation before God, the cult contributed to the constant education of the people with regard to the nature and meaning of their relationship with God and the necessity of fidelity to the covenant. In this way, it facilitated an ever more intense and personal awareness of the God of the covenant who set up his tabernacle in their midst. The juridical and liturgical structures of the covenant created the possibility of a profound personal experience when the individual interiorised the spirit of the Decalogue and participated in the cult with proper dispositions. However, these structures were not magical. Observance of the law could easily degenerate into legalism, participation in the cult into mere external routine. It would be the task of the prophets to reawaken the hearts of the people to pass beyond external observance and routine to an ever deepening encounter with the God of life and love.

Worship in Israel, therefore, refers first of all to the cult that was practised and celebrated in the precincts of the sanctuaries and later on in the Temple. But 'to serve Yahweh' meant more than encountering God in the cultic festivals. At the entrance to the sanctuary, worshippers were asked to perform an examination of conscience (cf. Pss 15, 24) concerning their conduct in daily life. And so the life of worship maintained links with daily living and true worship in turn influenced community living by motivating ethical conduct. Nevertheless, worship was a special event in the service of Yahweh, the source of all life and activity because Yahweh's mighty deeds in history, including creation, were recalled and remembered. Worship also had a future aspect that involved waiting for the Lord, hoping for the universal fulfilment of the destiny of Israel in the world of the nations.

SACRIFICE [3]

The notion of sacrifice is now so alien to people that it is almost incomprehensible. This is compounded by the fact that sacrificial ritual is at the very heart of the Pentateuch and demands an effort on our part to grasp such an elusive concept.

The Meaning of Sacrifice

Sacrifice is an essential act of worship in all the major religions and one of their chief forms. The ancestors of Israel built altars and worshipped their God (Gen 12:8; 13:18; 15:9-10,17; 21:33; 22:1-19; 35:7). Sacrifice is an acted out prayer, a symbolic action that gives expression to our deepest instincts. It is part of our response to the mystery of being, to the experience of the numinous that inspires awe, wonder, reverence and obedience. It is a way of acknowledging God as the source of our being and indeed of all created beings. From God we have come and to him we shall return at death. Sacrifice symbolises the surrender of one's life to the One to whom it belongs in the hope of establishing right relations with him. It signifies a turning around and facing in God's direction. Conscious of their finitude and estrangement from God, human beings wish to acknowledge God as absolute Lord in order to obtain his favours, to be liberated from alienation and sin, so as to enter into fellowship with him. Sacrifice is the outward manifestation of these attitudes. The offering of a gift functions as representing the offerer and manifests the intensity of his inner devotion. In the act of offering, the gift is withdrawn from profane use and handed over to God together with the offerer in the hope of mediating a relationship between them. It is the transfer of ownership of something precious, and embodies love and surrender, not the placating of an angry Deity.

The religion of Israel may be described as a search for communion with Yahweh, the God of Israel. By means of the prescribed rites, regarded as given to Moses by God, the sacrifice offered is accepted by God, guilt is taken away and union with God is achieved. It is essential though that the external act expresses the true inward sentiments of the worshipper since its efficacy is intimately bound up with them.

The altar[4] was the place of sacrifice, understood as symbolising God. The victims offered were usually domestic animals or vegetable produce, both of which were needed to sustain life. By offering them in sacrifice, the worshipper no longer lays claim to them for they are totally or partially destroyed or burnt upon the altar. As a result, they acquire a spiritual form as they arise in smoke from the altar upwards to God. The blood of the victim, regarded as the seat of life, is poured out at the base of the altar, or rubbed on the horns of the altar.

The rites used in Israelite sacrifice were of ancient origin and were similar to those practiced by the Canaanites who inhabited the land prior to the advent of the Israelites. When they settled in the Promised Land, the Israelites adopted and adapted these borrowed rites to serve their own specific purposes. The extensive ritual of sacrifice in the book of Leviticus, although compiled for use in Second Temple Judaism, does contain ancient elements going back to the time of the monarchy and beyond. The essential forms of the cult, therefore, were in place before the Exile, but obviously there was development. The two most frequently attested sacrifices in the Old Testament are holocausts and communion sacrifices. To these may be added sacrifices for sin and sacrifices of reparation which gained prominence in the post-exilic period.

Kinds of Sacrifice

The characteristic of the holocaust (*'olah*)[5] is that the entire victim is burnt on the altar. The victim is usually a domestic animal together with flour mixed with oil and a libation of wine. The blood of the victim is poured out at the base of the altar. Blood, the seat of life, belongs to God in a special way. In time the holocaust became the regular sacrifice offered in the Temple and was also offered on solemn occasions. The holocaust functioned as an act of homage to God. By the unreserved transfer of the gift to him, God's power and lordship is acknowledged.

In communion sacrifices[6] the victim is immolated and is shared between God, the participating priest and the offerer. The blood is poured out at the base of the altar and the fat is burned on the altar. The offerer's portion is consumed as a holy thing in the company of family and friends in the Temple precincts. Communion sacrifices can assume different forms:

sacrifice of praise (*todah*) offered on the occasion of a solemnity; freewill offering (*nedabah*) offered out of private devotion; votive offering (*neder*) as part of the fulfilment of a vow. Communion sacrifices were joyful occasions in which God and the offerer were united by partaking of the same victim and the bond of communion between them was thereby maintained or strengthened. This type of sacrifice was common in Israel from the earliest days.

Expiatory sacrifices served to re-establish good relations between the worshipper and God after they had been severed. They originated from an awareness of a fault committed and the need to be restored to favour with God. They were of two kinds: sacrifice for sin (*chatta't*) and sacrifice of reparation (*'asham*), although it is now difficult to determine the proper function of each. In sacrifices for sin, blood played an important part. It was rubbed on the horns of the altar or sprinkled before the veil concealing the Holy of Holies. They took on a particular solemnity on the Day of Atonement when the High Priest entered the Holy of Holies and sprinkled the propitiatory, God's throne. The offerer received no part of the victim. Sacrifices of reparation, in contrast, seem to have envisaged only individuals. Expiatory sacrifices were usually offered first to deal with any trace of sin or impurity that may have come between God and the worshipper. When the rite of purification was completed, holocausts and communion sacrifices could then be offered.

The Israelite sacrificial system, therefore, rested on the idea of representation. God is worshipped by means of an extensive sacrificial system minutely set forth in the book of Leviticus at the centre of the Pentateuch. In the course of the liturgical year, especially during the great feasts of Passover, Pentecost and Tabernacles, it served to bring about expiation, purification, restoration and communion through the offering of victims in sacrifice. Although the essence of sacrifice is union of the worshipper and creation with God, since humans are sinful beings, sacrifice takes on added aspects of deliverance from estrangement and guilt, purification, healing and atonement. During the course of its history, the Israelite sacrificial system tended to become more and more replacement or substitution rather than representation. The prophets condemn the hollowness of a sacrificial system that does not truly represent the spirit of the worshipper.

Characteristics

Although the cult was the normal means by which the community encountered God, it was open to many abuses. That is why criticism of the cult was expressed in varying degrees of severity beginning with Samuel's criticism: 'Has the Lord as great delight in burnt offerings and sacrifices, as in obeying the voice of the Lord? Surely, to obey is better than sacrifice, and to heed than the fat of rams' (1 Sam 15:22). But prophetic criticism was not the whole story, for the cult also sustained the framework of Israelite belief, and its role in the formation of Old Testament literature is often underestimated. A widespread view used to be that the pre-exilic prophets were opposed to the whole sacrificial cult. What is clear, at any rate, is that they were inflexibly opposed to the cult as it was practised in their own day. To honour God by means of an empty recital, but not in real life by proper conduct, was no honour at all, and God must repudiate such meaningless worship. When the inward tie between the worshipper and the means of worship was severed, the prophets had to emphasise the primacy of a personal relationship with God and the ethical conduct that this entailed. Beginning with Amos, the pre-exilic prophets made violent attacks on Israelite worship, especially the offering of sacrifices (cf. Am 5:21-27; Hos 6:6; Is 1:11-17; Mic 6:6-8; Jer 7:1-8:3). They contrasted the futility of sacrifice with obedience to Yahweh, especially with regard to the practice of justice and righteousness. The external worship offered to Yahweh was presumably in accordance with the prescribed rites and so the expression of the prophets' condemnation has to be understood in context. The prophets also condemned the cult of their day because it was contaminated with pagan practices and ideas and became syncretic or idolatrous worship (cf. Hos 2:13-15; 4:12-14; 13:1-2).

Since sacrifice held such a central place in Israelite religion, it is surprising to find such harsh condemnations of it in the prophetic literature. But the prophets were first and foremost preachers and it would be wrong to mistake their critique for an objective systematic treatment. Their sermons were delivered in a highly charged atmosphere with a mixture of hyperbole, rhetoric and even polemic. Because the language is direct and unconditional, it is easy to misinterpret it to mean the condemnation of sacrifice and of the whole cult. In the Hebrew language an absolute statement or direct contrast is often made where in English we would use a comparison. For example, in Hosea 6:6: 'For I desire steadfast love and not sacrifice, the knowledge of God rather than burnt offerings,' the laws of Hebrew parallelism require that the first phrase be understood in the same comparative sense as the second. The prophets then did not condemn the cult *per se* and the prophet Ezekiel even outlined a programme of renewal for a restored Israel with all its external rituals (cf. Ezek 40-48).

Pre-Exilic Prophets

Amos preached in the northern kingdom of Israel towards the end of the reign of Jeroboam II (c. 786-746 BC) when Israel was enjoying a period of material prosperity. But this prosperity concealed the seeds of social decay – injustice, exploitation of the poor by the rich, unscrupulous merchants, corrupt judges. Yet in spite of this, the royal sanctuary at Bethel was full of activity with its magnificent display of liturgy that gave a false sense of security since it had little influence on daily living. The practice of religion had become an alibi for a lifestyle devoid of justice and concern for the poor. It was from within this situation of economic prosperity, political stability, social and economic inequality together with formalism in religious practice, that the prophet Amos spoke. There were pilgrimages to the shrines of Bethel and Gilgal to offer sacrifices, the giving of tithes and the offering of prayers that Amos sarcastically points out were occasions of sin: 'Come to Bethel – and transgress; to Gilgal – and multiply transgressions' (Am 4:4). Amos exaggerates for effect since they became a substitute for justice towards the poor (cf. Am 3:9-4:3). He is castigating the participants, not condemning the cult. God does not accept such sacrifices, holocausts and chants at the expense of justice. Religious practice seems to have become a drug to tranquillise conscience rather than a symbol of sincere offering of self to God. True worship, on the other hand, is a means of seeking God and his will: 'Seek good and not evil, that you may live; and so the Lord, the God of hosts, will be with you, just as you have said' (Am 5:14).

In 5:21-25, Amos begins with a harsh denunciation: 'I hate, I despise your festivals, and I take no delight in your solemn assemblies' (v. 21). This is followed by a passionate rejection of cultic festivities. Different kinds of sacrifices with their cultic offerings are rejected together with the accompanying festivities, singing and music. What God wishes is that justice and righteousness flow like a stream that never dries up, bringing fertility and life with it. Although such lavish sacrifices and offerings were not available during the desert period because of material circumstances and undeveloped legislation, Israel remained faithful to God's law. If the worshippers refused to alter their lifestyle, then God must intervene in a drastic manner.

Hosea, a contemporary of Amos, preached mainly against the idolatry and syncretism prevalent in the northern kingdom: 'I will punish her for her festival days of the Baals, when she offered incense to them and decked herself with rings and jewellery, and went after her lovers, and forgot me, says the Lord' (Hos 2:13). Even when Israel did return to the Lord, it was a short-lived and shallow repentance prompted by God's threat of punishment. Their love of God was as ephemeral as the morning fog or dew that vanishes at sunrise. God desires authentic covenant love and knowledge of him, and rejects their meaningless sacrifices (cf. Hos 6:4-6).

In the southern kingdom of Judah, Micah's preaching was

directed against officials in the Jerusalem power elite (Mic 3:9-
12). They had perverted justice, constructed imposing buildings
in the capital with the proceeds of extortion and murder.
Princes, priests and prophets are accused of greed in carrying
out their duties. When the prophet pronounced judgement
against them, they replied with a misplaced reliance on God's
presence: 'Surely the Lord is with us! No harm shall come upon
us' (Mic 3:11). In 6:1-8, God himself recalls the saving acts that
constituted Israel as his people, a summary of sacred history
from the Exodus to the conquest of the land. There follows a request for cultic guidance, for the speaker imagines that ritual
acts alone will constitute a fitting response – holocausts, sin-
offerings, other sacrificial acts, even the offering of the first-born
are proposed. But the very thought of such sacrifices is rejected
as appeasement of the Deity. Instead, Micah recalls the forgotten
essence of true religion: 'He has told you, O man, what is good;
and what does the Lord require of you but to do justice, and to
love kindness, and to walk humbly with your God?' (Mic 6:8).

The issue for Isaiah was the virtual absence of social justice in
the Jerusalem of his time, but he is not a champion of an ethical,
cultless, moralistic religion, as is sometimes thought. Only a
complete misunderstanding of the circumstances that gave rise
to the polemic in 1:11-20, as well as a lack of appreciation of the
literary genre, could see a complete antithesis between cult and
justice. The pericope is homiletic and rhetorical, one that poses
the question of the relationship between worship and social justice. It begins with a summons to hear, while vv.18-20 extend and
interpret the message of vv. 11-17, making the instructions explicit
and the results of the people's choice clear.

Yahweh denounces a worship that is used as a screen to commit injustice with greater ease. He is weary of such hypocritical
worship: 'I cannot endure iniquity and solemn assembly' (Isa
1:13) – the extravagant ritual surrounding sacrifices on festival
days, pilgrimages and a multiplicity of prayers. The abundance
of sacrifices is contrasted with their futility in rhetorical fashion
to drive home the message. Even prayer itself is rejected because

'your hands are full of blood' (v. 15), a metaphor for acts of violence. There follows a series of imperatives that would pave the
way for a return to Yahweh. It is a call to repentance by ceasing
to do evil. Positively, conversion means learning to do good,
serving justice by defending and pleading the cause of the pow-
erless in society – the oppressed, the orphan, and the widow.
These, if sincere, will help bring about forgiveness and a new beginning. The human response to God's gracious offer of forgiveness will determine the future.

One of the most memorable events of Jeremiah's prophetic
career was his Temple Sermon (Jer 7:1-15; cf. 26:1-19). It was delivered on a major occasion, probably a feastday, when throngs
of people flocked to worship in the Temple. The sermon begins
with an exhortation to the worshippers to amend their behaviour so that they can continue to dwell in the land. Jeremiah then
castigates them for the superstitious belief that the mere presence of God's Temple in their midst would be enough to protect
them from their enemies, irrespective of their conduct. In
mantra-like fashion they chant: 'This is the temple of the Lord,
the temple of the Lord, the temple of the Lord' (7:4), while thinking they are free to go on committing every kind of crime and
abomination. The prophet calls for a radical change of lifestyle
as he spells out what is required if the people are to dwell securely in the land. The intensity of the prophetic rhetoric continues
by citing the Decalogue prescriptions to show the incongruity
between violations of the social requirements of the covenant
and worship of God. What Jeremiah finds astonishing is that the
people can go on violating the covenant stipulations and at the
same time continue worshipping in the Temple, all the while
claiming its protection. In these circumstances, the Temple is no
longer a place of worship but becomes a lair for robbers and will
be destroyed like the shrine at Shiloh had been. In 7:21-23,
Jeremiah reminds the people that at Sinai God called for obedience to the Decalogue that had to do with conduct rather than
the offering of specific sacrifices. He is not contesting the fact
that there were sacrifices in the Mosaic period, but that they

were less important than the covenant stipulations so little heeded by his contemporaries (cf. Jer 6:19-20).

Conclusion

The prophetic denunciation of the cult was never understood subsequently as a rejection of the cult itself. Indeed, Israel could not have preserved her distinctive religion without the protective framework of the cult and its rituals that also had the effect of guiding people in the moral conduct of their lives. With the rebuilding of the Temple and the reforms of Ezra (cf. Ezra 1:2-4; 6:3-12; Neh 8-9) in the post-exilic period, the cult was restored. Both the Torah and the prophetic word continued to be heard in the liturgy and in time came to form the two main divisions of the Hebrew Bible (Torah and Prophets). The message of the prophets was preserved, passed on and heard again and again right into New Testament times. The historical particularity of the prophetic critique was left largely untouched by those who edited the prophetic books and they served to provide a normative criticism of distorted religion for subsequent generations (cf. Isa 66:3; Mal 1:6-2:9). They continue to be a word of criticism against persistent and recurring abuses of religion that threaten authentic faith in every age. Mere performance is always a temptation for the worshipper. The prophetic criticism was meant to purify motives, not abolish the sacrificial system. Their struggle to align prayer and sacrifice with ethical conduct remains our struggle too.

DEVELOPMENT

Spiritualisation

The post-exilic community was essentially a worshipping community. Sometime after the reforms of Ezra took root, the Chronicler wrote his history to highlight the role of David as founder of the Temple and its liturgy. If the community was to have a future, it was by continuing to worship God according to the pattern set by David, handed down by priests and Levites, and kept alive by the remnant that survived the Exile. Around this time also, the Psalter, a collection of collections that originated largely in Temple worship, reached its final form as an expression of personal and communal piety that continued to form part of Temple liturgies. The offering of sacrifice itself was considered to be a form of prayer, but it was also accompanied by vocal prayer (cf. Am 5:23). Psalms were used and some even make reference to a rite (e.g., Pss 20:5; 26:6-7; 27:6; 66:13-16). Many of the psalms express a positive attitude towards the Temple cult and its liturgies (e.g., Pss 4:6; 27:6; 42:5; 43:4; 54:6; 66:13-15; 107: 21-22; 116:14, 18; 118:27). Some psalms, however, were influenced by the prophetic critique of the cult. Ps 40:7-9 stresses the priority of obedience to God's law over the offering of sacrifice. In Ps 50:8-15, animal sacrifice is unacceptable to God when there is a misunderstanding of its true purpose – that God needs to receive gifts or that he experiences hunger like the pagan gods. In contrast, true worshippers who 'bring thanksgiving as their sacrifice honour me' (v. 23). Ps 51:16-19 states that God takes no pleasure in animal sacrifice nor will he accept burnt offering from those who have gravely sinned. In that case, 'the sacrifice acceptable to God is a broken spirit; a broken and contrite heart, O God, you will not despise' (v. 17). This critique is modified in v. 19 to express unconditional approval of proper animal sacrifices and looks forward to a time when they will again be offered and accepted. There is emphasis on prayer in Ps 69:30-31: 'I will praise the name of God with a song; I will magnify him with thanksgiving. This will please the Lord more than an ox or a bull with horns and hoofs.' In Ps 141:2 the psalmist is hopeful that his prayer may be accepted like the incense offering and evening sacrifice that were part of the Temple ritual. No rejection of sacrifice is here implied. Elsewhere, the Psalter expresses strong approval of the Temple and its sacrifices that were taken for granted as a normal feature of worship. Nevertheless, a degree of 'spiritualisation' has taken place. Private prayer can in some circumstances take the place of Temple sacrifices.

Interiorisation

A parallel development can be traced back to the prophetic criticism which also contributed to making the cult a more interior experience for the worshipper. Israel's consistent failure to heed the prophetic warning led to a conflict that reached its extreme form shortly before the Exile. Jeremiah enacted in his own life the crisis of Israel. He suffered in solitude, in communion with God, under the disorder of a society to which he did not cease to belong. His 'Confessions,' fragments of a spiritual autobiography, are personal testimony to his interior struggles to remain faithful. He expostulates with God whose word only brings him affliction. The hostility he encountered because of his prophetic mission occasioned intense inner anguish. He was rejected as much as God whose spokesperson he was. Together with the biographical material (ch 36-44), they have to do with the failure of Jeremiah and so of God to change his people. The result was the loss of the land and exile to Babylon.

During the Exile there was no Temple, no public or communal form of worship, no sacrifice any more. The Exiles could no longer worship God in the accustomed way. This gave rise to the problem of how a right relationship with God could be kept alive, for this was the purpose of the cult. No longer able to celebrate the Temple liturgy, they could only suffer for the sake of their God and arrived at a new insight – that suffering could be a true sacrifice, a new form of worship. It could be offered not only on behalf of sinful Israel, but for the whole world.

The role of suffering was powerfully articulated by an unknown prophet of the Exile, conventionally known as Deutero-Isaiah (Isa 40-55). Four songs (42:1-4(9); 49:1-6; 50:4-9; 52:13-53:12) describe the vocation of a Servant whose task it is to bring the nations of the world into proper relationship with the God of Israel and this involves him in suffering to fulfil it. His message provokes hostility, persecution and physical assault. Nevertheless, he accepts this suffering as part of his vocation and persists in obedience, confident that God will come to his help (50:5-9). In the fourth song, an innocent person suffers. An anonymous crowd speaks of his birth and growth, suffering and passion, condemnation, execution and glorification. They undergo a change of attitude and confess their sins when they realise that there has been a divine purpose to the Servant's sufferings from which they have in some way benefited. Now they know that the very suffering which made them avoid him was a sacrifice of reparation ('asham, v.10), willed by God and freely accepted by the Servant. His suffering is vicarious as a representative sufferer.

> The order of being has revealed its mystery of redemption as the flower of suffering. It does not mean, however, that the vision of the mystery is the reality of redemption in history. The participation of man in divine suffering has yet to encounter the participation of God in human suffering.[7]

The identity of the Servant remains indeterminate throughout, perhaps deliberately so. Now every suffering just person, to the extent that he exemplifies in his own life the drama of the Suffering Servant, is mirrored in this portrayal (cf. Psalms of Petition; Wis 2:10-20). As well, it opens up to the expectation of one in whom all this will be entirely true.

Israel's experience of suffering during the Exile and the martyrdom undergone during the persecution in Maccabean times (167-164 BC) were believed to be a means of atonement for the people's sins (2 Macc 7:37-38). The vicarious surrender of one's life was thought to have sacrificial significance, and brought personal sacrifice and prayer into prominence as the equivalent of sacrifices offered in the Temple. These themes run parallel to each other throughout the remainder of the pre-Christian period. The experience of the Exile, then, together with prophets and psalmists provided the insight that a contrite spirit is a true sacrifice (Ps 51:17), and Israel began to grasp that the sacrifice pleasing to God is first and foremost a person pleasing to God and that prayer can be a true sacrifice. Ben Sira, a staunch supporter of the liturgy, regards obedience to the law as itself a fulfilment of ritual worship (35:1-10). Meanwhile, the Qumran community, unable to take part in Temple worship, interpreted its communal life and prayer in cultic terms (cf. IQS 8:5-10). For Diaspora Jews,

unable to frequent the Temple in Jerusalem, synagogue worship
stressed the holiness of everyday living and provided a substitute for the Temple sacrificial system. In the Hellenistic world by
the beginning of the Christian era a polemic against blood sacrifice was reaching its climax. Jews living in Alexandria came into
contact with this critique of the cult of the gods, and the concept
logike latria (thusia), sacrifice with spirit and mind, became increasingly important. It was into such a world that Christianity
was born.

FULFILMENT [8]

Jesus brings together the various strands of the Old Testament
that had remained separate. He did not condemn sacrifice as
such: he offered himself as a sacrifice (Mk 10:45), as the paschal
victim (1 Cor 5:7), as the sacrifice of the new covenant (Lk 22:20;
1 Cor 11:25). Jesus' self-offering is the perfect sacrifice in virtue
of the nature and dispositions of the offerer and victim, and by
reason of the manner in which it was performed. It is at one and
the same time a total self-offering to God, a communion sacrifice
more intimate than could have been imagined, an expiatory sacrifice sufficient to atone for all the sins of the world. As the perfect sacrifice, all other forms of sacrifice now become redundant.
The Temple could be destroyed, animal sacrifice could cease, for
what they represented is now fulfilled and even surpassed in
Christ who offered himself 'once for all' in a 'unique offering' for
our sanctification and redemption. His sacrifice avails for all and
need never be repeated (cf. Heb 7:26-28; 9:11-12, 24-28; 10:10, 12).
All this is dramatically indicated in the rending of the Temple
veil at the moment of Jesus' death (Mk 15:37-38). Access to the
true heavenly sanctuary of God's presence has now been
opened up for all.

In the New Testament eucharistic traditions, certain elements
suggest that a sacrificial interpretation is being proposed: the
framework of the institution is the Passover feast which was interpreted as a sacrifice because of the slaughter of lambs and the
shedding of blood; the words over the cup include 'the blood of

the covenant which is poured out for many' (Mk 14:24), an allusion to the Sinai covenant sacrifice and meal (cf. Ex 24:1-11); the phrases 'this is my body which is given for you' (Lk 22:19) and 'for many' recall the Suffering Servant (Isa 53:12); Mt 26:28 adds 'for the forgiveness of sins' associating it with sacrifices for sin; 'the cup that is poured out for you is the new covenant in my blood' (Lk 22:20) associates it with the new covenant foretold by Jeremiah (31:31-34); 'Do this in remembrance of me' (Lk 22:19; 1 Cor 11:24) recalls the injunction to celebrate the Passover (Ex 12:14).[9] In John, Jesus is 'the Lamb of God who takes away the sin of the world' (Jn 1:29,36), as a sacrificial offering provided by God (cf. Gen 22:8,13) to remove the world's sin (cf. Isa 53:7,8).

> Jesus, in accepting his death, gathers together and condenses in his person the whole of the Old Testament; first the theology of sacrifice, that is, everything that went on in the Temple and everything to do with the Temple, then the theology of the Exile, of the Suffering Servant. Now a third element is added, a passage from Jeremiah (31:31) in which the prophet predicts the New Covenant.[10]

All these associations are the result of a theological development based on the words and gestures of Jesus who interpreted his death as a voluntary self-offering to God, his Father: 'It was not primarily their own [the disciples] theological reflections, but above all the interpretative sayings of Jesus at the Last Supper which showed them how to understand his death properly.'[11] In the post-Easter period this was made explicit with the help of sacrificial terminology. For Paul, Jesus' self-offering on the cross becomes a present reality in the celebration of the Eucharist (cf. 1 Cor 11:26). The most systematic treatment of Jesus' death in relation to the Old Testament sacrificial cult, though, occurs in the Epistle to the Hebrews. By his self-offering as victim on the cross, Jesus removed once for all the burden of sin separating humankind from God and opened up access to God for all time: 'But when Christ came as the high priest of the good things to come, then through the greater and perfect tent (not made with hands, that is, not of this creation), he entered once for all into the Holy Place, not with the blood of goats and calves, but with his own blood, thus obtaining eternal redemption … For this reason he is mediator of a new covenant, so that those who are called may receive the promised eternal inheritance' (Heb 9:11-12, 15). The self-offering of Jesus in freedom and love is the kernel of what happened on Calvary and this is ritually made present in our Eucharist. Here at last is right worship, adoration 'in spirit and truth' (Jn 4:24). Christian liturgy, then, is one of promise brought to fulfilment, of the whole Old Testament and indeed of the whole human religious quest, but it has yet to reach its goal when 'the kingdom of the world has become the kingdom of our Lord and of his Messiah, and he will reign for ever and ever' (Rev 11:15).

Conclusion

As a result of Jesus' saving death, resurrection and sending of the Spirit, an entirely new meaning is given to sacrifice which is now focused exclusively on its personal core and from which ethical consequences can be drawn for living the Christian life of faith. Henceforth, Christians in union with Christ, can worship in a manner worthy of human beings: 'Present your bodies as a living sacrifice, holy and acceptable to God, which is your spiritual worship. Do not be conformed to this world, but be transformed by the renewing of your minds, so that you may discern what is the will of God – what is good and acceptable and perfect' (Rom 12:1-3; cf 1 Pet 2:5).

CHAPTER THREE

Johannine Perspectives on the Eucharist

Michael Mullins

Many terms have been used for the celebration of the Eucharist, some of the more well known being the Breaking of the Bread, the Sacrifice of the Mass, the Eucharist, the Lord's Supper and Holy Communion. Each term focuses on a dimension of the mystery being celebrated and the range of terms shows how there have been shifts of emphasis in understanding and appreciation of the mystery over the centuries.

Most people's images and understanding of the mystery are, however, not drawn from advanced theological study and biblical research, but arise in large measure from lived personal experience generated by upbringing and schooling, fed through devotion, art and music and, above all, through their personal experience of the liturgy. In addition to their experience of the central elements of 'the twofold table of the Lord's Word and Supper' their appreciation of the mystery is enriched by a whole array of prayers, hymns and ceremonies that have grown up around the 'core' of the celebration. Before the distribution of Holy Communion, for example, there is the appeal to the Lamb of God who takes away the sins of the world to have mercy on us and grant us peace. This is followed by the invitation to come forward to the supper of the Lamb with the proclamation, 'This is the Lamb of God who takes away the sins of the world, blessed are those who are called to his supper.' After the distribution of Communion the 'hosts' are placed in the 'Tabernacle' before which the sanctuary lamp burns to remind us of the 'real presence'. During the Mass the *Panis Angelicus* may be sung reminding us that the poor, the slave and the lowly can share the banquet of the Lord, or *O Sacrum Convivium* which praises 'the sacred banquet in which Christ is received, the memory of his passion is brought to life, and to us is granted a pledge of eternal glory.' After receiving the Body and Blood of the Lord, *Soul of my Saviour* is often sung with its appeal to be cleansed by the blood and water from the side of Christ.

Outside the celebration of Mass and Holy Communion, eucharistic devotions like Benediction, Holy Hours, prayer at the 'altar of repose' on Holy Thursday and the solemn Corpus Christi procession, in which eucharistic hymns such as *O Salutaris Hostia, Tantum Ergo* and *O Sacrament Most Holy* are sung, enrich our spiritual awareness. On the feast of the Sacred Heart the words of the Preface remind us that the blood and water which flowed from the pierced side of Christ are the fountains of the sacramental life of the church.

These inspiring ceremonies are the product of two thousand years of celebration, reflection and theological elaboration, and the gospel of John has been the inspiration for many of the prayers and hymns. Whereas Paul and the synoptic gospels focus on the central 'ritual' action whereby the paschal mystery, the Christian Passover, was instituted by Jesus at the Last Supper as a 'memorial' of his saving death to be celebrated 'until he comes', John focuses not on the 'ritual' by which the Eucharist was instituted and continues to be celebrated, but on the deeper significance of the mystery behind the ritual. Subsequent Christian celebration has knit together the more 'ritual' based texts of Pauline and synoptic tradition and the highly symbolic and theologically laden texts of the Johannine tradition which focus on Jesus as life-giver and revealer. This article focuses on the contribution of John to the understanding and celebration of the mystery.

J. R. Donahue and D. J. Harrington in their commentary on Mark in the *Sacra Pagina* series make a point about the Eucharist which is equally relevant to John as it is to Mark:

The eucharistic celebration of the church combines many perspectives: recollection of the Exodus deliverance, continuation of Jesus' presence through a meal, the sacramental re-enactment of his Passion and death, the foretaste of the heavenly

banquet, the presentation of Jesus as a model of loving service (the footwashing in John), and an anticipation of the
heavenly banquet. Mark's somewhat sober narrative stresses
above all the sacrificial death of Jesus 'for many' and so is a
caution against overstressing the communal meal as the
leading motif of the Eucharist. We recall not only a meal, but
the final meal of one who was to be executed as a criminal for
our sake…[The] reception of the Eucharist cannot be separated
from responding to the challenge of discipleship that permeates the gospel, though the failure of the chosen Twelve
serves as a warning that meeting this challenge is never complete. As a covenant 'in my blood' the Eucharist is a promise
that Jesus will be with the believer in the present and in the
future banquet of the kingdom.[1]

I. EMERGENCE OF THE TRADITIONS

A brief look at the biblical documents in their generally accepted
chronological sequence will throw light on the emergence of the
tradition(s).

The Pauline Tradition

Paul hands on the tradition of the institution of the Eucharist in
his First Letter to the Corinthians. This is the oldest written account and comes in the standard form for handing on tradition,
'I received … and handed on.'

> This is what I received from the Lord and in turn handed on
> to you: that on the same night that he was *betrayed*, the Lord
> Jesus *took* some bread, and *thanked* God for it and *broke* it and
> said, 'This is my body, which is *for you*; do this as a *memorial*
> of me.' In the same way he *took* the cup after the supper, and
> said, 'This cup is the *new covenant* in *my* blood. Whenever you
> drink it, do this as a *memorial* of me.' *Until the Lord comes*,
> therefore, every time you eat this bread and drink this cup,
> *you are proclaiming his death* … (1 Cor 11:23-26).

Using the ritualised language of a festive meal (*taking, thanking, breaking, sharing*), Jesus interprets the meal in terms of the vicarious nature of his death (*for you*), and how it initiates a whole new relationship with God (*the new covenant in my blood*). This is reminiscent both of the original covenant sacrifice and meal at Sinai (Ex 24:1-11) and of the atoning, vicarious death of the Suffering Servant (Is 53:12). The reference to a new covenant also associates the ritual action with the promise of a new covenant prophesied by Jeremiah (Jer 31:31-34). The command to 'do this in memory of me' recalls the injunction to celebrate the Passover (Ex 12:14; cf. Lk 22:19). St Paul reminds the Corinthians that this memorial will be celebrated until the Lord comes, and it will proclaim his death until he comes, that is, it will publicly acknowledge the salvific nature of his death, a triumph far removed from the intended disgrace. The meal itself and its salvific promise are set in the context of the betrayal that led to Jesus' death. Crucifixion was designed not only to destroy the victim's body but to disgrace him and eliminate his following, thus deleting all memory of him from the mind of humanity. Significantly, Jesus secures his memory in the command to 'do this in memory of me.'

The Synoptic Tradition

The Institution Narratives in the gospels of Matthew, Mark and Luke give an account of the institution of the Eucharist during the Last Supper (Mt 26:26-29; Mk 14:22-24; Lk 22:19-20). As in the Pauline passage from 1 Corinthians, the ritual actions of a festal meal – *taking bread, saying the blessing* and / or *giving thanks, breaking the bread* and *sharing/giving it*, (and similarly with the cup) – are solemnised and interpreted in the context of Jesus' impending death and its significance for a whole new relationship with God, a (new) covenant in his blood. The language of Mark and Matthew reflects the more Semitic tradition of referring to the accompanying prayer as 'said the blessing' while Luke resembles Paul in referring to it as 'giving thanks', *eucharistêsas*, from which the Eucharist takes its name. Luke resembles Paul also in instructing the disciples to repeat the action as a memorial and also in referring to a *new* covenant (though new is implied in the other accounts). The phrases *given for you* (Lk 22:19) and *poured out for many* (Mk 14:24; Mt 26:28) recall the vicarious suffering of the Suffering Servant. Matthew's addition of 'for the forgiveness of sins' (Mt 26:28) associates the Eucharist with the tradition of offering sacrifices for sin.

The Multiplication Narratives reflect the language of the Jewish festal meal, already established in early Christian eucharistic practice. It is reflected also in the accounts of the multiplication of the loaves, appearing in all four gospels, twice each in Matthew and Mark, six times in all (Mt 14:13-21; 15:32-39; Mk 6:34-44; 8:1-10; Lk 9:12-17; Jn 6:1-13). The double accounts in Matthew and Mark represent the messianic banquet for Jew and Gentile, a significance brought out by way of reference to location and by the use of symbolic numbers (of the people and the baskets of food left over). Significantly John uses the account of the multiplication of the loaves and fishes to open his lengthy chapter on the food that endures to eternal life.

In addition to the concentration on the words of institution one must pay attention to other essential aspects of the eucharistic mystery. The account of the disciples on the road to Emmaus (Lk 24:13-35) explores four modes of the presence of the Risen Christ. First of all, he is present in the journey through life where we are gathered in his name, like the disciples leaving Jerusalem for Emmaus perplexed and disappointed after their hopes had been dashed. Jesus was present to them as a stranger on the road sharing their story. Secondly, he was powerfully present to them in the opening of the scriptures whereby he caused their hearts to burn within them and moved them to invite him to share their evening meal and accommodation. Thirdly, he was present 'in the breaking of the bread' when their roles were reversed and, in a setting mirroring the Christian Eucharist, the guest became the host at the breaking of the bread. Fourthly, the presence of Christ in the church and in its leadership was confirmed when the Eleven and those who were with them proclaimed to the disciples returned from the road to Emmaus that

Jesus was truly risen and had appeared to Simon. Their individual experience of the Risen Lord on the road was confirmed within the communal experience of the church and its authority.

The Tradition in the Acts of the Apostles

In the Acts of the Apostles the term *the breaking of bread* signifies the celebration of the Eucharist. The practice of the first Christians in Jerusalem is described in the summary statement in chapter two: 'They remained faithful to the teaching of the apostles, to the brotherhood, to the breaking of bread and to the prayers … They went as a body to the Temple every day but met in their houses for the breaking of bread'(Acts 2:42, 46). The narrator in Acts, describing the visit of Paul and companions to Troas, states that: 'On the first day of the week we gathered together to break bread' and they broke bread following the raising up of the boy who fell asleep on the window during the lengthy sermon and fell three storeys to the ground (Acts 20:7, 11).

The Johannine Tradition

St John's Gospel comes later and, although it does not have an institution narrative like those of Paul and the synoptic gospels, it mirrors the eucharistic teaching and traditions through its own special insight, reflection and theology. The explicit references to the food that endures to eternal life are in the sixth chapter and they are a focus or funnel for the overall teaching of the gospel. Though there is no account of the institution of the Eucharist during the Last Supper, the focus on the washing of the feet, the sharing of the morsel, the farewell discourse(s) and the priestly prayer of Jesus on that occasion, bring out the deeper significance of the 'ritual' institution of the Eucharist in the synoptic and Pauline accounts. Furthermore, the various scenes on Golgotha are rich in highly symbolic imagery focusing on the birth of the church against the background of the paschal celebration.

On first approaching St John's Gospel one is struck by the

fact that the sixth chapter contains a lengthy treatise, with many well known sayings on the food that endures to eternal life: 'Do not work for food that cannot last, but work for food that endures to eternal life' (Jn 6:27); 'I am the living bread which has come down from heaven. Anyone who eats this bread will live forever' (Jn 6:51); 'Anyone who eats my flesh and drinks my blood has eternal life and I will raise him up on the last day' (Jn 6:54); 'The spirit is life-giving … the words which I have spoken to you are spirit and they are life' (Jn 6:63). The promise of eternal life in these statements stands in sharp contrast to the merely physical life sustained by the original bread from heaven, the manna in the desert. On further investigation one finds that chapter six opens with an account of the multiplication of the loaves and fishes which, like the synoptic parallel accounts, contains the ritual actions and words associated with the institution of the Eucharist in the synoptic and Pauline traditions: 'Jesus then took the loaves, gave thanks and distributed them to those who were seated' (Jn 6:11).

To be properly understood, the teaching and allusions in chapter six must be examined in the context of the chapter as a whole and the gospel as a whole. In turn, the Johannine text must be seen in the broader context of the Old and New Testaments, particularly in relation to two major roles of Jesus, that of *life-giver* and *revealer*, both of which are highlighted against the background of Jesus' teaching in the context of the feasts and institutions of the Jews.

There are several pivotal motifs in the gospel and they are so tightly interwoven and ubiquitous that it is difficult to treat them in isolation from one another. They give the gospel the character of a tapestry or even a seamless robe since they hold together the different, even contending, traditions in a weave of recurring and related themes. These themes are interwoven around the two principal functions of Jesus as *life-giver* and *revealer*, and they are explored in great measure in the context of the Sabbath, the feasts and the worship of the Jews. The various titles and functions of Jesus are also related to his two main roles of *life-giver* and *revealer* which are regularly presented in the gospel in terms of life and light.

II. LIFE AND LIGHT

Life/Life-giver

The pre-existent life of the *Logos* in eternity with God is high-lighted in St John's Gospel by the repeated use in the prologue of the verb *ên* (was), the imperfect of the verb 'to be' in its absolute and predicative uses. Its significance is reflected repeatedly in the 'I am' (*egô eimi*) proclamations of Jesus' ministry[2] where he refers to himself in terms that recall the revelation to Moses of the Divine Name at the burning bush, regularly translated as 'I am who I am', a name which focuses on the Divine Existence (Ex 3:14). The eternal existence of the Word with the Father is summed up in the final sentence of the Prologue in a participial phrase, *ho ôn eis ton kolpon tou Patros*, 'the one who is in the bosom of the Father'. This revelation is vital to the questioning throughout the gospel about where he dwells, whence he came and whither he goes.

A very significant aspect of the eternal pre-existence of the *Logos* is borne out in the statement 'in him was life'. The significance of the theme of life is seen from the fact that *zôê* (life) is used thirty six times throughout the gospel, seventeen times combined with *aiônios*, eternal. The corresponding verb *zên* is used seventeen times and the verb *zôopoiein*, to give life, three times. *Zôê aiônios* is a favourite expression of the gospel and First Letter of John. It is emphasised in the body of the gospel in Jesus' declaration that 'as the Father has life in himself so he has granted the Son also to have life in himself' (Jn 5:26). By command of the Father Jesus exercises sovereignty over his own life. This is borne out in the teaching about the ideal shepherd who lays down his life for his sheep. 'I lay down my life in order to take it up again. No one takes it from me, but I lay it down of my own accord. I have power to lay it down and I have power to take it up again' (Jn 10:18). Not alone has the Word made flesh, the Son (of God), the Son of Man, life in himself, but he has power to communicate that life to others.[3] He has received the command from the Father to do so (Jn 10:18 ff.). He states: 'As the Father raises the dead and gives them life, so also the Son gives life' (Jn 5:21). 'I have come that they may have life and have it to the full' (Jn 10:10). This is borne out most dramatically at the raising of Lazarus when Jesus declares that he is the resurrection and the life (Jn 11:25) and at the Last Supper when he declares: 'I am the way, the truth and the life' (Jn 14:6). Jesus sums up the purpose of his ministry in the saying: 'I have come that they may have life *(zôê)* and have it to the full' and this is reflected in the stated purpose of the gospel which was 'written that you may believe that Jesus is the Christ, the Son of God, and that believing this you may have life *(zôê)* in his name' (Jn 10:10; 20:31).

All life flowed through the Word. He is the giver and sustainer of life and this is reflected in the metaphors of life-giving water, life-giving bread, and life-giving vine. Jesus promises the Samaritan woman that if she asks he will give her 'living water … a spring that wells up to eternal life' and at the Feast of Tabernacles he promised 'rivers of living water' for those who believe' (Jn 4:10, 14; 7:38). The promise of eternal life comes through Jesus as a gift from the Father who sent him because 'He loved the world so much that he gave his Only Son so that those who believe in him might not perish but have eternal life' (Jn 3:16).

Light/Revealer

There is an intimate link between life and revelation, life and light. God's presence in creation and in history was a light in the world, particularly in the history of the chosen people. Creation, Wisdom and Torah reflected that light. In Christ, the true Light, the Light of the world has come. This is the ultimate revelation and Jesus' ministry is full of references to the light and its acceptance or rejection. Jesus declares himself to be the Light of the World during the Feast of Tabernacles in which there was great emphasis on the theme of light. His followers are told to walk in the light. 'He who follows me will never walk in darkness but will have the light of life' (Jn 8:12). Those who reject him reject the light and are aligned to the unbelieving world. They come under the judgement because 'the light has come into the world and people loved darkness rather than light because their deeds were evil' (Jn 3:19f).

Jesus, the Incarnate *Logos*, is the revealer who illuminates all existence. 'Through the gift of life given by the one sent by God there is the possibility of new life and the way to God is opened up.'[4] Jesus' life is the revelation of the Father. 'He who has seen me has seen the Father' (Jn 14:9). He links this revelation with the gift of eternal life when he says in the Farewell Discourse at the Last Supper: 'And this is eternal life, that they may know you, the only true God, and Jesus Christ whom you have sent' (Jn 17:3). This is the ultimate significance of the many references to Jesus as Light in the gospel. Putting his life-giving revelation in the overall context of his mission as revealer sent by the Father, Jesus says, 'I am the way, the truth and the life' (Jn 14:6), which is best understood as 'I am the way (because I am) the truth and the life, that is, I am the way because I am the revealer and the life-giver.'

In biblical language light is also a pointer to God's presence and glory. When the first two disciples approached Jesus he turned and asked them: 'What do you seek?' to which they responded with the question: 'Rabbi, where do you dwell *(pou meneis)*?' He replied: 'Come and see!' This exchange at the outset provides an interpretative key for the many uses of *menein/monê* (dwell/dwelling) in the gospel. 'Where', 'whence' and 'whither' recur throughout the gospel as disciples and people wonder where Jesus dwells, where he has come from and where he is going. This questioning about 'dwelling' recurs throughout the gospel and is very much in evidence in the Farewell Discourse(s) as Jesus promises the disciples a future life with Father, Son and Spirit–Paraclete so that 'where I am you may be also' (Jn 14:3).

III. FEAST / REMEMBRANCE.

To understand John it is necessary to understand the importance and role of the feasts and institutions of the Jews as they appear in the gospel. They were intended to reveal God, enabling the people to approach God, to be righteous before God and to savour the presence of God in their midst. As Christians re-assessed all these things in the early years of the church, and especially after the destruction of the Temple with its Divine Presence and its atoning rituals, the 'once-for-all' character of the revelation through Jesus encouraged a radical reassessment of many, if not all, of the earlier means of mediation. Beginning in the Temple with its sacrificial worship and atoning rituals, the story of Jesus in St John's Gospel unfolds through the succession of Jewish feasts, showing how Jesus fulfils and surpasses the older promise of institution or feast, opens up its meaning for the present and anticipates the future. Naming a feast not only creates an atmosphere for the reader as it conjures up a mood of celebration, but it provides the religious and theological frame-work for presenting the claims of Jesus and his ministry and en-ables the reader to come to an understanding of Jesus as the new temple, altar and lamb of sacrifice.

The papal encyclical *EdE* states at the outset that the church was born of the paschal mystery. St John's gospel is steeped in Passover/paschal imagery and celebration. It is during the first Passover Feast in his ministry that Jesus symbolically replaces Temple ritual and promises a new Temple. At the approach of the second Passover Feast he repeats the miracles of Moses when he feeds the crowd in the desert, saves the disciples from the sea, and then delivers the discourse(s) on the food that en-dures to eternal life. His death and glorification, and the birth of the church on Golgotha, take place during the third and final Passover of his ministry. Given this emphasis on feasts it is therefore very important to understand their significance for the Jews in order to appreciate their significance in John.

Celebrating the feasts enabled the participants to share in the history of God's dealings with the people, reviving their reli-

gious memory, sharpening their focus and heightening expectation for God's saving action in the present and the future. The
Hebrew name for a feast is *zikkârôn*, from the verb *zâkar*, to remember. 'Remembering' in the context of a feast is not just a recalling of the past, but a making present for every subsequent
generation of the experience of those who originally partook in
the saving event.[5] Ritual made the participants the contemporaries
of the events they remembered in celebration. The feasts collapsed time into the present time of the festival. In St John's
gospel Jesus steps into the context of the feasts, fulfils their
promise and opens up the future. He fulfils the promise embodied in the Temple and its atoning rituals and in the institutions
and the feasts of the Jews. In so doing he appropriates to himself
the cultic symbols of sacred space (Jn 2:2:19f; 10:36), sacred time
(Jn 5:17), bread (Jn 6:35,48,51), water (Jn 7:37-39), light (Jn 8:12)
and shepherding (Jn 1:1-18), all of which are associated with
Sabbath, Passover, Tabernacles and Dedication. Jesus now absorbs the feast in himself and his ministry, fulfilling its promise
in his own life, death and resurrection. Jesus himself becomes
the event to be remembered.

Originally the Passover *(Pesah)* probably combined an older
nomadic, pastoral feast celebrated with the slaying of a sheep or
goat and a settled agricultural feast of the grain (barley) harvest.
The Passover sacrifice has its origins in the nomadic times when
the shepherd sacrificed an animal and sprinkled the blood on
the tent pegs to ensure fertility for the flock and safety for the in-
habitants. The sacrificial meal was then eaten with bitter herbs
gathered in the desert, in the nomadic style of someone ready
for a journey. The feast of Unleavened Bread had its origin in an
agricultural celebration of the barley harvest when all the old
leaven was got rid of, and a new beginning was embarked upon
with bread made from the new grain. The consecration of the
first-born began as a feast recognising the gift of life from the
Deity, with the sacrifice of the first born of the animals and the
consecration of the first born of the children. The first-born was
believed to embody the best qualities. These older pastoral and

agricultural festivals were eventually combined and historicised into a festival celebrating the Passover, Exodus and Wandering which brought the people to Canaan. The slaying of the lamb recalled the escape from the plague of death visited on the first-born in Egypt. The sprinkling of the blood of the lamb symbolised the gift of life, and the sealing or anointing of the Israelites as the first-born of God. In its origin it saw the formation of a people and at many critical points of persecution and dispersion in their history the celebration of the Passover marked the people's experience of survival, gathering, restoration and new beginnings. It was a community building celebration.

The Passover in Jesus' time was celebrated as one of the three great pilgrimage feasts. However, between the lifetime of Jesus and the time when the gospel was written a change of seismic proportions had taken place. The Temple and its sacrifices were destroyed, Jerusalem was no longer the great focus of pilgrimage, and the Passover sacrificial meal evolved into the non-sacrificial meal celebrated in a domestic setting. The loss of the Temple with its sacrificial and atoning rituals occasioned the further development of the symbolic interpretation of the feast and its elements. As Christian Jews reassessed their position in the wake of the destruction of the Temple and the growing alienation from their mother Jewish community with its institutions, feasts and various religious and social celebrations and supports, the 'once-for-all' character of the revelation through Jesus encouraged a radical reassessment of many, if not all, of the earlier means of mediation. The story of Jesus came to be told with an emphasis on how he fulfils and surpasses the older promise of the institutions and feasts, and opens up their meaning for the present and future in the context of his own identity and mission.

The Lamb of God

In addition to the three Passover Feasts, the paschal dimension in John is heavily concentrated on the figure of the Lamb of God. On his second day of giving witness, John (the Baptist) testifies to an unspecified audience saying: 'Behold the Lamb of God who takes away the sin of the world' (Jn 1:29). No one is described as being present or responding at the first mention of the Lamb of God. It is as though John is presenting Jesus to Israel and the world at large. His second proclamation of the Lamb of God, this time to two of his own followers, results in their being the first two to follow Jesus (Jn 1:36ff). Using the Lamb of God image in this way at the beginning of the ministry opens up an image field that stretches right across the Bible and provides an umbrella term for many of the traditions woven into the fabric of the gospel. Several of these images are at work and are ultimately drawn together and focused on the crucified Christ who is elevated in death and glory.

First of all, the Lamb is called 'the Lamb of God'. When the reader of the gospel hears later that 'God so loved the world that he gave his only Son so that those who believe in him may not perish but may have eternal life' (Jn 3:16), it becomes clear in retrospect that the Lamb is above all the gift of God for the life of the world. The Lamb of God is seen in this context as a sacrificial offering provided by God. One thinks immediately of Abraham about to sacrifice his beloved son, sole heir to the promise and only hope for the future, and prevented from doing so by the divine gift of a substitute sacrifice (Gen 22:1-14). Like Isaac Jesus is bound and led away to the place, carrying the wood for his sacrifice on his back (Gen 22:6). In this case, however, he himself is the expiatory sacrifice provided by God, putting an end to all other sacrifices, and in this he is the Lamb who takes away the sin of the world. The sacrificial lamb was offered twice daily as a holocaust in the Temple, in the morning and between the two evenings.[6] At the spot where the holocaust was immolated one could offer a lamb as sin offering by placing one's hand on the head of the victim before immolation, dipping a finger in the spilled blood and smearing it on the horns of the altar before pouring the blood at the foot of the altar.[7] Elsewhere in the New Testament the First Letter of Peter says: 'You were emancipated … not with perishable things such as silver or gold, but with precious blood, as of an unblemished and spotless lamb, namely the blood of Christ ...'[8] The paschal lamb also springs to mind. The blood of the paschal lamb was sprinkled on the doorposts in Egypt to protect the Hebrews from the destroying plague. It marked them out as God's own first-born and so the marking of the doorposts with the blood of the lamb was in fact an anointing of the household as part of the people of God. It is very significant in St John's gospel that the crucifixion takes place on the eve of the Passover, a day earlier than in the synoptics. This means that Jesus is condemned and executed during the time when the lambs are being sacrificed for the Passover, a fact emphasised by naming the day and the hour. The lamb as the Servant of God also comes to mind. The Servant is presented in Isaiah as a Suffering Servant, and described as a lamb that is led to the slaughterhouse, like a sheep that is dumb before its shearers, never opening its mouth.[9] He takes away sin by vicariously suffering on behalf of sinners, taking their sins on himself as he prays all the time for sinners (Isa 53:11f). Significantly the Servant is lifted up, raised to great heights by God, to the amazement of those who had seen his former humiliation and suffering without understanding its significance (Isa 52:12ff).[10] Jesus promises 'when you have lifted up the Son of man then you will know that I am' (Jn 8:28) and 'when I am lifted up I shall draw all to myself' (Jn 12:32). When he is lifted up on the cross the narrator tells us the scripture is fulfilled which says 'they shall look on the one whom they had pierced' (Jn 19:37). The lamb of apocalyptic tradition was portrayed as the one coming from behind, from among the followers to take over the leadership[11] and to lead the faithful to victory in the war on sin.[12] The idea of the follower (of John) becoming the leader brings out the apocalyptic notion of the Lamb becoming the shepherd. The one from his own following proclaimed Lamb by John subsequently declares himself to be the Shepherd who lays down his life for his sheep (Jn 10:11, 15, 17, 18). The Apocalyptic Lamb takes away sin by leading the saints in the war against sin to destroy the power of evil.[13] Jesus defeats the ruler of this world and proclaims that he

has overcome the world (Jn 12:31; 16:33). The lamb as symbol of
innocence and victim of persecution is highlighted in the
prophetic tradition where Jeremiah is persecuted for his sermon
against the Temple. He described himself as 'a gentle lamb being
led to the slaughterhouse.'[14] Jesus follows suit in upsetting the
powers that be with his action and *logion* in the Temple. All
these dimensions of the lamb imagery are woven into the fabric
of John's Gospel.

The First Passover. The Temple

During the first Passover feast in his public ministry Jesus entered the Temple and began the process of fulfilling and surpassing the older promise of the institutions and feasts. The passage is framed by references to the Passover: 'Just before the
Jewish Passover ...' and 'During his stay in Jerusalem for the
Passover ...'(Jn 2:13, 23). The Lamb of God passes judgement on,
and replaces, the sacrificial system. He proclaims a new temple
in his resurrected body, which will ensure the divine presence
among the community of believers. This understanding is particularly important for Jewish Christians in the light of the destruction of the Temple and the growing alienation from their
mother Jewish community with its institutions, atoning sacrifices, pilgrimage feasts and various religious and social celebrations and supports. The Johannine scene in the Temple includes
but runs much deeper than a prophetic style action of simply
'cleansing the Temple', a designation by which the episode has
been popularly called.

Jesus may well have had a strongly critical attitude to the
Temple throughout his ministry. In this he was not alone in his
own day. The Hellenists, the Essenes and the Samaritans were
all less than enthusiastic in its regard. In having such a critical attitude Jesus would also have been in direct line of descent from
the prophets. The four accounts of Jesus' cleansing of the
Temple stand in continuity with this prophetic tradition. It was
commonplace for the prophets to adopt a critical stance on the
Temple, its worship, its authority and its ongoing role in the life

of the people. They issued stern reminders of the holiness of the Temple. It should be a place free from all kinds of corruption and venality, a place of true inner worship and a place which God would visit at some future time. Such conviction on the part of the prophets, often leading to persecution, prompts the Psalmist to say 'zeal for your house consumes me', a text which may well refer to the case of Jeremiah himself.[15] From the time of the Exile the prophets looked to an ideal future with a reformed, ideal Temple. Ezekiel spoke of a future ideal Temple from which the water of life would flow to bring life to all that was dead in the land. The prophets did not oppose the Temple as such. They opposed the attitudes, abuses and disconnectedness with moral living that grew up around it.

The scene in the Temple in St John's gospel has two parts. There is the action, usually referred to as 'the cleansing of the Temple', a generalisation that misses the main thrust and interpretation of the action as portrayed in this gospel, and the pronouncement (logion) of Jesus in response to the questioning of the authority behind his action. Each of the two parts ends with a quotation from scripture and a comment by the narrator about the subsequent belief and understanding of the disciples in the light of the resurrection.

The first part of the story deals with the action in the Temple. Unlike the synoptics John describes the making of a whip, the casting out from the Temple of the large animals, sheep and oxen, and the doves, in addition to the pouring out of the coins and the turning over of the money changers' tables. The distinctive character of the Johannine account highlights its meaning. The Temple rituals are the target, so the focus is on the animals and the doves. The sheep and oxen were the animals used for sacrifice, the doves for offerings. In the presence of the one who has been declared Lamb of God, the sacrificial offering supplied by God, the gift of God, the definitive Passover and sacrificial Lamb, these other atoning rituals lose their significance.

The second part of the scene deals with the pronouncement or logion of Jesus, set in the context of the challenge to explain the authority behind his action in the Temple. When challenged Jesus replied: 'Destroy this temple and in three days I will build it up again.' Thus St John's gospel in its own inimitable way lifts the whole discussion from the physical action in the Temple with its prophetic overtones onto the theological/christological plane where it fits into the gospel's ongoing discussion on God's presence and dwelling place and its rituals. The Temple incident points forward to the divine presence in the resurrected and glorified Jesus, the new Temple, through whose glorification the community of his followers will enjoy the divine indwelling through the gift of the Holy Spirit-Paraclete. Through the Spirit the community becomes the *topos* or location of the divine dwelling.

> After the resurrection the full meaning of what Jesus did and said became clear to his followers (Jn 2:17, 22). Jesus, the risen Messiah, had taken the place of the temple and all it stood for. The centre of God's presence among his people is no longer a place; it is henceforth a person (see 4:21-24). The new sanctuary is the risen body of Jesus. In this new temple dwells the fullness of the Spirit. And that Spirit comes to those who believe and dwells with them so that they in their turn, become temples of God.[16]

The Second Passover. Food for Eternal Life

Chapter six tells the story of Jesus in Galilee at the approach of the Passover festival. The multiplication of the loaves and fishes opens the chapter of the gospel in which Jesus develops the theme of food that endures to eternal life.

The Multiplication and Sea Crossing

The open spaces around the Sea of Galilee provide a setting reminiscent of the events of the Exodus-Passover. These events surrounding the foundation of Israel as a people are 'remembered' in the celebration of the feast as hope for the present and future is renewed and enthusiasm is enkindled through the festivities. The promise of the feast is fulfilled and the future anticipated in his person and mission as Jesus draws to himself the essentials of Exodus, sea crossing, wandering, manna in the desert, shepherding the people, covenant, Torah, Word and Wisdom, all under the rubric of *the food that endures to eternal life*.

The multiplication of the loaves and fishes is one of the few miracles recounted in all four gospels.[17] In fact it is recorded twice by Matthew and Mark. The two accounts in Matthew and Mark seem to refer respectively to a messianic banquet for the Jews and a messianic banquet for the Gentiles, a conclusion drawn by scholars from the locations of the multiplications and the symbolic numbers of the crowd and of the baskets of leftovers. John has one multiplication and, given its location in Galilee of the Gentiles and close to the pagan cities of the Decapolis, it possibly signifies a messianic banquet for a multitude made up of both Jews and Gentiles.[18] Both Matthew and Mark have two extended 'bread sections' in their gospels, containing the multiplication of loaves and fishes, a sea crossing, a request for a sign, teaching about bread, and a betrayal / passion theme leading to a demonstration of Peter's faith.[19] The Johannine account has all these themes or elements in chapter six, together with the murmuring of the crowd, the apostasy of many disciples, the profession of faith by Simon Peter and the prediction of the betrayal by Judas.

The scene in Galilee is a typical setting for a teaching, healing, feeding or commissioning sequence.[20] It reflects the role of the shepherd caring for the flock in the desert, an image spelled out explicitly by Mark in his introduction to the teaching and feeding of the multitude: '[Jesus] had compassion on them, because they were like sheep without a shepherd; and he began to teach them many things.' The various multiplication accounts refer to green grass, their need to rest after a long journey lest they faint on the way, and the fact that they ate, were satisfied and had food left over. All these elements recall Ps 22 (23): 'The Lord is my shepherd, I shall not want, fresh and green are the pastures where he gives me repose … he prepares a banquet for me … my cup is overflowing'. John mentions the green grass, eating their fill and gathering the fragments left over.

Among other expectations there was an opinion abroad that the Messiah would repeat the miracle of Moses' feeding the people in the wilderness.[21] Jesus' question to Philip: 'Where shall we ever buy bread for these people to eat?' recalls the circumstances of the Exodus-Wandering with its large groups of people needing food in the wilderness and the problems it presented for Moses. One remembers the desperation in Moses' questions to the Lord in the desert: 'Where am I to get meat to give all these people?' and: 'If all the flocks and herds were slaughtered would that be enough for them? If all the fish in the sea were gathered (LXX, *synagein*) would that be enough for them?'[22] This same theme is reflected in the psalm: 'They even spoke against God. They said, "Is it possible for God to prepare a table in the desert?"'(Ps 77/78:19). Jesus is portrayed in biblical fashion like Moses, posing the question to heighten the awareness of the problem and create an appreciation of the gift which follows and its sign value. The theological concern of the narrator that, in the event of these biblical allusions being lost on the reader, it might detract from Jesus' omniscience, probably prompted the remark that Jesus asked Philip in order to test him.[23]

Jesus, in this account of the multiplication, unlike the account in the synoptics, passes the bread around himself, as he did at the Last Supper in the synoptics. This is obviously a theological 'simplification' to highlight the word and action by then established in the eucharistic liturgy. The Greek term 'giving thanks', *eulogêsas*, is in line with Lucan and Pauline usage and contrasts with the more Semitic blessing as used by Matthew and Mark.[24] The focus of attention is on the bread rather than the fish, because the allusion to the eucharistic celebration is highlighted and also because the discourse on the bread of life is to follow.[25] The use of the verb *bibrôskein*, 'to feed on' (Jn 6:13,) prepares the reader, by using a related word, for the discourse on 'food *(brôsis)* that endures to eternal life' and for Jesus' statement that 'my flesh is true (or real) food *(alêthês brôsis)*' (Jn 6:27, 55). Food takes its significance from the hunger it satisfies, in this case the hunger for eternal life. The accounts reflect a strong influence of the liturgy of the first Christians with the use of the eucharistic formula, took the bread, gave thanks/said the blessing, and shared it around. The stylised liturgical words and actions of the multiplication bring out the specifically eucharistic allusions.

The verb *synagein* 'to gather', is used for gathering up the fragments *(klasmata)*. This usage is peculiar to this gospel, and emphasises the fact that the fragments are not a remnant, but a surplus. The gathering of the fragments recalls the gathering of the manna and with it the desert scenario of Moses and the Exodus-Wandering when the people gathered the manna each day, until they had what they needed (Ex 16:18, 8, 12, 16, 21). In fact the same verb is used in the LXX for the gathering of the manna. The noun *klasmata* has overtones of the breaking into shared pieces of the eucharistic bread and is so used to signify the eucharistic fragments in the Didache.[26] The verb *synagein* carries these overtones into the liturgy as it signifies the gathering of the liturgical assembly to celebrate the Eucharist.[27]

The episode on the lake which follows the multiplication of the loaves may be a variant of the story of the calming of the storm in the synoptics or of Jesus' walking on the water and, in Matthew's account, inviting Peter to join him on the storm tossed waves.[28] In John's Gospel the detail of the storm and the distress of those in the boat are described only sufficiently to create suspense and set the scene for what follows. The 'Mosaic' action of feeding the multitude is followed by another great miracle reminiscent of Moses and the Passover-Exodus event, leading the followers through the life threatening sea. The focus is not on the miracle of calming the storm but on the epiphany conveyed through the divine name, 'I am',[29] and the accompanying reassurance *do not be afraid*.[30] John places the incident here between the multiplication and the discourse on the food that endures to eternal life which will bring out the fact that Jesus not only *gives*, but *is*, the Bread of Life come down from heaven. If they truly understood the significance of the multiplication of the loaves they would realise who he is and consequently not be afraid.[31]

Discourse on the Food for Eternal Life. Jn 6:22-59

When the crowd, who had their fill of the loaves, go in search of Jesus in the hope of another miracle, they ask him for a sign, quoting the biblical example of the manna in the desert, seen as the greatest of Moses' miracles.[32] In a solemn 'Amen, amen I say to you' proclamation he tells them it was not Moses who gave their ancestors the bread from heaven in the desert, and goes on, with a change of tense in the verb, to say that it is his Father who gives the true bread. It is the true or real *(alêthinos)* bread, because it is the bread of God which comes down from heaven to give life to the world.[33] The crowd respond by asking him to give them this bread always. He instructs them not to work for food *(brôsis)* that does not last and he draws a sharp contrast between food that does not last and food that endures to eternal life. This food will be given by the Son of Man, the one credited throughout the gospel with life-giving power, the one 'on whom God the Father has set his seal' (Jn 6:27). In what is effectively a combination of two discourses, one on the bread from heaven, the other on eating and drinking his flesh and blood, Jesus goes on to develop the theme of food for eternal life.

Bread from Heaven. Jn 6:31-51

Deutero-Isaiah invites all who thirst, even those who have no money, to come to the water and drink, to buy corn, wine and milk, without money. Then he advises them: 'Why spend money on what is not bread, your wages on what fails to satisfy? Listen to me and you will have good things to eat and rich food to enjoy' (Isa 55:1-3). He compares the word coming from the mouth of God with the rain and snow that produce seed for the sowing and bread for the eating. The text from Deuteronomy, quoted by Jesus in the temptations, compares listening to the word with eating food: 'You shall remember all the way which the Lord your God had led you these forty years in the wilderness … and fed you with manna, which you did not know; that he might make you know that one does not live by bread alone, but one lives by everything that comes from the mouth of God' (cf. Mt 4:4; Lk 4:4; quoting Deut 8:3).

The concept of bread from heaven, manna, was a particularly apt symbol for the Torah.[34] The books of Nehemiah and Wisdom of Solomon associate manna and 'bread from heaven' with Torah, and the rabbinic tradition associated the 'bread' with the Torah that Lady Wisdom offered to those whom she invited to her banquet.[35] Torah became closely associated with Wisdom as it came to be seen as the great repository of divine Wisdom, and both are symbolised by the manna. The Wisdom tradition developed this in a personified way. Personified Wisdom issues an invitation to her banquet. The invitation comes in Proverbs in the words: 'Come and eat my bread, drink the wine I have prepared' and in Sirach, 'Come to me you who desire me and eat your fill of my fruits' (Prov 9:5; Sir 24:19). Sirach says of Wisdom: 'She will give ... the bread of understanding to eat, and the water of wisdom to drink' and speaks of the creation of an appetite for wisdom: 'They who eat me will hunger for more, they who drink me will thirst for more' (Sir 15:3; 24:21). The Wisdom of Solomon promises nourishment and immortality by way of a reputation that will never die: 'The various crops are not what nourishes man, but your word which preserves all who trust in you' (Wis 16:26). 'By means of her, immortality (memory) shall be mine' (Wis 8:13). 'The one who finds me, finds life ... all who hate me are in love with death' (Prov 8:35f). The invitation to eat and drink, therefore, is a metaphor for the call to hear, learn and obey the word of God, the commands of the Law and the dictates of Wisdom. Just as eating and drinking sustain physical life, so hearing, learning and obeying sustain 'spiritual' life, and lead one along the paths of life. The divine origin of the manna is emphasised in the biblical accounts and also in writers like Josephus and Philo who were contemporary with the New Testament. Speaking of the manna, Josephus describes it as 'divine and miraculous food'.[36] Philo allegorises the manna as the divine gift of wisdom and even uses the words manna and *sophia* (wisdom), interchangeably.[37] The symbolic interpretation of the manna was well established long before St John's gospel in which Jesus repeatedly invites his listeners to eat and drink. Jesus' promise: 'the one who comes to me will never hunger, the one who believes in me will never thirst' (Jn 6:35), stands out in stark contrast to the traditional promise of Wisdom: 'He who eats of me will hunger still, he who drinks of me will thirst for more' (Sir 24:21). The ongoing search for wisdom is now replaced by the fully satisfying bread from heaven which will put an end to human hunger and thirst. It satisfies the hunger for eternal life.

The imagery of God as shepherd of Israel protecting, feeding and leading his people is here transferred to Jesus. The promise of life and revelation draws people to Jesus, the Bread of Life. He now has care of the flock. Those whom the Father gives him he will not turn away. Those who come will not be lost. They will have life here and hereafter. Jesus has been sent to carry out the will of the One who sent him, and that will is precisely to ensure that all he has been given will not be lost, and that all who see the Son and believe in him may have eternal life. This is spelled out in terms of resurrection on the last day. In chapter ten the full significance of the shepherd's role in terms of laying down his own life for his sheep is spelled out. The Risen Lord will in turn commit this role of shepherd to Simon Peter.

A solemn declaration, 'Amen, amen I say to you', introduces a summary of what has been said (Jn 6:47-51) in this first part of the discourse. It comes to a climax in the triple designation *ego eimi ho artos ho zôn ho ek tou ouranou katabas* which is usually translated as 'I am the living bread that has come down from heaven', that is, I am the bread that is life-giving and revealing. Translated in this straightforward manner *ho zôn* and *ho ek tou ouranou katabas* qualify *artos*. If understood as being in apposition to *egô* as in *egô eimi ho artos (ego eimi) ho zôn, (ego eimi) ho ek tou ouranou katabas* the *logion* would translate as 'I am the bread, (I am) the living one, (I am) the one who has come down from heaven,' in other words, 'I am the bread, (in so far as) I am the *living one/life giver* and *the revealer*. This parallels the other great triple designation *ego eimi hê hodos hê aletheia kai hê zôe* which is best understood as 'I am the way (in so far as I am) the truth and the life', in other words, 'I am the way because I am the *revealer*/revelation/truth *(alêtheia)* and the *life/life-giver (zôê).'*

The final statement or *logion* in this section of the discourse is: 'the bread that I shall give is my flesh *(sarx)* for the life of the world.' It forms a bridge between the two parts of the discourse. Here *sarx* reflects its use in the key statement of the Prologue, *ho logos sarx egeneto*, the Word became flesh, and signifies the whole person, now offered for the life of the world, recalling the gift of the Father who 'gave his only Son', and Jesus' own promise to lay down his life for his flock. The *logion*, 'the bread that I shall give is my flesh for the life of the world', may even have been the eucharistic formula (the words of institution) used in the Johannine tradition, where *sarx* is equivalent to *sôma* (body) in the synoptic and Pauline accounts. This brings to a climax that section of the discourse. The term *sarx*, however, functions as a link word with the second part of the discourse where it is used with a very different meaning. Probably the two parts of the discourse were originally separate discourses in different parts of the gospel during its formation. Be that as it may, as the text now stands the parts complement each other with very different aspects of the food that endures to eternal life, one focusing on revelation/teaching/words, the other on the imagery of the sacrificial banquet, with its emphasis on eating and drinking as in the Eucharist.

Flesh and Blood. Jn 6:52-59

The discourse is interrupted by reference to 'violent quarrelling' among the Jews about how Jesus could give them his flesh to eat. This reference to flesh, *sarx*, forms a bridge between the two very different parts of the discourse. It is next mentioned in tandem with *haima*, blood. This introduces a new concept. A solemn proclamation: 'Amen, amen, I say to you' warns that 'if you do not eat of the flesh of the Son of Man and drink his blood, you will not have life in you'. Here again the figure of the Son of Man emerges as the one who gives the gift of life. The warning is followed by the assurance that 'the one who eats/feeds on *(trôgôn)* my flesh *(sarx)* and drinks my blood *(haima)* has eternal life and I will raise him up on the last day'. This life is described in terms of 'remaining' or 'abiding' *(menein)* in Jesus. In a *logion* that could be seen as summing up the theme of life and life-giving throughout the gospel, Jesus says: 'As the living Father sent me and I live through the Father, so the one feeding on me *(ho trôgôn me)* will live through me' (Jn 6:57).[38] The emphasis on the physical act of eating is brought out very strongly with the four uses of *ho trôgôn,* 'the one who eats / munches / feeds on' (Jn 6:54, 56, 57, 58). It stands out in contrast to the more common usage of the verbs *phagein* and *esthiein*. In classical Greek *trôgein* is generally translated as 'munching', 'crunching', like munching hay, and usually used of animals. It eventually came into use as a description of human eating. Jesus further emphasises the concept of eating and drinking by saying: 'My flesh is real / true food *(alêthês brôsis)* and my blood is real / true drink *(alêthês posis)*.' The discourse ends with the contrast: 'This is the bread that came down from heaven. Not as our fathers ate *(ephagon)* and died. The one feeding on *(trôgôn)* this bread will live forever.'

There is broad agreement among scholars that this passage is eucharistic. It may have formed part of a Last Supper discourse in an earlier stage of the formation of the tradition. The repeated use of *trôgôn,* with its emphasis on the very physical act of eating, is a strong reason why some scholars think that the discourse in Jn 6:51-58 may originally have formed part of the Last Supper narrative with its eating and drinking. The use of *sarx* rather than *sôma* (which the Pauline and synoptic traditions use) as partner to *haima* here in John is undoubtedly influenced by the sacrificial language of separation of flesh and blood in sacrifice. Furthermore, the emphasis on eating and drinking corresponds to the ritual of the institution of the Eucharist in the synoptics. In John, however, the eating and drinking shows a strong resemblance to a communion sacrifice, where God, the participants and the victim shared the life of the victim (though strictly speaking the eating of the flesh and not the drinking of the blood was the shared meal). In the synoptics, on the contrary, Jesus in-

terprets the elements of the meal as his body and blood in relation to his saving death and the new covenant in his blood, re-
sembling a sacrificial meal on the occasion of the ratification of a
covenant.[39]

The consuming of blood was forbidden to the Jews and accounts in part for the strong reaction to Jesus' statement about
eating his flesh and drinking his blood. The prohibition on blood
is contained in the command to Noah, 'You must not eat flesh
with life, that is to say blood, in it.' It is found also in the prescriptions in Leviticus, 'never eat either fat or blood', and in
Deuteronomy, 'take care not to consume the blood, for the blood
is the life, and you must not consume the life with the flesh …
but pour it out like water on the ground'.[40] The hostile reaction
of the crowd[41] is accompanied by the falling away of many disciples who said 'this is a hard *(sklêros)* saying' and went on to ask:
'Who can hear it?' that is, 'who can understand and accept it?'[42]
The telling of the story of Jesus in St John's gospel replays and
fulfils many aspects of the Old Testament story. The murmuring
and quarrelling here recall the murmuring and quarrelling of
the people in the desert. But the story of Jesus also reflects the
circumstances and issues of the early Christian community. It is
possible that the emphasis on the quarrelling about consuming
the flesh and blood also reflects disagreements arising from mis-
representation and misunderstanding of the Eucharist in the
early Christian community.[43] The link between Eucharist and
betrayal and all that followed is maintained. The chapter ends
with the prediction of the betrayal, and a statement by Jesus that
he himself had picked the one who would betray him. In the
light of the gospel teaching that Jesus knew what was in everyone's heart (Jn 2:25), it can be concluded that he knew his betrayer,
Judas, son of Simon Iscariot, and still chose him. The references
to betrayal anticipate the third and final Passover in Jesus' public ministry. They foreshadow what was to take place 'on the
night he was betrayed.'

The Third Passover. The Night He Was Betrayed. Love to the End
The 'Last Supper' which Jesus shared with his disciples is the
setting for the institution of the Eucharist in the three synoptic
gospels. In John's gospel, however, the Last Supper is the setting
for Jesus' final symbolic actions which manifest the inner meaning and ongoing implications of Eucharist. He 'loved them to
the end' in spite of the impending betrayal by Judas and the denial by Peter. His love is manifested in washing the feet of the
disciples, sharing with the betrayer the morsel from the dish,
consoling them in the Farewell Discourse(s) and offering the
Priestly Prayer of their behalf and on behalf of those who would
come to believe through them. The meal took place in the overall
context of the Passover Feast, and the gospel emphasises the
Passover dimension by focusing on the fact that Jesus dies at the
hour when the paschal lambs are being slaughtered on the eve
of the feast.

The Washing of the Disciples' Feet. Jn 13:1-11
Laying aside his outer/festal garment and guest of honour/
teacher/master status he dresses as a servant and performs the
menial task of washing the feet of the disciples. A disciple was
expected to do for the teacher what a servant does for his master
except wash his feet, as this was regarded as too demeaning. A
Jewish slave was never expected to wash his master's feet.
Herein lies the significance of Jesus' action. In doing so he assumed the condition of a slave. He would not call them servants
any more, but friends, for he too is a servant. The washing of feet
could, however, be done as a gesture of hospitality for a very
honoured guest, so washing their feet also casts Jesus in the role
of host who will welcome them into his Father's house where
there are many mansions and whither he is going to prepare a
place for them.

   By dying for his followers Jesus will receive them into his
Father's house and the footwashing symbolically portrays this
redeeming, cleansing and welcoming nature of his forthcoming
death. This service from him they must accept if they are to be

part of him. Peter misses the point and protests, just as he does following the prediction of the passion in the synoptics (Mk 8:31-33//Mt 16:21-23). He protests at having to humble himself to accept the servant model of salvation by Jesus. As in the case of the cleansing of the Temple and the entry into Jerusalem, the disciples did not understand the significance of what was taking place, but they would understand later.[44] This delay in understanding highlights the fact that the footwashing is not simply an act of humility, a ritual of hospitality or a 'penitential' or 'purificatory' rite like those practised by John the Baptist or the Qumran community. The disciples would have been familiar with these 'rituals' and would not have needed any explanation. It is, however, a salvific act, an action that can only be understood when they have experienced Jesus' hour of death and glorification, that is, his death, resurrection and sending of the Paraclete.[45]

In response to Peter's objection, Jesus not only speaks of the necessity of the footwashing itself, but emphasises that he himself must perform it: 'If I do not wash you, you will have no heritage (meros) with me.' 'Having or sharing a heritage' has a well-established history in the Bible. The Septuagint uses meros to translate the Hebrew hêleq, heritage. Originally it referred to the God-given heritage of Israel, where each of the tribes except Levi received a heritage or share in the Promised Land (Num 18:20; Deut 12:12; 14:27). Later it came to signify a share in the afterlife and it is used in this context in Revelation (Rev 20:6; 21:8; 22:19). The 'heritage' is described in John specifically as a heritage with him, and this is subsequently spelled out in the Farewell Discourse as 'where I am you also may be' (Jn 14:3). This is reminiscent of the question put by the first disciples to Jesus, 'Where do you live?' and Jesus' answer, containing the invitation: 'Come and see'. The reader, enlightened by the Prologue, realises the profundity of the response because it is an invitation to join him where he is 'with God', 'ever at the Father's side' (Jn 1:1, 18). He is now returning to the Father and promises to prepare a place for the disciples but they must ac-

cept this saving death on their behalf, symbolised in the washing of the feet, if they are to share in this heritage.[46]

A second interpretation of the foot-washing follows. It can be
seen as a moral example of service to be followed by the disciples in serving one another. If the 'teacher and Lord' has acted in
a particular way, the disciples should follow his example. It is a
challenging reversal of roles and status. If he has done a menial
service for them, they should not consider themselves 'above'
doing the same service for one another. In addition 'leaving an
example' *(hypodeigma)*, in relation to the foot-washing, is seen to
be rich in biblical allusions relating to saintly and noble death.
Sirach says of Enoch and his death that 'he pleased God and was
taken up, an example *(hypodeigma)* for the conversion of all generations' (Sir 44:16). In Second Maccabees the martyrdom of
Eleazer is destined to 'leave the young a noble example *(hypodeigma)* of a good death' (2 Macc (LXX) 6:28; cf. 4 Macc 17:22f).
Jesus is asking his disciples to follow his example in doing for
one another as he has done for them, to repeat in their own lives
the loving gesture of footwashing which symbolised laying
down one's life for one's friend. Vicarious death is the ultimate
implication and deepest expression of service. In the Farewell
Discourse Jesus will spell this out as the supreme expression of
love. 'Love one another as I have loved you. Greater love than
this no one has than to lay down one's life for one's friends' (Jn
15:12f). This *hypodeigma* gives a Johannine emphasis to 'my
memorial'.

The Morsel (Psômion) and the Betrayal: Jn 13:21-30

The hospitality of Jesus shown in the foot-washing when, in
spite of objections, he insisted on washing the feet of the one
who would deny him, is now followed by his extraordinary gesture of hospitality to the one about to betray him. In keeping
with the oriental custom of inviting the guest of honour to dip
together with the host in the dish or offering the guest a choice
morsel from it, Jesus hands Judas the morsel. In so doing he illustrates the fact that the one about to betray him is one whom

he is treating as a guest of honour. This highlights the depth of betrayal and illustrates why Jesus quoted the Psalm: 'He who eats my bread raised his heel against me' (Jn13:18 f.; Ps 40(41):9f). This is the breaking of a sacred code of behaviour whereby the guest does not break the bond of fellowship with the host while sharing his table. Jesus' special gesture of hospitality is reciprocated with Judas' definitive decision and action of betrayal.

There is an interesting set of allusions to the Eucharist in the adaptation of the quotation from Psalm 40 (41) and the offer of the morsel to Judas. In the Septuagint version of the text, the verb *esthiein* is used for eating. However, John again uses the rather surprising verb *trôgein* here, the verb used four times in chapter six in the section of the discourse dealing with eating his flesh and drinking his blood. John (or his source?) obviously chose this verb deliberately for its eucharistic overtones. It gave special emphasis to the deliberate act of eating. Further eucharistic allusions are found in the adaptation of the quotation from Ps 40 (41) to read 'loaf/bread' in the singular, instead of the original plural 'loaves', as *ho trôgôn mou ton arton* replaces *ho esthiôn artous mou*. The eucharistic dimension is further strengthened by the references in chapter six to the fact that Jesus knew from the outset those who did not believe and who it was who would betray him, since the references to betrayal are an integral part of the institution narratives.[47] Jesus chose the betrayer, knowing full well his disposition. He told him to 'do what you do quickly' and on his departure to carry out the betrayal Jesus associates the treacherous activity of Judas with his own glorification. 'Now has the Son of Man been glorified, and in him God has been glorified.' The betrayal facilitates the return of the Son to the Father and all that follows by way of the disciples 'being with me where I am.' Just as baptism is a sub-theme in the foot-washing, Eucharist is a sub-theme in the sharing of the morsel.

Throughout the Roman trial scene the themes of silence and innocence, associated with the Servant, silent as a lamb led to the
slaughter, are very much in evidence. So too is the theme of the
Paschal Lamb. Jesus' ministry began with John's proclamation
to the crowd: 'This is the Lamb of God who takes away the sin of
the world' (Jn 1:29). Now his ministry is brought to its completion, or perfection, when he is condemned and led away to die as
the lambs are being slaughtered for the Passover. The day and
the hour are carefully noted to bring out the significance. It was
'the day of Preparation, about noon'. Jesus dies as the definitive
Paschal Lamb, the Lamb supplied by God the Father, and like
the Suffering Servant he is both led as a lamb to the slaughter
and 'raised up' before the gaze of those whom he will draw to
himself.

Like Isaac, the beloved son of Abraham, Jesus is loaded with
the wood for his sacrifice and led to 'the place', called the Skull,
and crucified there between two others. Jesus, already robed,
crowned and saluted as king, is now proclaimed king in the
three languages, Hebrew, Greek and Latin. These were the sacred
and secular languages of the day, three languages symbolising
all languages. He is enthroned before all nations, proclaimed
king in all languages. He is lifted up and draws all people to
himself. This is an hour of triumph, of glory. Far from being
abandoned, the crucified Jesus, ironically proclaimed King of
the Jews by Roman decree, is exalted, lifted up to draw all people to himself. A small group of family and friends, the nucleus
of the nascent church, including the Mother and the Beloved
Disciple, are drawn to the foot of the cross. The dying Jesus
hands over the Spirit, and from his wounded side flow the blood
and water, 'fountains of the sacramental life of the church'.[48] The
larger, representative crowd round about are drawn to 'look on
the one they have pierced' (Jn 19:37). The church is thus born
from the heart of the paschal mystery.

Removing the last vestige of the dignity of the condemned
man by leaving him to die naked emphasises the total loss of

everything material, but in John's gospel it is the occasion of a special detail of ecclesial significance. John's gospel uses the two words, garments *(himatia)* and robe *(chitôn)* for two different realities, and emphasises also the distinction between 'sharing out' and 'not tearing'. There is a rich seam of Johannine symbolism in the verbs 'they shared out' *(diemerisanto)* and 'let us not tear' *(mê schisômen)*. The personal garments of the executed person were regarded as the property of the executioners. On the symbolic level, at which John's gospel is telling the story of Golgotha, they represented the victim's legacy to the world. In this highly symbolic account of the episodes on Golgotha, the personal garments of Jesus represent for those who receive them their share in his 'inheritance' *(meros)*. They share in the *meros*, as *diemerisanto* means they shared an inheritance. The same vocabulary was used in Jesus' statement to Peter about sharing in his inheritance. Sharing his garments, symbolic of his person, life and work, points to the fact that the soldiers, his executioners, share in his inheritance.

However, the subjunctive 'let us not tear' *(mê schisômen)* in contradistinction to 'sharing', highlights another very important aspect of Jesus' legacy. The word *schizein*, to 'divide' or 'tear', and especially 'to divide or tear a garment', figures in the Old Testament in the context of division among the people. The prophet Ahijah tore his new garment into twelve pieces to symbolise the forthcoming division of the kingdom of David and Solomon (1 Kings 11:29-31). Several times in the gospel a 'division', *schisma*, is said to have occurred among the people. All through Jesus' Farewell Discourse and Final Prayer he emphasised the importance of unity, building up to the climax at the end of the prayer, when he prayed for the unity of all who hear his word, and constitute the community of believers. The seamless robe was not torn, unlike the other garments which were divided out in shares *(diemerisanto,* to each a *meros,* a share). Since the time of the Fathers of the church the undivided robe has been seen as signifying the unity of the community which Jesus left behind.[49]

A whole new note is struck in the account of the crucifixion when Jesus' family and friends are introduced. 'On the one hand the soldiers did these things but on the other there stood by the cross of Jesus his mother, and his mother's sister, Mary of Clopas and Mary of Magdala'.[50] To this group Jesus hands over the Spirit in his last gesture before death. A new family of Jesus is created as his human family and his family of faith are brought together around the cross. In the midst of this loving group, a final caring gesture of a dying son for his widowed mother and an act of trust in his Beloved Disciple provide the context and the personnel for the birth of the church. Referring to the scene, O. Treanor writes about the Mother and the Beloved Disciple:

> Close to the heart of the Crucified they stand at the foot of the cross in mystical communion with the Word made flesh, caught up through suffering in the ineffable love between Father and Son. They are the first fruits of Jesus' promise to draw all things to himself when he is lifted up from the earth; first fruits of his prayer that all might be one as he and the Father are one.[51]

The revelatory formula 'Behold ...' is used to describe the establishment of the new relationships. In this formula the one who speaks is revealing the mystery of the special salvific mission that the one referred to will undertake.[52] This formula sets in the context of the broader theology and literary style of the gospel what would otherwise be a straightforward last will and testament providing for the care of a widowed and bereaved mother: 'Woman, behold your son/behold your mother.' Several interpretations of the deeper significance of the exchange suggest themselves. Here on Golgotha in John's gospel we see a solemn endorsement of spiritual relationship of mother, son and brother (and sister, since the Beloved Disciple represents all disciples). 'Because of the cross and from the moment of the cross a new family of Jesus has been created.'[53]' The passage affirms the maternal role of the Mother of Jesus in the new family of Jesus established at the cross.'[54] Drawn to himself, sharing his *hour*, the woman becomes mother and the Beloved Disciple becomes her son, and thereby brother of Jesus, representing all disciples who are thus constituted his brothers and sisters. Now, lifted up from the earth, Jesus draws to himself the nucleus of the new community of believers. They share his *hour* as they stand representatively at the cross.

Two references to completion follow, the first a remark of the narrator that Jesus knew that all was now completed, the second, Jesus' own final words: 'It is finished / completed / perfected *(tetelestai)*' (Jn 19:28, 30). Highlighted between them is the cry of Jesus, 'I thirst.' The term *complete, finish* or *perfect* in this gospel has the meaning of 'bringing to conclusion or perfection and achieving the purpose' of the work Jesus was sent to do. Many times in the story of the ministry Jesus looks ahead to this completion: 'My food is to do the will of him who sent me and to complete his work' (Jn 4:34). 'The works that the Father has given me to complete, the very works that I am doing, testify on my behalf that the Father has sent me' (Jn 5:36). 'I glorified you on earth by completing the work you gave me to do' (Jn 17:4). 'Having loved his own who were in the world, he loved them to the end / to the completion' (Jn 13:1). Jesus' final word *tetelestai*, 'it is finished / completed / perfected', refers therefore to the whole purpose of Jesus' coming from the Father into the world. Placing the *I thirst* between these two affirmations of completion gives it a very high profile and alerts the reader to a meaning deeper than the physical thirst, a meaning further highlighted by the statement that Jesus' cry, *I thirst,* was to fulfil the scriptures.

Only in St John's gospel does Jesus call out 'I thirst'. Here the focus is on the asking for the drink. Jesus takes the initiative. A jar of sour wine, a bowl of vinegar, was there for the asking. Jesus had accepted the cup the Father gave him to drink. 'Am I not to drink the cup the Father gave me?' (Jn 18:11). The final request of Jesus is for a drink. The bowl of vinegar, the cup of suffering, brought his work to completion. This symbolises the full measure of suffering which he accepts. In this he has carried out the work of the Father to its ultimate completion, achieved its purpose, and brought it to perfection. The drink offering recalls the suffering and mockery of the just one in Ps 68 (69):22; 'For my thirst they gave me vinegar/sour wine to drink', but the text is not quoted. Though the psalm refers to a hostile gesture in the offering of sour wine to the victim, and it is so interpreted in the synoptic tradition, here the Johannine approach is brought into play. Instead of having the hostile gesture forced on him, Jesus invites the gesture, just as he invited the arresting party to take him, and release his followers, in the garden. In that case, too, his action is followed by a statement that it fulfilled the scriptures. The offering of the drink is an action common to all three synoptics and in fact Matthew and Mark have Jesus die immediately after the drink is offered. Jesus in John's gospel is seen to 'order' or 'invite' the final action that heralds his death. Jesus himself thirsts for, and requests, the fulfilment. In the irony of the gospel the reader remembers the importance Jesus placed on asking for the gift of God. He told the Samaritan woman that if she asked for a drink he would give her living water, the water of life. The Galileans at his prompting asked for the bread of life. In proclaiming his thirst Jesus asks for the drink which heralds fulfilment of the scripture, and the completion of the work the Father gave him to do.

Significantly the vinegar is offered on a hyssop stick,[55] a fact mentioned only in John's gospel. The hyssop was used for sprinkling the blood of the Paschal Lamb on the doorposts of the Israelites in Egypt to save them from the destroying plague, and to mark them out as God's firstborn.[56] Jesus, the Lamb who takes away the sin of the world, dies as the lambs are being slaughtered for the Passover. His final request results in raising aloft the hyssop, a powerful symbol of the historic delivery of the people through the blood of the lamb.

And now, finally, the Spirit is given. The Son has been glorified so the Spirit can be given (cf. Jn 7:39). Leaning his head forward to look down on those assembled beneath, he communicates to them the Spirit: 'He handed over the Spirit', *paredôken to pneuma*, does not mean 'he expired'. It is not a euphemism for death, unlike Mark and Luke who use the verb *exepneusen* 'expire' and Matthew who uses *aphêken to pneuma*, 'give up / surrender the spirit'. The Johannine Jesus bowed his head and handed over / delivered / entrusted the Spirit to the nascent church. The text does not say 'his spirit' in the sense of 'his breath of life', but 'the Spirit'. John's use of the active participle *klinas*, bowed, points to a deliberate action, not the falling down of the head of someone already dead but the leaning forward of someone still alive.[57] The image is of Jesus looking down on the assembled group and, now that the hour of his glorification has come, he gives the Spirit to his followers assembled at the foot of the cross.

Just before Jesus died he handed over the Spirit. Now following the piercing of his side, the gospel stresses the resulting flow of blood and water. This further highlights the significance of what has just taken place in the death of Jesus. Its importance is pointedly stressed by the narrator's comment that it is an eye-witness account by a truthful witness. The narrator stresses the truth of this witness in a manner more insistent than any other comment in the gospel, and says that the purpose of this witness is 'that you also may believe'. It is therefore to be seen as more than a simple description of a bodily function following a spear thrust into the side. It is another window on the divine plan of salvation unfolding on Golgotha. At the Feast of Tabernacles Jesus proclaimed: 'If anyone is thirsty let him come to me. Let the one come and drink who believes in me. As scripture says: "From his breast shall flow fountains of living water".' The narrator went on to explain: 'He was speaking of the Spirit which those who believed in him were to receive; for there was no Spirit as yet because Jesus had not yet been glorified' (Jn 7:37-39).[58] Now that Jesus is glorified the Spirit has been given.[59] The flow of water from his side first and foremost represents the gift of the Spirit. The blood is the blood of the Lamb that anoints and saves. It recalls the blood of the Passover Lamb which in the celebration of the Exodus-Passover became a sign of life given and protected by God, an anointing, symbolising Israel's position as

God's children. It symbolises also the blood of the covenant and the blood of the atoning sacrifice. Because life was seen to be contained in the blood, blood symbolised life and was central to the atonement rituals: 'This blood I myself have given you to perform the rite of atonement for your lives at the altar' (Lev 17:11). The blood signifies the atoning, sacrificial nature of Jesus' death, and the gift of life it bestows. It is the blood of the new covenant celebrated in the Eucharist.

Throughout the gospel Jesus has been portrayed as the *locus* of God's presence and revelation among the people. At Passover in the Temple he spoke of rebuilding the Temple of his glorified body in three days. At the Feast of Dedication he spoke of himself in terms reminiscent of the consecration of the Temple and the altar. At the Feast of Tabernacles he proclaimed: 'If anyone is thirsty let him come to me. Let the one come and drink who believes in me. As scripture says: "From his breast shall flow fountains of living water"'(Jn 7:37-39). This water symbolism was graphically symbolised in the promise of living water to the Samaritan woman (Jn 4:10-16). Ezekiel expressed the life-giving power of God's presence in the ideal future temple in terms of the water flowing from underneath the right side of the altar and bringing life to all the land. Now from the Temple and altar of Jesus' body the water of life flows as he is glorified.

St Augustine, in the tradition of the Peshitta and Vulgate, translates the 'piercing' as an 'opening'. He comments: 'He did not say *pierced through*, or *wounded*, or something else, but *opened*, in order that the gate of life might be stretched wide whence the sacraments of the church flow.'[60] The liturgical tradition of the church has given prominence to the sacramental interpretation of the blood and water that flowed from Jesus' side, the water of baptism (cf. Jn 3:5) and the blood of the Eucharist (cf. Jn 6:53, 54, 55, 56). The Preface of the Mass of the Sacred Heart speaks of the blood and water as 'the fountain of the sacramental life of the Church'. F. J. Moloney puts it succinctly when he says: 'Despite his physical absence, Jesus is still present in the blood and water of the practices of a worshipping community',[61] and W. Harrington is equally succinct: 'The drama of the cross does not end in death but in the flow of life that comes from death. The death of Jesus on the cross is the beginning of Christian life.'[62]

John points out that all this happened to fulfil the words of scripture: 'Not a bone of his will be broken' and 'They will look on the one whom they have pierced.'(Jn 19:36). In typical Johannine style, more than one reference is involved in both quotations. In regard to the first quotation one thinks first of the Paschal Lamb. Ex 12:46 (and its parallel in Nm 9:12) is a ritual instruction for the preparation of the Paschal Lamb. It states: 'It is to be eaten in one house alone, out of which not a single morsel of the flesh is to be taken; nor must you break any bone of it.' It fits into the Paschal Lamb motif of this gospel which is alone among the gospels in setting the crucifixion on the Day of Preparation and so canonises the allusions to the death of the Paschal lamb. One thinks also of the suffering of the just person: 'Hardships in plenty beset the virtuous man, but YHWH [Jahweh] rescues him from them all; taking care of every bone, YHWH will not let one be broken' (Ps 34:20). This description of YHWH's protection of the Just One, resembles also the Suffering Servant as described in Isa 52:13-53:12, the one led as a lamb to the slaughter, but before whom the crowds would stand in awe when he was exalted by God.

In regard to the second quotation one remembers that Jesus had promised: 'When I am lifted up I shall draw all to myself' (Jn 12:32). In fulfilment of his own words and the words of scripture he drew them to himself when he was raised up on the cross as 'they looked on the one they had pierced' (Zech 12:10). Looking on the one they have pierced and seeing the flow of water from his side recalls Zechariah's description of the fountain of God's mercy in the wake of the murder of the only son: 'But over the House of David and the citizens of Jerusalem I will pour out a spirit of kindness and prayer … a fountain will be opened for the House of David and the citizens of Jerusalem, for sin and impurity …'(Zech 12:10; 13:1,6). One thinks also of the crowd looking on as the Servant was glorified, raised to great heights: 'See my servant will prosper, he shall be lifted up, raised to great heights … as the crowds were appalled at seeing him … so will the crowds be astonished at him and kings stand speechless before him …'(Isa 52:14f).

V. THE RISEN LORD

For Jesus, being raised up on the cross was his hour of glorification, his return to the Father. For his disciples, however, it was their experience of the risen Jesus that heralded their new relationship with him as Lord. As Mary of Magdala stared into the empty tomb she was overcome with grief but when she 'turned around' and was addressed by the risen Lord she recognised the voice of the teacher, the ideal Shepherd who called her by name. She now had to adjust to a new relationship, symbolised by his 'ascending to the Father', as she in turn became apostle to the disciples announcing the good news: 'I have seen the Lord.' Appearing to the disciples, Jesus twice said: 'Peace be with you.' Between the greetings he showed them his hands and his side and they were filled with joy. The risen Lord showed them the marks of his glorification, the hands that held him aloft as he 'was raised up' to draw all to himself, and the wounded side from which the atoning, life-giving blood and water flowed. Now glorified, he breathed on them the Spirit and told them 'Whose sins you forgive they are forgiven.' Everything that went on in the Temple by way of atoning sacrifices and sin offerings and everything to do with the divine presence now take place in the new Spirit filled Temple of his risen body after the temple of his earthly body had been destroyed.

The scene on the shore of the Sea of Tiberias (Lake of Galilee) has strong ecclesial and eucharistic significance. Like the encounter with the stranger on the road to Emmaus in Luke's Gospel, this encounter with the stranger on the shore culminates in a meal with strong eucharistic overtones. In Luke 5:10 Jesus tells Peter and his companions that they will be 'fishers of people'. The same idea is contained here in the allusions embedded in the Johannine text. The theme of 'drawing' the catch of fish into the boat and then 'drawing' it onto the shore reflects Jesus' teaching that the Father draws people to him (Jesus) in faith, and that he (Jesus) would draw all to himself when he was lifted up and glorified.[63] The account further emphasises the all-embracing nature of the mission to people. The most likely explanation of the precise number of fish is that one hundred and fifty three represents the totality of human kind, since the zoologists at the time believed there were one hundred and fifty three species of fish in the sea. The statement that the nets were not torn is also significant because the same verb, *schizein,* is used which is used throughout the gospel for 'division' among the authorities and the people about Jesus and, most strikingly, it is used in the statement about the seamless robe, how it was not divided/torn at his crucifixion, signifying the undivided community of believers he had drawn to himself as he was 'raised up'.[64] Peter's role as leader who draws people and maintains unity is seen in the account. This will be made explicit in his appointment as shepherd, a role fulfilled by Jesus during his ministry and now entrusted to Peter as he is commissioned to look after 'my lambs, my sheep'.

At the multiplication of the loaves in Galilee, and here on the shore of the lake, the eucharistic formula 'takes the bread and gives it to them' is evident in both. The words *elaben/lambanei, artos, opsarion* and *homoiôs* occur both in Jn 6:11 and 21:13 The theme of abundance, brought about by Jesus' word, as a sign of the kingdom, is in evidence in the wine at Cana, the multiplication of the loaves in Galilee and here in the abundance of fish on the Lake of Tiberias. The risen Lord, through his disciples and especially through his chief shepherd, draws all to the abundance of his table, a table rich in the life-giving and revealing food that endures to eternal life. We come to that abundance each time we celebrate the Eucharist. For this let us give thanks, *eucharistōumen.*

CHAPTER FOUR

'Those who have eyes to see': The Eschatological Eucharist

Francesca Aran Murphy

1. The 'Eschatological Tension' of the Eucharist

The book of Revelation invokes a blessing on those who 'are called to the marriage supper of the Lamb' (Rev 19:9); *Ecclesia de Eucharistia* affirms that 'The Eucharist is a true banquet'.[1] These parallel lines point toward what *EdE* calls the 'eschatological tension' of the Eucharist.[2] John Paul II glanced at the book of Revelation in his 1980 Encyclical, *Dives in Misericordia*. He speaks here of the cross as the gateway between time and eternity, saying, 'the Cross of Christ … makes us understand the deepest roots of evil, which are fixed in sin and death; thus the cross becomes an eschatological sign. Only in the eschatological fulfilment … will love conquer, in all the elect, the deepest sources of evil, bringing as its … fruit the kingdom of life … and … immortality. The foundation of this eschatological fulfilment is already contained in the cross of Christ and in his death. The fact that Christ "was raised the third day" … constitutes the sign that foretells "a new heaven and a new earth," when God "will wipe every tear from their eyes, [and] there will be no more death …" In the eschatological fulfilment mercy will be fulfilled as love, while … in human history, which is … the history of sin and death, love must be revealed … as mercy … Christ's messianic programme … of mercy, becomes the … programme of his people … the church. At its very centre there is always the cross, for it is in the cross that the revelation of merciful love attains its culmination. Until "the former things pass away," the cross will remain the point of reference for the other words … of the Revelation of John: "Behold, I stand at the door and knock; if anyone hears my voice and opens the door, I will come in and eat with him and he with me".[3] Christ, precisely as the Crucified One, is the Word that does not pass away, and he is the one who stands at the door and knocks at the heart of every man.'[4] In *EdE*, John Paul reminds us that *Sacrosanctum Consilium* described the Eucharist as 'the sacrifice of the Cross perpetuated down the ages.'[5] The new encyclical pinpoints the Eucharist as the aspect of the cross which reveals the 'gateway' between human time and eternity. *EdE* states that 'the whole *Triduum paschale* … is … gathered up … and "concentrated" forever in the … Eucharist. In this gift Jesus Christ entrusted to his church the perennial making present of the paschal mystery. With it he brought about a mysterious "oneness in time" between the Triduum and the passage of the centuries.'[6] How does this link up with the book of Revelation?

2. The Connection: The Promise of Eternal Life

Revelation can be located in relation to the genre of apocalyptic. Its narrator describes a journey into heaven, and earlier apocalyptic voyages, like that of Enoch in the second century BC *Book of Watchers* put us on his trail. Inter-testamental apocalyptic literature re-thinks the after-life. It is no longer just the Sheol from which Saul recalls the shade of Samuel. The angels who guide Enoch around heaven point out the souls of the righteous, living upon a 'spring of water', and of whom it is said that 'righteousness flowed like water before them'.[7] This new anthropology, in which persons have souls destined to survive their bodies, created a fresh interest in the Adam and Eve story: and so we have Raphael pointing out to Enoch 'the tree of wisdom from which your old father and your aged mother … ate and learnt wisdom'; and the angel Michael explains that another 'beautiful fragrant tree' is that from whose 'fruit life will be given to the chosen' after 'the great judgement'.[8] This generic background ties up the threads of some of John's imagery. It shows what integrates the promises to those who 'come through' in the letters to the seven churches. The promise 'to eat of the tree of life,' not 'to be hurt of the second death', 'to eat of the hidden manna,' 'the morning star,' 'the new name,' and to be led to 'the fountain of waters' (Rev 2:7, 11, 17, 28; 3:12; 7:17) all suggest that death will be a gateway to immortality. The climax of John's vision is to behold 'a pure river of water of life … proceeding out of the throne of God and of the Lamb. And in the midst of … it … was … the tree of life … and the leaves of the tree were for the healing of the nations. And there shall be no more curse' (22:1-3).

EdE picks up this thread by speaking of 'the eschatological thrust which marks the celebration of the Eucharist (cf. 1 Cor 11:26): "until you come in glory."' The Eucharist, says the encyclical, 'is a straining towards the goal, a foretaste of the fullness of joy promised by Christ … it is … the anticipation of heaven, the "pledge of future glory." In the Eucharist, everything speaks of confident waiting "in joyful hope for the coming of our Saviour, Jesus Christ". Those who feed on Christ in the Eucharist need not wait until the hereafter to receive eternal life: they already possess it on earth, as the first-fruits of a future fullness which will embrace man in his totality. For in the Eucharist we also receive the pledge of our bodily resurrection at the end of the world: "He who eats my flesh and drinks my blood has eternal life, and I will raise him up at the last day" (Jn 6:54). This pledge of the future resurrection comes from the fact that the flesh of the Son of Man, given as food, is his body in its glorious state after the resurrection. With the Eucharist we digest, as it were, the "secret" of the resurrection.'[9]

But, when Jewish apocalyptic literature describes the ascension of a 'historical' figure into the heavens to survey the foreordained future which it contains, does that not reflect a certain despair of history within Second Temple Judaism? Bernard McGinn comments that

> the Christian text goes beyond its ancestors in identifying the liturgical context as the place where the integration of the vertical and the horizontal dimensions of the message is effected. Later Christian interpretations … have usually chosen to lay greater emphasis on one or the other pole of the original message, that is, chosen either to see the book as just a

prophesy of what is to come or else to interpret it ahistorically as about the soul's (and the church's) relation to supernal realities.[10]

Like the liberation theologians, McGinn objects to a concept of history which disjoins time and eternity. *EdE* articulates the value of the liberation theologians' position when it states that 'the Christian vision leads to the expectation of "new heavens" and "a new earth" (Rev 21:1), but this increases, rather than lessens our sense of responsibility for the world today'.[11] If John Paul II reads Revelation liturgically, this does not constitute separating its meaning from human time. Along with liberation theologians like Leonardo Boff who take Mary's *Magnificat* as their key note, *EdE* affirms that 'the Magnificat reflects the eschatological tension of the Eucharist. Every time the Son of God comes again to us in the "poverty" of the sacramental signs of bread and wine, the seeds of that new history wherein the mighty are "put down from their thrones" and "those of low degree are exalted" (cf. Lk 1:52) take root in the world. Mary sings of the "new heavens" and the "new earth" which find in the Eucharist their anticipation and … their programme and plan … The Eucharist has been given to us so that our life, like that of Mary, may become completely a *Magnificat*!'[12] John Paul II sees liberation as a gift, following de Lubac in taking liberation theology as a way of 'supernaturalis[ing] the natural', rather than a way to 'naturalis[e] the supernatural'.[13] One can hold the two poles of history and eternity together by reading John's Revelation eucharistically, and 'reading' the Eucharist eschatologically. We begin by mentioning three questions which John the theologian's voyage into heaven raises.

3. I was in the Spirit on the Lord's Day…
At the outset of the Apocalypse, John sees: 'one like the Son of man … And his feet like fine brass, as if they burned in a furnace … And he had in his right hand seven stars: and out of his mouth went a sharp two-edged sword' (Rev 1:13-15). My question when confronted with such passages is: 'Am I supposed to

picture this?' It's not that we cannot picture Jesus with a two-edged sword projecting from his mouth; at least Albrecht Dürer managed it. And yet, the verbal and visual over-determination of the text undermines its presence as a spiritual image – if picturing is how we are supposed to image it.

John goes up into heaven through a satisfyingly literal 'door,' and is taken to the place of the Throne. He beholds 'a Lamb as if it had been slain, having seven horns and seven eyes, which are the seven Spirits of God …'(Rev 5:6). Painters usually tackle the 'as if it had been slain' by depicting a butcher's abrasion on the Lamb's body. Perhaps some of us are too little and too much imaginative to appreciate this, because, for us, a Lamb that's been slain shouldn't be standing there with a scar on its throat, it should be either dead or falling under the knife.

The painters are following the lead of those theologians who grasp the lamb by the horns, and go for the 'sense' rather than the letter. In their way, Dürer and Jan van Eyck are allegorising the text. Some of the images of Revelation do offer themselves as allegories. The woman seated on a 'scarlet coloured beast' is defined by an angel as 'that great city, which reigns over the kings of the earth' (Rev 17:3). As an allegorical city, Babylon is neatly paired with the 'holy city, new Jerusalem, coming down from God out of heaven, prepared as a bride for her husband' (Rev 21:2). Thus John's two women become Augustine's two cities, the city of man and the city of God.

Allegories are abbreviated stories, fine stories have a beginning, a middle and an end, and Frank Kermode has described Revelation as a key narrative for the Western imagination, the one which gives us our 'sense of an ending.'[14] My second puzzlement over Revelation is whether it is telling us a story? It certainly begins with John on Patmos and ends with the heavenly new Jerusalem. There are numbered sequences throughout the book: the seven angels with their trumpets, each entering one after another, and the seven angels serially opening their vials. But the many commentators who have divided the book in seven have seldom succeeded in finding seven successive events in it.

What happens smack in the middle of the book throws it off course as a story. John asserts that he speaks from exile in Patmos, and most moderns come to the book with the background information that he wrote under one of the persecuting emperors, probably Domitian; the seven letters to the churches in chapters 2 and 3 reflect the lives of Christian groups which had been around long enough to be tempted by persecution, and by worldliness. If the book was written in the mid nineties, the primitive church described in Acts had been there for sixty years. Then we read Revelation 12 and come on this: 'And there appeared ... a woman clothed with the sun, and the moon under her feet, and upon her head a crown of twelve stars: And she being with child cried, travailing in birth ... behold a great red dragon ... stood before the woman ... for to devour her child as soon as it was born. And she brought forth a man child ... and her child was caught up unto God ... And the woman fled into the wilderness ... And there was war in heaven: Michael and his angels fought against the dragon ... And the great dragon was cast out, that old serpent called the Devil, and Satan ... And the dragon was wroth with the woman, and went to make war with the remnant of her seed, which keep the commandments of God' (Rev 12:1-17). I don't know whether, as a story, this is supposed to be a vision of the future, or a present fact, or a description of the past. If prophecy or present-day fact, why is Jesus being born again? If it is a description of the past, why is the infant taken up into heaven without any ministry or passion?

To visualise the Apocalypse is to make it a 'movie.' Cinematic techniques work for some aspects of scripture. Mel Gibson's *Passion*, for instance, uses the flashback to create a cinematic typology of the Eucharist-Passion. But the Apocalypse doesn't just flash back or forward. It seems to lack an overall temporal forward-moving dynamism. If the book breaks down into a letter dictation scene, a throne scene with the Lamb opening the book, and the scenario of the triumph of the elect over the dragon, then none of these three leads to, or follows from, the other. These are 'more like three one act plays' than a continuous story.[15]

The apocalyptic tradition which John of Patmos inherits delighted in binary oppositions: the Dead Sea scrolls divide humanity into 'sons of Light' and 'sons of Darkness,' and the Qumran 'War Scroll' contains battle plans for the warfare of the two groups. In Revelation, the 'sons of Light' and the 'sons of Darkness,' are netted in the same image, the 'dark' parodying the light. The 'simultaneity of liturgy and judgement is perhaps the most all-pervading leitmotif of the Book of Revelation.'[16] The Laodicaeans, whose lukewarm-ness invites the judgement of being 'spued out' of the Judge's mouth, also get the best promise: 'Behold, I stand at the door, and knock: if any man hear my voice, and open the door, I will come in to him, and will sup with him, and he with me' (Rev 3:20). When these words are later recapped as: 'Blessed are they which are called into the marriage supper of the Lamb,' (Rev 19:9) the promise is pursued by a war-scene, the Word of God riding out to battle, and an angel calling out to the birds: 'Come and gather yourselves together unto the supper of the great God; That ye may eat the flesh of kings … and the flesh of all men' (Rev 19:18-19).

This dividing of humanity into saved and damned lends its force to the interpretation of Revelation as a cinematic jump-cut to the Last Days. And so, my third question is, does John mean what he says? It's not easy to justify reading the first verse, 'The Revelation of Jesus Christ, to show … things which must shortly come to pass' as meaning much other than 'shortly come to pass'; this is followed by the statement, 'the time is at hand' (Rev 1:3).

4. Interpreting Revelation

It was because of the natural inclination to take those words literally, and thus to read Revelation as a prophecy about the imminent future, that the book's acceptance into the canon was slow and intermittent. Other biblical books remained 'uncertain' for a time; but, once 'in', they stayed. Revelation is the only canonical scripture which bounced in and out of the books deemed to be acceptable for reading in church. Listed as canonical scripture in the Muratorian Canon (at the end of the second century),[17] Revelation simultaneously came under critical scrutiny by Gaius, an anti-intellectual bully of a Deacon in Rome, who demanded to learn 'What good does the Revelation of John do me when it tells me of seven angels and seven trumpets, or of four angels who are to be let loose at the River Euphrates, and of the mighty host of ten thousand myriads of warriors and of a thousand times ten thousand horsemen in flame-red, dark, and hyacinth blue armour?' Gaius spoke to episcopal anxieties spurred by the rise of the first End Time enthusiasts, the Montanists. A bishop with a flock to control might take seriously Gaius' satirical comments on the statement that the saints will reign on earth for a thousand years: Revelation 20 is an obvious text for a puritanical parody of a very long, very drunken 'marriage feast'.[18] Fifty years later, Dionyius, bishop of Alexandria, was the first biblical critic to note Revelation's stylistic differences from John's gospel, and to deny its Johannine authorship. In the fourth century, citing the criticisms of Gaius and Dionysius, Eusebius of Caesarea havers as to the canonical status of the text, listing it both amongst the books acknowledged by all as scripture, and amongst those which are 'disputed' or 'spurious'.

Jerome summed up what made it difficult to domesticate Revelation when he wrote: 'I know how much difference there is among people … about the way in which John's Apocalypse is to be understood. To take it according to the letter is to "Judaise". If we treat it in a spiritual way (as it was written), we seem to go against the views of many older authorities: Latins, such as Tertullian … Greeks such as Irenaeus …'[19] Jerome also hit the mediaeval solution on the nose with the phrase, 'The saints will in no wise have an earthly kingdom, but only a celestial one; thus must cease the fable of one thousand years.' The contemporary scholars who figure that millennialism is better suited to Revelation than Jerome's 'celestial kingdom' call that 'Jerome's curse.'[20]

But it is Augustine who is today deemed the principal culprit for the medieval, 'eternalising' interpretation of Revelation 20:1-6. The vision here is of 'an angel descending from heaven, holding in his hand the key of the abyss and a chain. He seized the dragon, that serpent of old … and he chained him up for a thousand years; and he threw him into the abyss, and shut it up … until the thousand years should be ended … And the souls of those slain because of their witness to Jesus … reigned with Jesus for a thousand years. This is the first resurrection … Over them the second death has no power' (Rev 20:1-6).

Augustine's objection to a literal reading of Revelation is the same as that of Gaius or Dionysius of Alexandria:

> those people assert that those who have risen again will spend their rest in the most unrestrained material feasts, in which there will be so much to eat and drink that not only will those supplies keep within no bounds of moderation but will also exceed the limits even of incredibility. But this can only be believed by materialists; and those with spiritual interests give the name 'Chiliasts' to the believers in this picture, a term which we can translate by a word derived from the equivalent Latin, 'Millenarians'.[21]

Augustine's way to lift Revelation over this obstacle was to allegorise such images.

In his *Confessions* Augustine deconstructs time, retracting the future into subjective expectation, and the past into memory. This gives us some insight into how he makes the 'thousand years' an allegorical sign for the time of the church. The 'time of the church' is neither a 'physical time span' nor one individual's expectation, 'now' or 'memory'. It is a social or intersubjective human time frame. Distinguishing the 'eternal' kingdom which is to come at the end of time from the reign of the saints, Augustine says that 'it is from the church that the reapers are to collect the tares which the Lord allowed to grow together with the wheat until the harvest … they must be collected from this kingdom which is the church in this world.'[22] The time of the church is how historical meaning is publicly constructed, until the end of time. And thus Augustine writes: 'The thrones are to be interpreted as the seats of the authorities by whom the Church is now governed, and those sitting on them as the authorities themselves … the best interpretation of the judgement given is that referred to in the words: "Whatever you bind on earth will be bound in heaven; and whatever you loose on earth will be loosed in heaven".'[23] We know that, historically, there has been a great deal to apologise for in this exercise of judgement; what has been precisely Christian, and eucharistic, in this public use of Christian authority has been its exercise of mercy.

Augustine's idea of history is often contrasted with later mediaeval providentialism. Augustine is felt to have given us a 'secularised' sense of history, and one which tends to 'demythologised eschatology'.[24] Augustine's interpretation of Revelation is seen as having relegated 'meaningfulness' to eternity. Bernard McGinn complains that 'Few of Augustine's "mediaeval" readers show any sense that the arena of the *saeculum* and the events that fill it are not to be seen as an object lesson in how divine providence publicly rewards the good and punishes the evil.' McGinn believes that, for Augustine, the 'visible church is the … instrument, even the proleptic sign of the eschatological *civitas Dei* and the perfect heavenly church … but there can be no question of simple identification of the two.'[25] For Augustine, the 'thousand year' time of the church corresponds to the 'sixth day': the first five 'days' of creation were the time before Christ, and the sixth day is the 'time of the saints'. The seventh day, the Sabbath, is the eternity to come, after the end of time declared by the angel in Revelation 10:4.

There are occasions when Augustine makes 'the time of the church' coincide with eternal time, as when he states that: 'Ultimately, those people reign with him who are in his kingdom in such a way that they themselves *are* his kingdom.'[26] One may feel that he could have tied up the knot between time and eternity more securely if he had seen the Eucharist as their bond. Augustine does not do this in *The City of God*. But, interpreting the words: 'The souls of those who were slain because of their witness to Jesus' (Rev 20:4), Augustine does identify the church as the body as Christ, which thereby spans the gap between the living and the dead:

> For the souls of the pious dead are not separated from the church, which is even now the kingdom of Christ. Otherwise they would not be commemorated at the altar of God at the time of the partaking of the body of Christ … Why are such steps taken, unless it is because the faithful are still members of this body, even when they have departed this life? And therefore their souls … already reign with him while those thousand years are running their course. This is why we read … 'Blessed are the dead who die in the Lord …' (Rev 14:13). And so the church now begins to reign with Christ among the living and the dead.[27]

Augustine's early mediaeval heirs made a decent 'reverential reading' of his exegesis by placing the figure of Christ in Judgement over the porches of their cathedrals, as at Autun. The theologians likewise pushed the figures of Revelation further toward representation of the church. Thus, Bede, in his *Explanatio Apocalypsis*, sees the church giving birth to Christ in the woman of Revelation 12.[28] In France, Alcuin, and some time later, Berengaudus, conceive Revelation as describing, not two churches, one present and 'earthly', the other eternal, but '"one church" lasting forever.'[29] For Berengaudus, Revelation's paradise is the church, its fruit-trees the '*doctores ecclesiae*'.[30] One could call this the 'Christendom' interpretation, which blossomed in the art and architecture of the mediaeval church.

This vision is reflected in a mid-fifteenth century Antiphonal, in which 'An initial "A" introduces the … words of Revelation 21:4: "And God shall wipe away all tears from their eyes, and death shall be no more ..." The Lord is shown wiping the eyes of the faithful kneeling before him, thus confounding the huge, threatening, scaly dragon with fierce biting jaws which makes up the shape of the letter "A". The believer is here shown not as one of a group of the elect confidently proclaiming the Eternal Ruler but rather as a humble yet trusting servant of a gentle and above all merciful Lord.'[31]

For Bede and Berengaudus, Revelation reflects scattered points of light in the dark mirror of historical time. Because, on their reading, the 'time of the church' is 'contemporaneous'[32] with eternity, they find *ad hoc* glimpses of the eternity portrayed in Revelation in the here and now. So the exegesis of Joachim of Fiore (1135-1202) did not drop out of the sky like the contents of an avenging angel's vial. McGinn claims that the 'appeal of apocalypticism is the conviction it holds forth that time is related to eternity, that the history of man has a discernible structure and meaning in relation to its End, and that this End is the product not of chance, but of divine plan'.[33] What makes Joachim's procedure 'literally epoch-making'?[34] As against the piece-meal sightings of earlier commentators, Joachim mapped the whole of history against the text, aiming 'to show that there was an intelligibility in the entire historical process'.[35] Since he 'sees the entire book as presenting an historical message', and, correlatively, presents us with a single intuition concerning the entirety of history, Joachim uses Revelation to make 'forecasts,' or 'predictions.'[36] He saw Revelation as a story or a movie, that is, as a 'continuous account of the entire history of the church.' Joachim claimed that he saw the 'plenitude'[37] of the book in what he experienced as 'clarity of understanding in my mind's eye.'[38] Such imaginative clarity enabled Joachim to break with Augustinian tradition, and de-allegorise the 'thousand years'. Joachim views Augustine's 'sixth day,' the time of the church on earth, as evolving into a temporal seventh day, which begins within historical time. Whereas 'Christendom' had somewhat eternalised the temporal, Joachim temporalises eternity. This means that the 'Sabbath' or the return of paradise on earth is planted in the present and grows toward the future. '*Arbores*' bulked large in Joachim's imagination because 'in the image of the tree Joachim found the perfect expression of the Trinity conceived as at work in all history.'[39]

Joachim had many heirs, the first amongst the Spiritual Franciscans of the thirteenth century, authors of predictive Revelation commentaries.[40] In the fifteenth century, Saint

Vincent Ferrer nominated himself as the 'angel of the Apocalypse,' and, in a striking example of bolting after the horse, Cardinal Pierre d'Ailly (1350-1420) used astrology to dampen End Time anxiety, proving in his *Concordance of Astronomy and History* (1414) that Antichrist was not due until 1789.[41]

Some historians see millennial expectation positively: when Bernard McGinn states that, despite Jerome and Augustine, 'the horizontal dimension could not be expunged, but remained for those who have eyes to see' and follows that up with Joachim's description of Revelation as 'the key of things past, the knowledge of things to come'[42] he indicates that Joachim has hit on an accurate interpretation of Revelation. On the other hand, drawing on von Balthasar's research into 'modern gnosticism,'[43] philosophers like Eric Voegelin consider Joachimite apocalypticism as the forerunner to twentieth century political totalitarianism. Joachim saw his 'temporal Sabbath' as a 'third status,' the status of the Holy Spirit, following on the pre-Christian 'status' or era of the Father, and the status of the Son. One of the motifs which Voegelin understood modern 'political religions'[44] to have drawn out of Joachim was a tripartite division of history. He saw heirs to Joachim in Comte, in Hegel, and in the Nazi Third Reich. For Voegelin, what is wrong with these movements is a perverted desire for complete vision: he complains that 'Hegel excludes … the mystery of a history that wends its way into the future without our knowing its end.'[45] Joachim had a 'strong visual imagination'[46] and the metaphor of sight looms large in both the positive and negative assessments of Joachimism: for Voegelin, positing a direct *vision* of the divine is illegitimate; and he pushed this to the extent of regarding not only Karl Marx, but also Isaiah and Saint Paul as Gnostics.

One can make a different response to the question of why millennial frenzy emerged in the later Middle Ages. One may conjecture that these phenomena relate to the Eucharist. The church is at the centre of the Augustinian and 'Christendom' interpretation of Revelation. Joachim's vision of a pneumatic church in the Third Age of the Spirit, and his reading of

Revelation have nothing to say about the Eucharist. For a theologian like Thomas Aquinas, the church as the body of Christ is the means by which his grace is transmitted to his members: his soteriology is sacramental and eucharistic. Like Eastern Christians, he sees the Eucharist as the means by which we are immortalised, that is, as the way past 'original death'; but he simultaneously follows Augustine in understanding Christ's atoning work morally, that is, as the means of overcoming original sin. After the definitive schism with the East, and with the elaboration of penal substitution theories of atonement in later scholasticism, the Eucharist was perhaps not so much imagined as a gateway to immortality. The thirst for a sight of the End Times of the fifteenth and sixteenth centuries perhaps substituted for the contact with immortality and eternity which earlier Christians had experienced in the Eucharist. By dint of the Incarnation, Christian believers expect that historical, everyday events will sign to the 'Beyond'. Although in Catholic teaching, at least since Lateran IV, the Eucharist is far more than a 'sign,' still, experientially or phenomenologically, it does function as a 'sign' of the divine. If the Eucharist is displaced from this function other imaginative stimuli, exciting events, current wars, and contemporary heroes and villains may come to fill the role of signing eternity. My opinion, somewhat at odds with Voegelin, is that the human need to handle the sacred is irrepressible. John Paul II touches on this need to touch, see, and hear the inner sanctums of the Beyond when he says that, 'Contemplating' Mary, 'we see opening before us those "new heavens" and that "new earth" which will appear at the second coming of Christ. Here below, the Eucharist remains their pledge, and … their anticipation.'[47]

What was perhaps missing in the era preceding the Reformation, and which is not prevalent in our own times, was the sense of what John Paul II calls the 'cosmic character' of 'the Eucharist which is always in some way celebrated on the altar of the world'; that is, the sense that the Eucharist 'unites heaven and earth … the world which came forth from the hands of God the Creator now returns to him redeemed by Christ.'[48] If the divine mercy offered in the Eucharist is not integrated with one's understanding of the church, highly moral persons will question her permission of an admixture of good and evil. The Eucharist will then speak neither to the problem of human evil nor to the human problem of death.

The sixteenth century opens with the End Time eagerly awaited. Lateran V (1512-1517) denounced apocalypticism in vain: Thomas Müntzer was about in Bohemia, and a new view of the church was in the offing. Instead of mercifully permitting 'the tares ... to grow together with the wheat until the harvest', Müntzer urged the princes of Saxony to bring on the millennial kingdom by 'Driv[ing] God's enemies out from amongst the Elect: "The sword is necessary to exterminate them ... At the harvest-time one must pluck the weeds out of God's vineyard ... But the angels who are sharpening their sickles for that work are no other than the earnest servants of God ... For the ungodly have no right to live, save what the Elect choose to allow them."'[49] Müntzer perceived the inauguration of combat depicted in Revelation 19 in the Peasants' Uprising of 1524-5. Martin Luther shared in the futuristic apocalyptic euphoria of his times: he 'rushed his translation of the book of Daniel to the printers so that it would have a chance to warn people of the coming end.' He feared 'he would not get his translation of the Bible finished before the Second Advent.'[50] But he was equally afraid that the political millennialism of the Peasants, and the rampant Joachism of the Anabaptists would deter the princes from re-forming the church in the way he proposed. Luther therefore devised a novel exegesis of John's Revelation: relegating the text to the appendix of the 'unnumbered' books in his German New Testament, Luther advised his followers not to think about it.[51]

This may be the real beginning of the overly 'vertical' or ahis-torical and 'individualistic' reading of Revelation for which Augustine is nowadays indicted: when magisterial Protestants, and Catholic authority too, effectively put eschatology into cold storage. For common-sensical Protestants could think of no better way of discouraging chiliasm amongst those who were otherwise taught to take the Bible as verbally inerrant than to marginalise Revelation, and Catholic worship and architecture ceased imaginatively to recapitulate what John Paul II terms the mysterious 'contemporaneity' of 'the drama of Golgotha'.[52]

Thus, in the nineteenth century, whilst the churches left that eschatological power in the deep freeze, extra-ecclesial spirituality focused its search for eucharistic apocalypse elsewhere. Some of the greatest Romantics, like William Blake, relocated the Eucharist in art and eschatological transformation in artistic creativity. Amongst the middle classes, visual contemplation of art earned the place once accorded to the Eucharist, and a new clerical class was born, the priest-heroes of old reincarnating as artist-transignifiers of everyday life. According to David Barr's exegesis, the drama of the 'Apocalypse has the power to bring into existence the reality it portrays, to transform the finite province of meaning into the paramount reality of those who worship.'[53] What happens here, as in artistic creativity, is a shift in imaginative meaning. Such efforts at trans-signification of the world have left their monuments in galleries of modern art. A Catholic is bound to say that what Revelation calls for is a transformation not only of image and imagination, but of the earth and its fruits. 'Transubstantiation' is not just a piece of Tridentine jargon but a solid, and earthy articulation of Revelation. We can't see this unless we realise that the meaning of Revelation is not unilaterally 'eternal,' but simultaneously eternal and historical, hooked into the temporal reality of the Mass, just as the gospels are bound to the historical life of Christ.

5. Who Performs the Book of Revelation?

It could be that a failure fully to incorporate Revelation into their self-understanding contributed to the separation of Christians into Catholic, Orthodox and Protestant. And likewise, listening to what God has to tell us in Revelation could be a factor in our reunion. Although Athanasius listed it as canonical in a Festal Letter of 367, the Eastern Church did not recognise Revelation as

canonical scripture until the thirteenth century.When John Paul
II speaks of the appropriate artistic décor for the Mass, it is to
Rublëv's icon of the Trinity that he directs us for aesthetic guidance. But the 'great architectural and artistic works of the Greco-
Byzantine tradition' and the Eastern 'sacred art' whose 'sense of
mystery'[54] *EdE* commends are not prolific Revelation scenes – in
the formative period of Icon painting, the text had yet to be
canonised, in the East. Nonetheless, it is the Orthodox, icono-
graphic aesthetic of temporality as the mirror of eternity which
may help Protestants and Catholics to grasp the 'Apocalyptic
Eucharist'. Scholars of apocalyptic literature say that the sense of
time as 'predestined' is stronger in this Jewish genre than the
'pure' biblical sense of forward moving historicity. One of the
Qumran seers claimed that:

> My eyes have gazed
> on that which is eternal …
> On a fountain of righteousness …
> on a spring of glory
> (hidden) from the assembly of flesh.[55]

That could give us visions which swing round in circles. If the
book does present its visions as concentric circles, with Revelation
12 at the centre, then it does not tell a temporal or linear story,
but, rather, circles around the birth of the Eucharist from the
church.

Most observers conceive of the distance between Catholic
Mass and Protestant service as referring to the Catholic belief in
'transubstantiation'. This is seldom considered as a question
about whether eternity enters time. That is, the question about
the Eucharist seems closed, whereas that about the Revelation
remains open: is it a book about historical time, or about eternity?
Perhaps one should bring the two questions into proximity.
That is, Revelation is the text which Catholics should invite
Protestants to consider; and they can only do that seriously
whilst reading the Eucharist eschatologically.

Not that reminding ourselves of the eschatological character
of the Eucharist will make Protestants and Catholics waltz off

into the sunset to the music of the seven trumpets. In choreographing Revelation, Protestants and Catholics go into role reversal, a procedure liable to produce toe stamping. Stalwart 'hearers of the word' in many theological matters, Protestant become resolute visualisers when they open John's Revelation. Jacques Ellul's definition of Revelation was that: 'The apocalyptist is first of all a seer while the prophet is a hearer … the prophet also has visions, but what is … decisive are the words which are spoken to him … the apocalyptist also receives words, but he is first of all the one who sees the personages, the scenes, the scenario, the events.'[56] Likewise, Richard Bauckham speaks of 'Revelation's peculiarly visual character.'[57] On the other hand, iconocentric Roman Catholics come away from Revelation with the sound of harpers harping (Rev 14:2-3) in their ears. Catholic scholars like Elisabeth Schüssler-Fiorenza direct us to the centrality of the choruses in the text,[58] and the most striking twentieth century presentation of Revelation is Olivier Messiaen's *Quartet for the End of Time*. In this musical evocation of the seventh angel's declaration that 'time shall be no more,' (Rev 10:6), 'the composer abandons the attunement to measured progress that had been a feature of all Western music since the Renaissance.'[59]

When John hears the trumpet voice of Alpha and Omega at the start of Revelation, he says that 'I turned to see the voice' (Rev 1:12). This oral-visual metonymy is characteristic of the book. In his preface to the seventh movement of the *Quartet for the End of Time,* Messiaen wrote, 'In my dreams, I hear and see classified chords and melodies, known colours and forms; then … I pass into the unreal and submit in ecstasy to a wheeling, a gyrating interpenetration of super-human colours. These swords of fire, these blue and orange lava flows, these sudden stars: here is the jumble, here the rainbows!'[60] Revelation is neither purely musical nor purely pictorial, but synaesthetic: in this text, the eternally 'new song' comes from amongst 'golden vials full of odours, which are the prayers of saints' (Rev 4:8-9). The best aesthetic monument to oral-visual synaesthetic is theatre.

What both Protestant exegesis and Orthodox aesthetic intu-

ition have both grasped is the performative, dramatic quality of
Revelation. Bauckham claims that, since 'Revelation was designed for oral enactment in Christian worship services', the
effect would have been like 'a dramatic performance'.[61] The
Orthodox icons gesture toward illustrating Revelation with
their vast figures of Christ the Pantocrat, a dramatic, judging
Christ; although the centre piece in the apse nave at Ravenna is
the Lamb.

Orthodox and Catholic exegetes of Revelation ought to direct
their Protestant friends to the point that its central action is not a
human 're-imagining,' or 'storyfying' of the world but a divine
re-creation of it. The Orthodox monuments surpass the aesthetic,
depicting a dramatic moment of judgement: '"there is no place
in it which does not see you. You must change your life."'[62] This
indicates that the dramatic or performative character of the
Eucharist is not purely phenomenological, relating to human
decision, but theo-dramatic, theo-ontological. Those old stone
churches with Christ in judgement on the West door anticipated
the Last Judgement, even as the Eucharist 'sees' us before we see
it, and with 'the loving gaze of mercy.'[63] The Apocalyptic-
Eucharist does not just retell the story of the world, it remakes
the world itself: its narrator is John, but its chief actor is the
Lamb of God.

The paradox of Revelation is that its historical influence has
come from its imaginative power, and yet it defies imagination;
it speaks of that before which the senses fail: *'Adoro te devote,
latens Deitas,'* we shall continue to sing with the Angelic Doctor.
Before this mystery of love, human reason fully experiences its
limitations.[64]

PART TWO

Doctrine

CHAPTER FIVE

The Eucharist Builds the Church

Raymond Moloney SJ

The body and blood of Christ are the sacrament 'by which the church is built'. So wrote St Augustine in the twenty second book of the City of God.[1] This is the language which returns in the title of the second chapter of John Paul's encyclical, 'The Eucharist builds the Church'. This is also the title which I have chosen for this paper, for there is a theme here, which enshrines one of the basic principles of the encyclical. As Henri de Lubac once put it, 'Christ in his Eucharist is the heart of the church.'[2] Christ, church and Eucharist belong so intimately together that you cannot have one without the other.

In bringing before you this theme which binds these three together I am not only broaching a particular interest of my own but also raising an issue which points, I believe, to one of the major weaknesses in our standard presentations of this mystery today, and embodies one of the main challenges to our eucharistic preaching and practice. I think I can bring this issue into focus by posing the following question. What is the Eucharist for? What difference does it make in the world?

The Goal of the Eucharist?
To that question we can give several answers. There are standard lists of fruits of the Eucharist in the manuals and in the *Catechism of the Catholic Church*, and they are all true; but they are all so many trees within the wood; what of the wood itself? Looking to that broader perspective I answer my basic question as follows: the Eucharist is for the Body of Christ.

About this expression, 'the Body of Christ', there is a flash of prophecy, combining, as only prophecy can, more than one level of meaning. On one level it is the same body as that raised up in the one sacrifice of the New Law. On another level it is the sacramental body offered in nourishment to those who believe. On yet a further level it is the ecclesial body, Head and members, of which the New Testament epistles speak. What is the Eucharist for? It is for the Body of Christ on all these levels, embracing them all in one comprehensive mystery. In the ancient sources of the faith this all-embracing notion of the body of Christ is central to the meaning of Mass and sacrament, and unless this way of thinking comes alive for us today, we are missing out on one of the main riches of our eucharistic tradition. A primary challenge for our eucharistic catechesis lies in making this vision of the Eucharist a living truth for the people of God in our world.

The Goal of the Incarnation

To help us understand our initial question, I might put it into a larger context by raising a further question: what is the Incarnation for? The Eucharist is so central to Christianity and to our Lord's plan in the Incarnation that to ask what the Eucharist is for, is to ask what the Incarnation is for. Briefly and bluntly, the Incarnation is for the transformation of the world. It is our Lord's great project to take over the whole world, thereby to achieve the salvation of the entire race, and so to hand the kingdom back to his Father at the end of time. You will recognise there the great vision of Paul in 1 Corinthians 15:24. We might see it also in the great hymn to the Saviour in Colossians 1:15-20. The corporate Christ of that hymn is the eucharistic Christ, the Head in whom all fullness is found, in his own being reconciling everything in heaven and on earth to God.

In this project for taking over the world, our Lord's great means is the church. If the transformation of all things is the end or goal, the church is the means: not, of course, the church as simply the Pope and the bishops, but the church as Vatican II sees it, the church as all of us, a reality to which we all belong in varying degrees, a reality both visible and invisible, as the First Eucharistic Prayer sees it, but subsisting most visibly in the Catholic Church.

This church then, Catholic and universal, is the most visible means for the transformation of the world, not in so far as it is numerous or venerable or humanly powerful, but in so far as it is the Body of Christ in which Christ still lives on, continuing his work through his Spirit for the salvation of the world. Christ is the Head and we are the members; he is the Vine and we are the branches; and if the church is the primary means for the transformation of the world, the Eucharist is the primary means for the transformation of the church, so that it may be more completely the Body of Christ, making Christ visibly present here below, working towards a new heaven and a new earth. 'Humanity,' wrote de Lubac, 'must become the body of Christ in order to enter into God with him.'[3]

There are a number of references to such a vision of things in this encyclical. In #20 the Holy Father speaks of our commitment in the Eucharist to 'transforming the world in accordance with the gospel'. In #60 he speaks of 'transforming history', and in #62 he speaks of 'the transforming power present in the Eucharist', a power which points towards 'a world renewed in love'. In the first article of the second chapter his subject is the causal influence of the Eucharist, and he cites the teaching of Vatican II that in the Eucharist the unity of the faithful is both expressed and brought about.[4] This causal influence could be summed up by saying that in the Eucharist the Body of Christ makes the Body of Christ. It is the ecclesial body making the sacramental body making the ecclesial body. The Eucharist is a primary means for the building up of the Body of Christ, drawing us ever more deeply into its life and mystery, knitting us ever more closely as members of the Head and members of one another (Rom 12:5), so that the church may be, ever more clearly and profoundly, Christ made visible in his transforming of the world.

In presenting the Eucharist to you in this way, I should say that one of my main sources of inspiration is Henri de Lubac. He is the origin of that phrase which has become programmatic for our contemporary theology: the Eucharist makes the church.[5]

Later he expanded it in the form: the Eucharist makes the church and the church makes the Eucharist. One can see it in this form behind the language of the Holy Father in #26 of the encyclical.[6] By this phrase de Lubac was summing up the understanding of the Eucharist which his researches in the patristic writers had brought home to him. He was convinced, as I think we must be, that one of the main sources for the renewal of our theology today has to be the great patristic heritage of the church, where the implications of New Testament teaching were brought to maturity under a providence which the church has always seen as special.

However, in reading the patristic writers on this matter there are two major difficulties which block our entry into the rich legacy of our ancestors in the faith. Indeed these two aspects mean that we are so seriously out of tune with what we are reading that the rich flow of patristic thought can simply pass us by.

The Problem of Secularism

The first blockage in our minds arises from the spontaneous secularism of our world. We often speak today of theology from above and theology from below. It is a useful distinction, especially in Christology, but sometimes we can misapply it, often from a predisposition in favour of a theology from below, which in turn can lead to an exaggerated use of the method of correlation in theology.[7] It can happen in particular with regard to the sacraments, which lend themselves to analogies with the natural world.

We can, for example, approach the Eucharist under the analogy of a banquet, and we have good authority in the sources of revelation for doing so. All comparisons limp, however, particularly as between natural and supernatural orders, and if we lose sight of that fact and fail to bear in mind the reservations that must attend such an analogy, we run the risk of substituting the image for the reality. The Eucharist becomes simply a banquet, an anticipated fulfilment of the age-old human desire for God and for one another in God; and so our human eating and drinking together become the measure by which the whole event is to be judged, for instance in questions of intercommunion.[8]

To think in this way is to set the ancient theology of church and sacrament on its head. For the patristic writers liturgy begins from above, not from below. The initiative is God's, and it is his design which sets the standard for all subsequent development. Let us recall that, as well as the human yearning to belong to God, there is God's yearning to belong to us. Our hearts are restless till they rest in God, but God's heart is restless till it rests in us, and this is why the measure of what is happening in the Eucharist can only be a divine one, away beyond our ordinary ways of thinking, as the heavens are high above the earth and God's thoughts above our thoughts (Isa 55:9). Only such a measure can help to make sense of the extraordinary means the Lord has chosen in the Eucharist to fuse his life with our lives and so to enter into our minds and hearts and bodies to become one with them.

As a consequence of this fact, any movement to measure the Eucharist by a merely human measure, and to domesticate the mystery within our ordinary ways of thinking, can only be regarded by the church as a betrayal of its most precious heritage. It reduces what should be a celebration in the spirit to a celebration in the flesh, that flesh which profits nothing (Jn 6:63). This is the background to that reductive understanding of the mystery referred to in the encyclical (#10), where the banquet of the kingdom becomes simply a celebration of human togetherness and the ecclesial body of Christ becomes merely a human association.

The Problem of Individualism

There is, however, a further factor that creates an even more serious difficulty for us in approaching the ancient patristic tradition of the church; and in fact our consideration of the secularist factor was only to prepare us for this. In the view of the Eucharist which I set before you in the first part of this paper, it is clear that the collectivity comes first. Indeed the primacy of the collectivity is fundamental to the way the sacrament is understood both in scripture and in the patristic writers. The problem for us is that, in our minds and hearts, culturally and spontaneously, the individual comes first. I have in mind Christians in Western Europe and North America, here at the dawn of the twenty-first century, especially in the middle class. Of course, in our academic discussions and writings, we have no difficulty in putting the idea of the collectivity first; but we do not feel it. As a result, culturally, without realising it, we are quite out of tune with the way the Eucharist is understood in the main sources of our theological understanding; and as a result I ask myself to what extent are we even capable of really entering into what the Christians of that early period experienced in the Eucharist and into what they say about their experience. That is something which should give us pause.

It is true, of course, that in some areas of human life, we are quite open to the values of communal endeavour. The model of social partnership in Ireland has been one of the great achievements of our public life in recent years. Having carried the communal ideal so far in the secular sphere, it is ironic that in the religious sphere, the very sphere where the communal is of primary significance, here we seem to be lapsing further and further into individualism. We have only to listen to some of the things people commonly say about religion today. 'I am all for Jesus but not the church.' Contrast that with the perceptive viewpoint of the Greek theologian, John Zizioulas, that the church is really part of the definition of Christ.[9] Again, we often hear the remark, 'I have not much time for religion but I am all for spirituality.' In today's world spirituality is often a mask for individualist religiosity; it is the last refuge of the churchless.

The contrast between ancient and modern came home to me most forcibly while thinking about the common difficulty thrown up to teachers and pastors in our day, 'Mass is so boring.' The underlying concern in that complaint is so often, 'What do I get out of it?' How different is the mentality of the patristic church as revealed in a remark in third century Syria in a church order called the *Didascalia:* 'Let no one stay away from the [Sunday] assembly, since, if they do, they deprive the body of Christ of a member.'[10] The dominant concern in the modern complaint is, 'What will the church do for me?' In third century Syria the concern was, 'What can I do for the church?'

In a Centre of Faith and Culture, one might like to reflect on the cultural influences that have contributed to our contemporary mentality, for instance the Renaissance, the Reformation, the Enlightenment, reaching a high-tide in nineteenth century piety, which one might sum up in the phrase 'me and my Jesus'. Religion has been described as what you do with your solitude. Well, whatever else that is, it is not the religion of the New Testament, where we are all members one of another (Rom 12:5). But when we say this, we are voices from a forgotten age. Frank Sinatra was much more representative of our world when he sang, 'I do it my way'.

The Century of the Church

It is true, of course, that an appreciation of the primacy of the church, the Body of Christ, has been growing in theological circles over the second half of the twentieth century, beginning on the level of the magisterium with the encyclicals of Pius XII. *EdE* stands in that line of development. As I remarked at the outset, the title of the second chapter, 'The Eucharist builds the church,' is Augustine's language for what Henri de Lubac put more famously and more succinctly, 'The Eucharist makes the church'.

Among the theologians responsible for renewing our appreciation of the role of the collectivity, the work of de Lubac has been outstanding. His famous study of the Eucharist, *Corpus mysticum*, published in 1944, has been foundational for much that followed. In fact, de Lubac's concern goes back to the 1930s as reflected in his first major publication, *Catholicism*. It appeared first in 1938 and in the original French edition bore the sub-title, unusual for its time, 'the social aspects of dogma'. As with a number of Catholic thinkers of that period, this represented a response of Catholic theology to the secular collectivism of Fascism and Marxism. De Lubac had been stung by nineteenth century criticism of Christianity for its individualism and egoism.[11] To this he had replied with passion. In the introduction to *Catholicism* he deplored what he called 'the swamping of the spiritual life by the detestable "I".'[12]

In fact this recovery of a sense of the collectivity may be traced back further still. Among the writings of Hans Urs von Balthasar there is a study of St Thérèse of Lisieux. In it he considers her not only from the point of view of devotion and spirituality but also from that of theology, and there he finds her to be something of an innovator. He presents her as opening up a new path in theology in the way she understands and applies the doctrine of the Body of Christ. 'The little Thérèse,' he writes, 'is the first to rid contemplation of its neo-Platonic relics; this fact alone is sufficient to guarantee her place in the history of theology ... It is not the essence of her contemplation which is different, but her insight into its effects. She relates them more closely to the saving work of the church than any previous teacher had done.'[13] The reason she can do this lies in her putting the doctrine of the Mystical Body at the centre of her spiritual life. Again Balthasar writes, 'Just as she herself placed the doctrine of the Mystical Body at the centre of her doctrine, similarly she treats her doctrine as the heart of theology.'[14] The phenomenon by which Thérèse emerged from the world of 'me and my Jesus' and earned for herself the title Patroness of the Missions is a prophetic sign to us to follow her example in placing the Body of Christ at the heart of our theology.

The leading theologians of the twentieth century, people like de Lubac and Congar, helped to make of that century for theologians what the former called 'the century of the church', and to make its great council in Vatican II 'the council of the church'.[15] What I wish to emphasise is that, although all that might be true of theology and of formal church teaching, it has still a long way to go in shaping the mentality of the people in our congregations.

Making Sense of the Ecclesial Body of Christ

In the next section of this paper I would like to turn aside for a moment from direct consideration of the Eucharist and take up this other truth, the appreciation of which is a necessary presupposition for any deeper awareness of the corporate nature of the Eucharist. I refer to our teaching on what we call the Mystical Body of Christ. The meaning of that phrase is well summed up in the following quotation from Congar:

> The community of Christians, inspired by the same Spirit and acting on the authority of, and moved by, the same Lord, forms one single whole, the Body of Christ. What does this 'body' mean? It seems to mean this: just as our body is animated by our soul, makes it visible and expresses it in different activities, so the church is animated by Christ, makes him visible and expresses him in different activities.[16]

The adjective 'mystical', as applied to the ecclesial body, is not an altogether happy one since, as Louis Bouyer once put it, the adjective commonly swamps the noun, and the whole reality easily slips into a fog of pure metaphor.[17] I am convinced that the failure of our teaching and catechetics to give meaning to this truth is one of the major factors in our lack of appreciation of the essentially corporate nature of faith and worship. To make more real for people what life in the Body of Christ means is one of the key tasks for anyone involved in teaching and catechetics today. How in our individualised world can we make our life in that body a living truth for the ordinary people of God? That is the question I wish to address at this point of my paper.

One group of people who made something of this truth are the liberation theologians of Latin America. The Eucharist is the Christian Passover, and Passover for the Jews was and is the great feast of liberation for the people of God. Obviously this was grist to the mill of the liberation theologians as they applied it to our sacrament. The Eucharist has to be about other people as we all come to share at the one table – and sharing means not only love but justice for all.

While all that is very welcome, and we all need some sense of

these truths in our celebrations, liberation theology does not
have the same immediacy in the affluent countries of Europe
and North America as in Latin America, where society is so
often polarised into the have's and the have-not's. However all
of us need to see that the truth of the Body of Christ means more
than political and social responsibility. There is a deeper mystery at work, of which such social engagement for justice is only
one of the fruits to be hoped for. We must bring our sense of the
Body of Christ, and our social concern for others, back to the
profound and mysterious spiritual reality which is the real
source of our being members of one another.

Clearly a very special effort will be required if we are to lead
our people back from our technological and empirical habits of
thought to a more mysterious and corporate way of thinking,
but in this we might be helped by invoking the figure of Thérèse
of Lisieux, who, as we have seen, placed the doctrine of the Body
of Christ at the centre of her teaching and in time became
Patroness of the Missions without ever leaving her convent. We
might compare another nineteenth century figure, Cardinal
Newman, who said, 'I am a link in a chain, a bond of connection
between persons.' In our own day Paul VI put it this way:
'Because of a secret and loving mystery in the order of things,
human beings are joined together by a supernatural bond, so
that the sin of one injures others, and the holiness of one benefits
others.'[18]

The Theology of Baptism

One way of doing this might take as its starting-point the sacrament of baptism, which is, after all, the celebration of our public
entry into the Body of Christ. We do not always realise how radically our doctrine of this sacrament needs to be revised once we
take on board the teaching of Vatican II on the universal offer of
salvation to the world. Before this, baptism could be presented
in a straightforward way as our passport to salvation. Now that
we have learned to take a more optimistic view of world religions and of the availability of salvation outside the church of

explicit faith, we have a problem about the function of baptism. I would like to suggest that there is help in the ancient patristic doctrine of the priesthood of the baptised, putting to the forefront one aspect of that priesthood which is often overshadowed by others.

This priesthood is sometimes explained from interiority, sometimes from liturgy. I would like to bring out a third aspect, that of mediation. Interiority underlines how we all make offerings to God 'on the altar of our hearts', much as Paul puts it at the beginning of the twelfth chapter of Romans.[19] At other times this priesthood is invoked for liturgy as a basis for the participation of all the baptised in our various celebrations.[20] While these aspects are of course part of it all, there is more to it than that. A number of patristic writers stressed that priests are mediators, and the priestly people, consecrated by baptism and confirmation, are called to join with our Lord in mediating life to the world.[21]

The baptised are the ones with explicit faith, and the privilege of this knowledge brings with it a responsibility for others, in accordance with the knowledge that Christ gives us of our involvement with one another. There is a character in Dostoievsky, quoted more than once by the Holy Father, who says, 'We are all responsible for all.'[22] This statement puts its finger on one of the defining characteristics of a Christian. Though salvation might be offered to every human being coming into this world, grace is always a grace of Christ, mediated to humanity in the first place by Christ himself, and then in a participated way by each of us who are members of the priestly people. By baptism therefore we are marked down, not simply as the saved but as mediators, mediating life to others both inside and outside the community of explicit believers; and the basis of that mediation is the way we all belong to Christ and to one another as members in varying degrees within the ecclesial Body of Christ.

This truth might be expressed more immediately in the following manner. Each of us must become convinced that there exist certain souls, the quality of whose life before God depends on the quality of mine. These are what I call 'my souls'. I am a channel of grace for them, as they are a channel of grace for me. If I do what I should, they grow in love. If I fall down in the task, they are diminished in some way. St Paul seems to be referring in a veiled way to this truth when he writes: 'If one member suffers, all suffer together; if one member is honoured, all rejoice together' (1 Cor 12:26). It works both for good or ill. They help or hinder me; I help or hinder them. We all belong to one another, all members one of another (cf. Rom 12:5).

Who these souls of mine are I only partly know. Clearly they are my family, my friends, all for whom I pray. But they may well be souls I have never met and never heard of. The great exemplar of this truth, and the one who helped the church to discover it again is, as we have seen, Thérèse of Lisieux, who became Patroness of the Missions by the paradox of her hidden oblation. This then is the great truth of the Body of Christ which we have to recover, if we are to understand the Eucharist.

The Theology of the Resurrection

Another basis for a renewed appreciation of this mystery is our theology of the resurrection. One of the limitations in our understanding of the Eucharist in the past has been an imbalance in our presentation of the paschal mystery, with a one-sided emphasis on the death of Christ and a neglect of the role of the resurrection. This imbalance owed more to the spirit of the times than to the texts of the liturgy itself. It is probably to be put down to a certain view of the atonement as the propitiation of an angry God, and of sacrifice as essentially propitiatory immolation. I think it safe to say that soteriology today has moved beyond these positions and has recovered a more patristic view of the role of the resurrection. Of course Christ's love in dying for us will always be part of our eucharistic devotion. Greater love no one has than to lay down one's life for one's friends (Jn 15:13). This bond is a key Eucharistic value, but it is only part of the story.

As well as Christ's death, there is also his resurrection. In the teaching of Aquinas the resurrection clearly exercises its own efficient causality in our redemption generally, and so in the Eucharist.[23] While one aspect of this is the regeneration of our souls in grace, this is but part of a larger movement by which the Lord continues to be at work in the world. We should link in a special way the resurrection and the Body of Christ. The creation of this ecclesial body can be seen as the masterpiece of the risen Christ working out the redemption of the world.

When Christ rose from the dead, he was no longer limited within the confines of one human life. He rose into the lives of each of us, drawing us all into one Body with himself. The church is Christ for us, or as St Hilary put it, 'He himself is the church, containing the universal church in himself through the sacrament of his body.'[24] The truth of the Body of Christ means that Christ did not cease his work on earth when he became invisible at the ascension. The work goes on. Through the Body of Christ, the invisible Saviour continues to be visible through you and through me, working through the Spirit and through the church for the completion of his work. 'He who sees the church really sees Christ,' says St Gregory of Nyssa.[25]

Ultimately the visible church, his body, is the means through which the risen Christ continues the transformation of the world; and the Eucharist, in turn, is his main means for transforming us into being more adequate members of his Body and more adequate channels of the transforming activity of his church. This is why we said at the beginning of this paper that Christ, church and Eucharist belong together intrinsically. Henri de Lubac put it this way. The Eucharist is referred to the church 'as cause to effect, as means to end, as sign to reality.'[26] More recently, Cesare Giraudo wrote: 'The Eucharist exists for the church and the church is what it is as a result of the Eucharist; you cannot have one without the other.'[27] In the words of the encyclical: 'Church and Eucharist are united inseparably' (#52); and again: the church emerges in the Eucharist 'as what she truly is' (#61).

The Meaning of Holy Communion

I now come to the final section of this paper, and here I would like to draw my various points together with a reflection on the meaning of going to Holy Communion. Though this paper has been critical of an undue individualism in our attitudes, this was only to redress a certain imbalance. I am well aware that in certain circumstances there can be a legitimate individualism, for indeed an appreciation of the individual person is one of the great contributions of Christianity to our culture.

As a consequence one could consider two main lines of emphasis in our approach to Holy Communion, one more familiar and personalist, the other more mysterious and corporate. Indeed each aspect, far from threatening the other, only deepens it all the more. Setting these two aspects side by side, we may chose to relate the personalist aspect more especially to the death of Christ, and the corporate aspect more especially to his resurrection; and in the liturgy itself we can find two distinct but complementary models of the sacramental encounter, which correspond to the two lines of approach which I have just mentioned.

The first model is implied in a phrase from the centurion in the gospel, which unfortunately has been obscured in the 1974 English translation of the Mass, though it is quite clear in the Latin – and, I might add, in the Irish. 'Lord, I am not worthy that you should enter under my roof' (Lk 7:6). In fact the Holy Father refers to this at the end of #48 in the encyclical. The image it calls to mind is that of coming to Holy Communion as a friend to a friend. We are like Martha and Mary of Bethany, or like Zacchaeus or the centurion, welcoming Christ under our roof. As the encyclical remarks in #22: 'Each of us receives Christ ... Christ receives each of us.' Holy Communion embodies that love of Christ for his friends which reached a high point on the cross: 'Greater love no one has than to lay down one's life for one's friends' (Jn 15:13).

As well as the individual aspect there is the ecclesial aspect. I have already quoted the remark of de Lubac that Christ loves us individually but not separately.[28] Again he makes the point that it is only through union with the community that Christians are united with Christ. Here too the liturgy gives us a pointer. In the third Eucharistic Prayer we pray that we become one body, one spirit in Christ. References to this doctrine are scattered throughout the liturgy. For example, very appropriately, given Augustine's profound teaching on the Body of Christ, we ask in the post-communion prayer of his Mass that by our sharing in the table of the Lord we may be made his members – and then a very mysterious and very Augustinian phrase – and so become that which we receive. Out of phrases such as these comes our second model.

As well as coming as friend to friend, we come as member to Head, as branch to the Vine, to be nourished by the life that binds the Body into one. Here I like to apply a phrase of St Paul where he talks of how a man loves his body, how he feeds it and cares for it (Eph 5:29f). At the table of the Eucharist the risen Christ is caring for his own Body, feeding it with his own flesh, so that we might be made more effective members of this mystery, and so become more fruitful channels of his life to those other members of his Body who depend on us.

In #18 of the encyclical Pope John Paul gives us one of those remarkable expressions which he comes up with from time to time. He says that 'with the Eucharist we digest the secret of the resurrection'. By this he refers directly to the power of the sacrament to prepare our own resurrection at the end of time; but if one accepts what I have suggested, namely that the building up of the Body of Christ manifests in a special way the overflowing power of his resurrection still at work in us, then I think it is possible to see that our making this corporate grace our own is another way for that digesting of the resurrection of which the Holy Father speaks.

Conclusion

The main purpose of this paper has been to focus on one of the basic principles of the encyclical, expressed, for instance, in #21, that 'in the sacrament of the Eucharistic bread, the unity of the faithful, who form one body in Christ, is both expressed and brought about'. The problem we implied as regards such a statement is twofold. On the one hand, in the case of professionals in the matter, this kind of language is now so familiar that it too easily passes us by unnoticed. On the other hand, its implications are so far removed from the received ways of thinking of people today that it really conveys nothing to the ordinary congregations in our churches. This paper has been an attempt to try to deepen our appreciation of what is involved in bridging the gap between principles and practice, between liturgy and life, between the mystical depths of the ancient tradition, which the statement just quoted represents, and the concrete reality of our calculating culture and our experience-hungry world. After all these reflections, then, how can we now express what the Eucharist is for and what is its goal? One of the best answers to that question which I have come across is given in some lines attributed to Teresa of Avila:

Christ has no body now but yours –
    no hands, no feet on earth but yours.
Yours are the only eyes with which his compassion
    can still look out on a troubled world;
Yours are the only feet with which he can go about doing
    good;
Yours are the only hands with which he can bring his
    blessing to his people;
Christ has no body now on earth but yours.

CHAPTER SIX

The Presence of the Mystery of Christ in the Broken Bread

Liam Walsh OP

The architectural and mosaic splendours of the Christian East and West are a patrimony belonging to all believers; they contain a hope, and even a pledge, of the desired fullness of communion in faith and in celebration. This would presuppose and demand, as in Rublëv's famous depiction of the Trinity, a profoundly eucharistic church in which the presence of the mystery of Christ in the broken bread is as it were immersed in the ineffable unity of the three divine Persons, making of the church herself an 'icon' of the Trinity.

— Pope John Paul II, *Ecclesia de Eucharistia*, # 50

Ecclesia de Eucharistia offers headlines for a theology of the church, and concomitantly for a theology of the Eucharist. It is on one such headline for the theology of the Eucharist that I am going to invite you to reflect. It is a headline offered in the phrase I have used as my title, *The Presence of the Mystery of Christ in the Broken Bread*.

The phrase employs three concepts that are pivotal in the theology of the Eucharist: 'presence', 'mystery of Christ', the 'broken bread'. The first of the three might be thought to be the most pivotal. It might be thought to be the most distinctive concept of Catholic theology of the Eucharist. But before deciding on that, it is useful to look at how these three terms, and the concepts they evoke, emerged in Catholic theology, and at the role they have been given in the tradition of faith. What I am proposing to do is to review the tradition of eucharistic theology in the hope that this will help to clarify the meaning of these three terms and help one to get the best out of them in one's thinking about the Eucharist.

The place to start the review is with the last of the three, 'the broken bread'. It is the one that needs to be, and historically has been, the first to be analysed. The subject of the theology of the Eucharist, the thing that it is about, must always be the broken bread and the shared cup that are offered and taken in the church of Christ. The subject of eucharistic theology is not just bread and wine. The value of the term 'broken bread' is that it evokes the whole ritual of the Eucharist, brings to mind a liturgy. Theology asks what this taking of bread, the blessing of it, the breaking of it and the giving it, this taking, blessing and sharing of the cup of wine are, what they are for, who makes them be what they are, what do they do. Theology will answer its questions about the broken bread and the shared cup by understanding how the mystery of God in Christ, in which humanity and the whole universe is receiving the saving grace of eternal life, is realised in the church through the broken bread and shared cup, through them, with them and in them. This is the second pivot of eucharistic thinking and it is evoked by the expression 'the mystery of Christ'. It will be the task of the third pivot, 'presence', which comes first in the phrase I am examining, to state the relationship between the mystery and the broken bread.

The 'breaking of bread'

The 'breaking of bread' is a biblical expression for what we now call the Eucharist.[1] It is a shorthand for the other things that are done with the bread, and with the cup. It gives Christian thinking about the Eucharist a subject on which to focus its attention. It further gives it access to the first thing that must be said about the subject, before any other questions are asked or speculation undertaken. The action it evokes carries with it the words spoken by Jesus as he broke bread at the Last Supper. When the church breaks bread in what Paul calls the Lord's Supper, it proclaims the Lord's own words that the broken bread is his body given for us and the shared cup is the cup of his blood shed for us.

Questions about the broken bread: St Justin

Quite soon after the writing of the scriptures was completed and the direct apostolic witness to the actions and words of Jesus was closed, we find a Christian thinker making a statement about the broken bread and the shared cup that answers a question that is not raised directly in the scriptures – although it might conceivably have been on the mind of St John. It is a question that arises as soon as people begin to ask themselves why and how can the eating of this bread that is broken when Christians gather as church and this drinking of the cup of wine that is passed around in the church – how can this be an eating of the body, the flesh, of Christ and a drinking of his blood? Perhaps it was not Christians themselves who began to urge this question. Perhaps the question came from the sceptical and sometimes scurrilous teasing of their pagan neighbours who had got some inkling of what Christians did when they gathered for their assemblies. It was anyhow in a work of apologetics that the first attempt to answer the question is recorded.

St Justin Martyr – and he is writing around the year 150 of the Christian era – answers that the food of which Christians partake, and which he says they call Eucharist, is eaten and drunk 'not as ordinary bread or ordinary drink'.[2] The answer begins, then, with a negative statement about the broken bread. It says what the bread is not: it is not 'ordinary bread'. That was an important beginning and a headline that theology ought not to forget. It is allowing, as eucharistic prayers will continue to do, that in some sense the broken bread is bread, and that what the cup contains is wine. But it is saying that they are not bread and wine in the ordinary way that something is bread and wine. This is the basic recognition of what will eventually be expressed by saying that the broken bread and the shared cup are a sacrament. If what is being broken and shared does not somehow function as bread and wine, that can be conveniently eaten and drunk, it is not a sacrament; but if it is only ordinary bread and wine, neither is it a sacrament.

Justin follows up his negative statement about the bread and wine with words that give a further headline that the theology of the Eucharist will always need to follow. He has in mind the words that Jesus spoke about the bread and wine at the Last Supper and that accompany forever the broken bread. But before he speaks them he prepares the minds of his readers for understanding why the bread and wine are no longer ordinary food and drink. He says: 'just as, through the Word of God, our Saviour Jesus Christ became incarnate and took upon himself flesh and blood for our salvation, so, we have been taught, the food which has been made Eucharist by the prayer of his word, and which nourishes our flesh and blood by assimilation, is both the flesh and blood of that Jesus who was made flesh.' Words are spoken, words of prayer, about the bread and wine. What is said, as well as what is done, is in obedience to what Jesus ordered his apostles to do. Justin quotes from what he calls 'The Memoirs of the Apostles', and we hear there the words that accompany the broken bread and shared cup: 'this is my body, this is my blood'. This is why they are no longer taken as ordinary bread and ordinary wine.

Further questions about the broken bread: St Ambrose
Another question about the broken bread that we find being addressed by the fathers of the church could be formulated this way: how is it that it is not ordinary bread; what happened to it to make it no longer be ordinary bread like the bread we eat at our family table? The answer again is down-to-earth and common sense. It must have somehow been changed. St Ambrose is the one who establishes the notion of the bread and wine being changed in Western theology.[3] The explanation he gives of what brings about the change is basically the same as that given by Justin. It is the words of Christ, spoken as his about the bread and the wine that changes their nature, so that what was once bread is made to be the body. These words have the creative power of God in them.

The Bread and the Body: Augustine

Augustine raises another question about the broken bread and shared cup that must have begun to emerge in people's minds: if what we are eating when we take the broken bread at the Eucharist is no longer ordinary bread but has been changed to be the body of Christ, are we not doing the disgusting thing that the Jews at Capernaum thought Jesus was inviting them to do – eating human flesh? Augustine's answer begins to clarify the role of the bread and wine.[4] He does it by putting the accent on what is done with the bread and wine, on the verbs that say what is done with the bread and wine rather than on the nouns themselves: we eat the bread and drink the wine. He then proceeds to find adverbs or adverbial expressions to qualify the verbs: we eat and drink *in figura, in signo*. The broken bread and the shared cup of wine allow us to eat and drink; the reality, *res*, that we take into ourselves in them is the body and blood of Christ. Augustine is drawing on platonic-type philosophy to distinguish between the signs and figures of things and the things themselves; in this view the reality is not the sign but is really in the sign, even though it belongs to a different level of being. The sign has its own materiality: it is the make-up and the 'eatability' of the bread and the 'drinkability' of the wine that allows them to serve as figures or signs of the body and blood and so allows the faithful to eat and drink the body and blood of Christ.

With Augustine we have the introduction of philosophical ideas into theological thinking about the broken bread and shared cup. In the form given them by Augustine they will serve Latin theology well, not alone in thinking about the Eucharist but about all the sacraments of the church. The distinction between sign and reality allows theology to make the very most of the symbolism that bread and wine, and their being shared in acts of communion, have in the biblical and liturgical tradition. It allows this to be done in a way that gives full truth to faith statements that what is eaten and drunk is, in reality, the body and blood of Christ.

Philosophical ideas being welcomed into the theology of the Eucharist are, however, inclined to carry some hostages to fortune with them. 'Substance' will do so later on, as will 'presence'. Augustine handled his platonic thinking about sign and reality quite comfortably. Those who read him in the early Middle Ages would sometimes be a little ill at ease with his words.

There is another element of the thinking of Augustine about the broken bread that will be an important and sometimes troubling legacy to Latin theology. And it is an element that begins to shift the accent from the 'broken bread' to the second of our pivotal concepts, 'the mystery of Christ'. Augustine talks often about the body that is given in the broken bread without mentioning the blood that is given in the cup of wine. It is a kind of theological shorthand that will be often used in subsequent theology, and that will eventually be translated into sacramental practice in the Latin church when communion comes to be taken only by eating the broken bread, without drinking from the cup. But there is a deeper reason why Augustine, when preaching about the sacrament of the Eucharist, talks more often about the body of Christ in the Eucharist than about his blood. The word 'body' lets what Paul has to say about the 'body of Christ' enter into and become a central part of Augustine's thinking about the sacrament. He tells his people that, when they receive well, they are what they receive.[5] They are the body of Christ, the very body that they receive. He is drawing on what Paul said about participation in the one bread and the one cup in 1 Cor 10. Augustine's words are the sparkling and almost playful words of the preacher rather than the ponderous analyses of the desk-bound theologian. But they are profound and exact. He is not overlooking the truth that the body of Christ which is received in the broken bread is the body of the one and only Christ who now exists in glory at the right hand of the Father in heaven. He is, however, saying this in a way that allows him to also say that the Christ who is seated at the right hand of the Father in heaven is there as Head of those who believe in him and are being saved in him. The bread and wine are the sacrament of the *totus Christus*. He is there with his members. They are his body. Their being in his body, their life-receiving contact with the one who is their Head, is actualised in the eating of the broken bread that is his body.

So in Augustine, the accent in thinking about the Eucharist is already shifting from the 'broken bread' to the body of Christ, and to the mystery contained and manifested in that body. He is preparing the second of the two pivotal concepts. The accent on it will become even more prominent in medieval theology.

The Body in the Bread: Middle Ages

The subtleties of Augustine's philosophical assumptions about sign and reality, and the richness of his language about the body of Christ, was not easily understood or shared by those who, during the dawning years of the Latin Middle Ages, were offered this or that text of Augustine as an authority to guide them in their thinking about the Eucharist. When believers looked at the bread and wine there on the altar – and from the early Middle Ages on, they were beginning to look more fixedly at what was on the altar than they had been doing during the age of the Fathers – the words of Augustine began to trouble some of them. 'Is he saying,' they asked themselves, 'that when we look at the bread and wine after the words of Jesus have been spoken over them, we are looking at the body and blood of Christ, or just at signs of the body and blood? Is the body and blood there, or only signs of it?' And if the body is there, what body is it? Their faith told them that what they saw on the altar was the body and blood of Christ. 'But is that body,' they asked themselves, 'the very body that was born of Mary and the blood she gave him? Does he who is now seated in glory at the right hand of the Father come down from heaven? How can the same body be in every little piece of the broken bread? Is what is there some kind of spiritual form of body and blood that can join our minds to him? Or is it another body, a mystical body in which the church is joined to him?'

One of the interesting features of the debate about these questions was that the focus of the questioning shifted from the broken bread and shared cup to the body and blood that is given in them. The subject being discussed is still the broken bread and shared cup – what is now being called the *sacramentum* – but the thinking is focused on the body and blood that is given in the sacrament, and more particularly on the body: what body is it, what kind of body is it, and how does the body exist in the broken bread?[6]

It was in reference to the body, not to the bread, that the word *substantia*, was first introduced in the debate about the Eucharist. It came, not from philosophy but from the theological language of the Christian church. It had been used to talk about God and about the truth and reality of both the divinity and humanity of Jesus – the reality of what was being conveyed in what could be seen and heard about him in the apostolic witness. Substance meant the reality underlying appearances. The first known use of the term in relation to the Eucharist is in a text from a fifth century bishop from southern France, Faustus of Riez.[7] It refers there to the substance of Christ; it is not used *à propos* of the bread.

'Substance' then was seen to express a valuable theological concept that allowed one to speak about the reality of things and to distinguish between appearances and reality. It would help the medieval theologians to understand how Augustine's language about sign, far from calling into question the reality of the body and blood of Christ that is given in the Eucharist, was the very thing that made it possible to understand how the real body and blood is really given, without seeming to postulate some cannibalistic eating of it. The eating and drinking was done on the level of sign-making; the reality exists in the sign, and is wherever the sign was; because it is the eschatological reality of the glorified body of Christ it is accessible only to faith, faith that penetrates the sacramental signs, seeing in them not what normally stand under them but the mystery-filled body of Christ.

One of the ways the medieval theologians formulated their question about the bread and wine was to ask whether the body that was contained and given in them was the body born of Mary. The question was put this way in order to challenge the vagueness of recourse to some kind of spiritual or mystical body in answering the question of what is given in the Eucharist. The only way the body can be there in all truth *(in veritate)* is if it is the body born of Mary, because this is the only body that really exists. The theological theorising about the body born of Mary may have, however, lent some support to a tendency of eucharistic faith and devotion to be imaginatively realistic in its conception of the body that is received in the bread. It is in the early Middle Ages that stories begin to circulate of visions of a baby being seen in the consecrated bread. This kind of ultra, non-sacramental realism even found some echoes in a document of the Roman magisterium, in the first profession of faith required in 1059 of the first potential eucharistic heretic, Beranger of Tours.[8] Later theologians, including St Bonaventure and St Thomas Aquinas, would be critical of this document. They were obviously happy that it was replaced fourteen years later by another profession of faith that was more sober in its realism about the body that is given in the Eucharist.[9] This profession has the special merit of spelling out that the body and blood, into which the bead and wine are 'converted' are 'the true body of Christ that was born of the Virgin that, offered for the salvation of the world, hung on the cross, that sits at the right hand of the Father, and the true blood of Christ which was poured out from his side …'. The body that is there on the altar is not just an object that is given; it carries in itself the full mystery of salvation realised in Christ.

The second profession of faith had the word *substantia* and the adverb *substantialiter*. This was the word that eventually allowed medieval theology and the medieval magisterium to bring the medieval debate to a resolution. It comes to be employed in efforts to understand the 'conversion' that makes what was once bread be now the body of Christ. It was this application that yielded the word *transubstantiatio*. The principal merit of *substantia* and its derivatives in the theology of the Eucharist was to protect the church's faith about the Eucharist from a too imaginative understanding of how the body of Christ is given in the Eucharist. Substance as understood in medieval theology can only be perceived by the mind, not by the senses. As such it affirmed what belongs to the plane of the spirit, not of the flesh and the senses. The substance that is given in the broken bread is no longer the substance of bread but the substance of the body of Christ, into which the substance of bread has been converted when the prayer of consecration is said over it. This substance of the body of Christ is something that can only be attained by the mind, and specifically by the mind enlightened by faith. Whatever images of it might be seen by pious eyes in the host are not the real Christ, because the body of Christ that is in the consecrated bread is the body of the risen Christ, which in the time of waiting for the *parousia* is seen sacramentally, not visibly.

St Thomas

Substance is one of the pillars of Thomas Aquinas's theology of the Eucharist. It, and the particular application it gets in the theory of transubstantiation, is a very functional pillar, not a kind of proud Greek column to be admired for its own sake. It is helping him to answer, for the world and church of the Middle Ages, the age old question faced by Justin: how is it that this broken bread and shared cup – and for our eyes and our taste-buds they are bread and wine – how is it that they are the body and blood of Christ? It is helping him to answer it, not now to protect the Christian community from the calumnies of Roman rumour-mongers, but to protect Christian believers from an excessively materialised thinking and imagining about the Eucharist that people of his day were liable to lapse into.

Thomas's concentration on the *verum corpus* does not make him separate it from the 'broken bread'. He begins his theology of the Eucharist with a long question about the bread and wine

and about their symbolism and sacramentality for Christian
faith. He then explains how their very sacramentality is realised
in their being converted, on the level of substance, into the substance (i.e. the reality) of the body and blood of Christ, while
retaining their eatability and drinkability, and therefore their
sacramentality, as bread and wine. Transubstantiation is postul-
ated precisely so that the bread and wine can be signs of the reality
of Christ's body and blood.

Let me take just one text to illustrate Thomas's concern to reconcile realism with sacramentality, to affirm the body without
forgetting that it is being given in the broken bread. Among the
texts of St Gregory the Great, who had such an influence on
medieval piety, is one that explains why the ruler of the synagogue at Capernaum who asked Jesus to come to his house to
heal his son is reproved for seeking the *praesentia corporalis* of
Jesus in his house. The text found its way into theological discussion about the Eucharist. It appears as an objection in the
Summa Theologiae q.75, a.1 in which Thomas deals with the issue
of the true body and blood of Christ being in the sacrament of
the Eucharist, and being there not only as in a sign. The objector
seems to be arguing from Gregory's text that it is not according
to the gospel to be looking for the *corporalis praesentia*, the bodily
presence of Christ in the Eucharist. Thomas refutes the objection
by explaining what 'bodily presence' means in the theology of
the Eucharist. In the article he uses the term in the course of an
argument that reasons from the charity of Christ, the love he has
for us, to the truth of what he gives us in the Eucharist. He says
that it was out of love that Christ assumed, for our salvation, 'a
true body of our nature' *(verum corpus nostrae naturae)*. He then
uses his understanding of charity as friendship and argues that
the most distinctive thing about friendship is living together
with one's friends *(convivere amicis)*. From this he argues – no,
not directly to the Eucharist – but to what Christ promised we
would enjoy at the end of time. He uses a somewhat obscure text
about the *parousia* from Matthew 24:28 which says 'wherever the
body is, there the eagles will be gathered together' to argue, in a

piece of typically medieval exegesis, that at the end of time the blessed will be gather around the body of Christ. This is the great gift of love, the eschatological gift of living together as friends, that Christ promises us *(nobis)*. From the eschatological gift that is 'not yet' Thomas goes on to reason to the 'already' of this gift of living with Christ in his body: this is what is given in the Eucharist. 'In the meantime,' he says, 'he did not deprive us of his bodily presence during our pilgrimage but by the truth of his body and blood he joins himself to us in this sacrament.'

In his reply to the fourth objection, Thomas explains the sense he is giving here to Gregory's expression *praesentia corporalis*. He says one has to agree with Gregory's discouragement of seeking the *praesentia corporalis* of Jesus if by that one means a presence *per modum corporis*, that is to say in the way a body is normally present; and *in sua specie visibili*, that is to say in a way that is visible to the eye. But the stricture of Gregory does not hold if the *praesentia corporalis* is understood to happen *spiritualiter*, that is to say invisibly and after the manner and in the power of the Spirit *(id est invisibiliter, modo et virtute spiritus)*. So the bodily presence of Christ in the Eucharist is a spiritual presence, realised by the power of the Spirit. He is present as the embodied Christ, because that is the only Christ that really exists now, risen gloriously and in heaven. But he is not present to us in the way one embodied person is present to another in the world of time: he is present to us spiritually in the sacrament of the broken bread and the shared cup. We are present to him spiritually by the faith we express in the sacrament.

Thomas and others in the Middle Ages, for all the attention they gave to the *verum corpus* of Christ himself that existed in the broken bread, did continue with Augustine to find the *totus Christus*, or the full mystery of Christ, in the sacrament. While they saw the personal body of Christ as the *res et sacramentum* of the Eucharist, they saw the *corpus mysticum* as its *res*. There were subtleties there that were not always appreciated by later scholastic theology. And the fact that eucharistic adoration rather than Eucharist communion became the most common way for the christian people to experience the sacrament of the Eucharist did not help the keeping together of *verum corpus* and *corpus mysticum*.

The other risk of the medieval concentration on the *verum corpus* was that of letting theology lose the sense that the broken bread is the sacrament of the broken body, of the body given in sacrifice on the cross. The theologians of the High Middle Ages devoted no special question to the Mass. The sacrifice is present all through their discussion on the sacrament because the body that is in the sacrament is the body given in sacrifice; the celebration of the Eucharist is the sacramental memorial of the death of Christ. Later medieval theology found itself having to cope with new questions about the Mass. They arose at a time when sacramental communion, the eating of the bread and the drinking of the cup by the faithful taking part in the Mass, was no longer common practice. The theologians began to look for answers to the questions about the Mass in the general theology of sacrifice, rather than in the theology of the sacrament of the Eucharist. That made them concentrate more on who offered rather than on what was offered. Left to itself, and dependent more and more on devotional experience centred on adoration of the sacrament, rather than on the sacrificial action of breaking bread, the theology of the Eucharist became more and more a theology that would bring into play and concentrate on the third of our pivotal concepts, a theology of what would be called the 'real presence'.

'Presence': the being of the body of Christ in the broken bread

The text of Thomas that I have been analysing is, to my knowledge, the only text in which he uses the word presence about the Eucharist. And to my knowledge, he never uses the expression 'real presence'. The language of presence can, however, be found in texts that are contemporary with Thomas, and which may even have owed something to him. The liturgical office for the feast of Corpus Christi was introduced to the bishops of the church by Pope Urban IV in 1264 with the encyclical letter

Transiturus de hoc mundo. In explaining how the Eucharist is *memoriale* this text says that in it we not alone bring to mind the work of our redemption but 'have indeed the advantage of the bodily presence *(corporali praesentia)* of the Saviour himself'. It goes on to explain that 'when we remember other things we hold them in our spirit and mind, but we do not by that very fact enjoy their real presence *(realem eorum praesentiam)*'. The Eucharist is different: 'In this sacramental commemoration of Christ, Jesus Christ is present with us *(praesens est nobiscum)* in another form, indeed, but in his very own substance *(in propria vero substantia)*'.[10] One can find the word *praesentia* and the expression *praesentia realis* quite often in the writing of the Blessed John Duns Scotus (1265-1308) on the Eucharist. I have not been able to find any research that would uncover a reason why he came to adopt this language and whether it was he who introduced it or popularised it in discussion about the Eucharist. A century after Scotus, *praesentia* is being used by John Wycliffe, but to deny rather than affirm it. Among the errors for which he is condemned by the council of Constance is saying that Christ is not in the Eucharist *identice et realiter (in) propria praesentia corporali*.[11] Interestingly, however, when the Council is formulating the church's teaching positively, in a series of questions which Wycliffe will be required to answer, it does not use *praesentia* in any of the three statements it proposes to him about the Eucharist.[12]

The Council of Trent and the Introduction of 'Presence'

It is in its decree about the sacrament of the Eucharist that Trent introduces the term *praesentia* and *praesens* into the official language of the church. The decree elaborates a teaching about the Eucharist as sacrament separated from any consideration about the sacrament as sacrifice. Consideration of the sacrifice comes in the decree about the Sacrifice of the Mass promulgated ten years after the decree on the sacrament. There are understandable historical reasons why the two aspects of the Eucharist are dealt with separately by Trent. What is harder to understand is why the teaching of the first seems to be so little drawn upon by the second. Perhaps it is because the theology of the sacrament has moved from being centred on the realness of the body of Christ that is given in the Eucharist to a preoccupation with understanding the manner in which that realness is ensured. Protestant doubts about the manner were being taken to be doubts about the fact. Catholic teaching about the fact had to be supported by Catholic teaching about the manner. Suspicions about the faith of Protestants were compounded by their rejection of Catholic practices, such as public adoration of the sacrament and communion under one species. The defence of these practices required a clear teaching on the manner in which the real body comes to be and remains in the sacrament.

It is in such a setting that the council of Trent introduced the word 'presence' into the theology of the sacrament. It did so in a cautious and less than dogmatic way. The word is not used in the canons about the Eucharist. The *Acta* of the council show that the words *praesentia* and *praesens* appeared in some of the drafts for the canons that were presented to the fathers. The *Acta* record both objections to *praesentia* and support for it; they do not, unfortunately, provide much information about the reasons given for either position.[13] Eventually the words disappeared from the text of the canons as they were finally approved by the council.[14]

Praesens and *praesentia* do, however, appear in the chapters of the decree, where Catholic doctrine on the Eucharist is expounded positively, although without the dogmatic authority of the canons. *Praesens* appears twice. The first chapter contains an explanation of why there is no conflict between believing that our Lord Jesus Christ should be always seated at the right hand of the Father in heaven and that he should be sacramentally present to us in many other places. He is in heaven according to his natural mode of existence *(iuxta modum existendi naturalem)* whereas in other places he is sacramentally present to us by his substance *(multis nihilominus aliis in locis sacramentaliter praesens sub substantia nobis adsit)*. The text goes on to speak of this being

sacramentally present as a *ratio existendi*. The being present is to
be understood as a mode of existence, and that mode is qualified,
not by an adjective but by an adverb, the adverb *sacramentaliter*.
Presence, then, is understood as given in the act of being, rather
than as an object of description.

The second use of the adjective *praesens* is in chapter 5, on the
cult of the Eucharist. The reason given for the Catholic practice
of adoring the sacrament is that, although the Lord Jesus instituted the Eucharist to be eaten, God is believed to be present in it
(Deum praesentem in eo esse credimus). The Eucharist is to be
adored because God is in it, and God is to be adored. It is the
presence of God that is being formally affirmed but, of course, of
the God that Jesus is. The scriptural references are to the way
Jesus was adored as God during his life on earth.

But it is in the title of chapter 1 of the decree that the most influential use of presence occurs. And there it is joined to the adjective that will make its fortune. The title is 'On the real presence *(de reali praesentia)* of Our Lord Jesus Christ in the
Sacrament of the Eucharist'. These chapter titles carry some
weight because, although they were not debated by the fathers,
they were approved by them at the council itself.

Catholic Theology of the Eucharist after Trent

It is understandable how the phrase 'real presence' could pass
from being included in the title of this first and most important
chapter of the council's teaching to becoming a convenient
shorthand label for the entire teaching of the council about the
sacrament of the Eucharist. It came to stand for the principal
theological truth that had to be established in a Catholic theology
of the Eucharist. It stood for the thesis of Catholic theology that
seemed to most separate it from Protestant theology. To that extent the pivot of Catholic theology of the Eucharist shifted from
the 'broken bread' and from the embodied 'mystery of Christ' to
the 'real presence'.[15]

But 'real presence' was more than a theological theory. With
time, and faithful to the inherent realism of Catholic thought, it

began to be a name for the reality affirmed by that teaching. One could speak about the faithful worshipping 'the real presence'. It is a process that has parallels in Catholic practice. The term 'Sacred Heart' was originally an evocation of something about Jesus that nourished devotion: the heart is a symbol of his love. But eventually the term comes to stand for Jesus himself. When we are told 'the Sacred Heart' appeared to St Margaret Mary Alacoque we are being told that Jesus appeared to her, under this particular visual form. One can see how a doctrine, a dogma, about a person comes to stand for the person herself in the statement that Bernadette heard from Our Lady: 'I am the Immaculate Conception.' Because 'real presence' passed from expressing a doctrine about how Jesus is in the broken bread to expressing the reality of Jesus himself present in the bread, it would not be inappropriate for a Catholic to talk about praying 'in the presence of the real presence'.

Theologies of the Real Presence

In the Middle Ages the term 'substance' was developed theologically by the use of Aristotelian philosophical analysis. I am not in a position to say whether or not 'presence' gained from any comparable philosophical analysis. But there has surely been some philosophical input into Catholic theology's use of these terms 'presence' and 'real presence'. I suspect that when 'presence' was introduced into the theology of the Eucharist it was taken as the equivalent of 'being'. But could it be that the term gave a providential opportunity to Catholic theology to open itself to the 'turn to the subject' that is said to be an important feature of modern philosophy? While 'being' evokes beings, 'presence' evokes subjects. Could it be that, while the verb 'to be' is the language of ontology and metaphysics, the verb 'being present' carries one into the domain of phenomenology? A phenomenology of presence can certainly bring to light the personal and subjective features of the sacrament and the full human reality of the contact that takes place in it. Contemporary sacramental theology has drawn widely on personalist philosophies to un-

derstand sacramental presence. Catholic teaching on the real
presence has lent itself to this kind of theological development:
the accent on presence is open to explanations of how the sacrament provides Christian believers with a person to person encounter with the Saviour: it is the making present of him to them
and them to him. A personalist analysis of presence can also
make good sense of the Tridentine teaching on concomitance:
the body of Christ that is sacramentally present in the Eucharist
is given, not as an isolated part of Christ but as carrying with it
his entire divine-human person: the body, as the normal medium of encounter between human persons, makes Christ, in the
fullness of his personal being, present to other humans.

Reliance on phenomenology carries risks. It can put realism
at risk. The debate that occurred in the theology of the Eucharist
during the sixties about transignification and transfinalisation
as alternatives to transubstantiation, illustrates it. Those who
put forward these alternatives provided some brilliant analyses
of the notion 'presence' and these certainly have enriched the
theology of the Eucharist. The dogmatic problem, however, was
whether or not these analyses could stand alone as explanations
of the reality of the Eucharist as Catholic faith affirms it. The
weight of Catholic theological opinion eventually turned
against saying they could. It became important to look once
again at why the adjective 'real' is added to the substantive
'presence' in the theology of the Eucharist. The magisterial
phrase of Paul VI quoted in *EdE*, #15, made the point: 'Every
theological explanation which seeks some understanding of this
mystery, in order to be in accord with Catholic faith, must firmly
maintain that in objective reality, independently of our mind,
the bread and wine have ceased to exist after the consecration,
so that the adorable body and blood of the Lord Jesus from that
moment on are really before us under the sacramental species of
bread and wine.'

Once the ontological ground of 'presence' is secured the
word can serve Catholic theology well. However, it is not a
word that can stand alone for very long. It needs adjectives –

and several others besides 'real' – to go with it. Because it is of and for and by other things and persons, it needs other nouns and verbs to have its meaning pinned down. One could do an interesting arrangement of the words that qualify 'presence' in the theology of the Eucharist on the basis of the causes of the presence. The arrangement could be instructive. For example, the qualification that is used with *praesens* when the word is first introduced in the teaching of Trent is the adverb *sacramentaliter*. Christ is said to be *praesens sacramentaliter*. The fact that an adverb is used suggests that the action that brings it about, and the agents that are at work in it (the infinite power of God, the word of Christ and the grace of the Holy Spirit, the priestly mediation of the church and its ministers) have to be affirmed before the adjective 'sacramental' can be used to qualify 'presence'. In formal terms, this qualification 'sacramental' is the first and most indispensable qualification that must accompany the word 'presence' when it is used about the Eucharist. It is only because it occurs sacramentally, and as such is different from the presence of Christ in heaven, that it can be real; it is because it is sacramental that it has to be substantial. The teaching of Trent about the true, real and substantial presence of Christ in the Eucharist is literally unthinkable unless the presence is being thought of as sacramental.

Presence and the Eucharist in Vatican II

Two particularly important things happened to the theology of eucharistic presence in the twentieth century. Firstly, it became less necessary to fight the battles of the Reformation around it. The theology of 'real presence' could no longer be a kind of end in itself; it came to be integrated in a full theology of the Eucharist. Theology was being helped by biblical studies to begin its thinking about the Eucharist from an open, non-apologetical reading of the scriptures. It was being helped by historical studies to draw more tranquilly from the patristic and even the medieval tradition. The discussion about presence could be put in its appropriate place, historically and theologically.

Secondly, theology was helped by liturgical practice and studies to overcome the separation that might have seemed to be canonised by Trent between the sacrament of the Eucharist and the sacrifice of the Mass. The theology of presence became integrated in a theology of the Eucharist that saw its subject to be the full liturgical action of the eucharistic sacrifice.

This is the theology of presence that one finds in the Second Vatican Council. The term is introduced in the first chapter of *Sacrosanctum Concilium*, #7. This is the passage that explains how Christ is always present to his church, especially in her liturgical actions. In the first sentence it uses the verb *adest* by itself to affirm that Christ is always with his church. Subsequent sentences about the different ways in which he is there in the liturgy begin with *praesens adest* … Among these is *maxime sub speciebus eucharisticis*. All the presences are sacramental, and the presence in the species is the core of sacramentality. Paul VI, wanting to affirm that what was being expressed here was the traditional Catholic doctrine of the real presence, but not wanting to separate this from the other presences said, and his words are quoted in *EdE*, #15 : '[the presence] is called "real" not as a way of excluding all other types of presence as if they were "not real", but because it is a presence in the fullest sense: a substantial presence whereby Christ, the God-Man, is wholly and entirely present'.

The encyclical Ecclesia de Eucharistia
The encyclical *EdE* is sensitive to the same concern to give 'presence' a servant rather than a dominant role in the theology of the Eucharist. The traditional Catholic doctrine of the real presence is strongly present in the encyclical. But presence is never dealt with for its own sake. And there is no particular discussion on real presence. The words 'presence' and 'present' are woven into statements about the Eucharist that develop in one way or another the arrangement of the three pivotal themes that I have been analysing. It is this kind of theology of the Eucharist that allows the Pope to present the church in eucharistic terms.

There is a wonderful concordance built into the text of the encyclical that is given on the Vatican website. In it you can check every use of every word. It is fascinating to do it for the words 'presence' and 'present', and for the words 'real' and 'really'. There are few words that appear as often as they do. But what is fascinating is to look at the words that 'presence' is neighbour to. 'Presence' is not passing on the other side of the road, with its own business to attend to, like the priest in the parable of the good Samaritan. It is caring for the broken bread and the broken body. It is bringing to light the sacramentality of the broken bread and letting it reveal and be the mystery of the broken body. This paper has been an exploration of how the theology of the Eucharist has followed a long road and worked itself out through many toils and troubles; how it has concentrated at different times on different truths, going from the broken bread to the mystery of the body and from there to the realism of the presence. It seems to me the theology of the Eucharist can be reaching a significant time of peace and balance in our day. I find that peace and balance beautifully headlined in John Paul's phrase 'the presence of the mystery of Christ in the broken bread'. It is this theological moment that has allowed John Paul II to draw on the theology of the Eucharist to frame his vision and hope for the church. It is a vision which he finds modelled by *The architectural and mosaic splendours of the Christian East and West [which] contain a hope, and even a pledge, of the desired fullness of communion in faith and in celebration.* It is a vision that, he says, *would presuppose and demand, as in Rublëv's famous depiction of the Trinity, a profoundly Eucharistic church.* And that church would live in a faith and in a celebration [and one can surely add, in a theology] *in which the presence of the mystery of Christ in the broken bread is as it were immersed in the ineffable unity of the three divine Persons, making of the church herself an "icon" of the Trinity* (cf. EdE, #50).

CHAPTER SEVEN

A People of Priests

Patrick Gorevan

The Holy Father speaks about the apostolicity of the Eucharist in Chapter III of the encyclical and concludes: 'the faithful join in the offering of the Eucharist by virtue of their royal priesthood, yet it is the ordained priest who, "acting in the person of Christ, brings about the Eucharistic sacrifice and offers it to God in the name of all the people" (*Lumen Gentium*, #10)' (*EdE*, #28).

EdE stresses the difference and relation between the way ordained ministers and all the faithful participate in the priesthood of Christ. This paper looks at how the liturgy of the Eucharist presents, firstly, the ministerial priesthood (notably as Romano Guardini and Robert Sokolowski explain this) and secondly the priesthood of all the faithful.

We might start, however, by recalling the events told us in Genesis 32. Jacob has been left alone, after sending his family across the river at the ford of Jabbok. A man wrestles with him till daybreak, wounding him, and giving him a new name (Israel, the man who wrestles with God). Towards morning, the man asks Jacob to release him, but Jacob refuses to let him go unless he blesses him. This passage has hidden eucharistic resonances and may help us to approach the dimensions of the Eucharist (sacrifice, communion, presence) in a fitting way. The Eucharist is a 'treasure' indeed, but we do not gaze at it in a detached way as we might gaze at the treasures of a museum, for we are to grapple with it and be challenged by it, it touches us to wound us, offers us a new name or identity, and we are not to let go until we receive a blessing. With that determination, we can approach the mystery.

Liturgy and priesthood: Guardini

Romano Guardini (1885-1968) was a German theological thinker of Italian origin. One of his most original works is entitled *The End of the Modern Age* (1950). It is sometimes described as a prophetically 'postmodern' text, written long before postmodernism came to be an issue. For Guardini the modern era, based on the eighteenth century enlightenment ambitions of totalising knowledge and, as a result, unlimited progress at all levels, was rapidly coming to an end. It was becoming increasingly difficult to place one's trust in human reason *sans plus*, and a new style, a more tentative and less domineering approach to the world, would have to characterise the 'postmodern' age.

Guardini was one of the central figures in the twentieth-century liturgical movement, and he felt that the great patterns of the spiritual life could emerge freely in the liturgy: the great human realities of flesh and spirit, individual and community, freedom and rigour, heart and mind, often opposed to one another, are given a space there to dwell in unison and enrich the interior life. The church, he felt, was now 'awakening in souls', and the liturgy permitted the growth of a more engaging human and supernatural form of worship, leaving behind the individualist forms of the nineteenth century.

For Guardini's liturgical phenomenology, liturgy was an example of the truth that the body is the icon of the soul. Signs of all kinds (one of his most influential works is called, simply, *Sacred Signs*) shadow forth the realities of our faith, our redemption and our sanctification. People who live by the liturgy will come to learn that the gestures, actions and material objects which it employs are of the highest significance. In man lives a soul, but the life of that soul is not itself visible; it is unable to express itself alone. To do so, it must first become gesture, act, word; it must translate itself into the language of the body so that we can grasp it.

The action of our redemption had to follow that process: it was distilled into liturgical rites, words and symbols, and thus remained part of the life of the church. It became possible to commemorate it regularly, as part of the everyday life of the People of God. Someone who saw *The Passion of the Christ* remarked that the Mass now meant much more to him, because Mel Gibson tries to point there to the link between the Mass and the Cross. But for Guardini the Mass does not try to connect in this dramatic way, not even with the Last Supper: the spontaneity and the immediacy of the moment are left aside and we use strictly prescribed words and gestures. He sums it all up by saying that 'the memorial of the Mass is celebrated not in the form of a play, but of a liturgy. The object commemorated is not imitated, but translated into symbols.'[1]

Romano Guardini expresses the identity of the Mass in memorable terms: 'Christ faces God as high priest of the world. And though his sacrifice was made in time, in the historical hour of his death, it is celebrated eternally, in the endless present … In all eternity there remains but one sacrifice, forever current in the words: do this in remembrance of me (Luke 22:19). In holy Mass this offering is constantly renewed, for it cannot be repeated.'[2]

The church does not present the sacrifice to us in dramatic terms, step by step, as may have happened in the *agape* in the early church, or as in passion plays. The Mass presents the sacrifice sacramentally. Bread and wine are given a new, additional significance in a liturgical, ceremonial setting. 'Do this' is the Lord's command. 'This' is now done in a ceremonial, ritual way, without the breath of everyday life which we find, for example, in the gospels, even in the account given there of the comings and goings of the Last Supper. The liturgy brings things into a different sphere of reality, a more stylised and detached one.[3]

Ministerial priesthood: Robert Sokolowski
This aspect of Guardini's vision of the liturgy has found a recent echo in Robert Sokolowski's *Eucharistic Presence*.[4] Fr Sokolowski, Professor of Philosophy at Catholic University of America, is an expert in Husserlian phenomenology. He has argued that phenomenology, the analysis of what is given to the mind in appearances, is able to examine Christian religious beliefs, particularly

the sacrament of the Eucharist, since the way that things appear is a succession of revelations of what they are, rather than just subjective impacts which at best only hint at things and at worst actually prevent our understanding them. Although the Eucharist is the centre of his focus in eucharistic presence, he brings this 'theology of disclosure' to bear on other issues in Christian faith, such as the Christian understanding of God, creation, the incarnation, redemption, and biblical revelation.

In eucharistic presence Sokolowski also finds that the Eucharist is a non-dramatic presentation of the sacrifice of Christ. He argues that if the Eucharist, and particularly its central moment, the Eucharistic Prayer and the institution narrative, were presented to us as a drama performed before the congregation, this would have the unfortunate result of shifting the focus of the liturgy from its relationship to God the Father to an axis between priest and people. The liturgy would cut away from its presence before God, which had been established in the preface and sanctus, and it would be centred on the dramatic impact of the priest acting before the congregation, as audience or participants.[5]

In true phenomenological style, Sokolowski refers to the time of the Eucharist, for the sacrament relies on time: it re-enacts an event which once happened in the world. The succession of time is the raw material for the Eucharist. But it re-enacts the event as occurring before the Father, in the endless present to which Guardini alluded, so that time has become an image of eternity and succession, which for us, in the natural order, is the ultimate setting for everything, now becomes an image, a moving image of eternity. Succession now lies against something which has no before or after, the eternal life of God.

He then gets down to analysing the rite itself, in the spirit of Josef Jungmann, whom he quotes: 'The rite makes it clear that the priest, when he begins the words of consecration, is no longer merely the representative of the assembled congregation, but that he represents now the person of Christ, because he does what Christ did.'[6]

Sokolowski's analysis of the appearances shows how this is done. Firstly, he reminds us that we don't get to the passion directly, as in a passion play. The Mass re-enacts the death of Christ indirectly, through the mediation of the Last Supper, in which Christ himself anticipated his death. So there is a blend of memory and anticipation in our own celebration, not merely as psychological states: we are re-enacting and pre-enacting things which God has done and will do. We remember something which anticipated something. We have a double perspective on the death of Christ.

This shift of perspective – from that of the church celebrating the Eucharist here and now to that of Christ at the Last Supper – is brought about by a remarkable shift in the language, the grammar of the eucharistic prayer. Throughout the eucharistic prayer, from the beginning of the preface to the great 'Amen', the priest speaks in the first person plural. He says that 'we' come before the Father, that 'we' ask him to give us his blessing, that we pray for our Pope and bishops. He is speaking in the name of the local community and of the church as a whole '*in persona Ecclesiae*', allowing Christ to gather her together as a communion.

At the central point of the prayer, however, and within the narrative of the Last Supper which is also spoken by 'us', the celebrant begins to quote the words of Jesus at the last Supper, and in this quotation he speaks in the first person singular: 'This is my body …' This is not just linguistic, for Sokolowski. We, in Maynooth in 2004, are now brought together to the time, place and perspective from which Jesus, at the Passover he celebrated with his disciples, anticipates his own sacrificial death. The church, he says, is brought back to the upper room in Jerusalem when her priest, in a quotation, allows Christ to say, 'this is my body'. St Ambrose spoke here of an 'interruption' of the priest by Christ in the institution narrative.[7]

The gestures are quotational: they are meant to 'be' actions of Christ, but not in a dramatic way. The priest lends voice and hand to Christ, to say the words, over the bread he is holding, but not as an actor might, for he does something, in the liturgy, which Christ almost certainly did not do: he bows slightly. This slight bow, for Sokolowski, amounts to 'gestural quotation marks'. The quote ends when he ends the bow and raises the bread or the chalice, actions which are quite different, done by the priest in his own right, in order to facilitate the congregation.

But, you might say, very interesting, we're always quoting people and re-living their actions in this non-dramatic way: 'did you hear the latest about Joe? He came over to me and said: "…"' This doesn't mean that Joe does it again! Certainly not: but in the Eucharist, the quotation is expressed and made alive again before the eternal Father, in a prayer addressed to him, before whom the original sacrifice of the cross is always present. It is God who takes the initiative; the priest simply lends voice and hands to Christ, he doesn't order or 'conjure' him.

Finally, Sokolowski reminds us that for St Thomas, in his treatise on the sacraments, this use of the first person singular is different from its use in the other sacraments. In the cases of baptism and penance, he speaks in his own voice when he says: I absolve you, I baptise you. But in the Eucharist, he does not. The 'my' uttered is the 'my' uttered by Christ and only quoted by the priest: 'The minister who accomplishes this sacrament does nothing except to state the words of Christ' (*tertia pars*, q.78, a.1, c). He 'does this' in answer to the Lord's command.

Do this: the cosmic Eucharist

'Do this': these words ring down through our Christian history. As Gregory Dix, the Anglican liturgical scholar put it:

Was ever another command so obeyed? For century after century, spreading slowly to every continent and country and among every race on earth, this action has been done, in every conceivable human circumstance, for every conceivable human need from infancy and before it to extreme old age and after it, from the pinnacles of earthly greatness to the refuge of the fugitives in the caves and dens of the earth. Men have found no better thing than this to do for kings at their crowning and for criminals going to the scaffold; for the proclamation of a dogma or for a good crop of wheat; for the wisdom of the Parliament of a mighty nation or for a sick old woman afraid to die; for a schoolboy sitting an examination or for Columbus setting out to discover America … one could fill many pages with the reasons why men have done this, and not tell a hundredth part of them.[8]

This passage is now re-echoed in the encyclical by the Pope's evocation of his own life: 'When I think of the Eucharist, and look at my life … I naturally recall the many times and places in which I was able to celebrate it … I have been able to celebrate Holy Mass in chapels built along mountain paths, on lakeshores and seacoasts; I have celebrated it on altars built in stadiums and in city squares ... This varied scenario of celebrations of the Eucharist has given me a powerful experience of its universal and, so to speak, cosmic character. Yes, cosmic! Because even when it is celebrated on the humble altar of a country church, the Eucharist is always in some way celebrated on the altar of the world … He, the Eternal High Priest who by the blood of his cross entered the eternal sanctuary, thus gives back to the Creator and Father all creation redeemed'. (*EdE*, #8)

The altar of the heart
In speaking of the cosmic Eucharist, John Paul II has spoken of the altar of the world: the cosmic liturgy, reverberating through all of creation! I would like to turn for the second part of this paper to a similar phrase from St Peter Chrysologus, the fifth century bishop of Ravenna, who remarked that every Christian should set up another altar: the 'altar of the heart'. Quite a contrasting vision, but one which brings me to that other feature of the quotation with which we began: 'the faithful join in the offering of the Eucharist by virtue of their royal priesthood' (*EdE*, #28), which is linked, in turn, to an earlier remark: 'Christ has also made his own the spiritual sacrifice of the church, which is called to offer herself in union with the sacrifice of Christ' (*EdE*, #13).

The rest of this paper will look at the links between this royal priesthood of the faithful and the liturgy of the Eucharist.

The liturgical altar

In the first place, the liturgy's presentation of the sacrifice of Christ offers us the parameters of our own. Most of us will have seen the ceremony of dedication of an altar. The church goes to great lengths on these occasions, with relics, anointings and incense, for she sees the Christian altar as a sign of Christ, the priest, the victim and the altar of his own sacrifice.[9] She also proclaims that each member and disciple of the Master is a spiritual altar, on which the sacrifice of a holy life may be offered to God.[10]

This is also a common theme in early Christian preaching on the priestly people (1 Pet 2): 'Since you are a human being, be God's sacrifice and his priest. Do not throw away the privilege granted you by the divine authority. Put on the vestment of holiness: buckle on the belt of purity ... set up the altar of your heart. And so, without fear, bring your body to God as his victim'[11] and '[What] could be more ... priestly than to consecrate a pure conscience to God and offer on the altar of the heart the spotless sacrifice of its devotion?'[12]

The Mass : teacher of the Christian sacrifice

Secondly, the action of the Mass itself also teaches and instructs all the faithful about our priestly role. In a letter on the Eucharist written in 1980, *Dominicae Cenae*, Pope John Paul stressed that while 'those who participate in the Eucharist do not confect the sacrifice as he does, they offer with him, by virtue of the common priesthood, their own spiritual sacrifices represented by the bread and wine from the moment of their presentation at the altar ... The bread and wine become in a sense a symbol of all that the eucharistic assembly brings, on its own part, as an offering to God and offers spiritually' (*DC*, #9).

In some of the prayers which the celebrant says *in persona ecclesiae*, references are made to the offerings and self-offerings of the people:

Merciful Lord,
make holy these gifts
and let our spiritual sacrifice
make us an everlasting gift to you
(Prayer over the gifts, Friday of the third week of Easter)

The Pope makes an appeal that this pedagogy resound in our celebrations: he puts a particular accent on a phrase at the end of the presentation of the gifts: the priest asks the faithful to pray 'that my sacrifice and yours may be acceptable to God, the almighty Father'(DC, #9). These words, he says, express the character of the entire eucharistic liturgy and the fullness of its divine and ecclesial content. The 'ecclesial' content, the sacrifice which is offered by the faithful and has just been figured forth in the presentation of the gifts, does not lose its distinctiveness by being taken up into the sacrifice of Christ, from which it receives its identity and significance.

The late Fr Brian Magee, CM, former editor of the *Liturgical Calendar for Ireland* and a foremost liturgist, has responded to these ideas with some warnings about the rite of the present-ation of the gifts. It began with the Christian people going to real trouble to make and provide the materials for the Eucharist and it continued with money and other gifts for the sustenance of Christ's body. He is concerned about the merely symbolic gifts which sometimes are presented, at graduation Masses for exam-ple, which, he felt, didn't cost anyone anything. Bread and wine are what count, and beyond that, let people be encouraged to make gifts which really take something out of them, represent-ing a true self-giving rather than a mild sense of nostalgia. Otherwise the power of the rite can be lost in a schmaltz which is unable to transform the energies and idealism of those present into an offering which is truly worth the candle.[13] A far cry from St Augustine's stern reminder: 'At a great table you have sat …'!

The priesthood of the faithful is demanded by the Mass
Secondly, the Mass seems to need the priestly life of the faithful. As Paul McPartlan put it, 'the priestly people, when they bring

the world to the altar ... and then take the new life and holy communion that we receive in return back out into the world are the bridge without which the altar is an island cut off from the world. What a calling! What a responsibility!'[14]

Pope John Paul, who is not renowned for speaking frequently about the liturgy, has also referred to this: 'The Roman liturgy is brief: basically, because there is much to be done outside the church and this is why we have the dismissal *'Ite missa est'* from which we have the word 'Mass': the community is sent forth to evangelise the world...'[15] This very brevity could be seen as another lesson from the liturgy. As a circle has its centre, the Mass should be at the centre of the Christian's life. But a circle also has a circumference and that circumference is, to a great extent, the secular life of the faithful. In a particular way the lay faithful have the mission to transform the world from within, by their expertise and commitment, bringing the inspiration that they have received at the altar into their workaday lives. References to the priestly mission of the lay faithful in *Christifideles Laici*,[16] the Pope's reflections on the 1987 synod on the vocation of lay people, were immediately followed by a chapter on their secularity, which is not just a sociological classification but defines a profound theological role and mission: it means that God has handed over the world to lay women and men that they may share in the work of creation, free the world from the influence of sin and seek holiness in the midst of earthly realities.

This emphasis on a priestly mission does not encourage an inward looking piety or a clericalisation of lay people. Their sharing in the priesthood of Christ is not even remotely by way of acting as agents or substitutes for the ordained priesthood, whether in the secular world, or just around the sanctuary. Rather, the church feeds them at the altar with the bread of life, and then profoundly respects their autonomy as, thus fortified, they strive to restore all things in Christ. This need hardly surprise us when we think of how St Peter's words concerning the priestly people offering spiritual sacrifices (cf. 1 Pet 2:5) are followed by an encouragement to go and 'declare the wonderful

deeds of him who called you out of darkness into his own wonderful light' (1 Pet 2:9).

This 'royal priesthood', so much part of the Christian vocation, would seem to offer a possible point of departure for a
spirituality of the earthly concerns and realities – including
work – which would form part of the subject matter of the spiritual sacrifices which this kind of priesthood involves. The
paschal mystery of Christ is found within these realities, by the
follower of Christ who is striving to live a life of co-redemption
precisely in the way that he or she works, gives thanks, or cheerfully unites suffering with the mystery of the cross.

Two writers who stressed the secular commitment of lay
people found that vision unthreatened by this 'priestly' dimension: Newman asserted that 'Christ by his coming sanctified
work as a means of grace and a sacrifice of thanksgiving, a sacrifice cheerfully to be offered up to the Father in his name;'[17] St
Josemaría, with his sense of the autonomy of the secular, also
threw down this challenge: 'Through baptism all of us have
been made priests of our lives, "to offer spiritual sacrifices acceptable to God through Jesus Christ" (1 Pet 2:5).'[18]

Conclusion

Much has been said and written about the relationship between
the ministerial priesthood and the priesthood of the faithful. The
Second Vatican Council took up the teaching which it had received from the previous magisterium by saying that these
priesthoods differ not in degree but in essence, and then went on
to make a point of its own by saying that they were ordered to
one another, without attempting to explain this ordering.[19] In
the years since the Council, one can notice a growing emphasis,
in papal and other significant texts, on a concept that is key for
interpreting this order: the 'gift' of the ministerial priesthood is
always at the service of the priesthood of the faithful, the return
'gift of the Bride' to Christ[20] (and through him and with him to
the Father), and the ministerial priesthood's greatest achievement in the church will be to do what within us lies as priests to

spread that love for God and concern for souls among all the
faithful people.

This brings me to conclude by borrowing once again from
the liturgy: the present translation of the Second Eucharistic
Prayer has given us the fine phrase: 'For our sake he opened his
arms on the cross …' There is something very priestly about that
embrace from the cross stretching out to draw all things to himself, echoed in the ancient Irish religious song:

The health of the Excelling-Man
Who stretched wide his limbs
Upon the tree of the passion …[21]

It is of course meant for us priests who say it, but not for us only.
Every Christian, as we have seen, is called to that mediating care
for souls, that priestly attitude of Christ. But that priestly love
will often be conceived in the womb of the church, in the hearts
of the faithful, as a result of our eucharistic ministry and the way
we go about it, as we wrestle with the mystery till daybreak; and
perhaps this will happen above all when we least suspect it.
May it be so!

CHAPTER EIGHT

The Priest Acting in persona Christi

Michael Spence

'It was the best of times, it was the worst of times …' These are the opening words of Charles Dickens' novel *A Tale of Two Cities*: words that could be used to describe the situation facing the church in the Western world at the present time. For the church in general, and for priests in particular, these are the best of times and the worst of times.

The large number of those who have turned away from the priesthood, the great decrease in priestly vocations in many countries, the increasing age profile of priests, the scandals regarding some clergy and the almost persistent media criticism of all things Catholic, ensure that these are difficult times – and these things do have a negative impact on priestly morale.

But these are also exciting times, as Pope John Paul II has reminded us in *Novo Millennio Ineunte*. Jesus' invitation to Peter 'to put out into the deep' for a catch ('*Duc in altum*', Lk 5:4) is given again to the church now. 'These words ring out for us today, and they invite us to remember the past with gratitude, to live the present with enthusiasm and to look forward to the future with confidence: "Jesus Christ is the same yesterday and today and for ever" (Heb 13:8).'[1]

One of the difficulties facing the church today is a crisis of identity among many priests. Addressing the 1990 Synod Cardinal Ratzinger acknowledged this.[2] In his encyclical letter *EdE* Pope John Paul II has reminded the church of the theological foundation of priestly ministry. 'If the Eucharist is the centre and summit of the church's life, it is likewise the centre and summit of priestly ministry. For this reason, with a heart filled with gratitude to our Lord Jesus Christ, I repeat that the

Eucharist is the principal and central *raison d'être* of the sacrament of priesthood, which effectively came into being at the moment of the institution of the Eucharist.'[3] In setting out this understanding of priestly ministry the Pope employs an expression that was used by the Second Vatican Council. That expression is *in persona Christi*.[4] In this article I wish to explore the history and meaning of this short but significant phrase.

The Origins of the Phrase 'in persona Christi'[5]
The expression *in persona* comes from classical Latin. It seems that the formula had a legal origin. The basic idea behind this legal use was that of doing something in place of someone whose part one took. This meaning was in line with the primitive sense of the word *persona*, which signified the mask, or the role, and was the equivalent of the Greek word *prosopon*.

A biblical origin?
Caution is required in discussing church organisation and ministry in the New Testament period. A complex picture emerges. The New Testament writings do not give a full description of how the early church was organised. Various groups are mentioned in addition to the apostles: deacons; presbyters (elders); *episcopoi* (overseers or bishops); prophets and teachers.

If the New Testament writings do not give us a full picture of organisation in the early church, it is also true to say that they do not give us a full picture as to how the early Christians understood this developing organisation and ministry. However there are clues. One text is of particular interest here for our investigation. It is in Paul's Second Letter to the Corinthians. St Paul writes: 'Anyone whom you forgive, I also forgive. What I have forgiven, if I have forgiven anything, has been for your sake in the presence of Christ'.[6]

The phrase 'in the presence of Christ' is significant. The original Greek phrase was *'en prosôpô Christou'*. In Latin, in the Vulgate translation, this was translated as *'in persona Christi'*. Interestingly, this Latin translation was in fact a mistranslation of the Greek. It changed the sense of Paul's assertion in 2 Corinthians 2:10. '*En prosopo*' means 'in the presence of'. '*In persona*' has the sense of 'in the name of' or 'occupying the role of'. However it was the Latin text that was then used by St Thomas Aquinas and interpreted in an immediately sacramental sense. St Thomas frequently referred to this text and he quoted according to the text of the Vulgate.[7] So it is in the exegesis of 2 Corinthians 2:10 according to the version of the Vulgate that the foundation is laid for the sacramental use of the phrase *in persona Christi*.

Patristic and early medieval period

In the patristic period the expression *in persona* was used in the biblical commentaries and it was used of biblical words, to attribute or refer to someone the words spoken by another, as if the one were represented in and spoke through the other.

This patristic application of the expression *in persona* was maintained up to the Middle Ages in the biblical commentaries. It is with Peter Lombard (1100-1160) that we find the first use of the phrase *in persona* in a specifically theological sense. Lombard is the first to use the expression *in persona ecclesiae*.[8] The *Sentences* of Lombard were to become the basic theological textbook of the late Middle Ages and so subsequent theologians would take up these phrases. Guerric of Saint-Quentin seems to have been the first to use the expression *in persona Christi* in regard to the words of consecration pronounced by the priest.[9]

St Thomas Aquinas

The systematic development in the use of the expression *in persona* was the work of St Thomas Aquinas. It was above all Aquinas who made the formulae *in persona Christi* and *in persona ecclesiae* classical ones. These phrases, especially *in persona Christi*, are often found in his writings. It is above all in the *Summa Theologiae* that we find the systematic use of *in persona Christi* in a strong theological sense.

The phrase appears in his treatment of Christ. In discussing the priesthood of Christ, Aquinas wrote: '… the priest of the Old Law was the type of Christ while the New-Law priest acts in his person. For what I have given, if I have given anything, for your sakes have I done it in the person of Christ …'[10] Here Aquinas refers to the whole ministerial priestly action as being action *in persona Christi*. Aquinas also used the term *in persona Christi* of the activity of the bishop as chief pastor having power over the church.

However, it was above all with regard to the action of the priest in the sacraments and especially in the Eucharist that he used the expression *in persona Christi*. The phrase therefore often appears in his treatment of the Eucharist. In discussing the form of the Eucharist, Aquinas noted that the form of the Eucharist is different from the forms of the other sacraments, which are pronounced by the minister speaking in his own name (as when he says, 'I baptise you'). 'But in this sacrament the form is pronounced as in the person of Christ himself speaking; by this we are to understand that the part played by the minister in the effecting of this sacrament is the mere utterance of the words of Christ.'[11]

Dealing with the issue of whether a bad priest can consecrate the Eucharist, Aquinas said: '… the priest consecrates this sacrament, not by his own power, but as Christ's minister in whose person he acts. However, from the fact of being wicked he does not cease to be Christ's minister, for the Lord has good and bad ministers as servants …'[12]

From these examples we can see that Aquinas used the expression *in persona Christi* in a technical sense, 'to mean that the consecratory words were spoken by the priest in the name of Christ, who so engages himself in the priest's speaking of the words that the deed is in fact his and not the priest's.'[13] For Aquinas, then, the phrase *in persona Christi* means 'to have power from Christ to act in such a way that one's acts are the acts of Christ'.[14] Moreover, 'this power to act *in persona Christi* is conferred through the sacrament of priestly ordination, because there the priest is configured to Christ by the sacramental character, being made to share in Christ's priesthood'.[15]

To give fuller expression to the action of the ordained minister in the liturgy, Aquinas also took up the phrase *in persona ecclesiae*. The role of the minister is to act as the mouthpiece of the praying and believing community. This is evident from Aquinas' treatment of the issue of whether the Mass of a bad priest is worth less than the Mass of a good priest. Aquinas says: '… in so far as [the prayers of Mass] are said in the person of the whole church, of which the priest is the minister … the prayers even of a sinful priest are fruitful, not only those of the Mass, but also those he says in the ecclesiastical office in which he acts in the person of the church.'[16]

Aquinas was keenly aware of the two dimensions of the ministerial priestly action. The ordained minister performs sacramental celebrations and particularly the Eucharist, and he acts simultaneously *in persona Christi* and *in persona ecclesiae*. We see this in his treatment of the case of the excommunicated priest. 'In reciting the prayers of the Mass the priest speaks in the person of the church. In consecrating the sacrament, however, he speaks in the person of Christ, whose role he plays by the power of Holy Orders. If therefore, a priest cut off from the unity of the church celebrates Mass, since he has not lost the power of Holy Orders, he consecrates the true body and blood, but because he is apart from the unity of the church his prayers have no effectiveness.'[17]

To sum up Aquinas' thinking, the phrase *in persona Christi* is used predominantly in a eucharistic context. It is above all the priest's role in the Eucharistic celebration that is described as being *in persona Christi*. The formula *in persona Christi* expresses the fact that it is Christ who acts as the principal cause. The minister's role is explained in terms of instrumental causality. The minister is an instrument, in and through whom Christ acts.

After Aquinas

With Aquinas the phrases *in persona Christi* and *in persona ecclesiae* entered into mainstream theological language. Theologians followed Aquinas's use of the expressions, although contrary to what one might expect, the Council of Trent did not use the phrase *in persona Christi*.

Catholic authors who trace the history of the Sacrament of Orders agree that the lengthy period from about 1600-1950 was, theologically speaking, quite uniform. The phrases *in persona Christi* and *in persona ecclesiae* were widely used by theologians, and the use of the phrase *in persona Christi* in particular, with its strong Christological emphasis, no doubt influenced certain schools of spirituality, which began to emerge.

A phenomenon known as the 'French School' emerged in the seventeenth century and was to affect priestly self-understanding. For the French School, the priest was pre-eminently a man of prayer, and therefore an acceptable mediator. The priesthood called for perfection. The French School's influence was not limited to France. Through the Vincentians and others it spread through the seminaries of Europe and had long-lasting effects. From the writings of Cardinal Mercier we get an idea of the direction priestly self-understanding took: 'The priest ... is bound to live in union with God and with his Christ because his priesthood is Christ's. His priestly duties identify him with the High Priest of the New Covenant. Christian tradition well expresses this truth in what has become a kind of theological aphorism, *Sacerdos alter Christus*, the priest is another Christ.'[18]

In the Catholic theology of the first half of the twentieth century the Sacrament of Orders was seen 'as a sacrament which represents, represents in the strongest possible sense of that term, the unique ministry of Jesus Christ himself.'[19] We can see this in the papal writings of this period: the priest is referred to as 'another Christ'.[20]

Vatican II

The phrase *in persona Christi* developed at a time when the understanding of church was becoming impoverished and when the role of the Holy Spirit had been neglected. This narrowing of vision was also apparent in the theology of Orders, with priesthood being focused on the Eucharist. The Second Vatican Council was to change this. The renewal in ecclesiology and pneumatology associated with Vatican II was accompanied by liturgical renewal and a renewal in the theology of priesthood itself.

Within this new theological framework the Council continued to use the phrase *in persona Christi*. The expression is used three times in *Lumen Gentium*.[21] But instead of the expression *in persona ecclesiae*, it used *nomine Ecclesiae*.

With its renewed ecclesiology, the Council insisted that all the baptised share in the life and mission of the church. There are no passive members of the church. All are called to be active members, sharing in Christ's threefold office. *Lumen Gentium* explained how the common priesthood of all the baptised is related to the ministerial priesthood, and in doing so it used the phrase *in persona Christi*. 'Though they differ essentially and not only in degree, the common priesthood of the faithful and the ministerial or hierarchical priesthood are none the less ordered one to another; each in its own proper way shares in the one priesthood of Christ. The ministerial priest, by the sacred power that he has, forms and rules the priestly people; in the person of Christ he effects the eucharistic sacrifice and offers it to God in the name of all the people (*nomine populi*) …'[22]

In turning to the hierarchical structure of the church, the Council fathers asserted the sacramental nature specific to the episcopacy. The episcopacy became the fundamental category for understanding the ordained ministry. Presbyters by definition are helpers and collaborators of the episcopal order. 'In the person of the bishops, then, to whom the priests render assistance, the Lord Jesus Christ, supreme high priest, is present in the midst of the faithful … Bishops, in a resplendent and visible manner, take the place of Christ himself, teacher, shepherd and priest, and act as his representatives (*in eius persona*)'.[23]

Finally, *Lumen Gentium* stated: 'It is in the eucharistic cult or in the eucharistic assembly of the faithful that they [priests] exercise in a supreme degree their sacred functions; there, acting in the person of Christ and proclaiming his mystery, they unite the votive offerings of the faithful to the sacrifice of Christ their head, and in the sacrifice of the Mass they make present again and apply, until the coming of the Lord (cf. 1 Cor 11:26), the unique sacrifice of the New Testament, that namely of Christ offering himself once for all a spotless victim to the Father' (cf. Heb 9:11-28).[24]

With the renewal in liturgical theology, the liturgy is recognised as an action of Christ and of his Body, the church. All the baptised then are called to participate actively in the liturgy. The priest presides over the liturgical assembly. He acts *in persona Christi* and *nomine ecclesiae*. *Sacrosanctum Concilium* asserted that '… the prayers addressed to God by the priest who, in the person of Christ, presides over the assembly, are said in the name of the entire holy people *(nomine totius plebis sanctae)* and of all present'.[25] On the subject of the divine office, *Presbyterorum Ordinis* said that priests 'pray to God in the name of the church' *(nomine ecclesiae)*.[26]

Finally, the Decree on the Ministry and Life of Presbyters, *Presbyterorum Ordinis*, also made use of the expression *in persona Christi*. '… Priests by the anointing of the Holy Spirit are signed with a special character and so are configured to Christ the priest in such a way that they are able to act in the person of Christ the head.'[27]

It is clear that the fathers of the Second Vatican Council found in this traditional expression, *in persona Christi,* a useful tool by which to express their understanding of the ministerial priesthood.

Understanding 'in persona Christi' after Vatican II
The use of the expression *in persona Christi* by the Second Vatican Council ensured that it will remain a key phrase for the understanding of priesthood today and in the future. However the expression can only be adequately understood today in the context of the theological framework set out by the Second Vatican Council.

Sacramental context

With the Council a new ecclesiology emerged. In this new ecclesiological framework the church itself is recognised as the basic sacrament, and the sacramentality of the church can only be understood in reference to Jesus Christ, who himself is the primordial sacrament.

The priest is a sacramental person at the heart of the sacramental church. So the Christian priesthood is of a sacramental nature, not only in the transitory act of ordination, but also in the person of the priest. He is a member of Christ's body. But what is distinctive about his place in the body? Precisely that it is he who represents Christ as the Head of the body, to the body itself. The ordained minister is the living sign and instrument of the risen Christ to the church. He does not simply represent Christ: all the baptised together as a body represent Christ to the world. The ordained minister represents Christ precisely as Head of the faithful.

The church needs the active presence of its Head and Shepherd so that it can maintain its sacramental nature – so that it can really be his sign and instrument in the world. It is priests who are the living signs and instruments of that presence of Christ to his church. The ordained minister represents Christ to the church so that the church can be the representative and ambassador of Christ to the world. Fink puts it like this:

> For Christ to gather the church into his own prayer, sacrifice and saving mission, he requires that some provide him with a human body for the task. He requires that some be set in relation to the many and humanly enact his own relationship to them. He requires, in other words, embodiment in the church.[28]

In *Pastores Dabo Vobis* (on the subject of vocations) Pope John Paul said that priests 'are called to prolong the presence of Christ, the One High Priest, embodying his way of life and making him visible in the midst of the flock entrusted to their care'.[29] It is within this sacramental context that the phrase *in persona Christi* is to be understood.

The whole church most clearly expresses its sacramental nature in its sacramental rites and especially the Eucharist. If this is so for the church, it is equally true for the priest. He expresses his sacramental nature in the most intense way in the sacramental actions reserved to him, especially the Eucharist, where he acts *in persona Christi*. The true perspective of the phrase *in persona Christi* is sacramental. The priest is not impersonating Christ. No human reality substitutes for Christ. Nor does the phrase *in persona Christi* wish to exalt the priest into a quasi-incarnation of Christ. What is at issue here is the nature of sacramental signification and the question of how persons (and not just things like bread and wine) may be signs, living instruments of Christ's presence and action.

One mode of Christ's presence

Vatican II affirmed that Christ is always present in his church, especially in her liturgical celebrations. The Council acknowledged four modes of Christ's presence: the Word, the priest or minister, the assembly and the consecrated bread and wine.[30] The phrase *in persona Christi* must be understood within this context. Christ is always present in his church. The ordained priest therefore does not stand in the place of an absent Christ. Rather he makes Christ's presence sacramentally visible. He is to be a sacrament of Christ in the deepest sense of the word – 'not to substitute for Christ, but to serve Christ who is present and who reaches out from within [the ordained minister's] own human person and ministry to touch and transform the people of the church'.[31]

According to Fink, the insight captured by the term 'transubstantiation' can help us to understand correctly the phrase *in persona Christi*.

Just as bread and wine still look like and act like bread and wine after consecration, so ordained human beings still look and act like human beings after the consecration prayer has been prayed. Moreover, just as bread and wine must be food for that particular mode of Christ's presence to accomplish its [his] purpose, the ordained person must be a human being for yet another mode of Christ's presence to achieve its distinctive and intended purpose.[32]

Fink proceeds to draw out the implications of this comparison. 'Here I think is the final paradox of that noble insight called transubstantiation: to be something it is not, it must be precisely what it is. When consecrated bread and wine cease being food, they cease to be the body and blood of Christ. When a priest ceases to be a human being, he cannot be the presence of Christ envisioned by the phrase *in persona Christi*. In order to be something he is not, namely, the *persona Christi*, the priest must be precisely what he is, a human being.'[33]

'By the anointing of the Holy Spirit …'
Pneumatology had been a neglected theme in Western theology for some time. Vatican II corrected this. The epiclesis in the new eucharistic prayers was one concrete expression of this renewal in pneumatology and this development is particularly relevant for our understanding of the phrase *in persona Christi*. We can formulate the question narrowly as follows: who is the agent of the consecration in the Eucharist? Is it the priest as the representative of Christ in the sacramental action in which Christ's words are re-used, or is it the Holy Spirit as invoked in the epiclesis?

To consider the question about who is the agent of the consecration is to become involved in a much broader issue – namely what is the relationship between the activity of Christ and the activity of the Holy Spirit in the Eucharist? However, with the epiclesis question, as with so many other questions in theology, it is not a matter of an either/or. To ask whether the agent of the consecration is the priest acting *in persona Christi* or the Holy Spirit, is to ask the wrong question.

In God's plan of salvation, while each one has a distinct role, the activity of Christ and that of the Holy Spirit are inseparably entwined. The Spirit was not only sent by Christ from the Father after his ascension, he was at work in the Incarnation itself, and in Jesus' life and mission, and in his resurrection from the dead.

In *EdE*, Pope John Paul II has drawn attention to 'the joint and inseparable activity of the Son and of the Holy Spirit'. 'The joint and
inseparable activity of the Son and of the Holy Spirit, which is at
the origin of the church, of her consolidation and her continued
life, is at work in the Eucharist.'[34] The consecration of the sacred
gifts then, 'is the act of Christ, the sovereign high priest who is active through his minister and through the Holy Spirit'.[35]

As noted earlier, the decree *Presbyterorum Ordinis* said: '…
priests by the anointing of the Holy Spirit are signed with a special character and so are configured to Christ the priest in such a
way that they are able to act in the person of Christ the Head'.[36]
A pneumatological understanding of ministry is evident here.
The priesthood is a sacrament that derives from and is dependent on the Spirit. In the ordination liturgy the consecrating
words are words of prayer in which the Holy Spirit is invoked
upon the ordained: 'Renew within him the Spirit of holiness.'[37]
The true power that is associated with ordained ministry is
nothing else but the fundamental empowering by God that is
named the Holy Spirit. So if 'the priest presides over the people
in the person of Christ, we must remember that all ministry is
animated by the Holy Spirit'.[38]

Threefold office

Turning to the renewal in the theology of priesthood itself, the
Council set out its understanding in a theological framework
that was Christological, pneumatological and ecclesiological.

In developing a Christological framework for its theology of
Orders, the Council confirmed that the priestly ministry could
only be understood in relation to Christ. It appealed to the threefold office of Christ. Christ is prophet, priest and king. Bishops
and priests then participate in this threefold ministry of Christ,
and not simply in his priestly ministry.[39] Sacramental activity is
only one dimension of the priestly ministry. But this cannot be
separated from the ministries of preaching, teaching and pastoral leadership. Priests 'are consecrated in order to preach the
gospel and shepherd the faithful as well as to celebrate divine
worship as true priests of the New Testament'.[40] It is interesting

to note the order in which the offices are listed, with preaching first. The decree *Presbyterorum Ordinis* elaborates on this preaching role of the priest. 'It is the first task of priests as co-workers of the bishops to preach the gospel of God …'[41]

Traditionally, *in persona Christi* had been used of the priest's Eucharistic role. Vatican II continued to use the expression in this context. But we could also say that the Council extended the use of the phrase to include his pastoral and teaching roles. As noted earlier, the decree *Presbyterorum Ordinis* said: '…priests by the anointing of the Holy Spirit are signed with a special character and so are configured to Christ the priest in such a way that they are able to act in the person of Christ the head'.[42] Here the whole ministerial priestly action is referred to as action in the person of Christ the Head. In *Pastores Dabo Vobis* Pope John Paul II also used *in persona Christi* in this wider context. '… Priests exist and act in order to proclaim the gospel to the world and to build up the church in the name and person of Christ the Head and Shepherd'.[43]

The fact remains, however, that the expression *in persona Christi* tends to be reserved predominantly for the priest's role in the eucharistic celebration. No doubt this is because it is precisely in the eucharistic celebration that the priest acts most intensely *in persona Christi*. Here the action *in persona Christi* reaches its climax. According to *Lumen Gentium*, in the Eucharist priests '… exercise in a supreme degree their sacred functions; there, acting in the person of Christ …'[44] The three priestly roles of teaching, governing and sanctifying in the name of Christ reach their climax in the Eucharist. The 'other sacraments, and indeed all ecclesiastical ministries and works of the apostolate are bound up with the Eucharist and are directed towards it'.[45] The Eucharist is '… the source and the summit of all preaching of the gospel …'[46] Preaching comes to its highpoint in the Eucharist in which the death and resurrection of the Lord is proclaimed. Moreover the Eucharist is the source and summit of the pastoral mission. In the Eucharist Christ the Shepherd continues to gather his people.

Pope John Paul has reminded us of these things in *EdE*: 'If the

Eucharist is the centre and summit of the church's life, it is like-wise the centre and summit of priestly ministry'.[47]

Concluding comments

Christian writers from the earliest days of the church have had to face the problem of language – how to express the church's understanding in a way that did justice to the truth it held, with-out watering down that truth. They faced such language prob-lems in attempting to express the church's understanding of the ordained ministry. We have only to look at the New Testament to see these language problems. Various names were given to those holding office in these early times: presbyters, overseers, deacons. As their faith sought understanding, theologians in the twelfth and thirteenth centuries began to make use of the ex-pression *in persona Christi* in their writings on the priesthood and the Eucharist.

The phrase *in persona Christi* arose within a scholastic theo-logical framework. Vatican II's continued use of the expression has ensured it a place in future theological discussion on priest-hood. Today, however, the phrase *in persona Christi* must be un-derstood within the Second Vatican Council's theological frame-work.

Prior to Vatican II priesthood was conceived very much in terms of 'power' and the phrase *in persona Christi* developed within this conceptual framework. A definition of priesthood which focused on power, tended to move theological thought away from the New Testament understanding of ministry as service. Vatican II did not say that this 'power' approach was erroneous, but it did attempt to place the theology and practice of ordained ministry on the basis of service, rather than power.

Ministry means service. Luke's gospel records Jesus' saying, 'I am among you as one who serves'.[48] In Mark's gospel Jesus recommends his example to his followers: '… Whoever wishes to become great among you must be your servant …'[49] Like St Paul, the presbyter is called to be a servant of the gospel;[50] a ser-vant of the Church;[51] a servant of Christ Jesus;[52] and a slave to all.[53] The expressions *in persona Christi* and *in persona/nomine ecclesiae* acknowledge that priestly ministry is indeed one of service. They highlight that the priest is an instrument of Jesus Christ, a servant of Christ, and he is also at the service of the church.

Perhaps the Pauline text that provides us with the key to a proper understanding of the phrase *in persona Christi* is 2 Corinthians 5:20, and not the problematic text of 2 Cor 2:10.[54] St Paul writes:

> All this is from God, who reconciled us to himself through Christ, and has given us the ministry of reconciliation; that is, in Christ God was reconciling the world to himself, not counting their trespasses against them, and entrusting the message of reconciliation to us. So we are ambassadors for Christ, since God is making his appeal through us; we entreat you on behalf of Christ, be reconciled to God.[55]

God speaks the word of reconciliation through the apostle's mouth. As co-workers of the episcopal order, presbyters share in this apostolic mission. Like Paul, the bishops and priests are ambassadors of Christ. It is as though God speaks through them. It is precisely this understanding of the ordained ministry that the phrase *in persona Christi* tries to capture.

Pastoral planning

Pope John Paul's reminder to the church that the Eucharist is the centre and summit of the church's life and that it is likewise the centre and summit of priestly ministry, is a timely reminder to the church in Ireland, and in the Western world generally, at a time of decreasing vocations to the priesthood. With a smaller number of priests the current level of service offered in Ireland will not be sustainable within five to ten years time. The Pope acknowledges that 'it is easy to understand how priests face the very real risk of losing their focus amid such a great number of different tasks'. This will be an important consideration for pastoral planning for the future. Many of the tasks currently being undertaken by priests are not at the centre of priestly life. Many of these tasks could be taken over by trained lay people.

In the early church, changing circumstances resulted in the

delegating of ever growing responsibilities to a new group of people, later to be called 'deacons'.[56] Surely we have something to learn from this for our pastoral planning today. The Pope has reminded priests that the Eucharist is the true centre of priestly life and ministry.

Eucharistic living

Finally, the expression *in persona Christi* is both a statement of fact and a statement of mission. The priest is the sign and instrument of Christ as Head of the church by virtue of his ordination. The mission demands that he continually strive to live and act in such a way that he may be a more effective sign and instrument. Perhaps sentiments of Augustine, though admittedly used in a different context, are nevertheless appropriate here: 'become what you are'.[57] Priests are already the signs and instruments of Christ, but they are called to become what they are.

In *EdE* Pope John Paul says that all who take part in the Eucharist should 'be committed to changing their lives and making them in a certain way completely "Eucharistic".'[58] In the rite of ordination to the presbyterate the ordinand is reminded of this responsibility. As the bishop presents the newly ordained with the paten and chalice to be used in the celebration of the Eucharist, he invites the newly ordained to accept from the holy people of God the gifts to be offered to him and then he adds, 'Know what you are doing and imitate the mystery you celebrate: model your life on the mystery of the Lord's cross.'[59] That is the challenge given to all priests. Some are called to make the ultimate sacrifice. The figures of Ignatius of Antioch and Polycarp of Smyrna, from the second century, come to mind. Both men died for having preached the gospel. Ignatius even referred to his impending fate using eucharistic terminology: 'I am his (Christ's) wheat, ground fine by the lions' teeth to be made purest bread for Christ.'[60] In *Novo Millennio Ineunte*, however, Pope John Paul has reminded us that we should not think of the martyrs in distant terms, as though they belong only to the past. In our own times there are those who in different ways are living the gospel in the midst of hostility and persecution, 'often to the point of the supreme test of shedding their blood'.[61] This includes many priests.[62]

Henri Nouwen, in his book *The Life of the Beloved*, offers one interesting interpretation of what eucharistic living involves. Focusing on four actions of Our Lord at the Last Supper – taking, blessing, breaking and giving – he explores how these four words summarise the life of every Christian. The same four words, I suggest, can also capture the essence of priestly life and ministry.

Turning firstly to priestly life, the priest is taken or chosen by God. He is blessed and is broken, in common with all humanity. He is given by God to the service of his people. As regards the priestly ministry, his mission is to remind God's people that they are eucharistic people. They too are taken or called by God by virtue of baptism and they have been blessed. He is to minister to God's people in their brokenness. He is called to remind God's people that the road to happiness involves giving, as the Lord himself said (in words recorded in Acts and not in any of the gospels) 'there is more happiness in giving than in receiving'.[63]

'Imitating the mystery we celebrate' is inevitably a costly business, but then the business of living and growing in holiness necessarily involves struggle. St Paul in his letter to the Philippians acknowledged two things that supported him in his struggle – the prayers of the Christian community and the help of the Spirit of Jesus Christ.[64] The prayers of the people of God and the help of the Spirit of Jesus Christ continue to support those who struggle to imitate the mystery they celebrate in the Eucharist.

Finally, Pope John Paul has reminded us that the Eucharist itself is a source of spiritual strength for the priest. In the Eucharist 'priests will be able to counteract the daily tensions which lead to a lack of focus and they will find in the eucharistic sacrifice – the true centre of their lives and ministry – the spiritual strength needed to deal with their different pastoral responsibilities. Their daily activity will thus become truly Eucharistic.'[65]

CHAPTER NINE

Communion: The Trinity and the Eucharistic Life of the Church

Thomas Norris

This essay will explore the role the Eucharist plays in 'mediating' between the mystery of the Blessed Trinity and the life of the church, taking its cue from *Ecclesia de Eucharistia*.[1] Our understanding of the Eucharist has in fact made considerable progress in recent decades, thanks to two themes that have emerged with fresh vigour during and since the Second Vatican Council. These are the themes of the Blessed Trinity and the ecclesiology of communion.[2] The former had slipped away from the practical devotional life of Catholics to the point that a certain 'Islamisation' of the God and Father of our Lord Jesus Christ had occurred as the centuries unfolded.[3] In the public arena, particularly in the liturgy, we were 'trinitarian' indeed, but in the private sphere we were more 'unitarian.' Certain authors had even begun to speak of 'the defeat of Trinitarian theology.'[4] The Council, however, inspired a recovery of the mystery of which St Augustine had written, 'There is no subject in which error is more dangerous, inquiry more laborious, and discovery more fruitful.'[5] Within three decades of the ending of the great Council, an Italian theologian could write that 'the Trinity has become the very grammar of all theology.'[6]

As for the second theme relevant to our topic, the theme of the church, the conciliar constitution, *Lumen gentium*, has opened up an 'ecclesiology of communion' with a perspective firmly rooted in Trinity and Eucharist.[7] *EdE* cannot conceal its delight in recalling the fact that the Extraordinary Synod of 1985 declared that communion was the key idea of the whole Council.[8] What has since come to be called 'eucharistic ecclesiology' is unmistakably present in the great texts of the Council.[9]

Thus, to take but one example, the Decree on Ecumenism teaches: 'In his church, Christ instituted the wonderful sacrament of the Eucharist by which the unity of the church is both signified and brought about.'[10]

This article will have three sections. In the first, we will look briefly at the Trinitarian mystery of Christ as the context of the Eucharistic mystery. The second section will look at the content of the mystery of Christ as encapsulated in the Eucharist in order to be the central mystery of the church's worship of God, the Holy Trinity. Finally, we will see how the Eucharist teaches the law of Christian life as an art of loving that builds up the concrete communion of the church on earth.

I. THE LEVELS OF THE TRINITARIAN EVENT: CONTEXT FOR THE EUCHARIST

The mystery of God as One in nature and Three in person, together with the paschal mystery of Christ, are the two central mysteries of divine revelation. All the other mysteries of faith, such as creation, incarnation, grace, eschatology, redemption and Mariology, occur within their parameters. In a unique fashion the Holy Eucharist occurs in that very milieu. In fact, the Eucharist manages to be 'the cup of synthesis' (Irenaeus) of the two central mysteries and therefore in some fashion of all the others as well. The scriptures of both the Old and New Testaments love to describe, in a salvation history perspective, the levels of the two 'co-ordinating mysteries' of Trinity and Passover. It would be helpful to consider briefly 'the levels' of the event of the Trinity: it will show how the theological context for the proper understanding and – what is more important – the living out of the Eucharist is the revealed mystery of the 'immanent' and 'economic' Trinity.

The God of the patriarchs and the prophets commits himself to the way of history. The covenant of creation is deepened by the covenant with Abraham and his children (Gen 12:1-3; 15:1-21), which in turn is deepened by the covenant with Moses (Ex 24:1-8) only to be identified in the time of the prophet Jeremiah as the prelude to the 'new covenant written in the heart' (Jer

31:31-4; Heb 8:1-13). Finally, in the fullness of time, having spoken in varied ways through the patriarchs and the prophets, he speaks through his eternal Son as the figure of his substance and the splendour of his glory (Heb 1:1-3). The same Letter to the Hebrews hurries as it were to remind the reader of the purpose of the Incarnation: 'Since … the children share flesh and blood, he himself likewise shared the same things … He had to become like his brothers and sisters in every respect'(2:14, 17).[11]

The Holy Spirit is the divine Person who 'has spoken through the prophets' (Nicene-Constantinopolitan Creed). He accompanied Israel's dramatic adventure with the Lord of all history.

In 'the fullness of time' (Gal 4:4; Rom 8:15; Mk 1:14) he comes upon the Virgin Mary (Lk 1:37) enabling the eternal Son to take on our humanity and all that was creaturely. The Son takes on what is ours in order to give us all he brings. What does he bring? He has the life he has drawn eternally from the Father and which he yields back to the Father in the love that is the Holy Spirit. The life of infinite love circulating among the divine Persons now circulates among created persons. 'As you, Father, are in me and I am in you, may they also be in us' (Jn 17:21). The scattered children of God are called into one and are now to be raised in glory by the Father to a new level of being, which is participation in the very life of the Trinity (Jn 11:51-52).

The incarnate Son, then, has lodged this life of giving in humankind and history. However, in giving humankind the life of his Trinitarian homeland, the Son also gives humankind to the Father in the love of the Holy Spirit who then cries out in the hearts of that 'new creation' (2 Cor 5:17; Gal 6:15), 'Abba! Father!' (Gal 4:4). In the words of St Augustine, 'By being born from you [Father] and becoming your servant, your Son made slaves into servants.'[12] The Son becomes man, yes indeed, but, as the fathers loved to repeat, in order that men and women might become God (by participation) – to enter the life of the Son's homeland.

Humankind, then, and creation are called into the life of the

Blessed Trinity. The 'place,' however, where this happens is the church. That is why the Second Vatican Council, in its *Constitution on the Church* and quoting St Cyprian and St Augustine, could describe the church as 'the people made one with the unity of the Father, the Son, and the Holy Spirit.'[13] The church is the communion of the Trinity brought down to earth so that humankind might live a new life, the life that was hidden in God and that has appeared to us (1 Jn 1:1-4). Within such a perspective it is no exaggeration to say that the church is the created heaven of the Trinity, while the Trinity is the uncreated heaven of the church. *O admirabile commercium!*

Concentration: the Eucharist

Through the wonder of his divine and human imagination, Jesus 'invented' the Eucharist as the means by which he could perpetuate and concentrate all he had brought from the eternal Father and in the Holy Spirit, and also continue for ever the return of humankind and creation to the bosom of the Father (Jn 1:18). The Eucharist contains the very 'mystery of Christ' (Rom 16:25-26; Eph 1:9; 3:9-12; Col 1:26) and so of the economic Trinity in concentrate: it recapitulates (Eph 1:10) all that 'Jesus did and taught' (Acts 1:1) as the sacrament of the ages. This is the theology contained in the command to 'do this as my memorial' (1 Cor 11:24, 25; Lk 22:19). It stands out in the discourse on the Bread of Life in St John. There, one verse, a masterpiece of Johannine brevity, has Jesus say, 'Just as the living Father sent me, and I live because of the Father, so whoever eats me will live because of me' (6:57). That verse connects Trinity, Christology, Eucharist and Eschatology. A brief analysis seems desirable. To that end, the text might be laid out as follows.

Just as *(kathôs)* the living Father sent me,
and I live because *(dia)* of the Father,
so whoever eats me will live because *(dia)* of me.

The second clause directs the reader's attention to the life of the Son with the Father in the bosom of the eternal Trinity. This is the source of all life, here identified by the word *zôê* that John

uses to distinguish it from merely human life or *bios*. The first
clause points up the mission of the Son: the Father sends him
and this involves the Incarnation whereby the Son becomes
flesh (Jn 1:14; 6:51-55). The third clause, however, identifies the
Eucharist – 'whoever eats me' – as the summit of the Son's mission. In the Eucharist we will receive the life he had eternally
from the Father: 'whoever eats me will draw life because of me.'
As if to put his meaning beyond all possible confusion, John
then sets up a contrast between the effect of the manna in the
desert and the effect of 'the bread which has come down from
heaven' (6:58).

St Hilary of Poitiers seems to capture the divine freshness of
what is being affirmed as to the Eucharist encapsulating the
mystery of the economic Trinity when he writes, 'While the
Word is in the Father by the nature of his divinity, we on the
contrary are in him by the nature of his bodily birth, and he
again is in us by the mystery of the sacraments. From this we can
learn the unity which has been achieved through the Mediator;
for we abide in him and he abides in the Father, and while abiding in the Father he abides in us. In this way we attain to unity
with the Father.'[14] The Eucharist, as Hilary stresses, is 'the sacrament of this perfect unity.'[15] In God's most wise design (Eph 1:9)
the components of reality are brought into unity, a unity in distinction of the many.

Still, all this has to happen under the law of time. The glorified Lord has indeed reached the end of time, being in fact the
Lord of history. He has assumed and 'redeemed the time'. As
the vigil liturgy of Easter so succinctly puts it, 'all time and all
ages belong to him'. 'What is not assumed is not saved', was the
principle worked out by the Cappadocian fathers. In the mystery of Christ our very time is already assumed by the enfleshed
and eucharistic Son as the summit of his love for us and the contemporaneity of the Eternal with us who live in time.[16] More
precisely, the Eucharist is the place where we receive the life of
the Trinity from Christ so that we already possess the life of the
eschaton in the tension of 'the already now but still not yet'.

'Those who eat my flesh and drink my blood *have* everlasting life' (Jn 6:54).

Expansion: a Network of Relationhips

In divine revelation, one perceives a set of relationships that constitute the whole of reality, for revelation connects God, humankind, society, the world and history in what scripture calls 'the mystery of Christ' (Rom 16:25-26; Eph 1:9; 3:9-12; Col 1:26). At one and the same time, that set both reveals our life with God, the Holy Trinity (Eph 2:18) and hides this life with Christ in the Father (Col 3:3). Jesus enables us to participate in his eternal relationship as Son to his Father. This fact is underlined in various ways in the New Testament. For St Paul, there is the truth that Christians are identified as 'being in Christ' on no less than one hundred and sixty-four occasions. This location makes us sons and daughters of the Father: the Spirit enables us to cry out in Jesus, 'Abba! Father!' (Rom 8:15; Gal 4:4; 1 Cor 12:3). Here, then, the indispensable 'Trinitarian ethos' of Christian existence comes into full view.

It would be no surprise if the Eucharist highlighted and nourished this Trinitarian ethos. As the third and final sacrament of Christian initiation, this is precisely what it does. It 'christens' the prepared recipient, divinising him in his spirit and flesh. By mixing the flesh of Christ that has been vivified by the Holy Spirit with our flesh, the Eucharist divinises us in body and soul. We become 'other Christs.' The Eucharist divinises us, then. However, God the Son can only exist in God, the Holy Trinity. This means that the Eucharist makes those who have received the sacrament 'worthily' (1 Cor 11:27) enter into the bosom of the Blessed Trinity.[17] There they will cry out, 'Abba! Father!'

It is at this point that another set of relationships comes into view. If the Eucharist enables each individual to participate in the crucified and risen Son's relationhip to the Father in the Holy Spirit, divinising each one in that fashion, it does the same to all the others as well. Since all become God by participation, all are one with one another. They are no longer many but 'one

Body', as Paul explains in First Corinthians (10:17). They are all together in God, the Holy Trinity, 'having access to the Father through the Son in the Holy Spirit' (Eph 2:8). The reality which the Eucharist brings about is the church as Henri de Lubac has shown.[18] The church, therefore, becomes that unique 'we' born from the eternal 'We' of the Blessed Trinity, yes, 'a people made one from the unity of the Father, the Son and the Holy Spirit,' as we have already seen.

It is at this point that a further dimension of the 'Trinitarian ethos' comes into view, that of a Trinitarian relationship among people who are members of each other and called to 'live in love, as Christ loved us and gave himself up for us, a fragrant offering and sacrifice to God' (Eph 5:2). The eucharistic Body has 'made' the many into the 'Mystical Body' of Christ. A modern author writes of these 'Trinitarian relationships' in these terms:

> Our being one in mutuality is the crucial point where the Trinity becomes visible for the world. A Trinity that floats above us can no longer be considered relevant to life. Only if we are ready to live the Trinity among us will the Trinity show itself to us in a new way. This is the true sense of the connection made in the gospel of John between the three levels of unity: the unity of Jesus with the Father becomes the unity between Jesus and us, and in this unity we become one thing in reciprocity.[19]

In our third section, we will be focusing on the eucharistic law of communion that inspires the Christian life and manifests its beauty.

II. THE CONTENT OF THE EUCHARIST:
TRINITARIAN WORSHIP AND COMMUNION

Since Paul is the first author in the New Testament, it is appropriate to turn to his texts in order to expound his insight into the mystery of the Eucharist. In the First Letter to the Corinthians, itself one of the earliest documents of the New Testament corpus, he provides a mini-treatise on the mystery of the Eucharist (chs

10-11), albeit tailored to address the precise situation of the
Corinthian church and her specific needs and difficulties. This
means that Paul has to keep in mind the factions that are a mark
of this church (cf. 1:10-17; 3:1-9) and that emerge again, rather
dramatically, in the context of the celebration of the Eucharist
(11:18). As if to exacerbate matters further, the issue of the food
offered to idols arises for the second time, the first occasion having drawn from his pen the fascinating account of the freedom
of the Christian that can be lived out only with the help of the
wisdom that comes from loving (chs 8-9). The lack of this wisdom
surfaces a second time as the Corinthians abuse their freedom
during the elaborate celebration of their *agape* and Eucharist.
'When you come together it is not for the better but for the worse
… Each of you goes ahead with your own supper, and one goes
hungry and another becomes drunk … In this matter I do not
commend you!' (11:17, 21, 22). The love-feast or *agape* that
should have prepared the celebration of the Eucharist has only
served to deepen the division between the factions!

The key and integrating concepts seem to be those of *koinonia*
and proclamation. Paul writes of the Eucharist in these terms as
he grapples with their apparent denial in the factional attitudes
and liturgical irregularities abounding in Corinth. 'The cup of
blessing that we bless, is it not a sharing (*koinônia*, Vulgate: *com-
municatio*) in the blood of Christ? The bread that we break, is it
not a sharing (*koinônia*, Vulgate: *participatio*; New Vulgate: *com-
municatio*) in the body of Christ? Because there is one bread, we
who are many are one body, for we all partake of the one bread'
(10:16-17). The text enjoys such clarity that brief commentary is
adequate. Perhaps the insight of John Chrysostom, who is typical
of the Greek East, is enough. His comments, 'profound and perceptive' as the encyclical notes,[20] are striking, 'For what is the
bread? It is the body of Christ. And what do those who receive it
become? The body of Christ – not many bodies but one body.
For as bread is completely one, though made up of many grains
of wheat, and these, albeit unseen, remain nonetheless present
in such a way that their difference is not apparent since they

have been made a perfect whole, so too are we mutually joined to one another and together united with Christ.'[21]

In the course of his *Confessions*, St Augustine adds the following explanation of how we become a 'collective other Christ' spread out in space and time as the Body of Christ: 'I am the food of grown men: grow great and you shall eat of me. And you shall not change me into yourself as bodily food, but you shall be changed into me.'[22] As 'the nourishment of the strong,' the Eucharist reverses the ordinary process of eating and digestion. Whereas human beings being stronger than the everyday food and drink they eat, transform these into themselves, in the Eucharistic food and drink it is the reverse process that occurs. Jesus as Eucharist is stronger than we are, and he changes us into himself. The one Christ makes the many, spread out in space and in time, into himself.

The originality of the concept 'Communion'
Sustained and careful research would have us attend to the roots of the concept of communion in order to appreciate its specific deployment in the eucharistic texts of the New Testament.[23] To this end it is useful to look at the Greek and Old Testament roots of the term and then at some of its usage in the New Testament outside specifically eucharistic contexts. One may detect accumulating and converging insights in these various roots. In the first instance we will look at the use of the word '*koinônia*' in Greek philosophy.

Contrary to the Old Testament, the Greek world entertained the notion of a *koinônia* between the gods and humankind. In Plato's *Symposium* there is an extensive discussion of the reciprocal communion of the gods with humans as the deepest content of every offering made to the gods. It is in this context that Plato coins a wonderful expression which is a kind of aspiration towards the Eucharist when he says that worship is nothing but 'the healing of love.'[24] In the Hellenistic religions, a *koinônia* between human beings and the gods was the central idea. However, the real goal of this religion was not communion but union. 'In the end it is not relation, but identity, that stands out.'[25] Plato recognised in this communion 'the healing of (human) love.'

When one turns to the Old Testament, one meets at once with its unequivocal repudiation of Greek polytheism: 'Yahweh is one Lord', as the *Shema* repeats (Dt 6:6). He is simply transcendent. However, as 'merciful and gracious, slow to anger and abounding in steadfast love' (Ps 103:8), he enters unilaterally into relationship with his chosen people. The resulting bilateral relationship is expressed centrally in the reality and concept of covenant *(berith)*. In Hebrew the word corresponding to *koinônia* is *chaburah*. It denotes, since the second century after Christ, the minimum quorum of rabbis for the celebration of the *Pascha*. *Chaburah* never describes the relationship obtaining between God and humankind, only interpersonal relationships. Between God and humankind there is no *chaburah* or communion, but rather the relationship of covenant, which guarantees the holiness and transcendence of God even as it expresses his loving relationship with his chosen. The church is the *chaburah* of Jesus and his members who celebrate his Pasch in his family, the church, which is 'the Israel of God' (Gal 6:16).

The word *koinônia* as used in Plato and in the Old Testament is, therefore, quite distinct in meaning from its later New Testament usage. This difference, however, serves to show up the amazing originality of the New Testament usage. The Eucharist does bring Christians into a communion with God, but not into an identity with him by which they would lose their being through an absorption into God. The fact that God is a Trinity of persons pre-empts this possibility. Cardinal Kasper stresses the fact that

the Greek word *koinônia* (Latin *communio*) does not originally mean "community" at all. It means participation, and more particularly, participation in the good things of salvation conferred by God: participation in the Holy Spirit, in new life, in love, in the gospel, but above all participation in the Eucharist.[26]

The Eucharist leads to participation in the enfleshed Son who then raises the eucharistised, 'through him, with him and in him,' to the Father and in the love of the Holy Spirit. This participation-communion is the most marvellous fulfilment of Plato's 'healing of human love' imaginable. As for its relation to the Old Testament, the Eucharist is the new Pasch, for 'Christ our Pasch has been sacrificed' (1 Cor 5:7). The effect of this celebration, however, is precisely the setting up of an unheard of participation: the indwelling of God in humankind and humankind in God. 'Those who eat my flesh and drink my blood *abide in me, and I in them*' (Jn 6:56).

The words of Cardinal Ratzinger make the point in personal categories: 'Eucharistic communion ... breaks open the I of the human being and makes a new We. Communion with Christ is necessarily communication also with all who are his.'[27] The Eucharist is that 'alchemy' dreamt of by medieval thinkers and searchers but actually given to us on a plane higher than any imaginable: our human being is gathered up and preserved in the being of Christ so that through him we become a new reality, his Body in the world. The vertical 'communion' of each individual believer is *also and necessarily* the horizontal 'communion' of believers with one another.

Where Christ is, however, there is the Father and the Holy Spirit. As we have already said, the Son exists in the Father (Jn 10:38) and the Holy Spirit. In making the many into his 'other self', he has by that very gift lodged and relocated them in his own eternal relationship with the Father. They enter into the bosom of his Father. The Eucharist, in other words, enables those who receive it worthily (11:27-34) to participate in the communion of the Blessed Trinity. It is by virtue of the fact that God is the communion of the Trinity, and so an eternal dialogue of love between Persons who are self-subsisting relations, that God could communicate himself substantially to humankind in the missions of the Word and the Holy Spirit. This divine self-communication now makes possible, through the wonder of the Eucharist on earth, the 'entry' of eucharistised humankind into the bosom of the Blessed Trinity. The doxology concluding the eucharistic prayer highlights the fact that the eucharistic Christ takes his members, 'through, with and in' himself, to the Father in the unity of the Holy Spirit. O Christians, recognize your dignity! It was for this reason that this paper had to begin with a brief consideration of the 'levels of the Trinitarian mystery' as the indispensable context for a better understanding of the content of the eucharistic mystery.

In First Corinthians (11:23-25), Paul employs a 'tradition/handing on' formula to remind the Corinthians of the origin of the Eucharist. The same formula is repeated a few chapters later in regard to the early kerygma (15:3-5). When one considers that Paul is that most vibrant, original and innovative of spirits, the one called by the risen Lord on the road to Damascus to suffer many things for the Lord and to bring his name before kings and powers (Acts 9:15-16), it is fascinating to see his wholehearted obedience to the tradition of faith that precedes him. It is that *traditio* which he receives with gratitude and 'traditions' with authority. Having vigorously reminded the Corinthians of the source of their eucharistic faith, Paul adds his own 'doctrinal' commentary: 'For as often as you eat this bread and drink the cup, you proclaim the Lord's death until he comes' (11:26). The liturgy of the Eucharist is a proclamation of the death of the Lord: it proclaims Christ crucified. This means that to eat this Bread and to drink this Blood is to have 'communion' with the death and, by implication, with the resurrection-glorification of Jesus until he returns in glory.

The Proclamation of the Cross

The eucharistic liturgy, then, is a proclamation of the paschal mystery of the Lord's death and resurrection, 'until he comes'. It thereby exerts the 'drawing power' of the risen *Kyrios* on the whole of the eucharistised community. In this way the liturgy is 'the fount and apex of the whole Christian life.'[28] The Cross enjoys a unique centrality in Paul's writing. First of all, it is enough to look at his *traditio* of the Eucharist to see this. 'This is my body which is given for you'; 'This chalice is the new covenant in my blood' (11:24, 25). The words are heavily indebted to the Servant Songs of Second Isaiah, particularly the fourth song (42:1-4; 49:1-6; 50:4-9; 52:13-53:12), as well as to the prophecy of the 'new covenant' in the prophet Jeremiah (31:31-34). Both of these Old Testament antecedents point towards the mystery of the cross that is activated in the eucharistic liturgy.

With regard to Second Isaiah, the context of this book is the Babylonian captivity. The Temple has been destroyed and with it the liturgy. Israel can no longer celebrate the liturgy of God's praise, in particular, the Passover. Denied the means of worshipping God through the Temple liturgy, Israel was driven to worship God by the offering of her sufferings in love and out of love. This was the message of the prophets who interpreted the deportation in that fashion and then asked Israel to live by a new experience of suffering offered out of love. This was to be the new worship that would be pleasing to God. Although God's people Israel bore the burden of her incapacity to live in the space opened up by her historic calling. This explains the great paradox at the heart of the hymns of the Servant: on the one hand, there is Israel's vocation as the Servant of God to be the representative sufferer not only for herself but also for the whole world. On the other hand, Israel is in practice quite incapable of fulfilling this calling, and this opens up the hope and expectation of the one who alone can fulfil the mission of Israel to the whole world.[29]

After the Last Supper Jesus went to suffer for the many. It is in him, and in him alone, that the great expectation opened up by Second Isaiah can be fulfilled. In the suffering of Jesus there occurs the liturgy of Israel and the whole cosmos. He is total 'being for you' (1 Cor 11:24): he offers himself in the place of all, even unto death, 'letting himself be taken for a sinner' (Isa 53:12). This is a presupposition of the eucharistic theology of Paul.

The implications of this truth are manifold. First of all, the death of Christ may be read in cultic categories. This is what

Paul will do later when, in the Letter to the Romans (3:25), he writes, '[God] put Christ Jesus forward as a sacrifice of atonement *(hilasterion)* by his blood, effective through faith.' The *hilasterion* is the Hebrew *kapporeth*, the mercy seat of the ark which was sprinkled with the blood of the sin-offering. Paul sees Jesus as the one who in the Eucharist, which incorporates the cross, is the living and eternal sacrifice of atonement. Paul can say, earlier in First Corinthians (5:7) 'our paschal lamb, Christ, has been sacrificed.' The Passover continues, indeed, but at a higher level, in the event of Christ's Passover to the Father as this is encapsulated in the eucharistic sacrifice.

The words over the cup highlight the fact that he is instituting the 'new covenant' in his blood (11:25). As we have seen in the first section, Christianity is a religion of covenant. The various covenants of the Old Testament lead up towards the promise of a 'new covenant' in Jeremiah (31:31-34). In accepting his death and in encapsulating that death in the Last Supper, Jesus has already 'recapitulated' the whole of the Old Testament religion (Eph 1:10). He recapitulated the worship of the Temple which was a sacrificial liturgy, and then the representative suffering of the Servant that had personified the 'second exodus' (Isa 42:9). With Jeremiah there enters a third element which has nothing to do with carnal descent from Abraham or with the fulfilment of the Law. Instead, it comes from the new love of the God who is the God of the evermore, promising the new covenant. This becomes fact with the entry of the Eucharist as it gathers into itself the mystery of Calvary.

What does this mean? The new covenant is communion between God and humankind in the God-Man. In his suffering unto death and in the giving of his blood, 'which is poured out for many for the forgiveness of sins' (Mt 26:28), the Son lifts up all his sisters and brothers to the Father (Jn 12:32) and 'gives' the Father to them as their Father (Jn 20:17). He sets up the definitive communion-covenant between God and humankind, greater than which none can be thought. He throws open the door that we cannot of ourselves open to enter into the holy of holies, communion with the Father through his Son and in the Holy Spirit. He becomes our communion with the Father. This makes the church a living relationship, or set of relationships: through the love of Christ made concrete in Eucharist and cross, thereby encapsulating and summing up both the aspirations of human-kind and the revelation already made through Israel's history and liturgy, a new wonder exists in the world – the 'Body of Christ' (1 Cor 10:16-17). This communion is both vertical in that it is a participation in the communion of the Blessed Trinity (Jn 6:57), and horizontal in that that same vertical relationship makes the many both one body and members of each other.

III. THE LAW OF THE CHURCH'S LIFE: THE ART OF LOVING

The Holy Eucharist, then, brings about an extraordinary wonder. This miracle is a source of wonder for believers, and wonder is the attitude Pope John Paul wishes to foster in *EdE* (##5-6).[30] Wonder in fact is not only the root of all knowing but also the perfect antidote to boredom with life and religion. The Eucharist does nothing less than communicate to humankind 'the eternal life that was with the Father and was revealed.' This life then generates communion on earth, 'a fellowship with the Father and with his Son Jesus Christ'. The practical impact of all this is that 'our joy is complete' (1 Jn 1:3, 4). The Eucharist, in other words, has the effect of generating joy in us, joy over the extraor-dinary truth that 'There is a "We are" which has precedence over an "I think"' (Gabriel Marcel). Since the celebration of the Eucharist is the proclamation of the death and the resurrection of Jesus (1 Cor 11:26), it is by that very fact in the genre of 'gospel'. It is through the Eucharist, as *EdE* stresses (#34), that the church 'constantly lives and grows' and 'expresses her very nature'.

Those who participate in the Eucharist are under an impera-tive: Be what you are! If God is love and if because he is love he is Trinity, if this immanent Trinity has become the economic Trinity, and the economic Trinity has encapsulated itself in the mystery of the Eucharist, making the many one, then all are under the imperative of loving. This explains why the Pope in his earlier Apostolic Letter for the Third Millennium, *Tertio millennio ineunte,* could write: 'To make the church the home and the school of communion: that is the great challenge facing us in the millennium which is now beginning, if we wish to be faithful to God's plan and respond to the world's deepest yearnings.'[31]

How can this imperative to love be detected? We do not have to invent it; it is there from the outset as the very heart of the 'morality' of the gospels. As one reads through their pages, one discerns the style or art of loving, which is appropriate to the new men and women (2 Cor 5:17; Gal 6:15) who are eucharistised in Christ, participants in the life of the Trinity already now (1 Jn 3:2-3), and in training for future blessedness. It is now time to describe this art of loving by which Christians can 'walk in love' (Eph 5:2) worthy of their vocation (Eph 4:1). There are various strands in this art.

First, Christians have the vocation to love *all*. With the example of the one who gave himself up for all (Rom 8:32) before them, Christians are moved to love all. They are sent to love enemies as well as friends (Mt 5:43-48), the old as well as the young, the refugees as well as the neighbours (Mt 25:35), the non-Catholics as well as the Catholics. The truth is that, as the eucharist-inspired text of 1 Timothy teaches, 'Christ Jesus gave himself a ransom for all' (2:6).

Next, Christians are called to be *the first* to love. After all, 'God loved us first' (1 Jn 4:19). Since this is the case, no one can be the first to love God who loved us 'while we still were sinners' (Rom 5:8). However, we can be the first to love others in imitation of Christ. This is a primacy we should actively seek. The eucharistic love of Christ inspires the Christian not to wait to be loved, but to take the initiative and to aspire to this primacy. A eucharist-inspired proactive disposition comes into view with most practical implications.

In the third place, this love is *concrete and practical*. As the First Letter of John formulates it, 'Let us love, not in word or speech, but in truth and action' (3:18). The Eucharist shows us a

Christ who loved by a Unique Deed, that of his paschal mystery which was the goal of his whole life (Mk 8:33). His love 'cost him not less than everything' (T. S. Eliot). This love had a content, and that content was the gift of himself (Mk 10:45), 'even to death on the cross' (Phil 2:8). To receive the Eucharist is to be sent to love with deeds and with facts, not remaining in the area of sentiment only. *EdE* quotes St John Chrysostom in this regard: 'Do you wish to honour the body of Christ? Do not ignore him when he is naked. Do not pay him homage in the temple clad in silk, only then to neglect him outside where he is cold and ill-clad. He who said, "This is my body" is the same who said, "You saw me hungry and you gave me no food," and "Whatever you did to the least of my brothers you did also to me".'[32]

In the fourth place, the love taught in the Eucharist portrays an art of making ourselves *one with the other*. In the First Letter to the Corinthians, Paul tells the 'secret' of his apostolic ministry, the style by which he loved the various peoples he encountered. 'For though I am free with respect to all, I have made myself a slave to all … To the Jews I became a Jew, so that I might win more of them … To the weak I became weak' (9:19, 20, 22). For Paul, the love of Christ for us 'urges us on' (2 Cor 5:14). It involves 'rejoicing with those who rejoice, weeping with those who weep'(Rom 12:15). The eucharistic Christ is the *ne plus ultra* recalling the abysmal depths of the Son making himself one with the whole human family even to the point of 'making himself sin who knew no sin' (2 Cor 5:21).

Finally, if two or more live these steps together, then the phenomenon of *mutual love* arises, and this mutual love is the fulfilment of the commandment which Jesus calls both 'his' and 'new'(Jn 13:34; 15:12). As 'his', it is the deepest desire of his heart, as 'new,' it is the law for the Eucharist as 'the new covenant in [his] blood' (1 Cor 11:25; Lk 22:20). The measure of this love has to be that of the cross and the Eucharist: 'Love one another *as I have loved you*.' Of this commandment, St Augustine writes: 'It is true that love renews those who hear, or rather those who obey; but not any love, only that love which the Lord distinguished from natural love by adding the words: "As I have loved you." Such love renews us: we become new men, heirs of the New Testament, singers of a new song.'[33] It is little wonder that Jesus teaches that when the art of loving reaches this stage, 'everyone will know that you are my disciples' (Jn 13:35). The will of God the Holy Trinity is now done on earth as it is in heaven.

It is one thing to celebrate the Eucharist as a 'sacrament of unity, a sign of love, a bond of charity.'[34] However, it is quite another to live eucharistically. Such living requires conversion to the love of God the holy Trinity and to the resolve to live by that love. That love will always be the 'still more excellent way' (1 Cor 12:31) than all others. In fact, it is this art of loving that would bring about the full implementation of *Sacrosanctum Concilium*, and the building up of the church desired by *EdE* (##21-25). Now as always, it is the linking of liturgy and living that is the key to the faith-life of believers, and, *a fortiori,* to the renewal of the liturgical celebration of the Eucharist.

CHAPTER TEN

Creation and Eucharist:
A Philosophical Consideration

Thomas A. F. Kelly

Introduction

What follows is written from the perspective of a philosopher, and, moreover, one with strong theological interests. The kind of theology I am professionally interested in is what used to be called rational or natural theology, and which I prefer to call 'philosophical theology'. Such a philosophical theology is the task of working out what we can know about the existence and nature of God on the basis of the application of reason to human experience, and, precisely as philosophical, unaided by revelation. This kind of philosophy is mostly associated with the Catholic tradition, and was practised by such thinkers as Anselm and Aquinas, who also of course practised theology as this is normally understood, namely a commentary on, and explication and interpretation of, the revealed truth which constitutes the deposit of faith.

I should begin by submitting certain considerations in regard to the legitimacy of this kind of philosophy – it runs contrary to many fixed opinions regarding what philosophy can and should be or do: philosophy we are told, is talk about talk, not talk about the world, and as such is incapable of making any existential claims. Moreover, suspicions, if not hackles, will be raised by any mention of the Eucharist in a philosophical context, and I can expect to be accused, at the very least, of a methodologically improper blurring of discipline boundaries.

These are large questions, and a systematic consideration of them would take us well beyond the confines of a short essay. However there are certain sketch-maps to where I think answers may be found, and these I would like to offer. I wish, though not in any exhaustive way here, to challenge the notion that philosophy can make no substantive claims about the nature of reality. It is my opinion that a cosmological argument for the existence of God, at least coherent with, if not implied by, the logical paradigms which must underlie all reasoning – and obviously also, scientific reasoning – about the world, can be successfully constructed.[1] This means that there can be at least one existential claim made by philosophy.

But this brings us up short at the question of what philosophy is, and of its relation to Revelation, of the relation between reason and faith.

Although these two pairs are sometimes presented as antitheses with no common ground, the truth is more complex. Some fear that philosophy / reason loses itself in the context of Revelation / faith. But if what I have asserted above is correct then there is a vector, inherent in philosophy, inherent in reason itself, towards the Divine. This vector is not reducible to the argument I have mentioned, but must be coterminous with what philosophy itself is, with what reason itself is. Reason as capacity for truth is capacity for Being, and the Divine, which is what Being is. Philosophy is the self-realisation – in both senses of the word 'realise' – of reason. In this sense philosophy is the actual harmonisation of all our diverse quests for truth – whether as personal goal or as a variety of rational endeavours – as theocentric. The ultimate task of philosophy then becomes the construction of a theocentric anthropology in which what the earlier Heidegger would have called the *existentialia* necessary to human dwelling in Being, and hence being towards God, are delineated. Such a delineation is what metaphysics is. In this sense, philosophy / reason is a preparation for Revelation, the human side in a (for the human) constitutive Divine-human dialogue; for it is vital in such a delineation that God be not reduced to some form of *a priori* structure proper to my or to our humanity, and in that way become lost, as indeed happens in the thought of the earlier Heidegger, to any real other. For all its being a 'Being with others in the world', proto-Heideggerian *Dasein* possesses no real Other than just such an *a priori* structure of the *Dasein* that is always mine to be.[2]

From the other perspective, Revelation may be other, but it cannot be alien. If there is to be Revelation, not only must it be in terms capable of being grasped by humans on pain of being vacuous, but it must also transform what we take ourselves to be, not into the utterly alien but along lines which a profound understanding of what it is for us to be must have anticipated, though not predicted. This is simply another example of losing oneself in order to find oneself. Reason and philosophy find themselves fully transformed into what they are ultimately capable of being in Revelation, just as I find myself most fully myself there too. If this is so, if Revelation is genuine, it makes harmony of what was dissonant in human life, it weaves into a tissue of wholeness the apparently disparate tendencies and desires which compose our moment-to-moment existence and posits a supreme Good in which alone all the littler goods that I am attracted by can be meaningful. In genuine Revelation my little absurdities are redeemed in a meaningful whole.

This means that – and this comes as no surprise to Anselm and Thomas – Revelation can be a guide for philosophical thinking. The proof of Revelation as guide comes as the appearance of philosophical discovery. Discovering something new under the guidance of Revelation does not mean assuming things without justification, or placing them beyond philosophical question. It means being able to arrive at certain discoveries which are vindicated, not as a function of any religious commitment, but by the richer insight they bestow on understanding, and by ordinary philosophical analysis as valid in themselves. Anselm may have gained from faith the insight that God can only be *id quo majus cogitari nequit*, but the insight this mediates can be philosophically investigated and vindicated.[3] Moreover, this very process of 'grounding' Revelation is the appreciation of its depth, its application and interpretation. We find on every page of Aquinas a manifold investigating, reasoning, grounding, such that whether any particular argument is religious-theological or rational-philosophical can become blurred, but such censoriousness is an attitude deeply out of sympathy with so big and so vital a thinker as Aquinas.

It is precisely this approach that I propose in the juxtaposition of Eucharist and creation in my title. Not only, as I hope, that these points that I have been making will be more intelligible by way of example, but also that the philosophical consideration of creation in the light of Eucharist and of the Eucharist in the light of creation may deepen our understanding of the truth of the one and of the other. Much is covered – even obscured – by this word 'truth', but when it occurs here it is not necessary to take it as merely equivalent to 'correspondence' or the like, however important this meaning may be in its rightful place. 'Truth' here has apparently opposed connotations, in being both something to be lived and therefore immediate, and something revealing the ultimate, and therefore removed. But the oppositions are little more than mere appearances, for the truth is always a thing to be lived, even when, even because, it touches what is ultimate, for this is always most intimate to what it is to be the kind of being that we are.

Finally I wish to suggest what it is that I understand by the word 'Eucharist'. This understanding is fully informed by and, I hope, fully in conformity with, Catholic teaching on this subject. In preparation for my First Holy Communion I learned that Jesus Christ, God and man, is really, truly and substantially present under the appearance of bread and wine in the Eucharist, and that the Mass is identical to the sacrifice of Calvary, and is the way God has chosen to make that sacrifice available to the faithful in every age and place thereafter, so that Calvary, Eucharist and church form an irrefrangible and inseparable unity. Since that time I have not reneged on this view, and it is still my belief today. While there may be many questions to be asked and answered with regard to the overall truth of Christianity, given that the claims made by Christianity are true, there can be little doubt, I believe, as to what This is: no misbelieving talk of 'mere symbol' can be apposite here, and this way of talking was never taken until Zwingli. We would do well to treat It as the Holy and the Awful, the Real Presence, at once most fair and most fearsome, and even when we merely speak of It, to be sure we discern It for what It is, as the apostle recommends (cf. 1 Cor 11:29).

Creation

Let us begin then, with the notion of creation.

It might be easier to start by saying what creation is not. Many people, scientists among them, talk about creation as the first event in the history of the universe, before which there was no existence, and consequently no space or time. If we understand creation in this way we are liable to fall into error. The error consists in seeing the universe as perhaps – and I emphasise this 'perhaps' – originating in Divine activity, but as proceeding independently of the Divine in every subsequent moment of its history. In such a picture, the universe in its long history, except for its very beginning, is independent of, indeed indifferent to, the Divine. Here we see a closed universe, operating and evolving according to its own inherent laws, with no place for the Divine within it.[4]

This picture of creation however is erroneous, and can be known to be so without recourse to Revelation. The best metaphor which I can think of for creation, for the relation between God and the world, is not that of, say, a carpenter and a table or a sculptor and a piece of sculpture. Such a metaphor is unsuitable for various reasons. However talented the sculptor or carpenter may be, however imaginative and creative they are, they always need material to work on, stone, bronze or wood, and in their activity have to take account of the limitations imposed by the medium.

Likewise, Michelangelo's David has long outlived Michelangelo, but we would not – most of us anyway – want to say that the universe is capable of outliving God.

No, we need a better image of creation. Where are we to find it? I suggest we look to music, and in particular to singing. The singer needs nothing other than her own power to sing, all things being equal, in order to sing. The song exists only insofar as the singer sings, and then not as a whole but note by note, each note being a temporal duration, a possibility realised over a time-interval, rounded and shaped by the singer's art. Each moment is at once promise and fulfilment: promise as opening new possibilities of resolution, fulfilment as resolving old ones. Only the current note exists, but it is the culmination of the ceased notes and intends those yet to be. If she is composer also, the singer gives voice to a logic which she both creates and respects: in music, manipulation of this logic is never possible, on pain of the singer's producing mere sounds and not music – the music lies in the logic, but exists only as sung note by note and moment by moment, as made real by what is other than it, and beyond it. The universe is a polyphony in infinite parts, with melodies constantly starting or falling silent. And yet, this worldly polyphony is made by just one voice.

That, I take it is what creation means. God creates the world as the singer/composer creates and performs the song. What I wish to do now is to unpack what this metaphor means, point by point.

First of all, we said that the singer needs nothing other than her own power to sing, all things being equal, in order to sing. In Genesis God says, 'let light be', and light is. Here is the central truth of creation: God grants existence. God doesn't make things yellow or green or hot or light: finite causes do that. God makes things to be, to exist in an absolute sense. Creation is the sheer granting of existence by God to something which of itself cannot be.

And here is another vital point. Everything in the universe is the sort of thing that of itself cannot be. Of itself, such a thing might be possible, but that possibility is insufficient to make that thing be. If it were, everything that is possible would be actual, and the universe would be a totality of mutually exclusive actualities. I, for example, am possible. I know I am possible because I exist. But that possibility alone is insufficient by itself to guarantee my existence – if my parents had never met, I wouldn't be here. That which turns possibility into actuality is what the word 'cause' means; a cause realises some possible situation which, without it, would remain merely possible.

But the whole universe is like this. The whole universe is an actualised possibility. Although I am not going to work out a full-blown argument for God's existence here, this point is very relevant to such an argument. When we think of the universe, we usually picture it as the largest possible class of objects, to which everything that is belongs, or we think, perhaps less prosaically, of what we can see in the night sky. But in so doing we are likely to forget that the universe is not static. Constant transformation, change and movement constitute the nature of the universe. What I see in the night sky is the stars as they were millions of years ago, for it has taken the light whereby I see them, travelling at 186,000 miles a second, that time to get to my eye from the place where it originated. Likewise, the desk at which I write is not a solid substance, but is mostly empty space and consists of tiny electric fields whirling about one another at great speeds. Likewise the hand that writes and the eye that sees were both sculpted by natural selection through thousands of generations of human and pre-human evolution. The form called 'hand' or 'eye' has a history that is shared in by more than one species. The sun itself has a long, though not an endless, lifespan, and matter itself is not a thing but an ongoing polyphony of 'voices' coming into being and passing away. That is why music is such a good metaphor for it. The essence of music is change, and any stasis within it is really the remaining constant of a variable.

We also said: the song exists not as a whole but note by note, each note being a temporal duration, a possibility realised over a time-interval. Only the current note exists, but it is the culmination of the ceased notes and intends those yet to be. The only bit of any entity that exists is the present moment, the current state. Now is the only real bit of time, and past and future are the no longer real, and the yet to be real. So it is with the universe and the entities which compose it. It is possible for me to be a child of seven or a man of over forty, but not at the same time. Since being the one means not being the other, both of these states cannot be realised together, but only serially. We often treat time like a landscape in space, with ourselves travelling across it. Events in that scenario loom and recede as do the features of a physical landscape according as we approach them or leave them behind. But this is a misleading picture of time. If it were true, then my being seven, which involves my not being forty, and my being forty, which involves my not being seven, would be real together, and this is a contradiction.

And now we come to the really interesting part of time. If I am but a realised possibility, and require a cause for my existence, and if also the only part of me which exists is the present moment, it follows that I am a possibility being realised over a time interval.

To be material is to last for some temporal duration, however short or long. But this is also to say that in the case of something that is a realised possibility, what it is is *never* sufficient to realise the possibility of its existing, so that it *always*, for the duration of its existence, requires that it be made actual by something other than it and beyond it.[5]

And moreover it is God that, for as long as I exist, confers my existence upon me. For as long as I exist God creates me, God makes me be. Creation is a holding in existence, a sustaining, as much as it is a conferring of existence, and indeed the two aspects of it are inseparable. If a note is to exist, that is if it is to last for any time, it must be sounded by the singer for that duration. When she stops, it stops.

Without some cause of its existence, the universe and everything in it would be doomed to remain a mere possibility, and never achieve of itself the status of reality. And the only thing that can be such a cause is something which exists in its own right, that is, not as a mere realised possibility, for in that case it, and all that depended on it to be, would be and would remain, merely possible. And that which exists in its own right is what the mind in search of wisdom calls 'God'. God is the one and only thing which exists of itself. And we know that God exists, not by any analysis of the concept 'God', but because there exists a world which of itself is incapable of making itself real. As

Aquinas puts it, God does not have existence: God is identical with existence. Put another way, God is what it is to be, in the full sense.

It should be clear now why the 'craftsman god' and the closed 'universe as artefact' will not do: such pictures do violence to the intimacy that exists between God and the rest of what is.

And here a vital point immediately follows. God is identical to what it is to be, but the reality of the non-divine consists in being, precisely not this, in being less than this, in being of itself mere capacity for being. This is brought out when we look at the uses of the three meanings of 'is' in their application to God and the world respectively. Only the existential and identical uses of the verb to be apply to God. We can say that God is, in the sense that God exists, but to say God is love means that God is what love is, or better, what love is, is what God is: the 'is' in predications of some x to god is the 'is of identity'. But to say that John is intelligent is to say, not that John is what intelligence is, for then no one else could be (fully) intelligent without being John.[6] It is to say that John is an example, among possibly many, of what intelligence is. John thus participates in intelligence. To be is either to be what something is or to participate in what something is. This is the logical grammar of creation.

Thus, what God does in creation is to share with the universe something, namely existence, that God properly, uniquely and as of right has, with something, namely the universe, which does not and cannot otherwise have it. God shares what God is – in this case existence – with others who cannot hope of themselves to have it. The song exists only insofar as the singer sings. Without the singer, no song; without God, a merely possible universe, that is, no real universe.

This means that by virtue of God's creative act, the universe participates in existence, participates, that is, has a partial share in, what God pre-eminently, perfectly and uniquely is. But to exist is to be definite in various ways, and to participate is to participate, precisely, in qualities, in determinations which are shared with others. Merely to exist is impossible, existence can and must englobe qualities which are more than mere given-ness and actuality. Actuality is always the actuality 'of'. Thus to share existence is to share what it is, over and above the mere actuality that existence consists in. To have existence communicated is to share in what the source, as existence, must be.

One of the things that the liturgy does is to teach. It teaches us about participation. Recall the lines from the *Exultet*:

Qui licet sit divisus in partes, mutuati tamen luminis detrimenta non novit: This light, although shared out in parts, suffers no loss from its being borrowed.

If we replace the word light with 'existence', we have in that short verse a whole philosophy of participation. God suffers no loss, nor augmentation, through creation, but shares what belongs to God, creating resemblances to Divinity in and as what is not divine. One might further add, creates things which in their existence, as themselves, are *imagines*,[7] icons of the Divine, are, if we may so put it, miniature gods.

I return again to what I said above: if she is composer also, the singer gives voice to a logic which she both creates and respects: in music, manipulation of this logic is never possible, on pain of the singer's producing mere sounds and not music – the music lies in the logic, but exists only as sung note by note and moment by moment, as made real by what is other than it, and beyond it.

In real terms this means that God creates a free universe. If the universe were merely God's puppet, it would not truly exist. To exist is to be able to act as oneself, and to be able to produce acts that are attributable to one self and to no other. Thus, when God creates, what is created is always, according to its nature, free. It is no secret that God loves us. But to love us is to want us to love him, our ultimate good and goal, in return. But this is possible only for creatures that are free. This freedom is the logic we spoke of which the Divine composer always respects. And we might say that God thinks so highly of freedom that God allows us to abuse it, that is, to choose what is other than God, to choose what is other than good.

Eucharist

Let us turn now to consider the Eucharist.

In all history only one Mass is ever celebrated, the sacrifice and sacrament which is that of the Saviour in his one act of atonement to the Father. The inner essence of the Eucharist is precisely this. Yet, if it were possible, it is more than this, for in it that which is always present in God is available in the most intimate way to each individual, and this is the meaning of Communion. It is the Eternal made present in all times and places, by the love of God, for our benefit, and by being received, becomes the being of the one who receives it. Let us unpack some of these ideas.

We turn to our great teacher, the liturgy. One of the prayers of the Offertory in the Tridentine Rite runs as follows:

Deus, qui humanae substantiae dignitatem mirabliliter condidisti et mirabilius reformasti, da nobis per hujus aquae et vini mysterium, ejus divinitatis esse consortes, qui humanitatis nostrae fieri dignatus est particeps, Jesus Christus Filius tuus Dominus noster.

O God, who in a wonderful manner founded the worth of human nature, and still more wonderfully reformed it; grant that by the mystery of this water and wine, we may be made partakers of his Divinity, who deigned to become partaker of our humanity, Jesus Christ your Son our Lord.

I choose this version of the prayer rather than the simpler 'By the mystery of this water and wine may we come to share the Divinity of Christ, who humbled himself to share in our humanity' of the New Rite, because there is an explicit 'history' and relation to creation in the older version.

This prayer, significantly, accompanies the mixture of a drop of water in the chalice filled with wine. At the moment when one substance becomes mixed in another, but without losing its own identity as the stuff it is, we are told what the significance of all that is happening or about to happen is, and it is simply and stupendously this: why did God become human? – so that human beings might become God.

What is in question here is the apex of the history which

leads to the Incarnation, the very goal that this and all the other mysteries were designed to effect – the divinisation of the human person, the exchange and the reform which makes humanity more than human. But more than this, it is not an abstract humanity which is in question, but the human being I actually am and you actually are. However unlikely we are as candidates for divinisation – and no-one is likely – the transformation begins, and in a way is accomplished, here and now, with the me I am.

And it is effected by an act which perfectly reflects what its truth is – by eating and drinking, by the taking of nourishment into ourselves and thereby becoming part of what we receive – rather than the usual course of events, which is that what I eat ceases to be itself and instead becomes what I am or what my body is. And yet it is participation, for one shares in a banquet, but nevertheless receives the Whole. And so also as the performance of a vital function, the act of eating is incorrigibly and finally mine, for no-one can do my eating for me just as no-one can do my breathing or my knowing or my loving for me. Communion is the reception of, and by me into, the Divine, without loss of what I am, without me ceasing to be who I am, as the water though now inseparable from the wine is no part of what the wine is, nor is what the wine is any part of what the water is.

And here we begin to see some of the connections between creation and Eucharist. We recognise, as it were, the brushstrokes of the master in his every painting. Just as existence is not ours by right, in virtue of what we are, but is given us by God's fathomless generosity, so too God wants to give us something which our natures are not capable of: a share in God's Divinity. Just as we are called to participate in existence in virtue of God's creative act, so too we are called to participate in God's own nature in virtue of the Son's redemptive act. Creation, which is nature, is a prefiguring of redemption, which is grace. And let us recall here that the word 'grace' has as one of its meanings, 'unmerited gift'.

For us these two, creation and redemption are diverse, but

not for God. Let us not delude ourselves. The fall, the serpent, the awful agony of Golgotha and the glory of the resurrection, came as no surprise to God, the all-knowing. For God, creation and redemption are one act in God's perpetual and eternal now. The Son, the Word whereby all things are made, in that making embraces human nature and its degradation in the cross. At the very first moment of creation, we might say without exaggeration, Jesus shoulders the cross.

Although perhaps we might not want to speak literally of a serpent and a garden and the pilfering of an apple, though we might wish instead to talk of a gradual hominisation in and of pre-human nature, we speak and must speak of the embrace of the non-Divine by the Divine, of the elimination of distance, which is always love's desire, but not the elimination of diversity, which never can be love's desire, for to wish it is to wish the ceasing to be of one of the partners. Such elimination of distance in the retention of diversity which love wants, is the kiss. And a kiss is essentially dual, is distanceless duality. And a kiss is welcoming intimacy too, for it is performed mouth on mouth. And although it may seem at first eccentric to put it thus, it is precisely as kiss that the Eucharist reveals the meaning of Being.

A word here about disgust. Dis-gust. The very opposite of the appetite and enjoyment of taste and texture of what enters the mouth as food. Disgust is a clamping constriction of the gullet and of the belly; it is elemental rejection, at only one remove from vomiting. Disgust is 'for' the unclean, the repulsive, and is not merely aimed at what cannot count as food. The repulsive and the disgusting is always what appals appetite. To take something into one's mouth, therefore, is to accept it into oneself in the most literal, concrete and, one is tempted to say, animal way. What is accepted or acceptable in this way is fundamentally what is meant by the word 'clean'.

The Eucharist as oral draws on all these meanings. It is food which is a kiss, a coming to be two-in-one, of the Divine and the divinised human. And at the same time it is an elevation, a making worthy, a making clean, a making fit of that which of itself is not elevated, is not worthy, at least with this worth, not clean, at least with this cleanliness, not of itself fit for this destiny. It is re-formation of that which is transformed, yet which remains as it-self, the same.

And as such it is the final truth of Being. It is this precisely which the Eucharist teaches us. In the Eucharist we have the eternal, made present without regard to history or to the gulfs of space and time which separate us from the first Good Friday. But we also have the future. We say the Creed, and we assert that we believe in the resurrection of the body and life everlast-ing. This remaking beyond time, beyond as at the end of time, as yet lies in the future, at least for us, although since we are free it is not a foregone conclusion. It is given to us as promise, as pledge, as a kiss is often given as a promise and a pledge, that is, as really here, but only to be experienced in its consummation there. As the old hymn, *O Sacrum Convivium*, puts it: *et futurae gloriae nobis pignus datur.*

And the pledge that is given is nevertheless the consumm-ation, the effective sacrifice of God the Son, which is a taking into the Godhead of that which is unworthy, which is unclean, the degradation which the cross epitomises, transforming that degradation which is not to be separated from human being heretofore, into participation in what God is. What we might have been is what the cross shows – consigned to suffering and death, facing a darkness in which God is hidden, knowing our-selves forsaken.[8] Indeed, not being born would have been preferable to such a fate. And what we might now be is shown in the resurrection. But the Jesus crucified is the Risen Jesus, and we cannot have the one without the other, in the Eucharist or anywhere else.

But the transformation of us into the risen and crucified which is wrought in the Eucharist is not all God's doing.

At Mass, we do not merely stand at the foot of Calvary as spectators. We remember that both the Virgin Mary and the Pharisees were present at Calvary, but with rather different in-tentions. The dying figure of the crucified is the death of what

we once were and once could not but be. What has died is replaced by what now lives in the resurrection, and which is now
what we are to be. The reconfiguration of what we are is real.
But it is possible for us to reject it. And there is no space given in
the mystery which is not that of the Pharisees or the Virgin, although there is space outside it. But that space is only distance
and ignorance. It is not ultimate in the divine history of Being,
whose essence and consummation are at one, given veiled in the
Eucharist. But within the mystery are only the two spaces, and
these are replicated in each of the actors mentioned in the scripture—in the Virgin and the Good Thief and the Disciples, in the
Pharisees and the Unrepentant Thief and in Judas: in the *fiat mihi
secundum verbum tuum*, which she lives as much at the place of
her Son's torture as she did at the moment of his conception, and
which is Jesus' own attitude to the Godless darkness, and in the
In manus tuas. The family resemblance between mother and son
here is indeed great. That space is also one in which sin sees itself as it is and asks for the forgiveness which is some remembrance in the kingdom. I am not loveable, but love me still. Over
and against these are self-sufficiency and despair.

Self-sufficiency is the assertion of the prior good, of what is
unregenerate in the face of the gift of God's reconfiguration and
against it: this is what I am and all I am, and this I shall remain.
All we can be is what the law makes us. Yet the law in itself, and
more broadly, the economy of virtue, is a way to an incomplete
human good, which as incomplete is in need of redemption, and
one that comes as the very opposite of economy, as spendthrift
love. Despair too decrees that this is all I am and shall be, and
seals it by its suicide, amputating all possibility that I can be
other. In sum, we either eat in discernment or in sin, and so eat
and drink judgement on ourselves, though this judgement is not
an external decree, but is what we are to be.

And yet this end seems far off. To live well is to live the mystery of Being, which the Eucharist reveals. To live well is to live
the Eucharist, the thanksgiving which accepts the mystery of
Being day in day out, and which passes through the asking of

forgiveness to an ever-more secure 'Be it done unto me', 'Into thy hands', a remaking which is only possible in and through communion in the mystery, and which becomes more secure insofar as we who receive the unmerited gift with thanks thereby open ourselves to becoming the Repentant Thief, the Virgin and the Crucified, in the intimacy of the unrepeatable identity of who we are.

CHAPTER ELEVEN

Postmodern Philosophy
and J.-L. Marion's Eucharistic Realism

Philipp W. Rosemann

In his encyclical *Fides et Ratio* the Holy Father has spoken of the considerable ambiguities that attach to the term 'postmodernism'. It is not clear when exactly modernity should be considered to have come to a close and to have given rise to a fundamentally different historical period; moreover, there is dispute as to whether the advent of postmodernity should be regarded as a positive or a negative development. 'One thing, however, is certain', the Holy Father continues:

> the currents of thought which claim to be postmodern merit appropriate attention. According to some of them, the time of certainties is irrevocably past, and the human being must now learn to live in a horizon of total absence of meaning, where everything is provisional and ephemeral. In their destructive critique of every certitude, several authors have failed to make crucial distinctions and have called into question the certitudes of faith. This nihilism has been justified in a sense by the terrible experience of evil which has marked our age. Such a dramatic experience has ensured the collapse of rationalist optimism, which viewed history as the triumphant progress of reason ...[1]

In this essay, I should like to offer a contribution to the fair-minded assessment of postmodernism which *Fides et Ratio* calls for. I am by no means the first Catholic thinker to attempt such a dialogue. In recent years a number of Christian philosophers have set out to develop a postmodern articulation of the faith – just as the church fathers and medieval thinkers took up the task of rethinking the tradition in the light of the intellectual challenges that confronted them in their own day. One of the most respected and sophisticated postmodern Catholic thinkers is Jean-Luc Marion, who teaches at the Sorbonne in Paris and at the University of Chicago. In the context of the present volume, I shall comment upon one of the central themes of Marion's thought, a topic that has preoccupied him since his very first publications: the theology of the Eucharist.

But first, a brief introduction to the postmodern movement is in order.

1. What is Postmodern Philosophy?

Fides et Ratio draws attention to three central characteristics of postmodern thought. According to the encyclical, the latter typically engages in (1) *destructive critique* of certitude and meaning, indeed so much so that it frequently results in (2) utter *nihilism*. These tendencies are to be understood as (3) *a reaction to the collapse of modern rationalism,* which for many has become untenable given the experience of evil in the modern age. Let us further examine these characteristics.

Modernity is a complex phenomenon to which it is obviously not possible to do justice in a few sentences. Nonetheless, there can be little doubt that modern thinkers tended to espouse an excessive rationalism – excessive in the sense of regarding reason as a goal in itself. To be sure, premodern philosophy and theology recognised reason as a defining feature of the human being; this feature, however, was seen as ordered towards a higher good, one not reducible to human reason. Plato, for example, held that human life finds its ultimate fulfilment only in contemplation of the Good, which he considered to transcend human knowledge and indeed Being itself. For Christianity, man is made in the image and likeness of God. This means that human existence does not have its centre in itself, but in that of which it is the image: God and his inner-Trinitarian life. The tension between image and exemplar sets in motion a dynamism that longs to find ultimate completion in the beatific vision, its end or *telos*. Since this *telos* is not reducible to human reason, neither is, ultimately, the human being itself. It longs for more than itself, for more than it can comprehend.

Modernity, by contrast, recognises no goal and no limit – no *telos* – outside the unfolding of human reason. Thus, self-regulated rational progress is the ultimate goal of the modern age. Progress is no longer aimed at anything that sets limits to reason; at anything where rational movement would naturally come to an end (such as the Platonic Good or the beatific vision, which are understood as completing human nature). Rather, it is limitless and shapeless: without form, as traditional metaphysical language would put it. As reason unfolds in ever accelerating, self-propelling motion, it absorbs everything in the demands of progress; that which cannot be so assimilated is marginalised or destroyed.

Philosophically, this vertiginous dynamic is perhaps most impressively evidenced in the preface to Hegel's *Lectures on the Philosophy of World History*. In this remarkable text, Hegel systematically reduces all aspects of reality to reason or spirit: human history, which he believes follows an inherently rational, predictable course; faith, in which he allows for no element of mystery that could not be penetrated by the light of reason; and even God and divine providence.[2] Yet the totalising tendencies of modern reason are not limited to the theoretical sphere: most tellingly, in the same preface Hegel vehemently defends colonialism, arguing that peoples whose way of life does not correspond to his conception of reason possess no culture, history, and state worthy of the name. They must therefore be 'civilised', that is, absorbed into Western rationality, or wiped out. About the native population of North America, Hegel writes that, 'after the Europeans had landed there, the natives were gradually destroyed by the breath of European activity … Culturally inferior nations such as these are gradually eroded through contact with more advanced nations.'[3] Perhaps, in writing of the 'terrible experience of evil which has marked our age', the Holy Father had in mind not only the Holocaust and the wars of the twentieth century, but also the exploitation by Europeans of their colonies and brutal destruction of indigenous cultures. Often, however, the perils of modernity are considerably more subtle. Martin

Heidegger has provided an incisive philosophical analysis of the structures of technological capitalism, suggesting that it aims at nothing but ever-increasing efficiency: thus, both subject and object are dissolved in structures that increasingly elude human direction and for which there is nothing that could not be turned into a 'resource' for further growth.[4] To cite a topical example, in medical research involving human foetal tissue, even the human being itself is no longer regarded as an end in it-self, but rather as a mere means for 'progress'.

The main thrust of postmodernism is directed precisely at such totalising rationalism. Against the modern presumption according to which nothing is opaque to reason (conceived as calculative, technological, and autonomous), postmodern thinkers emphasise the irreducibility of that which is 'other' than ration-ality. In this manner, Kierkegaard set out to defend the integrity of faith; Nietzsche maintained that a high price has to be paid for the repression of the irrational, destructive, 'Dionysian' forces in human life; Foucault argued that reason is subject to history, rather than vice versa, as Hegel had claimed – so that there exists no universal reason but only particular incommensurable rationalities; and Derrida argues that language, far from being the obedient tool of reason, subverts any attempt to construct stable, unambiguous meaning: all human speaking remains on the way to a completion that is always 'deferred' (*différance*). From these examples, it is obvious what *Fides et Ratio* means when it refers to a postmodern loss of certitude. Justified as the postmodern critique of modern excesses may be, it often re-mains a mere counter-image of modernity, negating the latter without being able to point to meaning-ful alternatives. The re-sult is nihilism.

This nihilism is all the more serious as its consequences reach far beyond the modern age. Since Nietzsche, postmodern thought has pursued a 'destructive critique' of modernity that has sought the roots of the modern predicament in the development of the Western tradition from its earliest beginnings. This critique reached its paradigmatic form in Heidegger's philosophy. For

Heidegger, the 'task of thinking', as he called it, consisted less in the construction of philosophical systems than in the 'destruction' *(Destruktion)* of the Western tradition, which for him had found its logical culmination in modernity. It is important to note, however, that for Heidegger and his postmodern disciples, 'destruction' is not synonymous with 'destroying'. Rather, Heidegger understands 'de-struction' etymologically, as the painstaking 'un-building' (from the Latin *de-struere*) of the layers of thought that have, since Presocratic times, gradually led to a rationality which, instead of 'listening to' the mystery of Being, is merely interested in mastering beings.[5]

For Heidegger, such 'forgetfulness of Being' – of the mystery of the All – is inextricably tied to a metaphysics of presence. Since the ancient Greeks Western thought has privileged vision as access to reality, rather than, for example, the much more humble sense of hearing.[6] We imagine even abstract things as though we can see them. In contemporary English, for example, we constantly use phrases like 'I see' or 'let me throw some light on this issue', rather than expressing such ideas through other kinds of metaphors ('I hear'? 'I touch'?). But in order for a thing to be available to sight, it needs to be relatively static; any dynamism in which it may be engaged has to be arrested. This is why Western metaphysics has always regarded stable presence as the paradigm of being, rather than flux, process, dynamism. Even the Greeks themselves – as the later Heidegger concedes against a position he maintained earlier on in his career – no longer understood the implications of the etymology of the Greek word for truth, *alêtheia*.[7] *Alêtheia* is composed of the word *léthé*, 'forgetting', and the alpha privative (*a-* meaning *non-, un-*). Thus, in the Greek language, truth, etymologically understood, was not simply some (static) state of affairs, but a process of 'un-forgetting', in which something previously not present to the observer emerges into presence. Had being been conceived in this manner as a dynamism in which an initially hidden, 'mysterious' element is given to man (like a blossom bursting into bloom), perhaps Western philosophy would not have culminated in modern technology.

2. Christian Postmodernism?

Generally, postmodern thinkers do not exempt the Christian tradition from their destructive critique of Western metaphysics. For many – such as Heidegger – the Christian God forms an integral part of the metaphysics of mastery: God, as cause of Being, ensures the availability of reality to reason. Nietzsche, for his part, sees nothing more in the Christian faith than an attempt to repress the wild forces of Dionysian life in superficial morality. Against the background of such fundamental critique, what constructive dialogue can there be between postmodernism and Christianity?

Christian postmodernists take the critiques of Nietzsche, Heidegger, and their contemporary disciples very seriously. The metaphysics of presence, totalising rationality, and mastery of beings, coupled with a forgetfulness of Being, represent genuine dangers, which are at the root of many of the ills that affect the global civilisation of the twenty-first century. But how deeply is the Western tradition infected by these dangers? About this question, there is considerable disagreement. Some, such as the influential Anglo-Catholic movement known as Radical Ortho-doxy, deny that the seeds of the problems of modernity were sown in antiquity, and perceive a radical break between pre-modernity and the modern age.[8] In his early work on Heidegger and St Thomas, John Caputo, an American Derridean who is Roman Catholic, accepted much of Heidegger's critique of the Western tradition, but maintained that Thomistic metaphysics remains exempt from it: St Thomas did not 'forget' the differ-ence between beings and Being.[9] Jean-Luc Marion has been quite hesitant on the status of Thomism, sometimes criticising, sometimes commending St Thomas's thought.[10]

Whatever side is taken on the status of premodern thought, and of Thomistic metaphysics in particular, one point seems to be agreed upon by Christian postmodernists: a philosophico-theological articulation of the Christian faith must be cautious to avoid the pitfalls of modern rationalism. Authentically Christian thought can therefore learn much from the de-structive analyses of postmodern philosophers. Indeed, it faces the task of critically examining the Christian tradition itself, with the goal of identifying elements of that tradition which may unwittingly have succumbed to the metaphysics of presence, while emphasising those aspects of the tradition that are most immune to any form of subtle intellectual idolatry. In this context, it should come as no surprise that many contemporary Christian philosophers and theologians have rediscovered the strengths of Neoplatonism, with its consistent emphasis upon the mystery of the divine in its transcendence of both Being and knowledge.[11]

3. Jean-Luc Marion

Born in 1946, Jean-Luc Marion entered the philosophical scene in the nineteen seventies as an expert on Descartes. Following in the footsteps of one of his 'masters',[12] Étienne Gilson, Marion devoted several influential books to the topic of Descartes' relationship and indebtedness to the tradition. For, although Descartes famously declared the need to create a blank slate, a *tabula rasa*, in order to free philosophical reflection from the prejudices of the past, Gilson demonstrated that his thought was deeply rooted in the philosophy of his late scholastic predecessors. In *Sur l'ontologie grise de Descartes* ('On the Grey Ontology of Descartes'), Marion expanded upon Gilson's insights by showing how Descartes' philosophy was based upon a systematic subversion and redefinition of Aristotelian concepts.[13] Still more spectacularly, *Sur la théologie blanche de Descartes* ('On the Blank Theology of Descartes') presented Descartes as a Christian thinker in the tradition of negative theology: far from being some kind of closet atheist, Marion argued, Descartes was fundamentally motivated by a genuine desire to save God's transcendence from the dangers of late scholastic metaphysics and modern mathematical science.[14] With these and other groundbreaking publications, Marion quickly won recognition as one of the leading experts on the founder of modern philosophy. The relevance of Marion's theses, however, is not limited to the interpretation of Descartes. What is at stake is nothing less than the meaning of the philosophical project of modernity. According to Marion, modernity (at least in its Cartesian form) is grounded less in a deliberate rejection of Christianity than in a (misguided and problematic?) attempt to defend it.

While making a name for himself through his rereading of Descartes, Marion produced a steady flow of explicitly Christian, and indeed theological, writings. One of the first essays he ever published was devoted to the contemplation of the Blessed Sacrament: entitled *'La splendeur de la contemplation eucharistique'* ('The Splendour of Eucharistic Contemplation'), it appeared in the year 1969 in *Résurrection*, the review of a French Catholic lay movement which was founded by Fr Maxime Charles (1908-1993).[15] Fr Charles served as chaplain of the Sorbonne between 1944 and 1959, creating the influential Centre Richelieu there, which quickly became a vibrant centre of Catholic intellectual life. Later, until 1985, he was rector of Sacré-Cœur at Montmartre. After Fr Charles's death, some of his sermons were published in book-form, under a title that is significant in our context: *Guide de l'adoration eucharistique*, 'Guide to Eucharistic Adoration'.[16]

Marion elaborated on the reflections that appeared in 1969 in several subsequent articles on the theology of the Eucharist; these culminated in chapters 5 and 6 of *God without Being*. It is no exaggeration to say that Marion's thought is eucharistic in its very core. About all this, more in a moment. Three important books, *L'idole et la distance* ('The Idol and Distance'),[17] *Dieu sans l'être* ('God without Being')[18] and *Prolégomènes à la charité* ('Prolegomena to Charity'),[19] also belong to Marion's early Christian writings. They show a thinker profoundly influenced by the negative theology and mysticism of the Greek fathers, especially Pseudo-Dionysius the Areopagite; but also a contemporary philosopher in dialogue with Nietzsche and Heidegger.

More recently, towards the end of the nineteen eighties, Marion's thought has acquired a third axis: phenomenology. From its beginnings in Husserl, phenomenology has wrestled with the problems of the modern turn to the subject and, in part-

icular, Kantian transcendentalism. Husserl's famous battle-cry
was, *Zu den Sachen selbst!* ('To the things themselves!'). Is it at all
possible – and if so, how – to come to know things as they are
themselves, abstracting from the question of how their appearances are processed and formed by human rationality? More
technically put, what is the pure 'givenness' of phenomena? If
Marion's first writings, on Descartes, treated of the beginnings
of modernity, his publications on phenomenology address the
possibility of emerging from it – not by means of a simple (and
simplistic) rejection, but by working through modern thought to
its own logical conclusions. Thus, phenomenology ultimately
calls for the possibility of a phenomenon or of phenomena that
determine the conditions of their own givenness. In books such
as *Réduction et donation* ('Reduction and Givenness'),[20] *Étant
donné* ('Being Given'),[21] and, most recently, *Le phénomène érotique*
('The Erotic Phenomenon')[22] Marion has examined this possibility. As with his research on Descartes, his work on phenomenology has earned Marion a reputation as one of the finest experts
in this field. Yet the ultimate inspiration of this work is, once
again, Christian. Unless the 'saturated phenomenon' exists – a
phenomenon that makes us humans what we are, rather than
being made and formed by us, by human rationality – there can
be no God; or, more precisely, all discourse on God, all theology, would in the last analysis remain idolatrous.[23] It would impose human categories upon God, instead of allowing itself to
be formed by an experience of the divine. For Marion, love or
charity is the saturated phenomenon *par excellence*.

4. Jean-Luc Marion's Eucharistic Realism

Many of the important issues of postmodern thought that were
discussed in the previous sections converge in Marion's theology
of the Eucharist.[24] From his very first publications on the subject,
Marion has emphasised the need to avoid two different yet dia-
lectically related modern 'idolatries'. Both arise from mistaken
conceptions of the real presence. The first calls into question
liturgical practices (such as perpetual adoration and eucharistic

processions) that appear to reduce the Blessed Sacrament to a 'thing'. Such practices, the argument goes, reflect a misguided metaphysicisation of the eucharistic mystery: 'the substantial presence … fixes and congeals the person in a permanent, manipulable, and delimited thing that is at our disposal'.[25] Against the background of what we have said about the meta-physics of presence and its concomitant forgetfulness of Being, it is clear why Marion concedes: 'the objection is very profound.'[26] This does not mean, however, that he rejects the liturgical prac-tices that are at issue here; far from it. Rather, he is suggesting that, in order to understand and fully to appreciate eucharistic contemplation, we need an appropriate conception of the real presence.

The second idolatry concerning the Eucharist aims to avoid the shortcomings highlighted by the first, yet fails due to a simi-larly insufficient understanding of the real presence. Marion at-tributes this conception to certain 'liberal' theologies; for in-stance, the *Dutch Catechism* and Fr Edward Schillebeeckx.[27] For these theologies, the Eucharist is above all a meal through which Christ becomes present in the consciousness of the community. There is no reification of Christ in this conception, but only at the price of moving the real presence into the human subject. Christ is now no longer received as a gift through the priest who speaks the words of consecration *in persona Christi;* rather, Christ's presence is dependent upon the state of mind of the community itself. Attempting to avoid one idolatry, the 'liberal' theology of the Eucharist thus produces another.

In his own publications on the Eucharist, Marion responds to the contemporary crisis in eucharistic practice and theory by means of reflections that are both fully orthodox and take into consideration many of the concerns of postmodern philosophy. His reflections centre upon a dialectical analysis of the two terms that figure in the expression, 'real presence'. For Marion, 'reality' and 'presence' designate two closely related yet distinct aspects of Christ's body and blood in the Blessed Sacrament.

a. The Reality of Christ in the Eucharist

The term 'reality' is derived from the Latin word *res*, 'thing'. When the church speaks of a 'real' presence, it thereby indicates that in the Eucharist, God has become a 'thing', indeed an 'object'.[28] Now according to Marion, the reality of Christ's body and blood in the Eucharist is not without precedent in the economy of salvation, rather constituting the culmination of a progressively more intense, 'palpable' self-manifestation of the Infinite within the finite.[29] Out of infinite love, God has manifested himself in creation, at least to those capable of looking at creation with open eyes. Furthermore, he has spoken through his prophets, who have left us a text, sacred scripture, through which we may discover him – if we have faith. Still more radically, the Word has become incarnate, in a complete unification of infinite, divine and finite, human nature; yet even the divinity of Christ is open to doubt by unbelievers. Finally, and most dramatically, the outpouring of God's love has permitted the mystery of transubstantiation, in which the Son of God enters our finite world in the form of lowly food. Here, the danger of misunderstanding is at its highest.

In each of these stages of self-manifestation or theophany,[30] God embraces and penetrates the material world more thoroughly in order to offer us his love. Each of these forms of self-manifestation represents a completely gratuitous gift *(don)*. In each of these theophanies, God can also be said freely to 'abandon' his divinity in order to communicate his love. In the incarnation and in the Eucharist, however, this 'abandonment' *(abandon)* becomes extreme: in the former, Christ abandons his life for our salvation, subjecting himself to humiliation, torture, and death; in the latter, God's 'gift of self goes right to the point where he abandons himself as a thing'.[31]

God's *aban-don* (gift-abandonment)[32] on the one hand serves to show us his boundless love. On the other hand, by 'abandoning' himself, God freely exposes himself to the risk of not being recognised in his divinity. This risk is due to the fact that in each of his theophanies, there remains a distance between the Infinite and the finite.[33] Creation is not God but a sign of its Creator. Scripture is not God's unmediated voice, but his revelation through inspired prophets and apostles; it is a text that requires interpretation. Even in the incarnation, the difference between divine and human nature is not abolished. Christ is not merely a sign of God, he is God; yet he is also man. Similarly, in the Eucharist, the reality of Christ is conjoined to the species of bread and wine, which ensure a certain limited persistence of the finite (even though only as accidents). In each of these cases, the finite is never simply absorbed into the Infinite. In each of these cases, we therefore remain free to misread and misinterpret God's self-manifestation. The world around us does not have to be viewed as creation; it can be understood as material 'stuff' completely explicable through the laws of physics. Scripture, too, is open to the possibility of being read as an interesting historical document, rather than as the word of God. In this case, it is regarded as a sign without (divine) referent. Alternatively, the referent can be absorbed into the sign; for in Judaism, God has become 'a kind of prisoner'[34] of a legalistically interpreted text. Again, Christ does not force us to receive him as the Son of God; he can be – and of course has been – considered as merely a fascinating and inspiring historical figure. Those who crucified him saw in him a political and religious threat. As for the Eucharist, it is susceptible to being misunderstood as nothing more than a childish and perhaps even sinister superstition. Indeed, in the Eucharist, 'the possibility that one disrespect the person in it'[35] becomes an extreme danger – one that is not unknown even in Catholic circles, and which is closely related to the two idolatries mentioned earlier on. Despite its considerable theoretical interest, the reader of Marion's work on the Eucharist senses that it is above all inspired by sincere piety; that is to say, by a desire to promote liturgical and contemplative practices which will restore to the Blessed Sacrament all the reverence that it is due.

b. From Reality to Presence

We have to acknowledge that there obtains an irreducible distance between the reality of Christ's body and blood in the Eucharist, on the one hand, and his presence in this sacrament on the other. This distance is in complete accordance with the structure of God's self-revelation in creation, in scripture, and even in the incarnation. However,

> the more [God's] reality lowers itself, the more is it necessary to deepen the gaze that perceives the brilliance of [his] presence. The more the gift of God realises itself without reserve [*sans retour*], the more is it able to be rejected.[36]

Therefore, it is our 'gaze', our approach to reality, which needs to be modified so that we may become able to discern the presence of God in it: 'the distance which separates and unites "reality" and presence corresponds to the economy of our conversion.'[37] Note that, according to Marion, both the reality and the presence of Christ in the Eucharist exist 'independently of our mind[s]';[38] it is the *distance* between them that is due to the finitude and imperfection – in a word, to the fallenness – of the human gaze.[39]

In *God without Being*, Marion has developed a helpful distinction to describe two kinds of 'gaze' *(regard)*, two kinds of viewing the real: the idol and the icon. The idol, according to Marion, 'consigns the divine to the measure of the human gaze'. An 'invisible mirror', it allows man to grasp reality only according to the depth of his own intention.[40] The idol can be the result of an authentic religious experience; thus, veneration of, say, a river indicates less an absence of religious feeling than the critical shortcomings of the latter. The human being, not expecting the divine to transcend a certain measure, fails to 'transpierce visible things'[41] in order to discover the divine in a dimension that exceeds them. 'God', the idolatrous god, thus remains subject to man. The icon, by contrast, 'does not result from a vision but provokes one'.[42] Or, to use the language of phenomenology, rather than being determined by human conditions for the possibility of perception and knowledge, the icon itself determines, 'starting from itself and itself alone, the conditions of its reality'.[43] The icon makes man, rather than being made by man. The reality experienced as icon shapes the human being's gaze, breaks through the circle of reflexivity, and transforms man in(to) its own image.

The question, then, becomes one of how the Eucharist can be approached iconically. In the Eucharist seen as an idol, a human being will discover nothing more than a wafer or, perhaps, a sign of Christ's presence in the community. In this manner, such a person will fail to acknowledge that there is a distance between the reality of Christ and his presence in the Eucharist, between the species of bread and wine and the divine person. This distance calls for conversion, for a training of the spiritual eye, as it were, as a result of which the believer will increasingly be able to see 'through' the accidents of bread and wine to Christ, who appears 'behind' them, as the substance of the Eucharist.

c. The Temporality of Christ's Eucharistic Presence

The difference between the idolatrous and the iconic approaches to the mystery of the Eucharist entails a distinction between two modes of 'temporalisation'. Marion terms these modes, respectively, 'metaphysical' and 'Christic' temporality.[44] His analyses on this subject are closely modelled upon the distinction between authentic and inauthentic time which Heidegger presented in *Sein und Zeit*. Marion himself explicitly acknowledges his indebtedness to Heidegger at this crucial point of theological reflection:

> According to *Sein und Zeit,* in fact, metaphysics deploys an 'ordinary conception of time' … through metaphysics, being is deployed in its Being only as long as its manipulable and assured availability endures. The presence available in the present – as the here and now – guarantees the permanence where spirit maintains a hold on being … This ontological overdetermination of a primacy of the present leads to a double reduction of the future and of the past: the one finishes and the other begins as soon as the present begins or finishes.

> Their respective temporalities count only negatively, as a double non-present, even a double non-time … What separates a good number of Christians from a theologically correct (if not adequate) comprehension of the Eucharistic present has to do with nothing less than the *'ordinary conception of time'* and hence with the metaphysical discourse of presence.[45]

Marion's move to invoke Heideggerian categories in the elucidation of one of the central mysteries of the faith is just as bold, I would suggest, as the use of Neoplatonic philosophy by the church fathers or the creative adaptation of Aristotelian philosophy by the theologians of the Middle Ages. We tend to take it for granted today that the faith can be expounded in terms of substance and person, participation, matter and form, and similar categories. These concepts, however, have nothing inherently Christian about them. They were derived from pagan sources by successive generations of Christian thinkers who had the faith, vision, and courage to engage in fruitful dialogue with the intellectual currents of their times. Our time is the postmodern age, and as Christians we have nothing to fear from the likes of Nietzsche, Heidegger, Foucault, and Lacan. Indeed, the religious impulses of postmodern thought are not difficult to discern beneath a surface of agnosticism or even atheism.[46] Our task, then, is to deepen the Christian intellectual tradition once again, by learning the philosophical language of our day.

But let us return to the passage just quoted. Christ's presence in the Eucharist is not exhausted by his objectification in the 'bread' and 'wine', an objectification through which he becomes available in the here and now like a thing – with the concomitant dangers of profanation that we discussed earlier on. For a 'theologically correct' comprehension of the Eucharist, such a metaphysical conception of time should be left behind in favour of a properly Christic perspective. This perspective must avoid any reductionism in which the present appears, in the final analysis, as the only dimension of time, such that the past is construed as the no-longer-present and the future as the not-yet-present. In this inauthentic (and un-Christic!) mode of temporalisation, man lives primarily in the present, rather than building the present out of the past into the future.

What could such an authentically Christian mode of temporalisation mean in connection with the Eucharist? To this question, Marion responds that 'the present must be understood first as a gift that is given' – given precisely by the past and the future. The Eucharist is, in its first mode of temporalisation, a memorial: 'Do this in remembrance of me' (Lk 22:19). However, this memorial does not have the purpose of reminding the Christian community of Christ's life, death, and resurrection, as for example the *Dutch Catechism* teaches.[48] Marion asks ironically: '[W]ould we be "Christians" if we had forgotten them?'[49] Rather, it is a matter of 'making an appeal, in the name of a past event, to God, in order that he recall an engagement (a covenant) that determines the instant presently given to the believing community'.[50] Marion thus views the Eucharist as taking up and perfecting the Jewish practice of praising God for the deeds whereby he confirmed his covenant with the people of Israel: 'This cup that is poured out for you is the new covenant in my blood' (Lk 22:20; cf. Mk 14:24). Just as on the cross Christ abandoned his life to the Father, so the priest celebrates the Eucharist in order to appeal to the Father that Christ may come again in glory so that the promise of eternal life may be fulfilled. The daily 're-presentation'[51] of Christ's sacrifice – to use terminology from *Ecclesia de Eucharistia* – does not have the purpose of adding anything to the work of redemption, which was completed on the cross; rather, the Eucharist defines the present as being situated within the distance, in the interstice, between Christ's self-giving to the Father, for our salvation, and his second coming. The presence of Christ in the Eucharist renews God's pledge of Christ's full presence that we eagerly await. In this way, the present, far from being self-sufficient, derives its meaning from the past.

And from the future! From the very nature of the Eucharist as memorial, its eschatological dimension has already become apparent. The two are, in fact, inextricable in their connection. For the cross, as the culmination and fulfilment of the covenant,

holds the promise of the *parousia*: 'I tell you, I will never again
drink of this fruit of the vine until that day when I drink it new
with you in my Father's kingdom' (Mt 26:29; cf. Mk 14:25).
According to a 'properly Christian temporality',[52] then, the present is constituted in the dynamic tension between the past and
the future; it is 'anticipation concretely lived'[53] (*epektasis*; cf. Phil
3:13) of the fulfilment of God's promise.

memorial of the covenant	present as concretely lived anticipation	eschatological expectation of the second coming

The Structure of Christic Temporality

There are consequences to this Christian, non-metaphysical understanding of the present. Most importantly, the present of the
Christian life appears as a gift of God's love. Outside of this love,
the present descends into meaninglessness: 'Each instant of time
sinks into vanity … if we do not endeavour to render the
Eucharistic Body present in it'.[54] In this context, one should not
forget that Jean-Luc Marion is the author of a book entitled *God
without Being*, in which he outlines a form of postmodern
Christian thought that is strongly influenced by the negative
theology of Pseudo-Dionysius. Marion believes, with much of
the Christian tradition, that Love is the first name of God, and
not Being. The world receives its Being from Love; the world
does not possess Being and, subsequently, God's love is added
to it. Without love, therefore, the world stands in danger of sink-
ing back into nothingness – a thesis, by the way, that Marion
illustrates through brilliant phenomenological descriptions of
the effects of melancholy.[55]

It is necessary, therefore, to revise our ordinary understanding of reality. The 'really real' is not, as modern philosophy has
taught us, that which stands before us in neutral 'presence-to-

hand' (*Vorhandenheit*, as Heidegger says in *Sein und Zeit*). Such presence in the frozen 'here and now' is, in fact, secondary and derivative. From a Christian point of view – and here Marion revises and deepens Heidegger's insights – 'only that attains to the status of reality which seems "mystical" to the ordinary gaze'.[56] We have previously seen that the term 'reality' derives from the Latin word *res*, 'thing'. The theological tradition has sometimes employed the term *res* to designate the matter of the sacraments, such as water in baptism, or bread and wine in the case of the Eucharist. Interestingly, however, there is a certain ambiguity in the use of the term *res*, such that it can also refer to the ultimate meaning of each sacrament: the ultimate 'thing' of penance, for example, is the remission of sins.[57] In the theology of the Eucharist, the 'thing' in this latter sense has traditionally been considered to possess two dimensions: the first *res* of the Eucharist is the body and blood of Christ, whereas the second *res* is the church, or Christ's ecclesiastical body. Marion comments:

> The bread and wine consecrated and transubstantiated into the Body and Blood are valid as *res* – Christ really given in the Eucharistic present – but, at the same time, they still remain a *sacramentum* [a sacramental sign] with respect to the ecclesiastical body of Christ, the church which they aim at and construct; only this ecclesiastical Body should be called purely *res*.[58]

What is 'really real', then, from a properly Christian point of view, are not the 'bread' and 'wine' – they are surface, though a tempting surface for our 'naturally blind gaze'.[59] The iconic gaze, the gaze informed by God's gift of charity, does not see bread and wine, but rather Christ in person. More than that: the iconic gaze perceives the kingdom of God, which already exists, albeit imperfectly, in his church. Thus, the reality and presence of Christ are reconciled: Christ's presence in the Eucharist is reality. The Eucharist calls us to a transformation of the real: leaving behind the lowly 'bread' and 'wine', we are called to ascend to that which is revealed in them. In this life, however, this ascent will never be complete: the distance between the reality and presence of Christ – a distance that God has completely traversed since the passion and the resurrection – remains, for us, a call to constant conversion, a 'conversion that requires the time of our entire lives'.[60]

5. Marion on the Eucharistic Site of Theology

We have already seen that, according to Marion, the tension between the divine reality and presence in the Eucharist – a tension that exists but for the human eye – is paradigmatic of the structure of all creation, understood as theophany: God's self-revelation is not without a moment of concealment. It is as though all of creation possesses the nature of a sign or a text, which requires interpretation for its proper meaning to emerge. Another way of framing this insight is to say that, for us in this life, all presence of the divine remains irreducibly tied to re-presentation: we do not live in the immediate presence of God that is characteristic of the beatific vision. The Eucharist, however, is a very special and privileged sign, for in the Blessed Sacrament the sign and that which it signifies coincide:

> Thus, only the coincidence of that which signifies (the 'bread') and of that which is signified in it (thing, referent) – of him who signifies himself in it – is able to privilege a signification ('body of Christ'), because only this coincidence, which imposes presence in the nexus of signs of the Word, transcends the insignificant and reciprocal circularity of that nexus.[61]

What Marion is attempting to explain in this rather technical passage is, in the end, quite simple: in all the signs that God has given us to manifest himself, he himself is not present in person. Creation does not contain God, nor does the text of scripture. We may dissect creation and interpret scripture as much as we want, we will never discover more in them than signs of the divine; we will never be able to move from signs of the Word to the Word himself. That, precisely, is different in the Eucharist, in which the Word signifies himself through the bread and wine accidents, yet is also genuinely present as substance.

Catherine Pickstock has criticised Marion's conception of the Eucharist because she believes that 'he insists on the idea of presence outside the sign'. Pickstock counters: 'So, whereas, for Marion, the Eucharist is something extra-linguistic which makes up or compensates for the deathliness of language, it is on the contrary the case that the Eucharist situates us more inside language than ever.'[62] I think that this criticism is not justified. As is obvious from the passage just quoted, according to Marion the Eucharist does not render God present outside the sign: such un-represented presence is something that can occur only in the beatific vision. The coincidence of sign and presence of which Marion speaks in the case of the Eucharist is not tantamount to the abolition of the sign.

Pickstock's mistaken impression that, for Marion, the Eucharist is something extra-linguistic stems from his discussion of the relationship between theology and the celebration of the Eucharist. Marion understands the theologian as, first and foremost, an interpreter of scripture. But how can the theologian overcome the 'gap'[63] that exists in scripture between the text and the event of which it speaks – between the words and the Word? Furthermore, how can he or she become an iconic theologian, one who refrains from imposing merely human meanings on the text instead of letting it speak for itself? The question again becomes one of how the phenomenon – in this case, the text of scripture – can determine, 'starting from itself and itself alone, the conditions of its reality'.[64] This requires a radical turning away from the modern subject, to (one might say) the 'sub-ject'; for it requires a subjection to the text of scripture: 'To do theology is not to speak the language of gods or of [an idolatrous] "God," but to let the Word speak us'.[65] Such being-spoken-by-the-Word occurs paradigmatically when the priest, *in persona Christi*, pronounces the words of consecration: 'the Eucharist offers the only correct hermeneutic site where the Word can be said in person in the blessing' – *où le Verbe se dit en personne dans la bénédiction*.[66] The French original is more radical than its English translation, for in French *se dire* suggests that, in the words of consecration, agency has passed from the priest to Christ, who 'says himself' in the blessing.

All of theology, then, must centre upon the abandonment of human agency which occurs at the central moment of the Eucharist. Theology is a matter of conforming oneself increasingly to the Word, by contemplating the words of God in scripture. Marion thus thinks theology in the most traditional manner, and that is, mystically. Theology is not a science, he declares, but rather a process of conversion: the theologian must be holy. *'[T]heology cannot aim at any other progress than its own conversion to the Word.'*[67]

And another consequence follows from Marion's eucharistic conception of theology: 'only the bishop,' who possesses the fullness of the priesthood, 'merits, in the full sense, the title of theologian.'[68] To be sure, the bishop may delegate the tasks of the theological hermeneutic. Any theologian, however, who breaks the ties of communion with his bishop, *ipso facto* forsakes the eucharistic site of theology and thus loses the legitimacy of speaking theologically. With this thesis, Marion does not mean to defend theological 'conservatism' but simply formulates a *conditio sine qua non* of any theological discourse that is to be more than a sophisticated form of idolatry. The indissociable tie between theology and the Eucharist does not negate the freedom of thought or the legitimate, and indeed necessary, multiplicity of theologies. In a very Augustinian vein, Marion affirms: 'The multiplicity of theologies – if these indeed Eucharistically merit *theo*logical status – ensues as necessarily from the unspeakable infinity of the Word as does the infinity of Eucharists.'[69] We will never be able completely to close the gap between the text of scripture and the divine persons of whom it speaks; but in our theological words, we can again and again utter our desire to live, one day, in the full presence of the Word. Thus the Eucharist, rather than detaching us from the text of scripture, immerses us ever more deeply in it.[70]

PART THREE

Tradition and Devotion of the Church

CHAPTER TWELVE

The Eucharist and Culture: Transcending Boundaries

Cardinal Paul Poupard

It is with joy that I respond to the invitation of the Irish Centre for Faith and Culture to compose an article addressing matters eucharistic and cultural, for the publication of the Acts of a conference which focused on the Holy Father's encyclical letter *Ecclesia de Eucharistia*. For me, as for all the faithful, this Year of the Eucharist is a special time to reflect on the august institution of the Most Holy Eucharist, as we prepare for the Eleventh Ordinary General Assembly of the Synod of Bishops, which from the 2nd to the 29th of October 2005 will address the luminous mystery of *The Eucharist, Source and Summit of the Life and Mission of the Church*.[1]

1. Transcending Boundaries

Definitions are curious things: by putting limits on concepts they help us to understand more. This means that by their nature they create boundaries and draw distinctions. Now it is well known that in our days many prefer to use their own arbitrary pleasure to take and manage what they want, when, how, and where they choose, in such a way that hard and fast concepts are as welcome as a cumbersome rock in a dinghy. Sometimes it seems it would be better to do without the clarity that definitions bring, in order to avoid the borders and divisions they entail. Indeed from this mindset the stuff of dogmas, absolute truths, fundamental norms, and authoritative language is often associated with fanaticism, the weird and the bizarre. Yet without definitions our words, symbols and images would lack that specific meaning we use them to convey. For definitions do serve a purpose. Without the Council of Trent's definition of transubstantiation,[2] our understanding of the Eucharist would not be so precise, so enriching, so focused. There are definitions too for 'church',[3] 'communion'[4] and 'our faith in Christ'[5] that are useful, and from time to time it is good to go back and consider them. Limits have been set out in order to help us understand what we mean by the Eucharist, and the encyclical *EdE* is intended to remind us of some of these.

Alas, there are other kinds of boundaries and walls. These are offsprings of our flawed humanity, conceits of our imagination and fall-outs from history. It is the fallenness of man that creates division, that destroys and impedes communion, and it was the life and work of 'that man' to overcome these faults of ours. Redemption from our sinful nature is our salvation, our happiness, our end. The bridge needed to cross that divide is given to us in a permanent fashion in the Eucharist. It implies an openness to the transcendent, and to change and continual reformation. Christ, the reconciler and healer of our weakened state, by the aid of the Holy Spirit restores our natural inclination toward the Father so often suppressed in our fallenness, and raises our lives to their true dignity. Turning back to him in the Eucharist, we refresh our memory, clear our awareness and are nourished plentifully. The Eucharist guides us on our pilgrimage through life as we seek to transcend those limits, build and cross bridges over the divides, and resolve our imperfections. Requiring that leap of faith to understand, it is also a mystery that brings peace by satisfying our ultimate need in making God present among us, for, as St Augustine confessed, 'our heart is restless until it rests in you'.[6]

2. The Faith-Culture Dynamic

Who is not familiar with the liturgy of the Eucharist, when 'earth unites with heaven to sing the new song of creation as we adore and praise you for ever'?[7] It is a timeless, and fearless, moment of unity. The Eucharist in its threefold dimension of sacrifice, presence and nourishment engages us in the eternal song of victory. By the work of the Holy Spirit, God-made-man offers himself for our sake, uniting us to him that we may reach our perfection in the participation and reflection of his eternal glory. The real presence of Christ, i.e., the presence *par excellence* that converts the substance of the bread and wine through which Christ becomes present whole and entire, is for us our salvation; it lifts us up to him, offering us a participation in the Transcendent. This dynamic activity is a far cry from the emptiness and soullessness which seem to strike some of our contemporaries who meander in the spiritual homelessness of those who find no peace, being without the God of Revelation. Our concern to share our joyful faith-lives with our contemporaries demands that we know them and their cultures, and thus re-echo the Psalmist's question:

> *Who is man that you should spare a thought for him?*
> *The son of man that you should care for him?* (Ps 8)

Since time immemorial people have sought to understand the human being: who he is, what he has and what he does. Many are the adjectives that are given to him – *homo faber, homo technicus, homo amicus, homo politicus, homo sapiens* and even *homo religiosus*[8] – but here I want to take the words of *Fides et Ratio*, where the human person is considered as both the child of a culture, and the parent of a culture.[9] As a human product, 'culture is an incarnation of liberty and of human transcendence'.[10] Whether we think of the arts or sciences, politics, values, customs or beliefs, culture is the oceanic reality by which we strive 'to achieve true and full humanity'.[11] This incorporates religious, spiritual, social and physical elements. Although the Romans used to say that *faber est suae quisque fortunae*, it must be remembered that although we have our training, our education, our formation and our culture, our destiny – our final end – is neither our creation nor our possession but a gift of God. To prepare for that, there is no such means as a perfect culture. There are just cultures more or less effective in making progress towards that perfection desired by God; there are cultures which are more or less marked by the gospel. The same psalmist gives us the key to understand the human person, and to understand cultures, by underlining our fundamental relationship with God. We are not alone. Made in the image and likeness of God, the human person is still minded by God. Cultures are not aimless, but by their exposure to the gospel they become more harmonious with our journey home to the Father.

This same thought was well-expressed during the 1974 Synod of Bishops, and was summed up in the Post-Synodal Apostolic Exhortation *Evangelii Nuntiandi*:

> The gospel, and therefore evangelisation, are certainly not identical with culture and are independent in regard to all cultures. Nevertheless, the kingdom which the gospel proclaims is lived by those who are profoundly linked to a culture, and the building up of the kingdom cannot avoid borrowing the elements of human culture or cultures. Though independent of cultures, the gospel and evangelisation are not necessarily incompatible with them; rather they are capable of permeating them all without becoming subject to any one of them.[12]

Cultures then can be shaped and moulded by the gospel. Aware of this, Pope John Paul II established the Pontifical Council for Culture to give to 'the whole church a common impulse in the continually renewed encounter between the salvific message of the gospel and the multiplicity of cultures, in the diversity of cultures to which she must carry her fruits of grace'.[13] The Eucharist is the source and summit of this missionary activity, and so in this article I wish to consider in juxtaposition two dynamic realities: the Eucharist and Culture. Bestowed on us for our perfection, they nurture, shape and bring us back to that blessed communion with God which is our ultimate end.

3. The Eucharist is the Sacrament of Sacraments

The Eucharist contains the church's entire spiritual wealth: Christ himself, our Passover and living bread. As the continuation of his sacrifice, its sacredness comes from Christ's action. Every grace is linked to the sacrifice and nourishment of the Eucharist; every gift of God is intrinsically bound up with the redemptive action of Christ. These truths are presented in the vocabulary of theological discourse, but through the more approachable symbolic and sacramental character of the Eucharist we enter more personally and more fully into the mystery of his life and work, death and resurrection. In it, what is intangible becomes tangible, what is ineffable becomes real, what is invisible becomes visible. St Thomas Aquinas gave an elegant description of these sacramental signs: 'A sacrament is a sign that commemorates what precedes it – Christ's Passion; demonstrates what is accomplished in us through Christ's Passion – grace; and prefigures what that Passion pledges to us – future glory'.[14]

Cultures are intimately linked to the signs, symbols, languages, mindsets, reference points and thought patterns that emerge from within them and shape them. In a certain sense, these render visible the invisible: cultures are known by their outward expressions. Each culture has its own symbols, beliefs, truths, ideas and concepts to transmit. Through dance, poetry, music, the written word, other visual aids, and politics, the sciences and culinary techniques, cultures find a way to express themselves, to grow and to facilitate the betterment of their component members; without symbols, without interpretative context, the messages would be void of significance and cultures would fail in their central purpose, which is to propel the person to a fuller realisation of his or her potential. The countless boundaries to transcend in this process of growth are transcended by what is passed on through the symbolism of cultures: memory, momentary action, and future guidance.

4. The Eucharist is a Sacrificial Memorial

'The Eucharist is the memorial of Christ's Passover, the making present and the sacramental offering of his unique sacrifice, in the liturgy of the church which is his Body'.[15] His command to 'Do this as a memorial of me' (Lk 22:19) is the basis of the apostles' priesthood and formulates a reminder of the past, a proclamation of the marvellous things Christ has done for us;

and the institution of the sacrifice of the altar is a gift to the
church that makes present the one sacrifice of Christ. As the
bread and wine become the body and blood of Christ all creation
is transfigured and called to transformation, change and true
conversion. Nothing remains closed in on itself, and by this
sacrament each person, each culture and indeed history itself is
'reopened'.[16] As such it is also a catalyst for the Christian to engage in the world. This final point is underlined by the Holy
Father in *EdE* by the citation of Homily 50 on the Gospel of
Matthew by St John Chrysostom (d. 407), a text previously used
in his encyclical *Sollicitudo rei socialis*, with its central theme that
whoever serves the poor person serves Christ, and whoever rejects the poor person rejects Christ. The sacrifice of Christ present in the Eucharist renews, regenerates and opens us up to
new horizons, new opportunities and new responsibilities. It is
not simply a static event that we watch passively, nor a means to
transmit our memory, but it is a provocative imperative increasing our sense of responsibility for the world.

When the Holy Father asked me to prepare the ground for
the 1991 Synod of Bishops, which in post-1989 Europe addressed the theme: 'We are witnesses to Christ who has set us
free', he thought it important to focus on Europe's gospel-rooted
culture, and so I outlined three central categories of Europe's
patrimony for special attention: memory, conscience and project.[17] It became clear that Christianity not only is a legacy that
shaped and created this old continent, but also that the gospel
imperative continues to be a catalyst that breaks down barriers.
So when we address the theme of Catholic culture, we do not
limit ourselves to the Irish Catholicism of generations past, nor
the fossilised memories of the Middle Ages when the Catholic
Church became a cultural factor as much as a religious one,
rather we must address the continually saving meeting of the
gospel and the cultures of our day. Although Europe's Christian
heritage is obvious to all, it would be complacent to rest on the
laurels of an old Christian culture – the old wineskins of Europe's
culture need to be renewed for the flood of new life which pours

continually from the Eucharist. Sacrifices built this old continent, and they are required again today to re-evangelise it
through the way of love. The Eucharist which builds the church
also urges us to transform our cultures by new sacrifices, in imitation of Christ, and so to reach out to today's people in all their
cultures in order that the gospel may come to be incarnated in
those cultures in new ways, with fresh vigour and with great
sensitivity. This is the call to hand on the faith at the heart of cultures which the 2002 Plenary Assembly of this Dicastery described as follows:

> It is directed to humankind, to every person and to the whole
> person, to make each one a child of the Father and a witness
> of the gospel, in the unity of the body of the church. It is a
> complex *process*: it takes place in *time*, and is directed towards
> *persons* who come from a particular *background*; it implies the
> *transmission* of content – *what has been revealed* – and an invit-
> ation to *life*, where *grace* encounters each person's *freedom*.[18]

5. The Eucharist is a gift

The Eucharist is a complete, sacrificial, ever-new, redemptive,
and transforming gift. It is for us a *mysterium fidei* and a *mysterium
caritatis*, a mystery of faith and a mystery of charity. It is 'the
promise of a humanity renewed by his love'.[19] Participation in
the Eucharist demands a commitment to changing our lives and
making them eucharistic. The seed of living hope that it gives to
us and implants in us supports those two other virtues that it
nourishes: faith in the completion of the Christian story and
charity towards all creation. It is this 'transfigured existence and
a commitment to transforming the world in accordance with the
gospel which splendidly illustrates the eschatological tension
inherent in the celebration of the Eucharist and in the Christian
life as a whole, "Come, Lord Jesus!".'[20] Christ has come as gift,
and, as we await in joyful hope the future coming of our saviour,
he remains given to us in the Eucharist.

Gifts involve a giver and a receiver. Giving is a moment in
which to bring out the absolute alterity of the other. This respect

for the other is a prerequisite for evangelisation. Often our friendships can be marred by an unconscious tendency to want to dominate or even possess the other. For Emmanuel Levinas this is a relationship doomed to failure. 'If one could possess, grasp, and know the other, it would not be other.'[21] The other person's alterity has to be totally respected, even if his or her presence is an 'irruption' into my life. 'The relationship with the other is not an idyllic and harmonious relationship of communion, or a sympathy through which we put ourselves in the other's place … the relationship with the other is a relationship with a mystery'.[22] And we can go even further by living as gift and surrendering to the other a real priority over us.

The transformation of cultures, a gospel imperative, must pay similar respect to the otherness of difference; diversity within unity is no barrier to the evangelisation of cultures. '[The church] takes the spiritual qualities and endowments of every age and nation, and with supernatural riches it causes them to blossom, as it were, from within: it fortifies, completes and restores them in Christ.'[23] It seeks neither to dominate them or be submissive to them, but to enrich them. This is evangelisation. It does not seek to threaten cultures or to suppress them but to bring them to fulfilment.

6. The Eucharist is the presence of Christ for us

There is something very gratifying about knowing that God became man *for us*. It is also very disturbing. Awareness of his self-giving act produces not just an intellectual response but also an emotional one. He poured out his heart for us in giving us the Eucharist: 'It is a sacrament of love, a sign of unity, a bond of charity, a paschal banquet "in which Christ is consumed, the mind is filled with grace, and a pledge of future glory is given to us"'.[24] It is engaging, because we continually find ourselves embraced by a God who so loves us that he gave himself for us. It is not just Christ, it is Christ *for us*. We too are called to cross that same boundary – to go beyond ourselves and live our life for others. The absolute alterity of the eucharistic sacrifice is our example.

'*Genus humanum arte et ratione vivit.*'[25] Man lives off culture; it makes him fully human, and makes society fully humane. Cultures exist *for us*, indeed when cultures or societies exclude man they often turn against him.[26] The plurality of cultures which meet in the new Areopagus of UNESCO were told in an extraordinary speech by John Paul II that cultures exist for man and that 'man lives a life which is truly human thanks to culture'.[27] From every perspective, including sociological and ethnological ones, there is but one purpose to culture: to let the human person attain to the fullness of humanity. It aids man to 'be', not simply to 'do'. What we have and possess is only relative, what counts is who we are. And part of who we are is our openness to the transcendent. As Pascal put it: *l'homme passe infiniment l'homme.*[28]

Nor can culture avoid this dynamic. It too should not be closed in on itself, despite the common tendency to fossilise cultures. While a solid foundation and good training let us stand on the shoulders of the giants of the past, it is culture's flexibility to change, adapt and grow, combining memory, consciousness and project, that ensures its ability to respect the human person. A rigid approach to culture, summed up in the assertive claim, 'that is what has always been done', kills the new life, the seed of the future that cultures should foster. Cultures seek to surpass their own limitations. After the model of the incarnation, the pastoral approach to culture seeks to ensure a new life-giving meeting between the transcendent God and mortal man.[29] 'Faith's encounter with different cultures has created something new: when they are deeply rooted in experience, cultures show forth the human being's characteristic openness to the universal and the transcendent'.[30] As authors of our cultures, we count upon our shared experience to transmit our values to others. When we cannot persuade with words and concepts, it is by our love and our heart-stirring action that the emotion which is in all of us comes into play, and provokes a distinctively Christian response: we go beyond ourselves. The love of God, and the love of neighbour, children, parents, relatives or the fellow who annoys us, are all consequences or expressions of the same self-denying love. Our existing for others in this way permits us to create something new.

7. The Eucharist is the source and the summit of evangelisation.
The Eucharist is the very heart of the church, and 'the church draws her life from the Eucharist'.[31] By Christ she is nourished and enlightened.[32] The Eucharist is celebrated in cultures and as such it evangelises them, taking on the splendour of a lived reality; it becomes contagious, and in a manner of speaking it 'warms our hearts'.[33] The Eucharist builds the church, giving its members the faith, hope and charity to press on in their journey through life, and places at its heart the command to go and spread the good news: *ite missa est!* Confident in the transforming power of the Eucharist, it is the responsibility of all who partake of it to share its fruits with all we meet.

Clearly, the culture of the people to whom we talk must be taken seriously if we are to win their respect. The new evangelisation must aim at the expectations of our contemporaries, not our own preconceived ideas. It is their worries, their concerns, their hopes that we share; the church shares the *gaudium et spes, lux et angor* of all the world. To do this, she uses the privileged forum of culture to find footholds for the new evangelisation. Centres for the study and awareness of culture such as The Irish Centre for Faith and Culture help find the moral and spiritual landmarks that people living in today's cultures can recognise and embrace, in order to lead lives worthy of our fundamental vocation. These are the words the Holy Father has written to that effect:

> Cultural centres offer to the church the possibility of presence and action in the field of cultural change. They constitute, in effect, public forums which allow the church to make widely known, in creative dialogue, Christian convictions about man, woman, family, work, economy, society, politics, international life, the environment. Thus they are places of listening, respect and tolerance.[34]

8. Conclusion

The salvation of Christ is universal. By it, 'the walls separating the different cultures collapsed'.[35] And through the field of culture the perceived limits of man are transcended: 'Man knows how to go infinitely beyond himself, as is clearly demonstrated by the efforts made by so many creative geniuses in order to catch and fix, in works of art and thought, transcendent values of beauty and truth, more or less fleetingly intuited as an expression of the absolute.'[36] Flooding out from these truths, we can be confident that the Eucharist, the sacrament that involves us most of all, is a preferential means to bring us to that fulfilment for which we were created. It is held in the bosom of the church, and it creates for us a spirituality of communion that is proper to the mystery of the incarnation, where the Word takes flesh and redeems mankind in ways that, with the help of grace, are then shared in ways that today's cultures can understand.

In the definition offered in *EdE*, the church is a communion 'both in its invisible dimension, which, in Christ and through the working of the Holy Spirit, unites us to the Father and among ourselves, and in its visible dimension, which entails communion in the teaching of the apostles, in the sacraments and in the church's hierarchical order.'[37] Such are the definitions that create limits – but which also help us to transcend our boundaries and reach our final aims.

Rapt in eucharistic wonderment, our lives and our cultures are caught up in the light of the gospel and through it we embrace our God in a foretaste of fulfilment. For in the supreme sacrifice which is the Eucharist, the furthest, the highest, the deepest, the widest and the longest – the bounds all creation – are consummated. And for that we join in the transcendent and limitless hymn of praise of our God the Redeemer:

Praise to the Holiest in the height
And in the depth be praise
In all his words most wonderful
Most sure in all his ways.[38]

CHAPTER THIRTEEN

'On the night he was betrayed'

Cardinal Godfried Danneels

It was on the evening of Holy Thursday that the greatest mystery of our faith was given to us, namely the mystery of the Body and Blood of the Lord Jesus. At first sight nothing could appear simpler. The table was set; on it was bread and wine; around the table were Jesus, Peter, and the Eleven. However, on that evening the Lord spoke as he had never spoken before, and he did things that he had not done before. Around that table was gathered the nascent church; or rather the church that was soon to be born was gathered around its Lord. With him it experienced a time of intense love and of great warmth, but also a time of suffering and shadow. Year by year the Holy Spirit invites the church to enter into the mystery of Holy Thursday, to understand more deeply the words and deeds of Jesus, and to enter with him into the paschal mystery. Happy are you who have been given all this, to live and to contemplate!

The language of wonder and of love
I could speak about this mystery of Holy Thursday in the clear and precise language of exegetes and theologians. Indeed the church will never be able to do without such language. However, I prefer to speak to you in the language of the heart, the language of wonder and love, the language of poets, great and small, of lovers, and of prayer. This language itself is but the feeble echo of what is said within God, when the Father speaks to the Son, and when the Son replies to the Father, 'Here I am, Father, ready to do your will!' Likewise it is the language of the Spirit, this breath of love within God which has become the breath of the church. I invite you to look with love and to contemplate what the Lord did on the night he was betrayed.

Here are four pictures to be looked at in faith, and to be gazed upon in love. These four pictures will invite you to pray.

FIRST PICTURE: THE WASHING OF THE FEET

Could St John have forgotten?
The gospel of John speaks about the Last Supper, but John did not mention what Jesus did with the bread and wine, nor did he report his words. Could St John have forgotten?

It would be hard to believe such a thing! Is not the Eucharist at the very heart of the paschal mystery of Jesus? Besides, is this not 'the hour' about which St John spoke several times, and the summit to which his entire gospel works its way up? From the miracle at Cana and the multiplication of the loaves, the whole gospel is waiting for this 'hour' with its table abundantly spread. How could John the Evangelist, the messenger of the good news, have forgotten, or how could he have omitted such good news – the good news *par excellence*? Maybe he was satisfied with the story of the Last Supper as recounted by Matthew, Mark and Luke, as well as Paul, each of whom told the story from his own point of view. These four had already spoken of this last meal of Jesus with his friends. As the fifth witness, John threw a fresh glance upon the same event. He had a message to communicate which the others had not mentioned. Let us listen to him with all the greater attention.

An in-depth look
No, John did not forget. For him, what is at the heart of things is invisible to the eyes. If we are to realise fully what Jesus did on that evening we must probe the very depths. John proposed to us a sort of X-ray of the Last Supper. He did not stop at what is visible: he forced us to rediscover what lies within. At the very moment in his gospel when we would have expected an account of the Last Supper, he proposes to the reader what seems to be a completely different picture, at least at first sight. In this picture Jesus is washing the feet of his disciples. The other evangelists, like St Paul, are artists who cling to shapes and colours. John, on

the other hand, goes straight to the invisible, to the very heart of the Last Supper. He comments, 'The meal had begun' (Jn 13:2), but does not stop there. He gazes into the distance. Beyond the Jewish Passover ritual, he invites us to discern what no human eye can see. Admittedly, Jesus was the thoughtful host who invited his disciples to eat with him. Certainly he was the priest of the New Covenant who offered himself as food to his own people. Yet, says John, Jesus is more than this. He revealed himself to his apostles and to the church as the slave, the Servant of God of whom the prophet Isaiah spoke (Isa 52:13-53:12).

He, the Lord and Master, washed the feet of his disciples; the greatest made himself small, smaller than all the others. The Master of the house took the humiliating role of a slave. At a Jewish meal it would have been a slave, or else the youngest child, who had the duty of fetching the basin of water to wash the hands of the guests. Jesus did more, he washed his disciples' feet, not their hands. Such is the framework; such is the profound setting of the fresco of the Last Supper. There was more taking place here than a meal, even a paschal meal. The greatest made himself the least. Because of his love, the Lord made himself the Servant. We have already perceived this gift of himself in the action of distributing bread and wine. We have understood as much from the words, 'This is my Body which will be given up for you.' Yet if John had not written we would never have begun to plumb the ultimate depths of this mystery. We would never have realised just how great was God's love for us: the Son of God made himself our slave.

God's love always comes first

What is love? The source of God's love is not found in the attributes or merits of the other person, whereas human love is based on the worth of the partner. 'You are beautiful, intelligent, kind and good; I love you because I find you lovable.' That is not how God loves, or Jesus. Their love does not depend on our worth. On the contrary, God's love finds its source in God himself. God's love is freely given, and it precedes our love. It does not presuppose any human qualities, but rather causes them. It was such a love that Jesus knew when he was in the bosom of the Father.

As John has revealed to us, 'This is the love I mean, not our love for God, but that God loved us first.' This is how Jesus loved men. He was always the first to move towards others. His whole life long he showed gratuitous love by his ministries of the word, of forgiveness of sin, and of healing. It was this love that led him to his fulfilment. In that hour of his agony, 'Jesus, who had always loved those who were his own in the world, now showed how perfect his love was' (Jn 13:1). It was at that moment when Jesus was beginning the night of suffering, the night when all abandoned him, that he showed his love to be stronger than any human scale could measure. It was like a torrent that is forced through a narrow passage: the narrower the passage, the stronger the river. And so the love of Jesus attained its fullness at the hour when he had to face the narrow passage of death. That impatient love became irresistible.

'Jesus got up from the table, removed his outer garment, and taking a towel wrapped it round his waist. He then poured water into a basin and began to wash his disciples' feet and to wipe them with the towel he was wearing' (Jn 13:4-5). Jesus rose, left the table and broke the convivial circle. From the moment of the washing of the feet until the cross, he was alone. He went his own way even in his manner of loving, and his loved ones were not able to follow him. His love had its own logic, which no one could understand until the morning of Pentecost, the day when the Spirit began to teach the church all that Jesus had said. The logic of the divine love is as follows: the master became the servant, the greatest took on the task of serving the least. Jesus knelt even before Judas, who had already betrayed him. Only John reported this scene. Is that because he was always the first to understand the love of Jesus? Is it not rather because it was his responsibility to bring the basin in which the others were to wash their hands? The Lord had forestalled John; he took upon himself that humble service. Could John ever have forgotten?

The washing of the feet: icon of love

John put that memory in writing and bestowed it on the church. He wrote it for us. 'Do you not see', St John is saying to us, 'that each time you gather to celebrate the Eucharist, that same scene is reproduced in all your churches. Invisibly, the Lord rises from the table and begins to wash the feet of each one of you, men and women, beginning with the smallest. Gaze deeply, you who were not present on the night he was betrayed. Let me declare it to you. At every Mass the Lord pushes his love to extremes. He pushes his love to the point of humiliation. He makes himself the servant of all.' That is what John is telling us.

And what about us? We are vacant or distracted. We are scarcely conscious of what is happening. We are not even disconcerted by this action, as Peter was. We are in the sound sleep of habit. We are scarcely touched by what our eyes are seeing and our ears are hearing. We see the table set with bread and wine; but it is difficult for us to see beyond the visible and to be touched by this action of the Lord who humbles himself before each of us, including the man or woman who is ready to betray him.

Who will rouse us from this sleep? Who, if not John himself, can restore to the church this deep, deep look, this look of love which sees with the eyes of the heart? Every year, on the evening of Holy Thursday, the church asks us the question that Jesus addressed to his own: 'Do you understand what I have done to you?' (Jn 13:12). It proclaims the gospel of the washing of the feet just as it has received it from the hand of John, the disciple whom Jesus loved. It invites us to contemplate at length this 'icon of extreme love', until this gospel scene is imprinted on the retina of our eyes and descends into our hearts, there to remain. With John, the church says to each of us, 'Come back once more without fear into the circle of the Twelve and find your place around the table. Put yourself in Peter's place, on the right of Jesus, and learn with Peter about repentant love; ask your question like Philip; become James, or Thomas or Andrew; and finally place yourself on the left, in John's place, the place of the beloved near the heart of Jesus. But beware of the duplicity of Judas!'

And Peter

Each year John wrests the church out of the apathy into which it risks falling. He shakes it, shouting 'Wake up! The bridegroom is coming!' And look at Peter: he is saying, 'Are you going to wash my feet?' (Jn 13:6) – Lord, how could you humble yourself before me? But Jesus did not reply to his question. He gave him to understand that he could not answer his question at that time: 'At present you do not know what I am doing, but later you will understand' (Jn 13:7). Then Peter burst out, 'Never! You shall never wash my feet!' (Jn 13:8a). That Jesus acted contrary to the accepted proprieties was one thing, but when he refused all explanation it was too much! Peter refused vehemently. Jesus replied with an equally vehement 'Yes!': 'If I do not wash you, you can have nothing in common with me' (Jn 13:8b).

This was not the first time that the Lord and Peter clashed. Far from it! There had been other occasions on which Peter spoke an emphatic No! For example, when Our Lord announced his passion for the first time: 'Taking him aside Peter started to remonstrate with him. But turning and seeing his disciples he rebuked Peter, and said to him: Get behind me, Satan!' (Mk 8:32b). That conflict centred around a matter of principle: Jesus could not countenance Peter's 'human ways of thinking, which were incompatible with God's ways' (Mk 8:33b). In the matter of the washing of the feet a problem arose which was no less vital, about the nature of divine love – which is always first. There was also the question of the humility of the church and of its 'yes' to God's unconditional grace. Like Peter, the church must know the profound nature of the Lord's love for it: it is loved by God first, and that love is beyond its capacity to return. Like Mary, the church learns that it is very small before God. It does not earn its salvation by its own efforts and by its own asceticism, but receives everything from God as a free gift.

In this story of the washing of the feet we can see the essence of Paul's experience: we are saved by the humble obedience of faith and by God's grace, not by works. John was merely writing some variations on this same theme. 'This is the love I mean, not our love for God, but God's love for us' (1 Jn 4:10). What Paul learned on the road to Damascus John already knew from the tenth hour of the first day spent with Jesus (cf. Jn 1:39).

'Let it happen to you'

'Long before any actions of your own, let yourself be purified by the Lord.' This is what we are told by the imagery in the account of the washing of the feet. The scene is profoundly eucharistic. Throughout the history of the church the inexhaustible spring of the divine mercy has been gushing forth. His body has been handed over, his blood has been poured out 'for us and for all, so that sins may be forgiven'. God acts first. He asks of us only one thing, namely to be sufficiently humble to let ourselves be loved by him. He asks of us only a disciple's heart, open to faith and to repentance. Let it happen to you; let yourself be overcome by divine love. That is the message of the washing of the feet; that is our part in the eucharistic mystery.

Christian tradition has always recognised in the washing of the feet the image and the source of the sacraments, which are occasions of divine grace for those who have a humble or a child-like heart. These sacraments are baptism, penance, and above all, the Eucharist.

Is God's forgiveness too easy?

Putting himself at the service of his church, the Lord made a slave of himself. Peter, and then the others, let Jesus do with them as he wished. 'In the kingdom', says Jesus, 'the Master becomes a slave; let the greatest of you become the least.' The world has been turned upside-down.

There is a trap here. One can reach the stage of counting on God's pardon even before one has committed a sin. At that point the free gift becomes a pretext for making no further effort. Abandonment to the mercy of God becomes laziness, presumption, and almost blasphemy. Mercy is inflated to the point where it disappears. If God has ceased to hate evil how can he forgive it? He has no longer any reason to do so, since there is no longer any fault. And so there disappears that tension between God's law which scrutinises us, and the mercy which pardons our fault. So too, the balance between justice and love, and between truth and forgiveness, is undermined. When we reduce God to the level of humanity he ceases to be God; he is only an idol to be adored, an idol made by our hands. St Paul says, 'However great the number of sins committed, grace was even greater. Does it follow that we should remain in sin so as to let grace have greater scope? Of course not!' (Rom 5:20b; 6:1). No, God is God! That is why Jesus, after he had served like a slave, put his garment back on and resumed his place at the table. He says to them, 'You call me Master and Lord, and rightly: so I am' (Jn 13:13).

If he did not continue to be Master and Lord, how could the church express wonder at the mystery of God's humiliation of himself out of love? 'His state was divine, yet he assumed the condition of a slave' (Phil 2: 6a, 7a). Jesus is both Master and Servant, God and man. No-one can break that unity. As John says, 'Any spirit that divides Jesus is not from God' (1 Jn 4:3). The same thing applies to the Eucharist: Jesus makes himself small, but beneath the humble species of bread and wine it is the Son of God who is present.

'I gave you an example …'
Let us take another step. The washing of the feet is not just a touching scene to be pondered and contemplated: it is not just a spectacle, it is also a demand, a mission to do the same for others. Jesus said, 'I have given you an example so that you may copy what I have done to you' (Jn 13:15). It is not sufficient for the church to look at what Jesus has done. It must do the same in its turn, every day, until he comes again. Its words and actions must conform to the attitude of its Lord, who washed the feet of his disciples. It must always be more humble than the littlest of

its children. It must assume the role of servant. In everything it does the church must serve: in its ministry of the word, in its pastoral work, and in its work of sanctification, it is the servant of everyone, even if it does not at the same time cease to be the Spouse of the Lord.

This humble service is not however reserved to the ordained ministers, the bishops, priests and deacons. All the brothers and sisters who together make up the church are invited 'to wash each other's feet'. Thus the Christian is called to a double kind of humility. First of all, to remain open to the grace of the Lord and to let him do as he wills. Secondly, not to keep that grace for oneself, but to pass it on to one's brothers and sisters by putting oneself at their service. And so, on the eve of his passion, the Lord Jesus entrusted this grace of service to his disciples, so that they would be transformed into servants of God, servants of the church and also of the whole of humanity, 'until he comes again'.

Where are the smallest ones?
It behoves us to listen to the words of the Lord, 'Go and look for the least in the church and in the world.' But where are they? They are the countless men and women who are hidden in the anonymity of the town, who never enter the wedding banqueting-hall to eat with us the Lord's meal. They are the ones who only enter a church when it is deserted, to pause at the places where Mary and the saints watch over the poor in the dim light of the side-chapels. There are also the thousands of young people who wander through the towns, without knowing where they are going or why they are living. The church must wash their feet also.

And what about the little children? They are welcome to our liturgy, we say. Deep down, however, there remains an unspoken persistent feeling: they disturb us by their noise and their impatience. They always talk at the wrong time! Yet the Lord is waiting for each of them to wash their little feet too. For there is no one so small that the Lord does not make himself smaller still! What about the stranger? How difficult it is to kneel before him and wash his feet. That is why Jesus tells us, 'Now that you know this, happiness will be yours if you behave accordingly (Jn 13:17).

SECOND PICTURE: THE LAST SUPPER

On the evening of Holy Thursday, John, with his deep and med-itative gaze, witnessed the washing of the feet. That was the hidden face of the eucharistic meal. Let us now turn to the Last Supper, which all the evangelists recount. For 'happy are your eyes because they see, your ears because they hear! I tell you solemnly, many prophets and holy men longed to see what you see and never saw it, to hear what you hear and never heard it' (Mt 13:16-17).

The entire city is waiting for this hour
Had Jesus been thinking for a long time about this last meal with his friends? He lived his whole life with this 'hour' in mind. He awaited it, shivering with apprehension, yet also trembling with joy. Jesus had foreseen everything. When the time came it did not take him by surprise. On the contrary, he is master of time and he rules it. He had longed so much to eat this Passover with his friends before he suffered (cf. Lk 22:15). He prepared for this hour carefully, like someone writing his will. He chose Peter and John and sent them to take charge of the preparations. It would be for them to help him as he would leave this world to go to the Father (cf. Lk 22:7-13).

One would almost think that the whole city was awaiting this 'hour', for it seemed that everything was ready when Peter and John arrived. Here was the man carrying the pitcher of water. He showed them his house, with its large upper room strewn with carpets. The only thing missing was the paschal lamb. God would provide, as he did for Abraham on the mountain. From this evening onwards Jesus himself would be the paschal Lamb.

Peter and John, the priesthood and love

Who are they, these men who are preparing the table of the kingdom? Peter and John. Or rather, they are the priesthood and love, the two pillars supporting the church and its Eucharist. The celebration of the Lord's meal requires from the church both the priesthood and the communion of love. It needs both Peter and John; the one cannot act without the other. They are inseparable, but they are not the same thing. The Eucharist needs the priest, and it needs the communion of love which is the church; each contributes its irreplaceable part. Healthy communities have no difficulty in linking the one with the other: the priest and the assembly face each other on the two sides of the altar. They are barely conscious of each other, so much is their attention drawn to the transfixed Lamb, which is standing upright on God's altar (cf. Rev 5:6). Yet when passions are roused in the church people turn away from the altar to look at each other and to ask that tortured question, 'Who is the greatest in the church?' Then Jesus takes a little child and places him before them and declares him to be an example to them. And so the fever subsides. It is at that moment that everyone resumes an attitude of contemplation before the humble gifts of bread and wine, in other words, before Jesus who has come to serve.

Two actions and two phrases

'When the hour came, He took his place at table and the apostles with him' (Luke 22:14). Then Jesus performed two actions accompanied by a few words. That was all. Yet it was enough to enable the church to live until the day when he will return to bring our history to a close. How can such riches be concealed in so little? That is how it is with most of the important events of men: the decisive event itself lasts but a moment; it is the effects that last far beyond. The yarn from a ball of wool seems to unravel almost endlessly as it is drawn out. It is the same with the death of a dear one: it is over in an instant, but it will be years before the spouse really grasps what has happened, and the children really understand that they are orphans. Likewise the 'I do' spoken by the fiancés at a wedding is just a single phrase that each one says to the other. Yet how important it is for their future, for their good days and their bad days, their times of joy and their times of trouble!

It is the same with the Eucharist. The entire history of God's dealings with mankind is concentrated within those words, and there all of creation finds its centre. As the bread and wine are transformed into him, Christ penetrates, so to speak, the heart of matter and places it on the way to the resurrection. Thus the Eucharist is the bridgehead of the new world. Since the advent of the Eucharist the kingdom of God pursues its course irresistibly, until God becomes all things in all, and the upper room in Jerusalem becomes the centre of the universe and of all its galaxies. 'How awe-inspiring is this place! This is nothing less than a house of God; this is the gate of heaven. Truly God is in this place and we did not know it' (cf. Gen 28:16-17).

'He took bread…'
'He took bread,' say the scriptures. Obviously: what else could he have done if he wished to give bread to feed his friends? And likewise for the wine.

All the gospels recount the same sentence: 'he took bread …' It could be said that they all insist upon it. If Jesus took bread and wine it means that he wanted to show to his church that he needed the things of creation – bread, wine – and of man's labour. He could have chosen other ways of being present: a written word, or a simple memory. He could have, but he chose not to. He wanted to make use both of what he himself had created and of what human labour produces. He did not want to be a passing stranger who hardly touches the earth, which he is already leaving to return to his Father. No, Jesus wanted to be one of us and to remain with us. That is why he wished to take on a body and to be born of Mary: there is no part of his humanity that he has not received from her. He wished to become truly man, and to take his place in the long line of human generations from Abraham, the father in faith of us all, even of Mary. In the same way that he came twenty centuries ago, he wanted to remain with his friends by embracing his own creation, taking on the appearance of bread and wine.

That is why the terrestrial realities and the work of man are so precious in the eyes of God. It is not only because they are the work of his creation, but also and above all because since Bethlehem he cannot look upon his creation without seeing the face of his Son. His only Son has, so to speak, taken root in the heart of our human world, and he stands in solidarity with the great family of man.

That is why the bread and wine are so precious in the eyes of Christians. It is not only because of the hunger in the world, which raises its loud cry to heaven, or indeed because of the scandal of waste. It is more than that; it is because the Lord made use of it to assure his permanent presence among us. One finds among poor people, and monks (the poor in spirit), a respect for bread that is almost religious. Watch how carefully they take it in their hands, break it slowly and eat it. They do so with actions that are almost liturgical.

Saint Francis: 'See, brothers, the humility of God'
'See', said St Francis, 'each day the Lord makes himself little to come onto the altar, exactly as he descended from his divine throne to enter Mary's womb … Listen, my friends! If the Blessed Virgin is so honoured, and rightly so, because she carried Christ in her saintly womb; if the blessed Baptist trembled, not daring even to touch the sacred head of his God; if the tomb in which lay for a time the body of Christ is surrounded with veneration: how holy, just and worthy should he be who holds Christ in his hands, receives him in his mouth and in his heart, and gives him as food to others! What wretched and miserable weakness, if while holding him in your hands you are concerned with anything else in the world. Let every man fear, let the whole world tremble, let the heavens rejoice when Christ, the Son of the living God, is present on the altar in the hands of the priest! See, brothers, the humility of God, and do him

homage in your hearts. You too should humble yourselves that you may be fit to be exalted by him' *(Letter to the Order).*

'He broke the bread …'
'He broke it …' Here is another detail which is underlined by three of the evangelists, and which seems to be an obvious fact, namely that the big round loaf must be broken so that everyone can partake of it and eat it. Yet that breaking of bread is much more than a practical action. Christian tradition has always understood that the action of breaking the bread had a further significance. The bread is broken, not simply for practical purposes but as a symbol of the passion. The Lord allowed himself to be broken, crushed by suffering. As Isaiah had written long beforehand, 'he was crushed for our sins' (Isa 53:5).

'Obedience' is a word that is often difficult for us to accept. It has a bitter taste and evokes rather disagreeable memories and experiences. Yet the word 'obedience' was not a negative one for Jesus. In his mouth it was charged with all the joy and tenderness of the 'Yes' which he utters unceasingly to his Father. From all eternity the Son has been obedient to all that the Father expects from him. It is this same 'Yes' that Jesus uttered when he became incarnate in Mary's womb: 'Here I am, Father, ready to do your will.' Jesus lived that total obedience all through his life, notably in the Garden of Gethsemane, and right up to the supreme 'Yes', when he consented to being broken on the cross. That this 'Yes' of Jesus was so painful did not necessarily follow from his obedience as such. It was our refusal to accept the Father's envoy that made that obedience so painful. In the heart of Jesus it was to be only a joy to abandon himself to the Father's will.

Obedience, joy and suffering
Only our 'Yes' is still missing from the obedience of the world. When all of humanity has got there, the universe will reach its consummation. Resistance to the love of God will give way to a confident Amen on the part of the universe. Just like Jesus,

creation will no longer be anything other than a docile 'Yes' to its Creator. 'Christ Jesus was never Yes and No: with him it was always Yes' (2 Cor 1:19). Jesus has made himself both food and drink, out of obedience, so that we can all say, 'You did not want sacrifice or oblation, but here I am! I am coming to do your will' (Heb 10:5, 7). In the beautiful words of St Cyprian, 'Each time you participate in the holy mysteries, that you eat his Body and drink his Blood, your own blood is also shed.' Paul adds, 'Think of God's mercy, my brothers, and worship him, I beg you, in a way that is worthy of thinking beings, by offering your living bodies as a holy sacrifice, truly pleasing to God' (Rom 12:1). Through the Eucharist, all that the Lord has lived becomes a part of our lives.

'This is my Body, this is my Blood poured out for you'
After the breaking of the bread Jesus said: 'This is my body which will be given up for you. This is the cup of my blood which will be poured out for you.' This foundational statement is the most important that Jesus spoke on Holy Thursday evening. He entrusted it to the Twelve, and through them to the whole church. Jesus gave himself over to the church completely. The words which he pronounced over the bread and wine mean, effectively, 'I am here for you; it is I entirely, body and soul, spirit, divinity and humanity, the eternal Word begotten by the Father and the child born of Mary.' The church lives those words, by which it receives the nuptial engagement of its Spouse. On the rough road of faith, the Lord is its only treasure and its only nourishment. It will eat this bread and drink this cup, until the moment when the dawning light of faith gives way to the mid-day sunshine of the bright beatific vision.

The church watches over these words of her Lord
The church cares for these words: indeed she lives by them. Like Mary she holds them in her breast in the silence of adoration. For centuries she has attentively cared for them. There is a real danger that these words might be stripped of the mystery of the

real presence of Jesus. Did not the Jews say, 'How can this man give us his flesh to eat?' (Jn 6:52). 'This is intolerable language. How could anyone accept it?' (Jn 6:60).

Such objections have not totally disappeared in the course of the church's history. In fact it is difficult to find a time when there was not a weakening of faith in the presence of Jesus in the Eucharist. It is reduced to an empty symbol, an image without content or solidity. However, the church clings to this mystery. It cannot forget that Jesus, when he was faced with the objections of the Jews, did not withdraw his assertions. On the contrary, he insisted more clearly still on the reality of his presence in the Eucharist: 'I tell you solemnly, if you do not eat the flesh of the Son of Man and drink his Blood, you will not have life in you' (Jn 6: 53).

At these words many left him and stopped going with him, shrinking from such a crude saying. Even the Twelve could have gone: 'What about you, do you want to go away too?'(Jn 6:67). Only Peter found the courage, and the words, to reply: 'Lord, to whom shall we go?' (Jn 6:68). Then his faith rose above his inner turmoil: 'You have the message of eternal life; we believe and we know that you are the Holy One of God' (Jn 6:68b-69). After Peter's confusion when placed before the Master's words, the most profound faith comes to birth in him.

This phenomenon has been repeated often in the course of the church's history. Faith in the real presence of Jesus in the Eucharist has been attacked ceaselessly, yet the 'scandal' caused by those shocking words of Jesus always gives rise to a deeper and a more steadfast faith. In moments of doubt, Peter's intervention was often decisive; but it may well happen, as it did in the sixteenth century, that it is the ordinary people, the poor and simple people, who take the lead in seeking new ways of expressing their faith in the Eucharist. That is how they discovered adoration, when they knelt for hours before the presence of this mystery of Christ's love-until-death. It was the common people who understood the words, 'There is something greater than Solomon here' (Mt 12:42).

God alone knows what is taking place in the hearts of these people who are 'worshipping in spirit and in truth', and who express their love by spending entire nights before the Blessed Sacrament. In the course of such hours, man is transformed into what he is adoring. He is taking part in the Pasch of the Lord, in his death and resurrection. In this way 'eucharistic man' is born, full of wonder and contemplation, full of joy and inner peace. And so too is 'Marian man' born carrying his Lord within him in faith. He has been visited by the Holy Spirit, and the gifts of the Spirit shine out in him. These are love, joy, peace, patience, kindness, goodness, trustfulness, gentleness and self-control (cf. Gal 5:22-23).

'Do this in memory of me'

'Do this in memory of me', said Jesus to the Twelve – and to the whole church. At the time of the Last Supper the apostles represented the entire church. They were at one and the same time the assembled community and the sacerdotal ministry. The church was still in an embryonic state and its structure was as yet rudimentary. The church was contained within the Twelve as a flower within a bud. Before the blossoming, they had to experience the cold night of the passion, and then live through Easter and Pentecost. Only then could the church unfold. Only then could the church assume that fundamental structure whereby the priest and the people are face-to-face. It was on the evening of Holy Thursday that the apostles entered into the mystery of the priestly ministry, according to the tradition of the church. The Lord said to them, 'Do this in memory of me', and made them participants in his priesthood. The proclamation of the Word, which is so important in the ministry of the priest, leads on to the meal, but the heart of his mission resides in his eucharistic ministry.

The fruits

It is only with difficulty that the church can be described as the fruits of the Eucharist, since they are beyond the scope of the church. It can say, along with the angel from the book of the Apocalypse, 'He showed me the river of life, rising from the throne of God and of the Lamb, and flowing crystal-clear down the middle of the city street. On either side of the river were the trees of life, which bear twelve crops of fruit in a year, one in each month, and the leaves of which are the cure for the pagans' (Apoc 22:1-2).

The fruit of participation in the Body and Blood of Christ is nothing less than 'transforming us completely so that we become what we are eating'. In that succinct sentence of Pope Leo the Great everything is said; the fruits of the Eucharist are all included. Let us enumerate them. We participate in the paschal mystery of Jesus, we die and we rise with him to live forever beyond death. 'He who eats my Body and drinks my Blood will live for eternity, beyond death. There is here much more than the manna which your ancestors ate in the desert: he who eats this bread will live forever' (Cf. Jn 6: 54-58).

In what does this superabundant life consist? It is that very life which the Son received in the bosom of the Father: 'As I who am sent by the Father, myself draw life from the Father, so whoever eats me will draw life from me' (Jn 6:57). The Lord is offering to us the fullness of life which he possesses: and we share too those emotions which animate and sustain him.

Communion in the Body and Blood of Christ has also the fruit of forgiveness of sins (cf. Luke 24:46-48). Besides, as St Paul says, 'Anyone who is joined to the Lord is one spirit with him' (1 Cor 6:17b). Finally, the church does not hesitate to speak of the fruits of eucharistic communion even with regard to our bodies: how many prayers after Communion speak of 'healing of body and soul'? This is not just a simple metaphor or form of speech. No, the church affirms that the Body of Christ does bring about cures. Conversely, anyone who receives unworthily the Body and Blood of the Lord does so for his own condemnation. 'That is why', says St Paul, 'many of you are weak and ill and some of you have died' (1 Cor 11:30).

Among all the actions which the church performs for healing –

such as the imposition of hands and the anointing of the sick – the most fundamental is communion in the Body and Blood of Jesus. There are concentrated all the powers of healing which come to us from Christ's glorious cross. That is why St Ignatius of Antioch calls it the 'remedy of immortality'. Other sacraments of 'healing', like reconciliation and the anointing of the sick, gravitate around the Eucharist like planets around the sun. It is the Body and Blood of Jesus which form the 'leaves which bring healing to all the nations' (Rev 22:2, cf. Ezek 47:12).

Teach one another

The Eucharist is the heart of the church; it is the ark of the New Covenant, the tent where God lives among his people. Yet it is precisely in this 'Holy of Holies' that there is division. Arguments between the different Christian faiths often centre around the Eucharist and the Sacrament of Holy Orders. We are no longer united around the same table to eat the same bread and drink the same cup. Catholics, Orthodox and Protestants all follow their own paths. That could not be the will of Jesus.

Admittedly, we should not deny the real differences between the denominations. Still less should we lessen the richness of the Catholic faith to a minimum that would be accepted by everyone; Jesus would not want that either. What he asks of us is that we take into account our common richness and that we recognise the positive elements in the eucharistic faith of the other denominations. 'Hold on to what is good' says St Paul (1 Thess. 5:21).

The Eucharist is a many-sided diamond, or a garden with many entrances. There are several access routes to this mystery, and they all lead unerringly to the same place. Thus the Latin tradition emphasises the Christological reality: Christ is really there, veiled but truly present. That presence is not a simple image or an empty symbol, it is completely real. Christ is present, not just for those of the participants who believe in him, but he is objectively present and his presence does not depend on the faith of the local community who are gathered to celebrate the Eucharist. Christ is present 'substantially': He is there, fully present, at once God and man, body and soul. This realism is certainly one of the greatest treasures of our tradition of faith. It is also indispensable, because without that real presence everything collapses. If the Lord is not truly present in the Eucharist, his sacrifice loses its substance and his meal is nothing more than mere ritual.

Of course the other traditions have their riches too. Although we share some of those riches, our separated brethren have given them a clearer emphasis. For example, the Eastern Church stresses the role of the Spirit. It is he who changes the bread and wine into the body and blood of Christ. Therefore the Spirit has a very honoured place in their eucharistic prayers, and this puts great emphasis on the *epiclesis*. Since Vatican II, we too have underlined the importance of the *epiclesis*.

As for the churches of the sixteenth-century Reformation, some of them are very far from sharing the Catholic concept of the real presence. Yet their tradition has its own riches. It declares, for example, that the faith of the participants is important, and indeed indispensable. The Eucharist presupposes faith. How would anyone benefit from participating in the Lord's Supper if he had no faith? Faith is essential for a fruitful communion. Thus these Christian denominations each emphasise a different aspect of the Eucharist. The Latin Church asks 'Who is present?' – and she replies, 'The Lord himself who died and rose again.' The Eastern Church asks, 'By whom does the presence of the Lord come about?' – by the Holy Spirit. The Protestant Churches, for their part, will first want to know what is necessary so that the Eucharist will bear fruit in the person who receives it: his personal faith. If faith is not born again in our hearts, what use to us is the birth of Jesus in Bethlehem? Needless to say, the faith of the participants does not cause the presence of Christ in the sacrament: that is the work of the Holy Spirit, through the ministry of the church. But it is faith which enables the sacrament to bear fruit in us. Whoever communicates without believing can be likened to a blind man: he does not extinguish the sun, but he is unable to perceive its light.

THIRD PICTURE: THE BETRAYAL OF JESUS

A shadow lingered over the meal on Holy Thursday. One of the Twelve, sitting at the table with the others, is about to betray his Lord. St John talked about it right from the beginning of his account, even before the washing of the feet. Scarcely had he spoken of Jesus 'loving his own until the end' (Jn 13:1) than the betrayal was announced: 'The devil had already put it into the mind of Judas Iscariot, son of Simon, to betray him' (Jn 13:2).

'At the moment of being betrayed'

Jesus knew about the betrayal, and he knew who was going to betray him. He could have prevented him had he wished, for he knew 'that the Father had put everything into his hands' (Jn 13:3). Yet he let him go ahead. He entered into his passion freely. He went to meet the one who would betray him, and knelt before him to wash his feet.

The Lord did not resist evil. That apparent passivity is difficult for us to understand. We say that we must oppose injustice, and that is true. Yet the language of the gospel is different: it orders us to offer the left cheek to someone who strikes us on the right, to give our cloak to someone who has taken our tunic, and to go two miles with someone who forces us to go one mile. We will never quite understand that passage. The logic that God follows is different from ours. His is the logic of love. God loves in a way that is different from our way, and he asks us to imitate him. One thing is certain: Jesus remained a friend of Judas even in that dark hour of betrayal. When Judas arrived at the garden with the soldiers, 'all with lanterns and torches and weapons' (Jn 18:3), Jesus said to him, 'My friend, are you betraying the Son of Man with a kiss?'

We do not know the origin of evil. It is caused not just by human error, or a sudden impulse, or even our ill will; evil is the work of someone, the Evil One. 'Satan entered Judas' (Jn 13:27). Only God can distinguish clearly the part played by human free will and the part played by the Evil One. Certainly we can commit sin by ourselves: that is the fruit of our freedom. Yet at the same time we feel that sin comes from someone else, from the great Tempter who makes us stumble. Our free will is engaged in that cosmic struggle which is mightier than we are.

The gospels suggest however that Judas had a more immediate and more concrete reason for betraying Jesus, namely money: 'He went to the chief priests and the officers of the guard, to discuss a scheme for handing Jesus over to them. They were delighted and agreed to give him money' (Lk 22:4-5). The heart of all sin may reside in pride, but the quickest way to get there is often by money! Throughout human history countless numbers of people have been betrayed and killed for a little money.

It is a friend who is betraying me

For centuries, the psalmists have described that pain of betrayal by a friend. Jesus did not wish to escape that great sorrow. He wanted to share fully, and share to the end, that suffering endured by so many other men before him. Henceforth the complaint of the psalmist would attain its deepest meaning. God placed it in the mouth of his own Son. With men of all time who have been betrayed by a friend, Jesus could say, 'Were it an enemy who insulted me, I could put up with that … But you, a man of my own rank, a colleague and a friend, to whom sweet conversation bound me in the house of God!' (Ps 55:13-15). 'Even my closest and most trusted friend, who shared my table, rebels against me' (Ps 41:9).

Henceforward the anonymous psalmist takes on the identity of Jesus of Nazareth, God's own Son.

'Night had fallen'

Jesus took the piece of bread which he had dipped and gave it to Judas Iscariot. Then he said to him, 'What you are going to do, do quickly' (Jn 13:26-27b). It was as though he was in a hurry. And Judas went off. John noted, 'Night had fallen' (Jn 13:30).

Each time that we take our places at the table of the Lord we should remember that night of betrayal. What if the Lord had said to us as well, 'Someone who shares my table rebels against me?' (John 13:18). When we approach the holy table we must 'recognise' the Body and Blood of the Lord (1 Cor 11:29). Anyone who does not is 'eating and drinking his own condemnation', St Paul tells us. We must not receive Communion in an automatic manner, without adverting to it.

The Lord does not reject anyone because of his weakness. You have only to think of Peter on the night of the passion. He does not reject someone who acts inadvertently: he calls out to him to waken him. However, he can not bear the duplicity of heart of a Judas. The latter really hurts him. 'Jesus was troubled in spirit', says St John (Jn 13:21), and adds, 'Satan entered him [Judas]' (Jn 13:27).

THE FOURTH PICTURE: THE FAREWELL DISCOURSE

Never had he spoken so openly
It was at the moment when everything seemed to be in darkness that Jesus began to speak with a clarity and a warmth which he had never shown before. That was the farewell discourse, which covers four long chapters of St John's gospel (Jn 14-17).

Never before had Jesus spoken thus to his disciples. The language he used was fresh and completely clear. No longer was he concealing anything; so much so that the disciples said to him, 'Now you are speaking plainly and not using metaphors. Now we see that you know everything' (Jn 16:29-30).

The words of this farewell discourse seem to be suspended between heaven and earth. Was he still here on earth among us, or was he already with his Father? Did he still have to suffer his passion, or had he risen already? The words which he uttered at that moment would not have been out of place in the mouth of the Risen Christ sitting on the shore of the Lake of Galilee.

Jesus had often spoken to his disciples about the kingdom and about many other things. Soon after this discourse he would remain almost silent except for the few sentences spoken during his trial, and the seven words uttered from the cross. Jesus was entering solemn silence. In the meantime he seemed to want to confide everything to his friends. He unveiled all his secrets. He talked about his Father, about the coming of the Spirit, about the church, about the world and about the Evil One. He spoke about himself as well. He had nothing more to hide.

'Show us the Father'

Jesus revealed himself to his friends. That evening, for the first time, they were able to catch a glimpse of who he really was, this Master whom they had accompanied from the days of Galilee until the Pasch before his death in Jerusalem. Now they could see that he was more than a prophet – that he was the only Son of the Father, that he had come from the Father and was now returning to him.

Jesus went further still. he led his friends to the very heart of God, so that they could get to know him. God is no longer just the person who revealed himself to Moses under the name of Yahweh, 'I will be with you'. He is the Father, the Father of Jesus, and in the Son, the Father of all men. No one has ever seen the Father. Now the One who is with the Father has revealed him to all those who listen to him and follow him. As the hour of his crucifixion approached Jesus spoke of the Father more and more openly. What he had done quietly by himself, praying in deserted places, he was now doing aloud so that everyone could hear him. 'Show us the Father', said Philip (Jn 14:8). Jesus replied, 'Look at me: whoever sees me sees the Father. Why do you say: show us the Father?' (Jn 14:8). The Father was revealed in Jesus, his only Son, and through him he showed himself to the disciples. Suddenly these were no longer servants but friends. Jesus had told them everything. He had initiated them into all his secrets: 'I call you friends, because I have made known to you everything I have learned from my Father' (Jn 15:15).

Spirit, Water and Blood

After the Father and the Son, Jesus spoke of the Spirit. God is Spirit, the Holy Spirit. That Spirit had always accompanied Jesus. John the Baptist had seen the Spirit descend on Jesus at the moment of his baptism in the Jordan. Now the time had come for Jesus to tell openly what the Spirit was working in him. Jesus was to be put on a cross. How many prophets before him had been killed by Israel? Would all his preaching and his miracles, and indeed his whole life, be negated on the wood of the cross? Had he lived in vain? No, for it was precisely from the cross that Jesus gave the Spirit. St John insists on this point: 'Bowing his head, he gave up his Spirit' (Jn 19:30). Henceforth, the way was open for Pentecost, when the Spirit began to speak to the disciples and to the church, and would do so until the end of time. 'He will teach you everything, and remind you of all I have said to you' (Jn 14:26). The Spirit was poured out with the blood and water that flowed from the wound in his side: 'Jesus Christ … came by water and blood; not with water only but with water and blood, so that there are three witnesses, the Spirit, the water and the blood' (1 Jn 5:6-8).

The Holy Spirit gave an entirely new meaning to the hour of darkness which Jesus was then entering. He was not going to die like a prophet who had failed in his mission. The Spirit was his advocate, and he, the Advocate, reversed the roles. The condemned man was freed, and it was the judges who were found to be at fault. He continues to play this role on behalf of the church, each time that it is brought before tribunals in any age.

On the cross, the forces of evil seemed to have sealed the lips of Jesus forever. All his teaching and all his educating seemed to have failed. However, a new teacher was given to the church, namely the Holy Spirit: 'He will teach you everything and remind you of all I have said to you' (Jn 14:26).

The World

Jesus did not stop there. He spoke for a long time about 'the world', and he set about unmasking it. The world is not innocent, he pointed out. It could not be considered a neutral ground, a simple backdrop where the drama of Jesus was played out. The world was no such thing. It hated both Jesus and those who followed him. It was the kingdom of the Prince of Darkness, the

Liar from the beginning, the *dia-bolos*, that is to say 'the one who sows discord'. The world is a place of despair and tears.

Satan had taken away all hope from the heart of Judas. Therefore Judas was no longer capable of repentance. Repentance is possible only if there is hope of forgiveness. Peter too had been sifted like wheat, but the Lord had prayed that his faith would not fail – and Peter came back.

The world knows only hatred for Jesus, and similarly for his disciples. 'If the world hates you, remember that it hated me before you … but because you do not belong to the world, because my choice withdrew you from the world, therefore the world hates you' (Jn 15:18-19). Without any reason, for in that way the words of scripture were fulfilled, 'They hated me for no reason' (Jn 15:25).

The Lord prayed for his own

In spite of everything, Jesus did not remove his disciples from the world. In the world was where they must stay. As he did for Peter, Jesus prayed for them to his Father: 'I am not asking you to remove them from the world, but to protect them from the Evil One. They do not belong to the world any more than I belong to the world' (Jn 17:15-16). That prayer was always heard.

Those whom Jesus has called cannot be wrenched from the hands of the Father. That is why 'not one was lost except the one who chose to be lost, and this was to fulfil the scriptures' (Jn 17:12).

Then Jesus lifted his eyes and looked beyond the Eleven. He could see the church, his Bride, for whom he would give his life. Suddenly the disciples seemed to be transfigured: they were no longer the poor uncomfortable sinners seated around the table in the upper room: they were 'the apostles', pillars of the church, servants of the Word, and Christ's messengers. They were the priests who would stand at the Lord's table in his church, and the servants who would lead the flock until the end of time. Jesus could see as well those people who would believe in him because of their preaching. He prayed for all that countless throng (cf. Jn 17:20).

In the course of his farewell discourse Jesus brought each of the *dramatis personae* out of the background twilight into full, clear light. Here they were revealed as they really are: the Father, the Son and the Spirit, the disciples, the world and the whole church. The scene was set, the actors were present, and so there could begin the drama of God's gratuitous love for us poor sinners.

The golden thread of love

All the *dramatis personae* were there! By his words of farewell the Lord displayed the golden thread which linked them all. Yes, all are linked. The Father loves the Son, and they both love the Spirit. The Son loves his Father and his Spirit, and the Spirit is that very Love which unites the Father and the Son. Jesus loves his disciples too, and they in turn cling to him. The disciples are linked to each other by the links of love, and so too, those who 'believe in the words of the apostles' are loved by the Lord. The whole church is woven out of the golden thread of love. Only the world, in so far as it rejects Jesus, puts itself outside this gratuitous love of God.

For their sake, Father, I consecrate myself to you

Here we have the final words of that long goodbye: Jesus consecrating himself. The liturgy of the word was ending, the table was set and the food was ready. To complete it all, Jesus offered himself to the Father on behalf of his own. His prayer of consecration was said over himself. This was the 'eucharistic prayer' by which he consecrated himself to the Father. However, that consecration of himself to the Father was done for the life of the world. 'For their sake, Father, I consecrate myself to you' (cf. Jn 17:19). In a long, solemn sentence, Jesus, the new Isaac, offered himself voluntarily to the Father for the life of men. This is the Lamb which the Apocalypse talks about, 'standing and already sacrificed' (cf. Rev 5:6). This gift of himself brought to an end the innumerable sacrifices of the Old Testament, offered over and over again; because there is something greater here

than the sacrifice of Abel or that of Abraham, and greater than
the bread and wine brought by the priest Melchisedech (cf.
Eucharistic Prayer I). At last he has come, he who has been pre-
figured by all the victims of the former sacrifices. In a mysterious fashion, and each in its own way, they foreshadowed Jesus.
This gift of himself Jesus the Lord has entrusted to his church,
which he invited to 'Do this in memory of me'. That is why,
when it celebrates this memorial – this meal and sacrifice of
Christ – the church repeats: 'Look with favour on these offerings, and accept them as once you accepted the gifts of your servant Abel, the sacrifice of Abraham, our father in faith, and the
bread and wine offered by your priest Melchisedech' (Eucharistic
Prayer I).

Brothers and sisters, that is what happened 'on the night he
was betrayed'. This is what happens on every Holy Thursday,
beneath the veil of signs. I invite you to participate wholeheart-
edly in the church's liturgy. Watch with him in the Garden of
Olives, as he requested. Follow him along the way of the cross
on Good Friday. On the night of Easter life will conquer death. It
will happen within us as well: you will share in the joy of the
resurrection!

CHAPTER FOURTEEN

'Amazement': Beginning and End
of Eucharistic Devotion

Michael Duffy OFM Cap

Introduction

In his fourteenth encyclical, *Ecclesia de Eucharistia* (On the Eucharist in its relationship to the Church), Pope John Paul sees himself as 'halting before the "eucharistic face" of Christ and pointing out with new force to the church the centrality of the Eucharist' (#7). The encyclical is more than a presentation of doctrine. It is also an expression of personal piety. It is a piety based neither on cold reason nor on sentimentality, but on the human will guided and enlightened by truth, by the Word in person, the Son, who breathes forth love, the *Verbum spirans amorem*.[1] In the words of Newman: *faith without charity is dry, harsh and sapless.*[2] It is evident that the Holy Father's faith is not without that love which is charity, neither is it dry, harsh or sapless. The opening words of the encyclical demonstrate this: 'The church draws her life from the Eucharist. This truth does not simply express a daily experience of faith, but recapitulates the heart of the mystery of the church' (#1). At the same time, the Holy Father is exercising what he calls elsewhere the hierarchy's '*diakonia* of truth' and, for that reason, the encyclical needs to be welcomed as an authentic witness to revealed teaching.[3]

The encyclical is the work of a teacher who is also a witness, one whose teaching would lose its clarity and vigour were it not also the work of a witness to the love manifested in the Eucharist. It offers a glimpse into the heart of a believer in his response to the mystery of the Eucharist. 'The thought of this leads us to profound amazement and gratitude … This amazement should always fill the church assembled for the celebration of the Eucharist' (#5).[4] In his Letter to Priests on Holy Thursday 2004, he gives expression to the same amazement: 'Before this extraordinary reality we find ourselves amazed and over-whelmed, so deep is the humility by which God "stoops" in order to unite himself with man!'[5]

The Holy Father describes lovingly the practice that sustained this amazement during fifty years of priestly ministry:

'For over a half century, every day, beginning on 2 November 1946, when I celebrated my first Mass in the Crypt of Saint Leonard in Wawel Cathedral in Krakow, my eyes have gazed in recollection upon the host and the chalice, where time and space in some way "merge" and the drama of Golgotha is re-presented in a living way, thus revealing its mysterious "contemp-oraneity". Each day my faith has been able to recognise in the consecrated bread and wine the divine Wayfarer who joined the two disciples on the road to Emmaus and opened their eyes to the light and their hearts to new hope (cf. Lk 24:13-35)' (#59).

What did Pope John Paul see in the host and the chalice that sustains such amazement?

He is, of course, contemplating the consecrated host and the chalice which is now 'the cup of my blood': he contemplates the body and blood of Christ, no doubt of this, but always 'under the appearances of bread and wine'. He is contemplating the body which is given for us, the body which bore the weight of the world's sin and the blood which is shed for us, blood shed to redeem us by undergoing an act of violence, as a man might con-ceive it; blood shed in the giving of birth, as a woman might more likely conceive it, seeing in the blood and water that flowed from his side, the sign of our re-birth in his love, and the birth of the church, his beloved Bride in time and eternity.

The Holy Father recalls with joy the many and varied times and places in which he was able to celebrate the Eucharist.

This particular passage in the encyclical is one with which any priest will readily identify. 'When I think of the Eucharist, and look at my life as a priest, as a bishop and as the Successor of Peter, I naturally recall the many times and places in which I was able to celebrate it. I remember the parish church of

Niegowic, where I had my first pastoral assignment, the collegiate church of Saint Florian in Krakow, Wawel Cathedral, Saint Peter's Basilica and so many basilicas and churches in Rome and throughout the world. I have been able to celebrate Holy Mass in chapels built along mountain paths, on lakeshores and seacoasts; I have celebrated it on altars built in stadiums and in city squares ... This varied scenario of celebrations of the Eucharist has given me a powerful experience of its universal and, so to speak, cosmic character. Yes, cosmic! Because even when it is celebrated on the humble altar of a country church, the Eucharist is always in some way celebrated on the altar of the world. It unites heaven and earth. It embraces and permeates all creation'.[6] Clearly, the Holy Father finds in the Real Presence, brought about by transubstantiation, a source of profound amazement: this is where Our Risen Lord exercises his governance of love over all creation, anticipating the fullness of the *parousia*, when God will be 'all in all', when we too will be fully his Body!

The conclusion of the encyclical

This affords the Holy Father a final opportunity to repeat his testimony of faith in the Most Holy Eucharist. He says: 'Allow me, dear brothers and sisters, to share with deep emotion, as a means of accompanying and strengthening your faith, my own testimony of faith in the Most Holy Eucharist' (#59). The entire conclusion will be appreciated only when one lingers over it in meditation, perhaps many times, taking time to absorb the thoughts and spiritual emotions contained in it. 'The mystery of the Eucharist – sacrifice, presence, banquet – does not allow for reduction or exploitation; it must be experienced and lived in its integrity, both in its celebration and in the intimate converse with Jesus which takes place after receiving communion or in a prayerful moment of Eucharistic adoration apart from Mass' (#61). In the conclusion the Holy Father shows that the kind of amazement he wishes to re-kindle is not one of the mind only, but rather an amazement that leads to devotion and eucharistic self-giving, an amazement that is not complete without these things.

SECTION I: AMAZEMENT

What is Amazement?

In the United States, amazement is commonly expressed, among the young, by the word 'wow'. Pope John Paul is no stranger to this word since his visit to the United States in 1979. On that occasion, he entered into a profound dialogue with an assembly of young people. The entire content of the dialogue was expressed in the word 'wow'! On that occasion, the Holy Father showed himself capable of entering into dialogue with a young audience, which responded to him with enthusiasm. However, let us not forget that it was the Eucharist, the celebration of which is central to all the Holy Father's pastoral visits, that created the 'space' for such a dialogue. My question now is this: How can one speak to a learned audience for an hour on something that is expressed in a three-letter word which uses only two letters of the alphabet, and which sounds the same whether you spell it backwards or forwards? Is there an opposite of amazement, in the same way that despair and presumption are on one side and the other of hope? Perhaps not. But there is certainly an absence of amazement. It does not have a name, but it is what every teacher/ communicator secretly fears and what every preacher/ homilist tries to anticipate. It is often written on the faces of the listeners and is expressed in an unspoken 'so what' or 'big deal'.

What is 'amazement'? It is like reverence, but more. Amazement leaves us wide-eyed, breathless, but not paralysed! St Thomas describes 'amazement' like this: 'He who is amazed shrinks at present from forming a judgement of that which amazes him, fearing to fall short of the truth, but inquires afterwards: whereas he who is overcome by stupor fears both to judge at present, and to inquire afterwards. Wherefore amazement is a beginning of philosophical research: whereas stupor is a hindrance thereto'.[7] St Thomas teaches eucharistic amazement both in his theological work in the service of the gospel and in his throwing down the pen after an experience of eucharistic amazement which took not only his breath away but his reasoning as well. He deserves special mention if for no other reason

than that he has the unique distinction of being mentioned or referred to three times in the encyclical (apart from the apostles,
second only to St John Chrysostom, who is quoted four times). I
was nearly forty when I began to read Thomas for myself. I
made an amazing discovery. Many have made a similar discovery before and since. I was taken by the comment of a woman
who made such a discovery long before I did. In fact, she wrote
about in the year I was born: 'But the *Summa* is becoming, not
quite a best seller – it is rather big for that – but something not
unlike a bedside favourite. It is exciting enough to distract from
daily worries, but not so exciting as to prevent sleep. Indeed, its
pervading sense of the happiness of living in God's world rather
disposes to trustful slumber'.[8] The writings of St Thomas give a
special kind of satisfaction to the mind; the satisfaction of understanding, as distinct from knowledge. It is a satisfaction or pleasure that prevents the mind from stagnating. Unlike knowledge
(scientia), which is extensive and occupies more 'brain space',
understanding *(intellectus)* is intensive and is no load to carry. It
is a point, a resting place for the mind. This activity may not
make me a better teacher, or preacher, or communicator: but it
makes me a better 'understander'. Again to my amazement, I
discovered that three distinct skills are exercised in the act of
thinking, namely, knowledge *(scientia),* understanding *(intellectus),* and wisdom *(sapientia).* I think it not far-fetched to maintain
that Thomas had a eucharistic mind: his mind functioned 'eucharistically', in awe before the gift of being, grateful and re-
spectful of all that is, finding rest in the contemplation of being.

A mind that lacks the capacity for amazement is not a fully
functioning human mind. A life without the excitement of
amazement lacks an essential ingredient for happiness and holiness. There is a special kind of pleasure associated with amazement. Writers of diverse interests have noted its increasing
absence with regret. 'The act of contemplation,' wrote one such
author, 'is thoroughly playful and thoroughly intellectual.' He
appeals for a return to enjoyment of things, the re-discovery of the
pleasure that is not diversion, but a rejoicing in the act of being.[9]

The common human experience of amazement in the presence of nature's grandeur and humanity's dignity and diversity, needs to be valued for itself and promoted as a means of healing and wholeness. The Holy Father has already written of this gentler and more contemplative approach to life.[10] Human beings are amazed, overwhelmed, sometimes by brightness (in medieval times), sometimes by bigness (in modern times).[11]

The truly amazing thing about eucharistic amazement is that it is so completely unsensational and unspectacular! Its appeal is to faith that comes by hearing. The eucharistic presence is not deception, but revelation. 'Under the appearances' does not mean magic, a conjuring trick. Admittedly, St Thomas, writing as a poet, says *visus, tactus, gustus, in te fallitur:* 'Seeing, touching, tasting are in thee deceived; how says trusty hearing? That shall be believed; what God's Son hath told me, take for truth I do; truth himself speaks truly, or there's nothing true.'[12]

The gospels are full of amazement, especially in the Infancy Narrative as told by Saint Luke: It is the kind of amazement felt by the mother of Jesus and the disciples when Jesus 'let his glory be seen' in the first of his signs given at Cana in Galilee. It was an amazement that opened the door to faith in Jesus.[13]

Specific Examples of Eucharistic Amazement
The eucharistic sacrifice creates a space where freedom, unity, peace – in a word, communion – is experienced:

Edith Stein walked into the cathedral in Frankfurt in 1916 and saw something that amazed her. It is highly significant that what she saw took place in a space created by the Eucharist. What she saw in the cathedral changed her life. This is how she described what she saw: 'A woman with a shopping basket entered and knelt down for a short prayer. This was something completely new to me. Here was somebody coming out of the midst of everyday work into the empty church as to an intimate conversation. I never forgot it.' She was truly amazed. The eucharistic sacrifice creates a space of freedom for those who would enter into its realm. The cost of admission is faith and repentance. The communally spoken 'I confess' liberates the soul by allowing us to accept and acknowledge guilt, while finding joy in our confident recourse to the communion of saints.

A seven year old received his First Holy Communion and soon came to learn (well, it took some years really: I was about thirteen when it dawned on me) that Holy Communion introduced him to a sacred space where everything was new: a safe space, a loving and welcoming space. Holy Communion led him into his own soul, led him to begin to discover the dimensions of his own soul. 'I have given you a soul which no man can measure.' I received my First Communion in Seville Place, Dublin, the church where Matt Talbot prayed on his way to work. I am often amazed at how well the church of the fifties succeeded in communicating the faith, especially faith in the Eucharist, to me and to others.

A young woman approached a priest after the liturgy of Easter celebrated in Moscow (reported in *Time* magazine, in the early 1970s). She wanted to receive baptism. The priest was puzzled, as she had no instruction whatever. 'I want that', she said, indicating the liturgy from which she had come. Clearly, she had been struck by an amazement that led her to enquire further and seek to be part of what she had witnessed in the liturgy.

A seven-year-old girl, preparing for her first Holy Communion, attended the Paschal Vigil with her mother. As the priest walked in, carrying the newly lit paschal candle through the thick darkness of the church, the little girl was heard to exclaim: 'Gee, Mom, look at that candle!' Once again, amazement, and in a eucharistic setting. It was a US Army base in Germany. The year was 1970 and I was the priest. And I too was amazed by the amazement of that little girl with her whispered exclamation. And I wonder sometimes: was it the brightness or the bigness that provoked her amazement?

Amazement is seen first in God, before it is seen in the human being. It is the enthusiasm of God for his own creation: 'God saw that it was good … God saw that it was very good' (Gen 1:25, 31). In Psalm 62, prayed every Sunday morning in the

Liturgy of the Hours, we have 'the Lord delights in his people'. Again, an expression of amazement. Eucharist is as much, nay more, about God's amazement and delight in us, as it is about our amazement and delight in God.

Our (human) amazement begins in Genesis, with the man's discovery of the woman as 'bone of my bone and flesh of my flesh'. The Holy Father's catechesis on the Song of Songs and the book of Tobias are particularly instructive here.

Like Mary, the church teaches us to 'treasure all these things and ponder them in our hearts'. It is a contemplative gaze. A habit of looking. The amazement experienced in the Eucharist is prompted by the wonder of God's love in Jesus Christ. The letter to the Hebrews, for all its complicated theological reasoning, is the New Testament writing, apart from the gospels, that is most insistent on the humanity of Christ and his astonishing solidarity with us, even in our sin and shame. There we read: 'He is not ashamed to call us his brothers and sisters' (Heb 2:11). Us! His brothers and sisters! He is one of us.[14] Jesus is never more clearly our brother than when he humbles himself in the Eucharist, giving his Body and Blood to each one of us, offering himself as victim for our sins and uniting us in his own Body.

The response of the Bride to her Lord in the liturgy is an ever-present source of amazement for those with eyes to see. See the way the church, both mother and teacher, *mater et magistra* (being mother gives her the right to be also teacher) oversees our life of prayer in the liturgy. All the sacraments and prayers of the church are designed in a way to prepare us for the Eucharist, for the mutual self-giving which take place there. See the way the church prepares us, for example, in the Divine Office. Psalms arranged beautifully, readings carefully chosen. Someone who is faithful to the Divine Office is treated throughout the year to a selection of all that is best in the writings of the saints and the ancient writers.

Saint Francis speaks of the Eucharist with a breathless, sustained 'amazement': 'Every day he humbles himself … Give yourselves wholly to him who gives himself wholly to us'.[15] In his writings, Francis speaks most often about the Eucharist, even more than about poverty. Francis marvels at the humility of God in caring for us. We ought not to doubt that the eucharistic presence of Jesus is an act of humility, it is a humble presence and a humble caring.[16] Saint Clare writing in the thirteenth century urges Agnes of Prague to 'gaze upon him for refreshment'. Though not referring directly here to the Eucharist, we know that the Eucharist is dear to her heart. Her special sign in iconography is the monstrance, which she lifts high in the face of the enemy, assured of the protection of Jesus.

Saint Thomas might appear to some to be dry and unimaginative. However, legend has it that a kind of competition was held by church authorities for the creation of a liturgy for the feast of Corpus Christi. All the great theologians were present. St Thomas' turn came to read his piece, while St Bonaventure, the Franciscan, known as the Seraphic Doctor and the Prince of Mystics, waited his turn, manuscript in hand, ready to follow Thomas. The story tells us that as he listened to St Thomas and became rapt with the piece, he soon drew his notes tightly into his fist, crushed them, and threw the crumpled pieces of paper into whatever corresponded to a wastepaper basket in medieval times. And as they say, the rest is history and we bask in the sunshine of the *Adoro, te devote*, and other beautiful eucharistic hymns. Yes, St Thomas was doubtless nourished by the Eucharist and captivated by amazement at the Saviour's loving and merciful presence. In fact, he made the eucharistic self-giving of Jesus the inspiration of his own self-giving to others: 'God gave him great wisdom which he faithfully taught to others; he passed it on to them without keeping anything for himself,' says the *Magnificat* antiphon for his memorial on 28 January in the Divine Office.

The Eucharist is an assembly of forgiven sinners who never cease to confess what they are. This characteristic of the eucharistic assembly forms no small part of our 'eucharistic amazement'. The logic of such forgiveness leads to the praise of the Triune God and the hunger to work for the restoration of relationships at many levels: family, society, nations, churches and ecclesial communities.

Important Effects of Eucharistic Amazement

It is amazing that God loves us, and demonstrates that love by becoming incarnate and by being 'made sin for us'. This is a recurrent theme in the documents of Vatican II and in the writings of Pope John Paul II: 'For, by his incarnation, he, the Son of God, has in a certain way united himself with every man and woman. He worked with human hands, he thought with a human mind. He acted with a human will, and with a human heart he loved. Born of the Virgin Mary, he has truly been made one of us, like to us in all things except sin' (Vatican II, *Pastoral Constitution on the Church in the Modern World*, #22).[18] This has implications for our appreciation of the Our Lord's passion. As Pope St Leo the Great put it: 'Anyone who has a true devotion to the Passion of the Lord must so venerate Jesus on the cross with the eyes of his heart that Jesus' flesh is his own' (Office of Readings, Lent, Week 4, Thursday).

It is even more amazing that divine genius found a way of carrying that love to us in history (not just in memory, through a looking back from the 'now' moment, nor only in anticipation, through looking forward from where we are now). Our Lord gives himself to us in the most intimate and personal way. The *in illo tempore* that used to precede every proclamation of the gospel, underlined the fundamental importance of time in the Christian mystery.[19] Without the ecclesial event of the Eucharist, God's incarnation is absent from time and his presence becomes one of spirit, determined by the individual believer. Postmodernism likewise sees truth and meaning determined not by the individual's assent to external reality but by personal perspective and determination. The quest for truth and worship is abandoned as illusory and meaningless.[20]

'By the gift of the Holy Spirit at Pentecost the church was born and set out upon the pathways of the world, yet a decisive moment in her taking shape was certainly the institution of the

Eucharist in the Upper Room. Her foundation and wellspring is the whole *Triduum paschale*, but this is as it were gathered up, foreshadowed and "concentrated" forever in the gift of the Eucharist. In this gift Jesus Christ entrusted to his church the perennial making present of the paschal mystery. With it he brought about a mysterious "oneness in time" between that Triduum and the passage of the centuries. The thought of this leads us to profound amazement and gratitude. In the paschal event and the Eucharist which makes it present throughout the centuries, there is a truly enormous "capacity" which embraces all of history as the recipient of the grace of the redemption' (#5).

Catholics have shown themselves capable of grasping this presence of Our Lord in history and, as a consequence, capable of being moved to amazement and gratitude. I remember the woman from Cork who said, with a wisdom she herself was un-aware of: 'I don't care what they take away as long as they don't take Him away!' The context was a conversation on a train, in the late sixties, about the changes in the liturgy that were being implemented at the time.

Coming naturally on the heels of eucharistic amazement is gratitude, followed by a deepening of faith, a sure hope and a more fervent love, along with unity and communion with one another. 'It is *right* to give him thanks and praise.' *Dignum et justum est*. Lord, make us a people of grateful memory!

When Paul VI wrote an Apostolic Exhortation on Joy in the year 1975, he devoted an entire chapter to joy in the lives of the saints. He draws up a list of saints in whom there was a special witness to joy. Then he compiles an even shorter list, of three, whom he considered to be the most noteworthy witnesses to joy. These were Francis of Assisi, Thérèse of Lisieux and Maximilian Kolbe. It will be helpful if we try to do something similar, by ob-serving eucharistic amazement in the lives and writings of the saints. I have chosen Francis of Assisi and Edith Stein.

The Eucharistic Spirituality of Saint Francis
Saint Francis' 'principle and foundation' for the spiritual life is

the gift of Our Lord's presence in the Eucharist. We are to live in imitation of Our Lord's self-giving in the Eucharist. When Mr and Mrs Adam stopped saying yes to their God-given humanity and set up a plan of their own by eating of the tree of the knowledge of good and evil, they broke the original covenant with God. It seems that they did not much like being human, that is, incomplete and limited. The behavioural sciences, from their point of view, confirm from their studies that human beings still do the same. These sciences have discovered in the hearts and minds of people a hatred of being human, a ferocious raging at being incomplete and in need.[21] The Adams sought a re-negotiation of the original agreement, but that was not available. So they walked out on the original blessing of creation. God, in his infinite love for us, sent his divine Son to do what Adam and Eve had failed to do. He became a man like us in all things but sin, and from the first moment of his existence ratified the original covenant. 'He made himself poor so that by his poverty (note! Not, "by his property") we might be made rich' (2 Cor 8:4). What we expect is that he will enrich us by giving us what he owns, depriving himself for us. But this is not the point. It is by his poverty, which expresses what he is as Son from all eternity, that he enriches us.[22] He said 'yes' to the humanity that is willed by God, in its vulnerability, powerlessness and limitation. And when he took the bread and the wine at the Last Supper, he offered us a new covenant that would be based on the acceptance of our God-willed humanity, where the human body becomes the expression and the means of accepting and showing covenant fidelity.

Sometimes people will say, in a well-intentioned manner, that what Jesus 'really meant' in saying 'This is my body' was 'This is *me*.' No, he knew very well what he was saying and why he was saying it. He was taking his 'self-emptying' to its logical conclusion (logical, in the sense of the divine logic of love and humility, a logic that is foreign to us and could never have been guessed before God revealed his mind to us). He meant what he said, and he said what he meant: 'body', body and blood, implying all the vulnerability and incompleteness of our humanity. To receive Holy Communion is to ratify the original covenant, to consent to live our humanity in the way God wants it to be lived. It is to allow the Holy Spirit to form within us that 'yes' to being created in a certain specific form. The eucharistic way of life is also teaching us how to live, even now, the life of glory. In the Eucharist, we eat without destroying anything, we nourish ourselves without 'consuming' others; we give ourselves, without losing our true selves. The only thing that is lost or put to death in the Eucharist is the Self. And that is not loss for us, but gain!

The root of all sin is in the refusal to live that 'yes', to devise a thousand other ways of living, what amounts to a re-negotiation of the terms of human life. That is why it is such a sacrilege to receive Holy Communion in a state of grave sin: it is a contradiction. The Eucharist is more than a ritual: it is a way of living. The Eucharist puts God back into our flesh. To betray our eucharistic faith is to betray all that we are, all that Jesus wants us to be. The Eucharist is culmination, not conundrum. It is not far-fetched. On the contrary, it makes sense of everything. It is nearly a hundred years since the church, in the person of Pius X, now Saint Pius X, began to urge the practice of frequent and even daily Communion. Ever since that time, the church is almost breathless in its desire to share the Eucharist and gather us, like a mother, into that place of warmth and security. At times, out of loving care for the integrity of the human conscience, the church will challenge us to examine ourselves.[23] But, make no mistake, by far the dominant thrust of the church over the past hundred years has been the spirit of the Lucan parable: 'Go out and compel people to come in' (Lk 14:23)! And it is right that it be so. Long may it continue.

Finite and Eternal Being
Since I read about Edith Stein's encounter in the cathedral in Frankfurt I have searched in her writings for explicit reference to eucharistic amazement, but without success.[24] Then it occurred to me that the book of her mature years, *Finite and Eternal Being,*

in its entirety, is an example of eucharistic amazement. She is in awe before the mystery of the human person, especially in its fragile hold on being:

> The being of the ego is alive only from moment to moment. It cannot be quiescent because it is restlessly in flight. It thus never attains true self-possession … My own being, as I know it and as I know myself in it, is null and void *(nichtig)*; I am not by myself (not a being *a se* and *per se*), and by myself I am nothing; at every moment I find myself face to face with nothingness, and from moment to moment I must be endowed and re-endowed with being. And yet this empty existence that I am is being, and at every moment I am in touch with the fullness of being.[25]

It is not difficult to imagine her seeing in the Eucharist a welcome and amazing answer to the questions raised by her philosophy and by her experience of life. The same might be said about her observations on our vocation to eternal life: 'The vocation to union with God is a vocation to eternal life … Rather, the soul is destined for eternal being, and this destination explains why the soul is called upon to be an image of God in a wholly personal manner.'[26] By the time she wrote those words she had already learned to partake of the Eucharist daily. It is hard to imagine that what she wrote in this section (cf. n. 23) in relation to human individuality could have been uninfluenced by her eucharistic experience. After all, she refers explicitly to Revelation 2:17 (the 'white stone' and the 'new name'), which easily connects to the experience of receiving the sacred host in Holy Communion. Pope John Paul has called Edith Stein a 'symbol embodying the deepest tragedy and the deepest hopes of Europe'.[27]

SECTION II: CULTIVATING ('RE-KINDLING') EUCHARISTIC AMAZEMENT: THE EXPRESS WISH OF THE HOLY FATHER

'I would like to rekindle this Eucharistic "amazement" by the present Encyclical Letter, in continuity with the Jubilee heritage which I have left to the church in the Apostolic Letter *Novo Millennio Ineunte* and its Marian crowning, *Rosarium Virginis Mariae* … From this "living bread" she draws her nourishment. How could I not feel the need to urge everyone to experience it ever anew? The Eucharist, as Christ's saving presence in the community of the faithful and its spiritual food, is the most precious possession which the church can have in her journey through history' (## 6, 7, 9).[28]

How can we communicate and cultivate amazement with regard to the Eucharist, in such a way that we can 'experience it ever anew'? The late Professor Balthasar Fischer, Director of the Liturgical Institute in Trier, used to say that he never expected liturgical reform to fill the churches: only faith can do that. Liturgy is no substitute for evangelisation and ongoing catechesis. It is the noble task of the church as mother to teach us how to live in continuous eucharistic amazement. The gift of the Eucharist comes as the completion of the initiation that begins with baptism. Our participation in the Eucharist is the culmination, not the beginning, of initiation into the Christian community.

What things need to be looked at in our Catholic heritage and revitalised? Eucharistic adoration, benediction, visits to the Blessed Sacrament, personal thanksgiving after Holy Communion, eucharistic poetry and hymns, all of these come to mind. Lord, make us a people of grateful memory, as we discover with amazement the glory of God 'deep down things' (G. M. Hopkins), deep down even the bad things, the shame and humiliation of the church in recent times, the answer to the prayer of the psalm: 'redeem us because of your love', not because we deserve it or because we have some 'redeeming features', but only because you love us and because all our confidence is in that very love, merciful love incarnate in the Eucharist.

It is pleasant to spend time with him, to lie close to his breast like the Beloved Disciple (cf. Jn 13:25) and to feel the infinite love present in his heart. If in our time Christians must be distinguished above all by the 'art of prayer', how can we not feel a renewed need to spend time in spiritual converse, in silent adoration, in heartfelt love before Christ present in the Most Holy Sacrament? How often, dear brothers and sisters, have I experienced this, and drawn from it strength, consolation and support! (# 25, urging eucharistic adoration).

The Second Vatican Council needs to be heard again in its call for true 'devotion' in the liturgy. 'Mother church earnestly desires that all the faithful should be led to that fully conscious, and active participation in liturgical celebrations which is demanded by the very nature of the liturgy … In the restoration and promotion of the sacred liturgy, this full and active participation by all the people is the aim to be considered before all else …' (*Constitution on the Sacred Liturgy*, #14). 'Active' participation has more to do with interior dispositions than external practices. The word is *actuosa*, which is more like 'energy-filled'. The measure of participation is not in the physical energy expended, but in the heart's devotion.

Relationship between Eucharist and Lectio Divina
The Constitution on the Sacred Liturgy (1962) laid it down as a principle that 'the liturgy of the word and the liturgy of the Eucharist form one single act of worship'. The Council urged that the treasures of the Bible should be opened more fully to the faithful. And this has undoubtedly happened. But much needs to be done to help the faithful make the treasures of the Bible their own. For the baptised the Bible is not a foreign land, though for many it appears to be. On the contrary, the Bible is the book of our people. It needs to be heard and received as the story of the people to whom we belong, and of which Jesus is the first-born among many brethren. The Bible is our story, my story. There are many methods of realising this ambition of the Council. For example, there is the option, for the homilist and others who care to follow it, of using the Lectionary in conjunction with the Catechism. Among the indices at the back of the Catechism is one that enables us to find references in the Catechism to hundreds of biblical texts. In this way, a Sunday gospel can be read in the context of a point of doctrine.[29]

However, by far the most widely used and promising method available to us today is the revival of *lectio divina*. The Holy Father himself has drawn attention to this: 'It is especially necessary that listening to the word of God should become a life-giving encounter, in the ancient and ever valid tradition of *lectio divina*, which draws from the biblical text the living word which questions, directs and shapes our lives' (*Novo Millennio Ineunte*, #39).

What can we say about *lectio divina* that will enable us to see the connection with 'eucharistic amazement'? The aim of *lectio divina* is to lead us to speak to God in words first addressed by God to us! This is nothing unusual: it is how every child learns to speak. The two parts which, in a certain sense, go to make up the Mass, namely, the liturgy of the word and the eucharistic liturgy, are so closely connected with each other that they form but one single act of worship (*Constitution on the Sacred Liturgy*, #56). The Holy Spirit put the words there so that we might hear them and, from hearing them, learn the language by which we can converse with God! Among the three criteria laid down in the Catechism for interpreting sacred scripture is the following: Read the scripture within 'the living tradition of the whole church'. According to a saying of the fathers, sacred scripture is written principally in the church's heart rather than in documents and records, for the church carries in her tradition the living memorial of God's Word, and it is the Holy Spirit who gives her the spiritual interpretation of the scripture.[30] Eucharistic devotion and adoration go hand in hand with love of the sacred scriptures. We find evidence of this in recently founded congregations, for example, the Spiritual Family of Christ, the Work, whose foundress died as recently as 1987. In a privately published booklet, there is a chapter which describes the love for the Eucharist that is characteristic of members of the Institute. In the same chapter the following is proposed as the ideal for each sister: 'The gospel is her favourite book. At the school of Saint Paul she has acquired the certitude that nothing can stand in the way of those who wish to live a life of love. True love is willing to be sacrificed and to give all it has.'[31]

Theology of the Body. A renewed theology of the body is essential for a renewal of eucharistic amazement and devotion. As it happens, such a theology is at hand in the writings of the Holy Father, where he develops the idea of the 'nuptial meaning' of the body.[32]

Thanksgiving after Holy Communion. 'The oyster opening to the dewdrop': The oyster sometimes opens its shell to receive a drop of fresh morning dew. On doing so it closes its shell.[33] This keeps the dewdrop pure and free from all contamination with seawater. It also enables the oyster to enjoy the pleasingly cool sensation of the dewdrop that came from the heavens. Something like this happens to the person who receives Our Lord's Body in Holy Communion with the proper dispositions. In order to obtain the fullest benefit from Holy Communion, it is very important to close one's mind and heart to all that comes from the outside. The eternal Son of God dwells within you touching you in your soul. It is necessary to focus all your spiritual energies on him. Close your eyes. Bury your face in your hands for a few moments. Pour out your heart to Jesus who is the Bread of Life and the pledge of Eternal Life. It is time to recite slowly a favourite prayer or short aspiration … Sacred Heart of Jesus… Jesus, I trust in you. We expect too little from the reception of Our Lord's Body and Blood in Holy Communion. We sometimes do not even know what to expect or what to ask for! The studies of the post-Communion prayers by Placid Murray are immensely rewarding in this respect. What we want to put the knife to, if we are to live lives of love, is self-will. As the old nun said: 'I'd be a saint only for myself.' Or put more theologically by the *Doctor Mellifluus*, the honey-tongued doctor, Bernard of Clairvaux: 'Let self-will cease and there would be no hell.' One of the principal healing effects of Holy Communion is the surgical removal of self-will. Only God can do it and he accomplishes this by bringing us into contact with his living body, touching us on the inside, not on the outside, when we literally eat his sacred Body and drink his precious Blood.[34] To return for a moment to the oyster: at the core of the oyster's being something very precious develops, namely, a pearl. Similarly, something very precious develops in the body of the person who receives Our Lord in Holy Communion, namely, that 'Amen', 'Yes' to our heavenly Father, to one another, to all creation, a 'Yes' that Jesus forms within us. That 'Yes' is indeed the pearl of great price, formed within our very bodies by our Saviour, the treasure in the field, which is worth all we have to give in exchange.

Consecrated life in the church lives from eucharistic communion and amazement or it does not live at all. 'By its very nature the Eucharist is at the centre of the consecrated life, both for individuals and for communities. It is the daily viaticum and source of the spiritual life for the individual and for the Institute.'[35] The Holy Father puts his finger on a crucial point of renewal for all religious when he writes: 'The call to holiness is accepted and can be cultivated only in the silence of adoration before the infinite transcendence of God: "We must confess that we all have need of this silence, filled with the presence of him who is adored: in theology, so as to exploit fully its own sapiential and spiritual soul; in prayer, so that we may never forget that seeing God means coming down the mountain with a face so radiant that we are obliged to cover it with a veil (cf. Ex 34:33); in commitment, so that we will refuse to be locked in a struggle without love and forgiveness. All, believers and non-believers alike, need to learn a silence that allows the Other to speak when and how he wishes, and allows us to understand his words." In practice this involves great fidelity to liturgical and personal prayer, to periods devoted to mental prayer and contemplation, to Eucharistic adoration, to monthly retreats and to spiritual exercises.'[36]

Amazement is undoubtedly a power for good in human life, eucharistic amazement powerful in a manner impossible to calculate. It should not surprise us, then, to find that amazement can be hijacked by the Evil One in order to lead us astray and cause confusion and damage. St Francis de Sales, among others, speaks wisely of this possibility: 'We are not to be surprised, therefore, if the devil – when he is up to his monkey tricks, deluding souls, scandalising the weak, passing himself off for an angel of light – brings about raptures in one or two souls insufficiently instructed in piety'.[37] The Doctor of Love, as he is called, has excellent teaching and very helpful advice and guidance in the matter of what he calls 'spiritual ecstasies': 'When it comes to spiritual ecstasies, however, they are of three kinds: ecstasy of intellect, ecstasy of will, ecstasy of activity. The first is towards enlightenment, the second towards fervour, the third towards good works; the first is caused by wonderment [what we have been calling 'amazement'], the second by devotion, the third by exercise.'[38] One should seek to be amazed, but at the right things, because amazement leads to devotion, and devotion leads to the gift of oneself to God in the doing of his will. '… If an ecstasy is more beautiful than good, more discerning than fervent, more speculative than stimulating, it is extremely dubious, highly suspect.'[39] The Eucharist is a safe path, safe from delusion, because it has us walk by pure faith.

Eucharistic amazement is especially suited to promote the practice of faith, hope and love; in this way leading us to a true ecstasy of activity, of life. These are the theological virtues; like all the virtues, skills for living, they are more specifically, 'the God-touching skills'. A word here about the practice of the virtues. The virtues make us new. It is not about saying new things, but about what makes us new. The virtues are the secret of originality and true newness. The virtues are useful and beautiful: they take us away from self and bring us to God. When we apply ourselves to the practice of a virtue we escape from self. Just as taking to the golf course gets us into the fresh air, application to the virtues gets us into the sunshine of the divine life. They take us away from self, they ensure that we will be real, not a stereotype or a copy of someone else. The virtues are the secret of variety and therefore of interest and excitement in life. What the flowers are in the vegetal kingdom these skills are in the spiritual life. There is variety in the spiritual life due to the existence of virtues. With each virtue there is variety. Patience never repeats itself. Nor does humility, or any other virtue. A field of daisies are recognisable as daisies, but no two are identical. It is the same with the virtues. They never repeat themselves. They are based on the attraction of the good, there is no sense of being pressurised or pushed. Pull, not push, is the secret of the virtues. We are attracted, not driven. It is by means of the virtues that we live the gospel life to which we are called by baptism. Every virtue, no matter how imperfectly practised, ends in God.

External Reverence. St Louis Marie de Montfort advised that we recite the Hail Mary with 'attention, devotion and external reverence'.[40] The last mentioned is crucial. Without it the other two cannot live – at least for long. Cardinal Newman emphasises the importance of a reverential demeanour before God. Not to have feelings of fear and awe is proof, according to Newman, that we have not truly realised or believed that God is present! I might paraphrase him like this: 'Show me how you genuflect before the Blessed Sacrament and I will tell you whether you believe.'[41] This reverence extends to the language we use in referring to the Body and Blood of Christ after the consecration. The external reverence to be cultivated in regard to the celebration of the Eucharist and its adoration is easily neglected, but at a cost. It is to be noted that external reverence has nothing to do with histrionics or rigidly exercised movements. External demeanour is a witness to what is within and enables one to bring the body into prayer. The crowds who flocked to Lourdes to see Bernadette were deeply moved and filled with wonder by one thing in particular: the way she made the sign of the cross.[42] The reverence of silence, sacred silence, is likewise of great importance in the celebration of the Eucharist, if the wonder of the Lord's presence is to be felt. One modern writer on matters religious has observed, 'without silence, there is no ecstasy'. She rates the 'mainstream churches' badly on this score, but claims that Catholics have the edge, because of the wonder of the Eucharist. 'The Sanctus feels like a door to me, opening onto eternity, where the angels and all the saints sing "Holy, Holy, Holy". Then, a few simple words are used to break open the world, and Christ becomes present, silently, in the sacrament.'[43]

Conclusion

The Eucharist is the fulfilment of a promise, Our Lord's promise to give us the bread of life. It is also the promise of fulfilment, the fulfilment of glory, when he raises us up on the last day. I would like to finish with an exclamation of wonder and gratitude found in the Revelations of Saint Gertrude. It is easily accessed because it is contained in the second reading for her memorial on 16 November in the Office of Readings. Having expressed gratitude to God for many supernatural benefits, she finishes: 'More still, you have so gently drawn me by the sure and certain promise of your favours when I die, favours to come when I am dead. Had I known no other gift of yours, for this life-giving hope alone my heart would go out to you.' May the Eucharist be, for each one of us, the fulfilment of a promise, and the promise of fulfilment, and for all this, may our hearts go out to him in love and gratitude, and sustain us in that profound amazement, which the Holy Father earnestly desires to re-kindle.

CHAPTER FIFTEEN

Eucharistic Adoration: the Worship of the Blessed Eucharist outside of the Mass*

Thomas Norris

The encyclical, *EdE*, radiates an air of awe in the presence of the Sacrament of the Altar. In fact, one objective of John Paul II in this gift to the church is precisely to reawaken in the faithful an attitude of awe and to revive in them wonder towards the Most Holy Sacrifice (cf. ##5, 6). This attitude of wonder is more than an affectionate feeling; it is actually at the foundation of every science, both theological and human. This was the conviction of Plato and Aristotle, for whom wonder is the generating motor for every search and for all human discovery. For this very reason, the adoration offered to the Eucharist is not without its importance for Catholic theology, especially eucharistic theology.

The text, in #25, speaks of worship outside the Mass. It begins in this way: 'The worship of the Eucharist outside of the Mass is of inestimable value for the life of the church.' It is not surprising that this worship is repeatedly recommended by the magisterium of the church, as *EdE* notes. The objective of this article is to consider certain aspects of this worship that are expressed in Benediction of the Most Holy Eucharist, in adoration and in eucharistic processions, especially those for the feast of Corpus Christi. We will consider the following themes: adoration and the building up of the church as the love of the eucharistic Christ spread out in space and time; the anthropological value of this worship; the philosophical importance of the theme of adoration with regard to the category of relation. Finally, there will be an examination of the Marian factor that is actualised through the worship of the Eucharist.

*An earlier version appeared in Italian in *L'Oservatore Romano* (25 June 2003, p 6)

Adoration and the building up of the Church: the ecclesiological value
It is not without significance that the central paragraph on the
worship offered to the Eucharist outside the Mass is found in the
second chapter of the encyclical. This chapter bears the title, 'The
Eucharist builds the Church.' The Pope cites St Paul by taking a
text from his 'mini-eucharistic treatise' in chapters 10 and 11 of
the First Epistle to the Corinthians: 'The cup of blessing that we
bless, is it not a communion *(koinonia)* with the blood of Christ?
The bread which we break, is it not a communion *(koinonia)* with
the body of Christ? Because there is one bread, we who are
many are one body, for we all partake of the one bread' (1 Cor
10:16-17). The communion with the Blood and Body of the Risen
Lord not only builds the vertical communion with the Risen
Lord, so to speak, it also builds the communion between all
those communicating with the Lord. Vertical communion causes
horizontal communion, while horizontal communion becomes
the very epiphany of this vertical communion. Communion
with Christ in the sacrament necessarily becomes communion
also with all those who receive him.[1] In that way the 'I' of the
human person opens up and a new 'We' is created. The
Eucharist builds the church (Henri de Lubac). In fact, the church
is the body of the Lord generated by the Body and Blood of
Christ, the head of humanity and Lord of history who desired to
give his flesh as food 'for the life of the world' (Jn 6:50).

In the Johannine tradition we find certain insights that throw
fresh light on this Pauline understanding to which we are referring. When Caiaphas as High Priest proposes that 'it is expedi-
ent for one man to die for the people, than for the whole nation
to be destroyed' (Jn 11:50), the evangelist interprets this advice
in the following manner, 'Jesus was to die for the nation – and
not for the nation only, but to gather together in unity the scattered children of God' (Jn 11:51-52). It would be difficult to find a
clearer affirmation of the purpose of the paschal mystery. It explains the prayer of Jesus to his Father when he is about to pass
from this world to the Father, 'may they be one in us, as you are
in me and I am in you' (Jn 17:21).

Now it is by means of' eucharistic communion that we attain such unity, being one single body, indeed the very Body of Christ, and in that way also being members of each other. How, then, should we live and act? The imperative is to love one another. Quite simply, there is no other way for Christians to live. St Augustine's thought on the matter is beautiful. 'Because there is only one bread, we, though many, are only one body. Here in this Bread it is suggested to you how you ought to love unity. As for that Bread, is it made out of only one grain of wheat? Were there not many grains of wheat?'[2]

Throughout the pages of the New Testament, we discover in the words of Jesus in the gospels an 'art of loving'. This art is a 'skill' or 'technique' by which we can be what we are, the 'eucharistised' body of the paschal Christ. Let us look immediately at the basic steps in this art and at the relevant passages in the Word of God. We must be the first to love. 'God loved us first' (1 Jn 4:19). Then we must, like Jesus who gave up his life for us all, *anti pollôn*, (Mk 10:45), love each and everyone we meet. It is not enough to love only friends, those who are dear to us, fellow-Catholics and those who are pleasant to us. The third step in this art is to love with actions and not only with words (1 Jn 3:18), since the important thing in love is to love. We love best by concrete deeds and gestures of service. In the fourth place, we can love by making ourselves one with others – in all things except evil. Are we not shown this step in the art of loving by the very mystery of the Eucharist? The Word, who is God, was made flesh from the flesh of Mary, and 'when he had loved his own who were in the world, he loved them to the end *(eis telos)*' (Jn 13:1). Therefore he made himself into food and drink for us, thereby showing us in a marvellous way the depth of his unity with us. And as soon as we are 'eucharistised', what should we do? We too must make ourselves one with others, as the apostle Paul urges us, 'Rejoice with those who rejoice; mourn with those who mourn' (Rom 12:15; cf. Phil 2:2). The importance, indeed the necessity, of eucharistic worship outside the Mass becomes clear at this point. In order to make up our Christian identikit, it is necessary to realise that it is a eucharistic identity. Adoration is a privileged moment to make this discovery since it is then that one realises the realities of the Eucharist, and realising is the very life of religion (Cardinal Newman).

We need to adore! We need to reawaken love inside of us, or rather to wake up to the love that sleeps inside us. It is this very love in fact that binds all authentic believers into a new humanity. This is an incalculable benefit that flows from eucharistic adoration: the realisation that we are the living members of one and the same mystical Body of Christ. There we find the energy to live by the art of loving. The humble and glorious love of the eucharistic Lord shows us our obligation to live by the art of loving even as he coaxes us into the resulting adventure. Mother Teresa of Calcutta used to repeat, 'When I look at the Most Holy Eucharist, I think about the poor, and when I see the poor, I remember the Eucharist.'

The anthropological value: the Eucharist reveals Man to man!
The great French theologian, mathematician and philosopher, Blaise Pascal, used to say: *'L'homme passe infiniment l'homme.'*[3] Aristotle had already perceived the same idea, to be followed by St Thomas Aquinas, his great admirer over a millennium and half later: *'Anima quodammodo omnia'* ('in a certain way, the soul is all things').[4] This means that man transcends himself, and does so to an unlimited degree. Not only that, but he feels the need to transcend himself towards Another who is immensely greater. Perhaps St Augustine chanced upon the best formulation: *'Inquietum est cor nostrum donec requiescat in Te'* ('Our heart is restless until it rests in you').[5] Modern culture recognises the greatness of the human being, even if it sometimes formally denies the existence of God. This yearning, constitutive as it is of the human person, highlights a question that cannot be hidden because it arises within the human heart itself, and that is: where and how do we find that Supreme Being, or rather, the One who is always Greater? That is the real question.

Visitors to Asia often meet peoples who, in their own way,

practice a *latria* (worship) towards their religious images. They bend down or get on their knees with heads to the ground towards concrete forms. And they offer some precious gifts. It is certainly a posture that expresses their essential devotion towards the One who is always greater. It expresses this constitutive desire of man to recognise his dependence on Another.

This gives us a perspective for understanding the human meaning of adoration. As we have seen, Jesus 'loved us and gave himself in our place as a fragrant offering and a sacrifice to God' (Eph 5:2). The invisible Son of the invisible Father becomes man, and being man and visible, he leaves himself totally present under the eucharistic species. This is the meaning of adoration: I recognise before me the mystery that encompasses me, I bow before the sacred host that contains the entire mystery of Christ as my mystery! 'You are who you are and I have the privilege of a lifetime to recognise this.' The Irish poet, Patrick Kavanagh, has writtten:

O Christ, this is what you have done for us:
In a crumb of bread the whole mystery is.

The founder of the Blessed Sacrament Fathers, St Pierre-Julien Eymard, lived a life that was an ongoing journey into the infinite treasures contained in the Eucharist. It was he who uttered the famous phrase: 'Our age is sick because it does not worship.'[6] In order to live an authentically human life in tune with who we are as creatures dependent upon Another, the one who is always Greater, we need to worship. Worshipping the eucharistic Jesus, we become what we are!

The Philosophic Value: 'Adoratio' leads to 'Relatio'
According to revelation, the human person is made in the image and likeness of God (Gn 1 :26). This means that each man and woman is a 'You' before God. This is why religion is not something added on to human nature as if it were an ornament. The truth is that the human person finds himself only in the generous gift of himself. To find and to live by this relationship which is constitutive of our humanity is to become persons fulfilled.

This is the famous teaching of the Second Vatican Council in *Gaudium et Spes* (#22). It runs through the entire teaching ministry of John Paul II.

In the New Testament, this relationality is emphasised. God is revealed as a Trinity of infinite Persons. Each divine Person is a *relatio subsistens* (subsistent relationship). They live in an eternal dance or *perichoresis* of love. This explains why Jesus, by bringing to earth and into history this trinitarian culture of loving, puts love of God and of others at the centre (cf. Mk 12:28-34). It means that *relatio* is the heart of human existence. Being a person means to find and to live from this relationality and for this relationality. In fact, Jesus both prays to the Father and suffers so that 'they may be one just as we are one, I in them and you in me' (Jn 17: 22-23).

Eucharistic adoration in its various forms must be seen in this perspective: in a truly magnificent way it helps human persons to become what they are. Actually, the worship offered to the Eucharist pushes a person to live out the relation with the Lord in the sacrament, yes, but also with all one's brothers and sisters. Adoration is not at all a denial of individual human dignity; rather, it reveals the true greatness of every human being. It stresses that I am myself only by establishing living relationships with God and others. Adoration teaches us that our life is realised if it is like an arrow in flight.

With the Eyes of Mary

With moving originality, John Paul II dedicates an entire chapter on the 'Woman of the Eucharist', the Blessed Virgin Mary. Mary is described as the 'first "tabernacle" in history' (cf. #5). It is here that the Pope brings to the fore an insightful parallel: 'There is a profound analogy between the *Fiat* which Mary said in reply to the angel, and the *Amen* every believer says when receiving the Body of the Lord.'

In every believer Jesus finds a tabernacle. We know that Mary 'treasured all these things and pondered them in her heart,' as Luke says (2:19). Surely this is an invitation to the whole church to discover ever more fully the gift that the Father makes in the sending of his beloved Son as proof of the eternal love of the Holy Trinity for humankind (cf. Jn 3:16; Rom 5:8; 8:32). Is this not the very *raison d'être* of the worship offered to the Eucharist outside the Mass? Mary is the shining model of this worship.

Urged on by the Love incarnate in her flesh, Mary visits Elizabeth impelled by the Love within her to love her cousin by her presence and practical assistance. In this way there begins the faith-pilgrimage of the Mother of Jesus, a *via Mariae* (cf. Pope John Paul II, *Rosarium Virginis Mariae*, #24). By means of adoration Christians feel the Lord's pull to walk in love along the holy journey that leads to God and to others, serving them with concrete acts of love and thereby becoming 'living Eucharists' for them.

CHAPTER SIXTEEN

At the School of Mary, 'Woman of the Eucharist'

Caroline Farey

'By adaptation to the changing conditions of time and place, the Eucharist offers sustenance not only to individuals but to entire peoples, and it shapes cultures inspired by Christianity. It is necessary, however, that this important work of adaptation be carried out with a constant awareness of the ineffable mystery against which every generation is called to measure itself. The "treasure" is too important and precious to risk impoverishment or compromise …' (*EdE*, #51).

The best ecclesial art follows the principles embedded in the words above, words that, in relating primarily to the liturgy of the Eucharist, also relate to art for the Eucharist. This article draws on examples of art from the fifteenth to the seventeenth centuries not necessarily to promote use of these particular artworks in the liturgy today[1] but to demonstrate how the same principles used by those artists can be used to guide art for the liturgy in our own time.

Let us look now at three principles we might derive from the paragraph quoted above. Firstly, it can be taken that liturgical art needs to be adapted to the people of its time; secondly, that it needs to manifest and promote an 'awareness of the ineffable mystery' of God's saving act in Christ, and thirdly, that the artwork needs to reveal this 'treasure' as a 'measure' to enlighten and elevate even the humblest and most hopeless of sin-filled worshippers. Art has magnificent ways of its own that are significantly different from the written word for proclaiming, often more powerfully for some people, this same faith.

Pope John Paul II entitles chapter six of his encyclical, *Ecclesia de Eucharistia*, 'At the School of Mary, "Woman of the Eucharist".'

He insists that 'If we wish to rediscover in all its richness the profound relationship between the church and the Eucharist, we cannot neglect Mary, Mother and model of the church.' Mary, he argues, 'can guide us towards this most holy sacrament, because she herself has a profound relationship with it' (*EdE*, #53).

The artworks chosen for this article follow the principles enunciated above and confirm the truth of the Holy Father's words as they each reveal how Marian art can display the richness and unity of the Catholic faith concerning the church and the Eucharist. In the tradition of Christian art and theology, as we have seen, Mary is understood as Mother and Model of the Church. This means that wherever one sees Mary in the paintings one sees the church *(ecclesia)*. Not only this, but most of the works from this period were painted for churches and, therefore, largely for the context of the liturgy of the Mass *(Eucharistia)*. One might say, then, that although the paintings may appear to be simply scenes of Mary's life with Christ, they are also scenes of the inner meaning of the eucharistic celebration, that is of the life of the Son of God handed over for us in the church. Not one of the paintings is of altars or priests and yet all the paintings manifest the *Ecclesia de Eucharistia* through Mary.

What is more, Mary is beautiful, and though the artists chosen here used different styles, they have each attempted to paint her with the utmost beauty. This helps give us a new sense of the church as beautiful, as the bride of Christ, rather than as the broken vessel she so often seems to be, as manifested in her members. The *Catechism of the Catholic Church* explicitly draws together the 'spiritual beauty of God … reflected in the most holy Virgin Mother of God' with the capacity of sacred art to evoke 'the surpassing invisible beauty of truth and love visible in Christ' (*CCC*, #2502).

Certain 'keys' used by artists to help them paint divine mysteries in two dimensional human scenes must be noted. For example, buildings frequently symbolise the church; a source of light would frequently symbolise God the Father or, at least, a heavenly presence or power, while the brightest, lightest part of a picture could indicate the focus or purpose of the painting – for example, in the annunciation scene by Blessed Fra Angelico, the brightest part of the whole painting is the white stonework of the building, that is the church, which 'houses' the extraordinary event taking place, that is, the divine Word becoming flesh; robes and dress are indicative of the inner state of the person, or the status, either in the eyes of men or in the eyes of God – for example, in the same painting by Blessed Fra Angelico, Mary is dressed not as a poor girl from Nazareth but as a young queen sitting on a throne. (It is mainly through the dress and the background of the painting that the artists show strong adaptation to their own time).

1. The Annunciation and the Eucharist
'Mary lived her Eucharistic faith … by the very fact that she offered her virginal womb for the incarnation of God's Word ' (*EdE*, #54).

The painting of the Annunciation by Blessed Fra Angelico OP (1432, tempera on wood, see page 321 below) which is found in the Museo Diocesano, Cortona, is one of many annunciation scenes painted by him. This one reveals through its many details, the great mystery of the moment of the incarnation and, at the same time, the mystery of the Mass, the place today where the same Word becomes flesh on the altar.

As we have said, Mary is painted as a virgin princess seated on a throne with a carpet under her feet and dressed in richly embroidered clothes. The angel has stepped inside the arched structure in this painting and the message is given in three lines of text flowing from the angel's mouth. It is also embodied by the angel pointing upwards to God the Father in heaven (symbolised by a carving in the stonework) and directly towards Mary's womb. Here one can see both words and embodiment, just as, in the scriptures and in the Mass, God reveals himself in words and deeds. The Holy Spirit, who Gabriel says to Mary 'shall come upon you', hovers above Mary as though waiting for her 'fiat', completing the Trinitarian presence that we are given in St Luke's gospel text.[2]

The purport of the message is reiterated again and again around the centrally placed angel. The angel, *angelos*, bringer of good news, evangeliser, is at the centre of the painting. If one looks at the left hand side of the painting one finds the story of salvation starting from the expulsion of Adam and Eve from Paradise. Adam and Eve walk out into a red-stained desert and into night. The desert turns to a dark forest[3] with occasional 'lights' like the prophets guiding the people of Israel. Then the scene changes at the picket fence[4] where, suddenly, an abundance of flowers bloom.

The tips of the angel's wings point out and pick up the story, from both sides of the fence, which the angel Gabriel is relating to Mary, revealing to her a new understanding of her identity as both Daughter of Sion and Mother of the Son of God. The whole scene is reminiscent of the Song of the Songs: 'He looks in at the window, he peers through the lattice. Winter is past, the rains are over and gone, the flowers appear on the earth' (Song 2:8-14).

At this fence there is also a palm tree reaching up and back as far as Adam and Eve, seemingly to rescue them.[5] At the foot of this tree are two large, bright white flowers like two shining witnesses of faith, Mary and the beloved disciple, at the foot of the cross. There is now a garden in place of the forest, where flowers, like waves of grace and beauty, flow down to the edge of the painting towards us into our time, the time of the church.

Not only is God's promise of a new Eve portrayed here, fulfilled in Mary, but God's promise to Abraham, our father in faith, is depicted in the skies above Mary and the angel. Where the roof of the house should be, there are instead a multitude of stars, 'As the stars in the sky, so shall your descendants be' (Gen 15:5). We are all children of Mary, the new Eve, and every Mass is a fulfilment of God's promises and a continuation of the story of salvation by Christ through his church.

2. Mary's disposition and the Eucharist

'*Mysterium fidei!* If the Eucharist is a mystery of faith which so

greatly transcends our understanding as to call for sheer abandonment to the word of God, then there can be no one like Mary
to act as our support and guide in acquiring this disposition'
(EdE, #54).

Nicholas Poussin was the son of a French farmer who made
Rome his home and who after intense study is reported to have
said himself that he 'neglected nothing'[6] in his paintings,
whether of religious or classical scenes. This attention to detail
can be seen in his painting of the Annunciation (oil on canvas,
1657, National Gallery, London, see page 321 below).

This depiction of the annunciation portrays very explicitly
Mary's 'sheer abandonment to the word of God'. Mary, her eyes
closed, is 'seeing' the message, the word, rather than the messenger. The dazzling angel is there for our sake, manifesting the
message in bodily form. The angel's abundance of white robes is
an indication of the purity of the message and its radiance that
brings light to a world in darkness. The content of the message is
more specifically portrayed by the two hands of the angel that
are positioned at the precise centre of this small devotional
painting. One hand, typically, points heavenwards; the other
points to the heart and womb of Mary which, here, is in deep
shadow:

> 'The people that walked in darkness has seen a great light;
> on those who live in a land of shadow a light has shone' (Isa
> 9:1).

> 'The loving kindness of the heart of our God
> who visits us like the dawn from on high,
> will give light to those in darkness,
> those who dwell in the shadow of death' (Lk 1:78-79).

The main light source for the painting is not the angel but, like
'the dawn from on high', it shines into the painting from beyond
it. The moment of the incarnation in Mary's womb has always
been recognised as an event of the Trinity and artists have often
indicated the Trinitarian presence in different ways. Here it is
achieved by both a sign and light for each of the divine persons:

God the Father is indicated by the ultimate light source and the pointing of the angel; the shining white brightness of the angel and the pointing finger indicate God the Son, and the Holy Spirit is presented as a dove in a halo of light.

Mary, meanwhile, is portrayed reading, sitting on a cushion with curtains stretched out behind her, as Isaiah had prophesied:

'Sing O barren one, who did not bear;
Break forth into singing and cry aloud
You who have not been in travail
For the children of the desolate one
will be more than the children of her that is married, says the Lord.
Widen your tent, and let the curtains of your habitation be stretched out
Your descendants will possess the nations …
For your Maker is your husband,
The Lord of hosts is his name'(Isa 54:1-5).

The open book always symbolises the scriptures. Although we know that books as such did not exist in Mary's day and that the New Testament had not been written, nonetheless, the book here symbolises the two covenants, the first and the second, with Mary, as we have seen, included in both covenants as Daughter of Sion and Mother of Christ. The light picks out Mary's knees, the embodiment of the two Testaments, Old and New.

The light and shadow are clearly significant in this painting. Light also catches Mary's face focusing our attention upon her reception and response to the message of the angel. Her inner disposition is, again, embodied: Mary receives the message of the angel with her head raised upwards in an attitude of reception and faith, with her 'fiat' visibly flowing like energy down her arms and out through her long fingers stretched towards us. The right arm particularly, in the golden sleeve picked out in light, is painted to reveal the pure beauty of such an 'Amen' like a river of molten glory pouring down from her face, down her

arm and on into pools on the floor on either side of her outstretched hand. The whole of creation will be touched by this
event and redeemed, as it is in the eucharistic celebration of the
Mass. Such is the result of 'abandonment to the Word of God'.

3. Mary's 'fiat' and the Eucharist

'… there is a profound analogy between the *Fiat* which Mary
said in reply to the angel and the *Amen* which every believer
says when receiving the body of the Lord' (*EdE*, #55).

In both paintings of the annunciation that we have contemplated, Mary's *fiat* has been key, either as hands crossed against
her breast or as arms thrown open to receive the Word in her
womb. Not only in her gestures do we see her reply but also in
the backgrounds of the two paintings: in the stretching back of
the curtains in Poussin's painting and in the open doorway in
the painting by Fra Angelico. An open doorway is a sign in religious painting of the inner chamber of a person's mind and soul.
In some paintings one sees an ascending stairway suggesting
another form of ascent, an ascent of the mind. In this painting it
is further emphasised by the angel's finger that points directly
towards the structural opening in the wall. The Holy Father implies in the encyclical that the same 'structural opening' can take
place deeply within the mind, will and conscience of each believer when he or she says 'Amen' to receiving the body of the
Lord with faith.

4. Grace, poverty and the Eucharist

'Above all, let us listen to Mary Most Holy, in whom the mystery of the Eucharist appears, more than in anyone else, as a
mystery of light. Gazing upon Mary we come to know the transforming power present in the Eucharist' (*EdE*, #62).

In the painting of Mary teaching Jesus to read (artist unknown), we unexpectedly see a painting of the Eucharist *par excellence*, as the Holy Father suggests we will. Here, 'gazing upon
Mary', 'the mystery of the Eucharist appears' and we see its
'transforming power'.

Angelico, Fra (1387-1455): Cortona Altarpiece with the Annunciation, Cortona, Museo Diocesano, © 2002, Photo Scala, Florence. Used by permission.

Poussin, Nicholas (1594-1665): The Annunciation, © The National Gallery, London. Used by permission.

To set the whole scene in context we see firstly that the archi-tectural background is entirely ecclesial, rather than domestic as in many other paintings of this genre. The painting draws upon actual architecture of a fifteenth century church (a clear example of what the Holy Father describes as the work of adaptation), thus bringing the reality of this scene shockingly close to those for whom it was painted. It is taking place within the church building in the central position where the eucharistic celebration occurs.

One can also see immediately that within the setting there are three elements: Jesus, portrayed as a tiny figure poorly dressed, sitting and held, together with a book, by Mary in the richest of robes. Is this an example of the complexities of tradi-tion overlaying the simple gospel account, so that the poor girl from Nazareth is now replaced by a medieval queen? Rather, we have here a deeply insightful application of the words of St Paul: 'Remember how generous the Lord Jesus was: he was rich, but he became poor for your sake, to make you rich out of his poverty' (2 Cor 8:9).

It is in the Eucharist, today, that Christ becomes poor that we might become rich. The poverty of the Christ child in a simple, collarless chemise, almost like a corporal for a dead body, con-trasts powerfully with the rich dress of the woman. Mary's dress, indicating, as we have said, the state or status of the per-son, is so important to the artist that he completely fills the lower half of the section with its voluminous, velvety folds. This demonstrates, with glorious abundance, Mary's fullness of grace.

Not only this, but here too is depicted the fullness of the Mass in the double aspect of Word of God (the scriptures) and body of Christ (the living child) both held lovingly and securely in the lap of Our Blessed Lady, Mother and Model of the Church, with whom and in whom the scriptures are always to be read, in the presence and in the light of Christ. Mary's dress, then, symbolises too, the grace lavished upon the church, in each of her members, at the celebration of the Mass. 'Blessed be God the Father of our

Lord Jesus Christ, who has blessed us with all the spiritual bless-
ings of the heavenly places … Such is the richness of his grace
which he lavished upon us' (Eph 1:1-8).

5. Mary at Christ's Sacrifice and the Eucharist

'Mary, throughout her life at Christ's side and not only on
Calvary, made her own the sacrificial dimension of the Eucharist'
(*EdE*, #56).

Raphael painted a crucifixion scene in 1503 for a side altar
dedicated to St Jerome in the church of San Dominico, Città di
Castello, in Tuscany. It is now in the National Gallery, London.
In this painting we see Mary, typically, again at Christ's side.
Here, she looks not at her son but at us, inviting and teaching us,
as the Holy Father suggests, how to make our own the sacrificial
dimension of the Eucharist which Mary lived throughout her
life.

If we look closely at the painting we will see how deliberately
eucharistic it is in its details. The most obvious sign of the eucharistic nature of this scene is given by the angels carrying chalices to catch the saving blood of Christ as it falls from his hands
and his side to be used directly at the eucharistic celebration.
Such is the sacrifice of the Mass, re-enacting the one sacrifice of
Christ on the one cross.

The dark cross in this picture rises from blackened and barren earth up through the centre of the painting right up to the
sun and moon. It rises through golden but still desert hillsides,
then through water, where the landscape becomes fertile and
then up into the skies. Such is the path of salvation from the
darkness of sin, by golden grace, through the water of baptism
to redemption brought about by Christ's paschal mystery, both
on Calvary and at the altar.

The figures are gathered at the foot of the cross in different
attitudes of prayer. St Jerome is the penitent asking for forgiveness, holding a stone to beat his breast in one hand and holding
out a white hand against the black ground to catch the blood
falling from Christ's feet and this outstretched hand shines in

'La Vierge et l'Enfant'. Photo © Musées royaux des Beaux-Arts, Brussels.
Used by permission.

Raphael (1483-1520): The Crucified Christ with the Virgin Mary, Saints and Angels
(The Mond Crucifixion). © The National Gallery, London. Used by permission.

the darkness, indicating faith seeking healing through the touch of Christ's blood.

Mary Magdalen, on the other hand, is kneeling in adoration and thanksgiving because of all that Christ has done for her by his love. Forgiven and radiant, her red cloak is touched with gold manifesting her inner self as she worships, kneeling peacefully and looking loving up at her saving Lord; the most appropriate disposition after communion.

St John and Our Blessed Lady look out of the painting at us, the onlookers. In sacred art such regards are always invitations. Mary, the pure one, invites us to penitence like Jerome for what our sins have done to her Son and our Lord; St John invites us to worship with thanksgiving like Mary Magdalen for our salvation by God's great love.

Mary, standing at Christ's side, mirrors the colours of Christ and his cross, black and red. In fact every figure on the ground wears red in some form, even St Jerome. His red girdle reminds us of the red cord used at Jericho allowing the Israelites to escape (this was recognised by the fathers of the church as a prefiguring of salvation by Christ's blood poured out).

To sum up, the Holy Father writes, 'The Mystery of the Eucharist – sacrifice, presence, banquet – does not allow for reduction or exploitation: it must be experienced and lived in its integrity' (*EdE*, #61). This painting portrays each of these three mysteries eucharistically. Christ's presence is quiet and without anguish. He is not portrayed as the suffering one calling out '*Eloi, Eloi, lama sabachthani?*' (Mk 15:34). He is presented more as the pale communion host adored at benediction. Christ's sacrifice is portrayed in the black cross and the outpouring blood touching and transforming St Jerome's hand and symbolised in the red worn by each of the figures. The banquet of the Mass is made evident in the chalices of blood held by the angels. The lifegiving qualities of the blood affect the animated angels who seem to dance together with their dresses and animated ribbons in sharp contrast to the still figures below. The Eucharist takes us from death to life, as the cross does too in this picture from the dark earth at the foot of the painting to the bright skies at the top, uniting heaven and earth by Christ's eternal offering of himself to his Father.

'Ave verum corpus natum de Maria Virgine, vere passum, immolatum, in cruce pro homine! Here is the church's treasure, the heart of the world, the pledge of the fulfilment for which each man and woman, even unconsciously yearns' (*EdE*, #59).

Sacred art, adapted to the liturgy of the people of each time and place, manifesting the ineffable mystery of the Eucharist and reminding the ordinary man and woman of their great dignity in Christ and the graciousness of God's condescension, is as necessary today as in the past. Liturgical art that truly reflects 'the church's treasure, the heart of the world', has a vital role in drawing people towards that happiness 'for which each man and woman, even unconsciously yearns' (*EdE*, #59).

CHAPTER SEVENTEEN

St Thomas Aquinas, Poet of the Eucharist

James McEvoy

He that is hurt seeks help; sin is the wound;
The salve for this I'th'Eucharist is found. *Robert Herrick*

The reader of *EdE* encounters St Thomas Aquinas several times
on the way through the document. Side by side with his theology
of the Mass and eucharistic presence stand allusions to the poetry
of the saint concerning the Sacrament of the Altar. When taken
all together, these references form part of the meaning of the letter, which actually comes to an end (#62) with a quotation from
one of the poems of the saint, *Lauda, Sion*:

> *Bone pastor, panis vere,*
> *Iesu, nostri miserere …*
> Come then, good Shepherd, bread divine,
> Still show to us thy mercy sign;
> Oh, feed us, still keep us thine;
> So we may see thy glories shine
> In fields of immortality.[1]

From the liturgy composed by Aquinas for the Feast of Corpus
Christi comes a reference to the Eucharist as 'the pledge of future glory' (#18).[2] The concluding exhortation of *EdE* opens with
the words *'Ave verum corpus natum de Maria Virgine'* (#59), and
continues with a personal testimony of the Holy Father that pro-
longs the words of Aquinas (taken from the poem *Adoro Te
Devote*) concerning the transcendence of the senses in and
through eucharistic faith.[3] The veritable theme song of the
Thomistic reflection on the Eucharist is evoked by means of a
thought from the *Summa*: 'In this sacrament is recapitulated the
whole mystery of our salvation' (#61).[4]

The Personal Eucharistic Devotion of Thomas

One of the biographers of Brother Thomas, William Tocco, brings out the special quality of his confrère's eucharistic devotion:

> He had a particular devotion to the Sacrament of the Altar; and no doubt the special profundity of his writings on this subject was due to the same grace which enabled him to celebrate Mass so devoutly. This he did every day, unless prevented by sickness; after which he would hear, and usually also serve, another Mass said by his *socius* or some other priest. We are told that at the elevation of Christ's body it was his custom to exclaim devoutly: *'Tu rex gloriae, Christe, tu Patris sempiternus es filius.'*[5] While saying Mass he was utterly absorbed by the mystery, and his face ran with tears.[6]

The Office for the Feast of Corpus Christi (Opusculum 54, 1264)

The attribution to Thomas of the entire Office for the Feast of Corpus Christi (i.e., both the liturgical hours and the Mass) goes back to an Italian Dominican, Ptolemy (Tolomeo) of Lucca, who wrote as follows:

> By order of the same Pope [Urban] brother Thomas also composed the Office for Corpus Christi – the second commission from the Pope to which I referred above.[7] This Corpus Christi Office Thomas composed in full, including the lessons and all the parts to be recited by day or night; the Mass, too, and whatever has to be sung on that day. An attentive reader will see that it comprises nearly all the symbolic figures (*figurae*) from the Old Testament, clearly and appropriately relating them to the Sacrament of the Eucharist.[8]

Ptolemy died in the year 1327, four years after the canonisation of Aquinas and some fifty-three years after his death.[9] His is the first testimony to Thomas's authorship of the office, and its lateness has led some to question the authenticity of the writing, on the grounds that no contemporary of Ptolemy lends independent corroboration to the attribution. However, the weight of opinion has of recent years swung heavily behind the credibility of this well-informed historical chronicler, who was a student and confrère of Thomas during the latter's years in Italy.[10] Ptolemy in fact spent the two final years (1272-74) of Thomas's short life living in the same convent, and he compiled a list of his Master's writings, even finishing one (*De Regno*, On Kingship) which was left incomplete upon his death.

Friar Ptolemy, in the notice we have quoted, goes to the very heart of the originality of the office, namely the constant employment its author makes of the Old Testament motifs, to which, just like Thomas, he refers as *figurae* (such as the bread and wine offered by Melchizedek, the sacrifice of Isaac, and the manna or 'bread from heaven'), which in some way or other 'prefigure' Christ the Bread of Life, and the Eucharist.

The Solemnity

The origins of the Feast of Corpus Christi are well known and need only be summarised here. It was originally on the initiative of an abbess, St Julienne (Juliana) of Mont-Cornillon in Liège, that a diocesan feast was instituted by the bishop, Robert de Thourotte, and celebrated on the Thursday (June 19 in that year) following Trinity Sunday (Thursday, recalling Holy Thursday). Eucharistic devotion in the territory of Liège grew up as a reaction to the Albigensian denial of the sacrament. St Julienne (1192-1258) was the object of a very revealing biography by one of her nuns. She directed a leprosarium, and combined administration with a life of intense prayer. She aligned her life progressively upon the objective of promoting a feast dedicated to Christ in the sacrament of his body and blood. Her personal spirituality was focused upon the love of Christ.[11] It so happened that an archdeacon of that city, Jacques Pantaléon, became Pope as Urban IV, and he took the decision to extend the feast to the whole church. This he did through the Bull *Transiturus*, promulgated on 11 August 1264. In compliance with the papal request Thomas Aquinas submitted a text for the office of the new 'Solemnity of the Body of Christ', but this (known from its initial word as *Sapientia*/Wisdom) was provi-

sional; it was replaced in the months following the first celebration (in the first half of 1264) by Thomas's definitive text,
Sacerdos in aeternum ('A priest forever, Christ our Lord, according to the order of Melchizedek, offered bread and wine'), the
one which appears in editions of his works. Thomas finished the
revision of his text in the early summer of 1264. It was a fruit of
his lengthy stay at Orvieto, where he was in the service of the
Pope between 1259 and 1265. Each copy of the Bull sent out from
Rome had folded within it a copy of the liturgy which was to be
obligatory for the celebration, and thus to replace the existing
Liège Office. Such was the exceptional importance attached by
Urban to the Office he had commissioned from the greatest of
living theologians. In fact the feast was not very widely celebrat-
ed until after 1317, when it was re-promulgated under Pope
John XXII.

The thirteenth century witnessed a significant rise in eucharistic devotion. Responsible in part for the new fervour were
the female religious orders and congregations (such as the
Cistercians and the Béguines) and the many recluses. If St
Julienne may in the eyes of the historian stand for this movement as a whole, it is St Thomas Aquinas who is emblematic of
the parallel development in theology and the schools.

Purpose of the Solemnity

In the fourth Lesson of the First Nocturne of the Feast, Thomas
himself analysed the aims of the Solemnity of Corpus Christi in
the following effective way:

It fits in well with the devotions of the faithful to have a
solemn recollection of the institution of a sacrament which is
such a bearer of salvation, and is as wonderful as this one is;
[1] in order to venerate the unsayable mode of the divine
presence in the visible sacrament; [2] to praise the power of
God which in a single sacrament works so many wonderful
things; [3] and to give the thanks that are due for a gift so
health-giving and so full of delight.[12]

The Old and the New in the Office

Ptolemy of Lucca, as we have seen, picked out as the most strik-ing feature of the Office the use of *figurae* coming from the Old Testament. The greatest living expert on the Office, Père Gy OP, writes: 'This office grants their full value to the Old Testament prefigurations of the Eucharist; it clearly refuses an allegorical interpretation of scripture and focuses attention as precisely as possible upon the exact meaning of the texts.'[13]

In what follows we will have occasion to advert to several motifs which illustrate the promise-fulfillment motif in the eu-charistic thought of St Thomas.

Personal stamp

The personal imprint of St Thomas's thought regarding the Blessed Eucharist is to be found everywhere in the text of the Office – even down to its silences, which, it has been shown, can be made in a way to speak. Gy has pointed out, quite strikingly, that Thomas never countenanced the eucharistic interpretation of Mt 28:20 ('I am with you always, to the end of the age') that was current among his contemporaries, and was indeed present in the Liège Office – as it would prove to be in the Bull *Transiturus*; theologians saw in this saying of Jesus a promise of his presence in the Eucharist.[14] As an alternative, Thomas's trawl through the Old Testament brought up Deut 4:7, 'For what other great nation has a god so near to it as the Lord our God is?'), identifying there an Old Testament motif that was to find its fulfillment in the New Covenant precisely through the pres-ence of Christ, God and man, in the Blessed Eucharist.

Thomas likewise declined to employ the idea of *praesentia corporalis* that was in common usage to designate the presence of Christ in the eucharistic elements. His motivation evidently was that the transubstantiation, or the conversion of the substance of the bread and of the wine into the body and blood of Christ, leaves the accidents intact, including that of 'locus', i.e., the acci-dent of being present in a place.[15] The notion of 'real presence' was closer to Thomas's own thought, and in fact it was to appear side by side with that of 'corporeal presence' in the Bull *Transiturus*. In the Lessons which he composed for the feast Thomas referred to 'the unsayable (*ineffabilis*) mode of the divine presence in the visible sacrament'. And in his *Summa* he turned the idea of localisation around in a way that is worthy of notice. Rather than making himself present to us as in a place, it is us that Christ makes present to him. It was in terms of the philosophy of friendship (which he himself had recovered through writing a commentary on the *Ethics* of Aristotle) that Thomas attempted to make the presence of Christ intelligible to believers:

> It belongs completely to friendship *to live with one's friends*, as the Philosopher says … and that is why Christ has promised us his bodily presence as a reward … But meanwhile, in our pilgrimage he has not wished to deprive us of his bodily presence, but through the truth of his body and blood he joins us to himself in this sacrament. Hence he says, "Those who eat my flesh and drink my blood abide in me, and I in them" (Jn 6:56). Hence this sacrament is the sign of the greatest love and the comfort of our hope, by reason of this very intimate union with Christ.[16]

The Aristotelian thinking which Thomas espoused throughout his life leaves a clear trace in the second Lesson which he composed for Matins: 'For the accidents exist in it without the subject, so that faith may have its place while the visible is received invisibly, hidden under another appearance, *and the senses, which judge about the accidents with which they are familiar*, are made safe from error'. The words placed in italics underline the value of the judgement made by the senses regarding the eucharistic accidents; the former may not seem to suit a liturgical context, but they are something like a personal signature of Thomas upon his writing.[17]

In the mature thought of St Thomas regarding the Eucharist the highpoint of his development, both intellectual and spiritual, can be studied. In the Office, he centred everything upon the mystery of Christ contained in the sacrament, to the point where he can say, 'Receive Christ', rather than 'Receive the body and

blood of Christ.' The notion of presence we have already underlined. There is also at work in the Office a kind of eschatological
displacement, in a way that became more accentuated as
Thomas developed. The sacrament is 'a pledge of future glory'
and 'the comfort of our hope'. The eucharistic thought of
Thomas fused with his theology of the tension of human existence towards the vision of God. The affective language of the
Office and of the prayers (*suavis refectio, dulcedo spiritualis:* sweet-
tasting nourishment, spiritual delight) invites us to accept the
credibility of Bartholemew of Capua, who claimed that Thomas
made a profession of eucharistic faith upon his deathbed, in the
following terms:

> I receive you, price of the redemption of my soul; I receive
> you, viaticum of my pilgrimage, for whose love I have stud-
> ied, watched, worked, preached and taught.

The Hymns of the Office

The hymns are three in number, to which the Sequence of the
Mass should be added as a fourth item (*Lauda, Sion*). Together
these productions bring the eucharistic-liturgical hymnody of
the Middle Ages to its highest point.[18] A word may be said about
each of them.

Pange, lingua, gloriosi corporis mysterium, is the most familiar,
and it ends with the two verses '*Tantum ergo sacramentum*' and
'*Gentori genitoque*', which have a firmly traditional place in the
service of Benediction.[19] The first line is borrowed from the
Hymn to the Holy Cross of Venantius Fortunatus.[20] The passage
from the observance by Jesus and the Twelve of the Old Law
('*observata lege plene*'), through the eating of the foods prescribed
in the Torah ('*cibis in legalibus*'), to the New, is marked by the
yielding of the Old Writing ('*antiquum documentum*') to the New
Rite ('*novo cedat ritui*') – requiring faith since the senses give no
guidance as to what is truly happening ('*sensuum defectui*'). F. J.
E. Raby judged, many years since, that the hymn, being 'beyond
all praise, for its severe and rigid beauty, its precision of thought
and adequacy of content, should be heard as the processional in

a cathedral on Holy Thursday ... [it] is one of the most sublime productions of sacred poetry'.[21]

Sacris solemniis juncta sint gaudia, which is the hymn for Matins, expresses joy and praise for the Feast. 'Let the Old give way, let all be made New!' ('*Recedant vetera, nova sint omnia*'). The verses mingle precise theological expression with fervent devotion, something indeed that characterises all the eucharistic hymns of Thomas. The '*agnum et azyma*' which Christ offerred to his brethren refer to the victim lamb and the unleavened bread (*azyma*, Gr.), as in Mk 14:1. The last two verses, beginning '*Panis angelicus fit panis hominum*', have been set to music many times and are well known. The concluding verse is addressed to the Trinity, asking to be led to the light and vision of heaven. The expert use made of the difficult asclepiad rhythm displays Thomas's always-skilful employment of metre, and his rhyming is impeccable in each of the poems.

Verbum supernum prodiens. In the hymn for Lauds, Thomas again borrows his first line (this time from an ancient Ambrosian hymn). This time he employs the popular 'Ambrosian' rhythm. The penultimate strophe, '*O salutaris hostia*', is extremely familiar from Benediction. The hymn in six verses closes with praise of the Trinity, and expresses hope for the Life '*in patria*'.

For the Sequence of the Mass, *Lauda, Sion, Salvatorem*, the metrical model was the *Laudes Crucis Attollamus* of Adam of St Victor (fl. ca 1140), who was in several ways Aquinas's predecessor in hymnody. 'Sion' stands for the church, in this hymn of pure praise of the 'living and life-giving Bread' ('*panis vivus et vitalis*'). The 'new Pasch' of Easter refers to Christ 'the paschal lamb [who] has been sacrificed' (1 Cor 5:7), thus bringing to an end the '*phase vetus*', or old dispensation.[22] This poem of twenty-three verses may be considered the most theologically sophisticated of the hymns, and its strophes can be aligned with the eucharistic teaching of Thomas. The Eucharist is referred to as '*panis angelorum*', the bread of angels, in a quite traditional way, and '*non mittendus canibus*' ('not to be thrown to the dogs') likewise went back to earlier centuries (and of course to Mk 7:27);

just as did the three *figurae* of the sacrifice of Isaac, the designation of the paschal lamb, and the manna given to the Fathers.[23]
The two concluding verses, beginnng '*Bone pastor*', are quoted at
the close of *EdE*; they express longing for the Land of the Living
and the table that awaits the faithful there.[24]

O sacrum Convivium

The origin of this celebrated prayer and hymn-text can be fixed
firmly in the Office of Corpus Christi, where it forms the
Antiphon of the Magnificat of the Second Vespers. The words
make up the most condensed summary of eucharistic doctrine:

> O sacred banquet
> In which Christ is received,
> The memory of the passion recalled,
> The mind filled with grace
> And a pledge of future glory given us.

The image of the 'pledge' (*pignus*) was employed more than
once by Aquinas. Among the numerous Antiphons and
Responses this one is the exception, being composed for the occasion; the others are all taken (or adapted) directly from the
Bible. The threefold structure of eucharistic time into past, present and future had a parallel in the oration in the Office and the
Mass: '*Deus, qui nobis sub sacramento mirabili ...*'

> 'O God, who under this wonderful Sacrament have left us a
> memorial of your passion, grant, we pray, that we may ven-
> erate the sacred mysteries of your Body and Blood so as con-
> stantly to feel the fruits of your redemption within us, who
> live and reign ...'

Adoro Devote

The judgement of authenticity regarding the celebrated *Adoro*
has taken more than one dramatic turn of recent years, and leading Thomistic scholars such as Gy, Torrell and Wielockx are
presently to be found arguing for Aquinas's authorship of it – in
the case of Gy, following a change of mind based upon freshly-
discovered, early manuscript evidence.[25] It is significant that in

the extensive (though generally late) manuscript tradition of the poem no attribution is ever made except to Thomas Aquinas. One is perfectly entitled to regard this devotional salute to the elevated species as a genuine work of the saint. The first lines were restored by Dom André Wilmart through textual criticism: *'Adoro devote, latens veritas/ Te qui sub his formis vere latitas.'* The word *figurae*, so widespread as a textual variant in the manuscript tradition of *Adoro*, is in Thomas's authentic thought assigned a firm meaning in relation to biblical typology, as we have noted earlier. Nevertheless, *figurae* was for centuries a firmly-implanted variant, and Gerard Manley Hopkins SJ rendered it:

> Godhead here in hiding,
> whom I do adore,
> masked by these bare shadows,
> *shape* and nothing more ...

The standard English translation on the other hand reflects the reading *formae*:

> O Godhead hid, devoutly I adore Thee,
> Who truly art within the *forms* before me ...

The most unforgettable verse in the beautiful Hopkins version is the one on the eucharistic *memoriale*:

> O thou our reminder
> of Christ crucified,
> living Bread, the life of
> us for whom he died,
> lend this life to me then;
> feed and feast my mind,
> there be thou the sweetness
> Man was meant to find.

The idea, which makes its appearance in *Adoro*, that a single drop of the blood of Christ (*'una stilla'*) would have sufficed to save the whole world, goes back to St Bernard, to whom Thomas twice attributed the notion in theological writings. Bernard spoke of *'una gutta sanguinis Christi'*.

Raby justly described *Adoro* as 'a pious meditation of incomparable beauty and closely-knit construction', and added that it has the 'strongest claim' to authenticity.[26]

The Prayers Before Communion and of Thanksgiving after Mass
Most missals print these prayers, which are among a total of twelve attributed in manuscripts to St Thomas.[27] They exhibit in microcosm the characteristic features of his eucharistic thought. The prayer of preparation asks for relief from sickness, blindness, poverty and indigence of spirit, and also for contrition and devotion to receive the sacrament, together with its full effect and power to incorporate the believer into the mystical Body.[28] It concludes with the hope of the viator for the pure contemplation of heaven, and with a trinitarian invocation. The thanksgiving praises the divine mercy, 'that this holy communion may not bring me condemnation and punishment but forgiveness and salvation'. Taking images from the letter to Ephesians, Thomas asks that holy communion may be a 'helmet' of faith for him and a 'shield' of good will. He prays that it may extinguish evil desire and augment the virtues (notably charity and patience); that it may unite him closely to the one true God, and that it may lead him safely through death to the heavenly banquet of fulfilment, perfect joy and happiness.

APPENDIX

St Thomas Aquinas, Lessons from the Office of Corpus Christi
This résumé of Catholic eucharistic faith was composed by St Thomas as Lessons (divided into four) for the Office of the Feast of Corpus Christi. It has been retained in abbreviated form in the revised breviary of 1973. Although it is admirably condensed it expresses the whole faith of the church in the gift of the Eucharist, and does so in terms that are very accessible.[29]

Lesson 1
The immense good done to us by the generosity of God and manifested to his Christian people confers upon the latter a dig-

nity beyond price. For there neither is nor was at any time such 'a great nation which had gods so near to it, as our God' is close to us (cf. Deut 4:7). The only-begotten Son of God, wishing to enable us to share in his divinity, assumed our nature, so that by becoming man he might make men gods.

Moreover, he turned the whole of our nature, which he assumed, to our salvation. For he offered his body to God the Father on the altar of the cross as a sacrifice for our reconciliation; and he shed his blood for our ransom and our cleansing, so that we might be redeemed from wretched captivity and cleansed from all sins.

Lesson 2

Now in order that we might always keep the memory of this great act of love, he left his body as food and his blood as drink, to be received by the faithful under the appearances of bread and wine.

How precious and wonderful is this banquet, which brings us salvation and is full of all delight! What could be more precious? It is not the meat of calves or kids that is offered, as happened under the Old Law; at this meal Christ, the true God, is set before us for us to eat. What could be more wonderful than this sacrament? …

Lesson 3

No sacrament contributes more to our salvation than this; for it purges away our sins, increases our virtues, and nourishes our minds with an abundance of all the spiritual gifts. It is offered in the church for the living and the dead, so that it may be beneficial to all, as it was instituted for the salvation of all.

Lesson 4

Finally, no one is capable of expressing the delight of this sacrament, through which the sweetness of the Spirit is tasted at its source, and the memory is celebrated of that surpassing love which Christ showed in his passion.

And so, in order to imprint the immensity of this love more deeply in the hearts of the faithful, at the Last Supper, when the Lord had celebrated the Pasch with his disciples and was about to pass from this world to his Father, he instituted this sacrament as a perpetual memorial of his passion. It fulfilled the types of the Old Law; it was the greatest of the miracles he worked; and he left it as a unique consolation to those who were desolate at his departure.

CHAPTER EIGHTEEN

Ut Unum Sint: Eucharist and Ecumenism

Paul McPartlan

'May they all be one, just as, Father, you are in me and I am in you … so that the world may believe it was you who sent me' (Jn 17:21). It is not often recalled that this prayer of Jesus, which constantly inspires ecumenical work, was actually uttered in the setting of the Last Supper. It is primarily a eucharistic prayer.

Jesus wanted his followers to be one most of all in the Eucharist. After all, he died so as 'to gather into one the scattered children of God' (Jn 11:52), and the Mass is the 'sacramental representation of Christ's sacrifice, crowned by the resurrection', as Pope John Paul teaches in his encyclical letter, *Ecclesia de Eucharistia* (#15).[1] This is the act which makes us one. In this celebration, we are refashioned in unity as the church. 'We must all be molten in that crucible of unity which is the Eucharist',[2] said the French Jesuit Henri de Lubac (1896-1991), one of the leading pioneers of Vatican II.

Jesus said in the gospel: 'if you are bringing your offering to the altar and there remember that your brother has something against you, leave your offering there before the altar, go and be reconciled with your brother first, and then come back and present your offering' (Mt 5:23-24). In accordance with this teaching, Christians of many different churches and traditions are involved in ecumenical dialogue today in the hope of resolving their differences so that they may be able to celebrate the Eucharist together. One of the great fruits of dialogue is a richer understanding of the Eucharist itself and that richer understanding is what I would like to explore in this chapter.

Pope John Paul makes a number of references to ecumenism in his encyclical on the Eucharist. He gives thanks for the ecumenical movement (*EdE*, #43) and notes the 'significant progress and convergence' that dialogue has achieved on two aspects of the Eucharist in recent decades, namely the relationship between priestly ministry and the Eucharist and also regarding the sacrificial aspect of the Eucharist (*EdE*, #30). He gives no reference at this point, but it would seem likely that the Pope is referring to the 'Lima Report' of the Faith and Order Commission of the World Council of Churches, entitled, *Baptism, Eucharist and Ministry* (1982), the most significant ecumenical agreed statement so far achieved, and one with full Catholic participation (the Catholic Church became a member of Faith and Order in 1968). Regarding the first of the two matters highlighted by the Pope, the Lima Report emphasises that, in the celebration of the Eucharist, it is Christ himself who 'gathers, teaches and nourishes the church'. Ordained ministers are 'representatives of Jesus Christ to the community', and 'may appropriately be called priests because they fulfil a particular priestly service by strengthening and building up the royal and prophetic priesthood of the faithful'.[3] Regarding the second matter, the Report carefully and exactly states: 'The eucharist is the sacrament of the unique sacrifice of Christ, who ever lives to make intercession for us.'[4] These are indications of remarkable ecumenical convergence in recent times on issues that sharply divided Catholics from Protestants at the Reformation, and should indeed give us cause for rejoicing.

Unfortunately, the encyclical makes no further reference to points of convergence, and there is no specific mention of the various agreed statements on the Eucharist that have been achieved ecumenically. However, there are many points at which Pope John Paul's own teaching in the encyclical actually resonates with themes that have emerged in ecumenical dialogue and been very important for the achievement of consensus, and I would like to highlight some of those themes here.

We should mention immediately one well-known point on which the teaching of the Catholic Church (and likewise of the Orthodox Church) is at variance with that of many other

Christian traditions, namely regarding the possibility of inter-communion, that is, regular eucharistic sharing between Christians of different churches prior to our visible unity. While happily acknowledging that, in particular cases of spiritual need, Catholic priests can administer the sacraments of Eucharist, Penance and Anointing to individual Christians of other churches (*EdE*, ##45-46), the Pope firmly states that full eucharistic sharing is the goal of ecumenical activity because it presupposes the communion of those who celebrate together (*EdE*, ##35, 38, 44). The Eucharist is, in fact, 'the supreme sacrament of the unity of the People of God' (*EdE*, #43; cf. #61), and not a means towards the achievement of visible unity. This teaching is clearly based on the instruction of Jesus in St Matthew's gospel recalled above, and also on the way in which St Paul holds strictly together the sharing of 'one bread' and being 'one body' (1 Cor 10:17; cf. *EdE*, #23). We might aptly say that the unity of the community which celebrates the Eucharist is itself part of the sacramental sign of the Eucharist, and a crucial indication of what the Eucharist actually is in God's plan, namely the sacrament by which the communion life of the blessed Trinity is shared with human beings in Christ. Pope John Paul II praises Rublëv's famous depiction of the Trinity as pointing to 'a profoundly eucharistic church in which the presence of the mystery of Christ in the broken bread is as it were immersed in the ineffable unity of the three divine Persons, making of the church herself an "icon" of the Trinity' (*EdE*, #50).

A Bigger Picture of the Eucharist
In his celebrated encyclical letter on ecumenism, *Ut Unum Sint*, in 1995, the Pope already emphasised 'the ecclesiological implication of sharing in the sacraments, especially in the Holy Eucharist',[5] and this is his primary theme in the new encyclical, as the title shows: *Ecclesia de Eucharistia*. The first sentence states: 'The church draws her life from the Eucharist' (*EdE*, #1). We would surely be justified in detecting strong hints of the work of de Lubac here and at various points later on. Pope John Paul

greatly admired de Lubac and made him a cardinal in 1983. It was de Lubac who coined the famous expression, 'the Eucharist makes the church'.[6] For de Lubac, this principle was a vital and explanatory complement to the more obvious fact that the church itself celebrates the Eucharist. In 1953, he said: 'the church makes the Eucharist, but the Eucharist also makes the church'; 'if the sacrifice is accepted by God and the church's prayer listened to, this is because the Eucharist, in its turn, makes the church, in the strictest sense'.[7] The encyclical notably echoes this double principle: 'the Eucharist builds the church and the church makes the Eucharist' (*EdE*, #26).

What de Lubac was opposing was the idea that receiving the Eucharist is simply a private, individual devotion. In the Eucharist, Jesus is not feeding lots of individual Christians, he is feeding his body, the church, and each of us as members of the church. 'True eucharistic piety', he said, 'is no devout individualism.' 'With one sweeping, all-embracing gesture, in one fervent intention it gathers together the whole world … [I]t cannot conceive of the action of the breaking of bread without fraternal communion.'[8] De Lubac saw that the primary task of the church in the midst of a fractured world was to restore the communion life for which humanity was made, when it was created in the image of the God who is Trinity. The Eucharist, in which we receive communion, is the focal point of the church's life, where together we receive the very gift we are to minister to the world. 'Humanity is one', he wrote, 'organically one by its divine structure; it is the church's mission to reveal to men that pristine unity that they have lost, to restore and complete it.'[9]

Joseph Ratzinger, also greatly influenced by de Lubac, has condensed de Lubac's double formula even further. 'The church is the celebration of the Eucharist; the Eucharist is the church; they do not simply stand side by side; they are one and the same; it is from there that everything else radiates.'[10] The bond between the Eucharist and the church has become a strong ecumenical theme. In words rather similar to Ratzinger's, the American Lutheran theologian, Robert W. Jenson, states: 'The

Eucharist does not merely enable or manifest the communion we call church, it *is* that communion.'[11] He himself then recalls an Anglican-Orthodox agreed statement which says: 'The church celebrating the Eucharist becomes fully itself: that is *koinonia* … The church celebrates the Eucharist as the central act of its existence, in which the ecclesial community … receives its realisation.'[12]

The Second Vatican Council taught that the Eucharist is 'the source and summit of the Christian life',[13] and that 'the principal manifestation of the church consists in the full, active participation of all God's holy people in the same liturgical celebrations, especially in the same Eucharist, in one prayer, at one altar, at which the bishop resides, surrounded by his college of presbyters and by his ministers.'[14] The Lima Report states likewise that: 'It is in the Eucharist that the community of God's people is fully manifested. Eucharistic celebrations always have to do with the whole church, and the whole church is involved in each local eucharistic celebration.'[15]

Strongly associated with this bond between the Eucharist and the church is the connection between the Eucharist and the future, because the church will only be fully realised on the Last Day, and the Eucharist gives us a foretaste of the final fulfilment we shall have all together in the heavenly Jerusalem. Looking to the end of time, and drawing on the teaching of St Augustine and others, Vatican II states: 'At that moment, as the Fathers put it, all the just from the time of Adam, "from Abel, the just one, to the last of the elect" will be gathered together with the Father in the universal church.'[16] The Eucharist mysteriously opens up that heavenly gathering to us already: 'In the earthly liturgy we take part in a foretaste of that heavenly liturgy which is celebrated in the Holy City of Jerusalem toward which we journey as pilgrims'.[17] In this way, the earthly community is progressively moulded after the model of the heavenly community, the 'universal church', and grows into what it is called to be; that is how the Eucharist makes the church. From a Lutheran perspective, Jenson says: 'The church is what she is just and only as anticipation of what she is to be',[18] and these words echo those of the distinguished Orthodox bishop and theologian, Metropolitan John Zizioulas, who, with reference to the repeated event of the Eucharist, says: 'She [the church] is what she is by becoming again and again what she will be.'[19]

It is primarily by means of the Eucharist, therefore, that the earthly church is itself a 'sacrament' of communion with God and of unity among human beings, as Vatican II taught,[20] both 'sign and instrument' of 'the full realisation of the unity yet to come'.[21] Jenson notably says: 'This teaching, that the church is herself a sort of sacrament, has become a centre not merely of Catholic ecclesiology but of ecumenical discussion.'[22]

How all of this happens is by the power of the Holy Spirit. Very significantly, Jesus himself promised the gift of the Holy Spirit in the eucharistic context of the Last Supper. He said: 'The Holy Spirit will teach you everything and remind you of all I have said to you' (Jn 14:26). Thus, it is the Holy Spirit who makes it possible for us to follow Jesus' instruction to 'Do this in re-membrance of me' (Lk 22:19; 1 Cor 11:24-25). Moreover, Jesus also said: 'When the Spirit of truth comes he will lead you to the complete truth ... and he will reveal to you the things to come' (Jn 16:13). In the Eucharist, therefore, the Spirit is powerfully ac-tive, not only enabling the memorial of Christ, but also revealing to the earthly church the wonders of the heavenly church, which itself is the great multitude gathered in communion with Christ in his glory by the same Spirit. The Spirit's gift is always one of communion (or *koinonia*, in Greek), as St Paul made clear when he prayed for the factious Corinthians that they might be blessed with 'the fellowship *[koinonia]* of the Holy Spirit' (2 Cor 13:13). In a most powerful statement, long before Vatican II, de Lubac already linked the Eucharist to the Holy Spirit and identi-fied the Spirit as the giver of the communion life we receive in the Eucharist: 'As the Spirit of Christ once came down upon the apostles not to unite them together in a closed group but to light within them the fire of universal charity, so does he still when-ever Christ delivers himself up once more "that the scattered children of God may be gathered together".' 'Our churches are the "upper room" where not only is the Last Supper renewed but Pentecost also.'[23]

We have seen that the Eucharist is fundamentally linked to the church, to the future and to the Holy Spirit. It is plain from the scriptures that the Eucharist was celebrated by the early Christians with a vivid awareness of these linkages. We might also mention the Letter to the Hebrews, read, as all the epistles were, first of all to a local community gathered for the weekly Eucharist, which teaches: 'what you have come to is Mount Zion and the city of the living God, the heavenly Jerusalem where the millions of angels have gathered for the festival, with the whole church [ekklesia] of the firstborn, enrolled as citizens of heaven' (Heb 12:22-23). In the Book of Revelation, John tells us likewise that he saw 'Jerusalem, the holy city, coming down out of heaven from God' (Rev 21:10). He saw a Lamb standing on Mount Zion surrounded by a great multitude (Rev 14:1; 7:9). Moreover, he saw all of this on the Lord's day, perhaps pointing us towards the Eucharist that he would presumably have celebrated that day with other exiles on Patmos, and he saw it because, as he says, 'I was in the Spirit' (Rev 1:10).[24]

However, these links are far from being vivid in our minds today. It would not be too much of a caricature to say that Catholics and western Christians generally tend to think of the Eucharist as an occasion when I as an individual encounter Jesus my Lord, who feeds me with his body and blood in a re-enactment of the past event of the Last Supper. This picture is by no means wrong but it is very incomplete. Inviting others to share it is inviting them into a rather small space. We have seen that this understanding of the Eucharist needs augmenting in three decisive ways: first, it is not primarily me as an individual that is being fed in the Eucharist, but rather the church, and me as a member of it; second, it is not only Christ who is present, but the Holy Spirit also; and third, the Eucharist is not only a remembrance of the past, but also an anticipation of the future. The small picture needs stretching into a bigger picture, and our minds and hearts need stretching likewise into this greater awareness of the mystery, in which neglected perspectives are restored. Inviting others to share this greater picture is inviting them into a big space, and there is ample evidence from recent ecumenical dialogue that Christians from many traditions who have been divided in their understanding of the Eucharist for centuries are able to find a home in this bigger space and reach agreements where previously there were only arguments.

There is not yet full agreement on all points. For instance, there would still be a lot of ecumenical reserve about the Catholic doctrine of transubstantiation. But the potential for solving issues is greatly determined by the framework in which they are set, and the bigger picture of the Eucharist that is now being established ecumenically is full of promise for progress on outstanding matters. De Lubac himself lamented that, whereas the Eucharist had been 'the mystery to understand' for the fathers of the church, in medieval times, at the hands of the scholastics and following major eucharistic controversy, it became simply 'the miracle to believe',[25] and the transformation of the elements of bread and wine became virtually the sum total of what was taught about the Eucharist. Eucharistic understanding was narrowed. The Eucharist was seen statically, as a 'presence' and an 'object', instead of dynamically, as an 'action' and a 'sacrifice'.[26] In particular, the ecclesial dimension of the Eucharist was gradually forgotten. When the transformation of the elements stands on its own like this it is much more difficult to comprehend than when it is seen in view of the transformation of those who receive, and ultimately in view of the 'new heavens and new earth' (2 Pet 3:13; cf. Isa 65:17; 66:22; Rev 21:5). We must recall that the church receives the body of Christ in order to *become* the body of Christ.[27] Dialogue with the Orthodox, who hail the gifts as 'Holy gifts for the holy people',[28] has helped enormously to restore this ecclesial dimension, and also more recently the cosmic dimension too, both of which help to give context and purpose to the transformation of the bread and wine.

Before turning finally to the cosmic dimension of the

Eucharist, which is also highlighted by Pope John Paul in his eucharistic encyclical, thereby giving another ecumenical resonance to his teaching, let us look more closely at what has been said ecumenically about the links between the Eucharist and the church, the Holy Spirit and the future, respectively, and let us also see how Pope John Paul is attentive to each of these links in the encyclical. Under each heading, I shall briefly consider agreed statements from three of the major dialogues in which the Catholic Church is involved: two bilateral, namely those with the Orthodox Church and the Anglican Communion, respectively, and one multilateral, namely the dialogue within the Faith and Order Commission of the World Council of Churches. There is not space to comment in detail on all of the quotations that follow. Part of my purpose in citing them is simply to give resources for reflection and for that stretching of minds and hearts that is an intrinsic part of the ecumenical task.

Eucharist and Church

The first Catholic-Orthodox agreed statement, in 1982, bore the weighty title, 'The Mystery of the Church and of the Eucharist in the Light of the Mystery of the Holy Trinity',[29] and one sentence serves to indicate the profound linkage between these mysteries that the statement explores: 'Taken as a whole, the eucharistic celebration makes present the Trinitarian mystery of the church.'[30] We may recall Pope John Paul's comment on Rublëv's icon, quoted above.

The statement says that 'the church finds its model, its origin and its end in the mystery of God, one in three Persons', and it therefore gives a programmatic role to the Eucharist, which communicates the life of the Trinity, in the organisation of the earthly church: the Eucharist is 'the criterion for the functioning of the life of the church as a whole'. 'The institutional elements should be nothing but a visible reflection of the reality of the mystery',[31] it says. What this means is that all of the church's organisation is somehow related to the Eucharist. For instance, the bonds of apostolic succession and collegiality among the bishops which unite the fabric of the church actually express through time and across the world, respectively, the unity of all the communities that have celebrated, celebrate today and will celebrate the Eucharist under the presidency of their bishops, because it is that celebration which most truly unites the church.

> The identity of one eucharistic assembly with another comes from the fact that all, with the same faith, celebrate the same memorial, that all by eating the same Body and sharing in the same Cup become the same and unique Body of Christ into which they have been integrated by the same baptism. If there are many celebrations, there is nonetheless only one mystery celebrated in which all participate ... Like the community of the apostles gathered around Christ, each eucharistic assembly is truly the holy church of God, the Body of Christ, in communion with the first community of the disciples and with all those [communities] throughout the world which celebrate and have celebrated the Memorial of the Lord. It is also in communion with the assembly of the saints in heaven, which each celebration evokes.[32]

In 1971, the first statement of the Anglican-Roman Catholic International Commission (ARCIC), which was on 'Eucharistic Doctrine', said more simply that the purpose of the Eucharist is 'to transmit the life of the crucified and risen Christ to his body, the church, so that its members may be more fully united with Christ and with one another'.[33] The dialogue subsequently stated that the idea of *koinonia* (communion) 'is the term that most aptly expresses the mystery underlying the various New Testament images of the church'. 'This theme of *koinonia* runs through our Statements. In them we present the eucharist as the effectual sign of *koinonia*, *episcope* as serving the *koinonia*, and primacy as a visible link and focus of *koinonia*.'[34] The second phase of ARCIC dialogue later specified that the ministry of *episcope* or oversight, which is entrusted in its fulness to the bishops and exercised especially in celebrating the Eucharist, has 'both collegial and primatial dimensions'.[35]

The Lima Report says: 'As the eucharist celebrates the resurrection of Christ, it is appropriate that it should take place at least every Sunday'. It continues with a very remarkable statement in the light of the widely varying eucharistic practice of the traditions, Catholic, Orthodox and Protestant, that were represented among its signatories: 'As it is the new sacramental meal of the people of God, every Christian should be encouraged to receive communion frequently.'[36] The bond between the Eucharist and the church evident both here and in the extract quoted earlier from the Report is repeated: 'The eucharistic communion with Christ who nourishes the life of the church is at the same time communion within the body of Christ which is the church.' The clear emphasis that the church, rather than just individual Christians, is being nourished by Christ, is reiterated in a dense and powerful summary of eucharistic doctrine that actually brings together all three of the links we are examining, namely those between the Eucharist and the church, the Holy Spirit and the future, respectively. 'The Holy Spirit gives a foretaste of the kingdom of God: the church receives the life of the new creation and the assurance of the Lord's return.'[37]

In his encyclical, Pope John Paul himself repeatedly highlights the life-giving link between the Eucharist and the resurrection (*EdE*, ##1, 6, 7, 11, 14, 15, 18, 22, 60), implicitly correcting another unfortunate Western tendency just to link the Eucharist to the cross, and he makes it plain that it is the church that draws its life from Christ in the Eucharist (*EdE*, #6); the church that is built up by the Eucharist (*EdE*, #24); and the church to which Christ gives himself in the Eucharist (*EdE*, #48). There are echoes of St Augustine, the great champion of the ecclesial nature of the Eucharist, when he teaches not only that each of us receives Christ in the Eucharist, but also that Christ receives each of us (*EdE*, #22), and that what is set before us is, in fact, the whole mystery of ourselves in Christ (*EdE*, #40). Moreover, since the same gift is made to each community that celebrates, none can cut itself off from the others and be 'self-sufficient'. Ecclesial communion with the local bishop and with the pope should be seen in a eucharistic light, as expressions of this necessary mutual openness (*EdE*, #39).

Eucharist and Holy Spirit

The Pope points out that Christ's flesh is 'made living and life-giving by the Holy Spirit' (*EdE* #1), and therefore that in receiving Christ we receive the Spirit also (*EdE*, ##17, 24, 60). There is an *epiclesis*, an invocation of the Holy Spirit, in the Eucharistic Prayer, by which the church 'implores this divine Gift, the source of every other gift' (*EdE*, #17), particularly so that those who receive Christ will themselves be sanctified (*EdE*, #23) and become one body, one spirit in him (*EdE*, #43).

These affirmations are important but also rather restrained. There are fuller statements about the Spirit's role in the Eucharist in the ecumenical texts we are considering, and of course especially in the Catholic-Orthodox agreed statement. One of the greatest ecumenical gifts of the Orthodox to Western Christians is a rich and ready recognition of the sheer scope of the Spirit's activity, by whose outpouring Jesus himself is 'the Christ', the anointed one. Jesus gives the Spirit but also, as the Christ, is given to us by the Spirit.[38] Pope John Paul says that the church was born of the paschal mystery (*EdE*, #3) and also that it was born at Pentecost (*EdE*, #5), which very alluringly invites us to see the latter as part of the former, as in St John's gospel in which the Spirit was given on Easter day (Jn 20:19-23). The Catholic-Orthodox dialogue is more explicit about the link, and forthright. 'Pentecost, the completion of the paschal mystery, inaugurates simultaneously the last times. The Eucharist and the church, body of the crucified and risen Christ, become the place of the energies of the Holy Spirit.'[39] Moreover, it clearly recognises that the Spirit is the agent of the transformation of gifts and people that occurs in the Eucharist, and the *epiclesis* is seen on a grand scale. 'The Spirit transforms the sacred gifts into the Body and Blood of Christ *(metabolê)* in order to bring about the growth of the Body which is the church. In this sense, the entire celebration is an *epiclesis*, which becomes more explicit at certain moments. The church is continually in a state of *epiclêsis*.'[40] 'By making present what Christ did once and for all – the event of the mystery – the Spirit accomplishes it in all of us.'[41]

The Lima Report says of the Eucharist that the Holy Spirit is 'the immeasurable strength of love which makes it possible and continues to make it effective'; 'The church prays to the Father for the gift of the Holy Spirit in order that the eucharistic event may be a reality: the real presence of the crucified and risen Christ giving his life for all humanity.'[42] ARCIC likewise acknowledges the Trinitarian configuration of the eucharistic prayer. 'Through this prayer of thanksgiving, a word of faith addressed to the Father, the bread and wine become the body and blood of Christ by the action of the Holy Spirit, so that in communion we eat the flesh of Christ and drink his blood.'[43]

Eucharist and Future

This statement from ARCIC leads into a remarkable passage which looks to the future and identifies the transformation brought about by the Spirit in the Eucharist as a foretaste of the new creation itself. 'The Lord who thus comes to his people in the power of the Holy Spirit is the Lord of glory. In the eucharistic celebration we anticipate the joys of the age to come. By the transforming action of the Spirit of God, earthly bread and wine become the heavenly manna and the new wine, the eschatological banquet for the new man: elements of the first creation become pledges and first fruits of the new heaven and the new earth.'[44] The Lima Report also includes the new creation in its account of the foretaste of the kingdom that the Eucharist gives us. 'The Eucharist opens up the vision of the divine rule which has been promised as the final renewal of creation, and is a foretaste of it. Signs of this renewal are present in the world wherever the grace of God is manifest and human beings work for justice, love and peace. The Eucharist is the feast at which the church gives thanks to God for these signs and joyfully celebrates and anticipates the coming of the kingdom in Christ (1 Cor 11:26; Mt 26:29).'[45]

Powerfully and succinctly, the Catholic-Orthodox dialogue states that the Eucharist is 'the foretaste of eternal life, the medicine of immortality, the sign of the kingdom to come';[46] it 'antici-

pates the judgement of the world and its final transfiguration'.[47]
There is a 'Jerusalem from on high' which 'comes down from
God' and founds the earthly community. 'The church comes
into being by a free gift, that of the new creation',[48] and, regularly
moulded and shaped by this future-gift, the ecclesial community
is 'called to be the outline of a human community renewed'.[49]

One of the most striking aspects of *EdE* is its own emphasis
upon the eschatological dimension of the Eucharist and upon
the manifold transformation that we anticipate when we celebrate it. 'The Eucharist is truly a glimpse of heaven appearing on
earth. It is a glorious ray of the heavenly Jerusalem which
pierces the clouds of our history and lights up our journey' (*EdE*,
#19; cf. #18). Therefore, it fills the church with 'confident hope'
(*EdE*, #1), so that we can be 'witnesses of hope' to the world
(*EdE*, #62). This hope is for the 'new heavens' and the 'new
earth', as the Pope repeatedly recalls (*EdE*, ##20, 58, 62). He
teaches that the Eucharist sows the seeds here and now of a 'new
history' (*EdE*, #58) and that it should bear fruit in us in the form
of 'a transfigured existence and a commitment to transforming
the world' (*EdE*, #20). With Christ we are called to 'transform
history until its fulfilment in the heavenly Jerusalem' (*EdE*, #60).

This is a cosmic vocation and Pope John Paul emphasises
that Christ's saving work embraces nothing less than the whole
of creation. In the Eucharist, 'the world which came forth from
the hands of God the Creator now returns to him redeemed by
Christ' (*EdE* #8). This reassertion of the cosmic dimension of the
Eucharist is of much greater ecumenical significance than might
be realised, because Orthodox theologians complain that
Western theology has seriously neglected this dimension ever
since the rise of scholasticism around the start of the second millennium, the very time of the historic rift between East and
West. Zizioulas says that, in the West, 'instead of being a blessing over the material world, the fruits of nature, and a reference
of it with gratitude and dedication to the Creator, the Eucharist
… became primarily a memorial service of the sacrifice of Christ
and a means of grace for the nourishment of the soul'.[50] If

Western neglect of the cosmic dimension of Christian faith and sacramental life was indeed a significant factor in the growing apart of East and West, then it stands to reason that the rediscovery of that dimension will be an important factor in our coming together again.[51] At the start of this chapter, we recalled that an awareness of our mission to the world has prompted Christians to strive to be one, so that the world may believe. If we have a mission not only to humanity at large but to the creation itself, the urgent demands of that mission, in a time of such concern about ecology and the environment, should surely draw us even more powerfully together.

It can readily be seen that Zizioulas' criticism of medieval theology of the Eucharist actually has various components and in fact touches upon the very points we have been considering. He is lamenting a growing focus at that time, and since then, just upon the individual soul being fed, just upon Christ himself being present, and just upon the event as a memorial of the past. We have seen that this incomplete picture of the Eucharist, over which Christians have disputed and divided, has been triply augmented in recent times, so as to establish a fuller picture in which the nourishment of the church, the presence of the Spirit, and the anticipation of the future are also properly recognised. We must work to strengthen our awareness of these neglected dimensions, not only so that we can have a fuller appreciation of the mystery of the Eucharist, but also because, as we have seen, they are extremely important for Christian unity. By itself strongly highlighting these dimensions, *EdE* makes a significant contribution to ecumenism.

CHAPTER NINETEEN

The Mass and Holy Communion in Current School Catechesis in Ireland

Breda O'Brien

Setting the Context

Some time ago, in my role as a RE teacher, I was discussing with a class the distinctive features of Christianity. The girls are about sixteen, and about 95% of them have spent about twelve years in Catholic schools of one kind or another. One girl raised her hand. 'Miss, you know the way you are talking about Jesus and the resurrection? Well, I've always wanted to know when and how he died again.' There were enthusiastic sounds around the classroom, and at least ten others looked at me expectantly, wondering if I was finally going to solve a mystery for them that had crossed their minds more than once. They were visibly amazed and sceptical, when I told them that the whole point was that he did not die again. In the same class, but later on, we were doing a revision exercise and they had to fill in blanks in a sentence. 'Jesus is fully human and "blank blank".' Almost no one could fill it in, and those who managed it were tentative and reluctant to offer their answer because they were so uncertain they were right. One outspoken young woman looked at me and said, after I had spoken about the centrality of this particular message: 'If it is such a big deal, how come I have never heard it before?'

Lest you think that I am a particularly inept teacher, I would wager that there are many, many others like these young women who have in fact been told this message over and over, but have never heard and internalised it, much less decided to live by it. Therefore, it is not surprising that knowledge of and devotion to the Eucharist tends to be minimal among young people. For example, in Desmond O'Donnell's survey of young educated adults aged between 20 and 35, missing Mass on

Sunday came twenty-sixth in a list of twenty-eight possible of-
fences.[1] Only contraception and living with someone you intend
to marry came lower. Sexual abuse of children ranked first. Even
granted that some very serious moral issues were covered, one
would have expected Mass to feature higher than third from
last. Mass attendance among those surveyed averaged at 52%
who attended weekly. Similarly, research by David Tuohy
among young people aged 17 to 24 shows that about 40% attend
Mass regularly. This is lower than the Greeley and Ward survey
which showed that the national average is 62%.[2] Sadly, in
Tuohy's study, the experience of Mass attendance is mostly negative. Those interviewed tended to see Mass as a 'ritual, empty
of meaning'.[3] Those who no longer attend Mass did so for a variety of reasons, but Tuohy comments:

> There seldom was any formal rejection on ideological
> grounds. Other things took over, be it work or relationships,
> and those assumed greater value and importance than any-
> thing associated with the church. When the social calendar
> filled up, church got crowded out.[4]

Since knowledge of Christ is so linked to devotion to the
Eucharist, it is interesting to look at the fact that in O'Donnell's
study, only 63% believe that Jesus is God in human form. (That's
how it is put in the survey.) A different question was asked
about a personal relationship with Christ. Adding together
those who have 'a personal relationship with Christ' and those
who have a 'very deep relationship' produces exactly the same
figure, 63%. There is an interesting statistic here. Belief in the divinity of Christ increases, if you experienced childhood before
1970, dips between 1970 and 1975, and increases slightly after
that.[5] It is not fanciful to link these statistics with the upheaval
that happened after the Second Vatican Council. The confusion,
even if it was sometimes mixed with exhilaration, led to very
strange things happening in religious education. A friend of
mine who is in her late forties, tells of a nun who taught them to
say the Rosary with great care, but who after the Council announced to them that it was no longer important. This unsettled

my friend's faith enormously, as she began to suspect that it was something arbitrary, which people were making up as they went along.

Where young people have a strong commitment to Mass, it tends to come from a strong family background of commitment to faith. Although, in recent times, I was heartened to be told by a young woman in Fifth Year, that although her parents did not practice, she and a small group of friends had started to meet together every Sunday in order to go to Mass. These girls may be unrepresentative, but as a teacher of RE you tend to take happenings like these and treasure them.

Catechesis

Many teachers do not categorise themselves as catechists, but as teachers of a subject, religious education. That is an important distinction, which is relevant to discussion of catechesis on the Eucharist. According to the *General Directory for Catechesis*, (*GDC*) 'Catechesis is that particular form of the ministry of the word which matures initial conversion to make it into a living, explicit and fruitful confession of faith.'[6] Already a problem presents itself. How many young people have made an initial conversion? Pope John Paul II has said, 'In countries with ancient Christian roots, and occasionally in the younger churches as well, entire groups of the baptised have lost a living sense of the faith or even no longer consider themselves members of the church and live a life far removed from Christ and his gospel.'[7] This may not be entirely the case in Ireland. Many young people consider themselves to be Christian, but have a hazy conception of what that means. They may say something vague like, 'Being nice to people,' if asked what being a Christian is about. However, the *GDC* acknowledges the fact that '... frequently, many who present themselves for catechesis truly require genuine conversion'. For that reason, they say that 'primary proclamation,' is necessary, that is, evangelisation. 'Catechetical renewal must be based on prior missionary evangelisation.'[8]

Some writers in the area of religious education would urge

caution about what can be achieved in a classroom. Patrick M. Devitt, in *Willingly to School*, says that even the best school teaching is unlikely to bring about 'increased Mass attendance among rebellious teenagers or make dishonest pupils honest overnight.' He says:

> Religion teaching in school has real and important aims, but they are quite limited. Religion teaching aims at knowledge, not maturity. Of course, the former may lead to the latter. But equally, it may not.[9]

The document issued by the Vatican Congregation for Catholic Education, in 1988, *The Religious Dimension of Education in a Catholic School,* distinguishes between religious instruction and catechesis:

> The distinction comes from the fact that, unlike religious instruction, catechesis pre-supposes that the hearer is receiving the Christian message as a salvific reality. Moreover, catechesis takes place within a community living out its faith at a level of space and time not available to a school; a whole lifetime.[10]

As has been demonstrated earlier, it is questionable how many young people participating in RE class view it as a 'salvific reality.' Catechesis in school happens as a result of the whole school operating in a way which reflects the values of the gospel, and only a small part of catechesis actually happens in the classroom. This is even more true, given the advent of the religious education examination syllabus, which will be examined in more detail later. As *RDECS* puts it:

> A Catholic school is not simply a place where lessons are taught; it is a centre that has an operative educational philosophy, attentive to the needs of today's youth, and illumined by the gospel message.[11]

As a result of his research among young people, Tuohy suggests different approaches for different cohorts within a second level school. He says that these approaches include pre-evangelisation, evangelisation, and support for the committed.[12] To what extent is this a realistic option in a classroom situation? It may not be realistic at all, because people at each of these stages are present in the same classroom. However, it may be more realistic for a school, that is the entire school community and not just the RE team, to consider activities that reach out to each group. The religion teacher will already be attempting in the classroom to juggle the needs of those in need of pre-evangelisation, evangelisation, and support because they are committed. Unfortunately, the teacher is often reduced to a form of teaching often known as the 'lowest common denominator'. As a result, there is even more need for the school community as a whole to provide activities for people at different stages of development in faith.

SPECIFIC CONTENT OF PROGRAMMES

Primary Level

It may be that more catechesis takes place at primary level than at second level, in particular in relation to the sacraments. Certainly, the teacher is working when preparing for first penance, and first Holy Communion, in a way that accords more closely with the six aims of catechesis as set out by the *GDC*. These are: 1. Promoting knowledge of the faith. 2. Liturgical education. 3. Moral Formation. 4. Teaching to pray. 5. Education for community life. 6. Missionary initiation.[13] Sadly, in the last aim, the missionary initiation may be to the child's own parents, who may be no longer practising.

The *Alive-O!* programme, produced on behalf of the Irish Bishops, works in a spiral fashion, introducing and then re-visiting concepts over the course of primary school. So, for example, in the early years, Jesus as healer and storyteller is the focus. When it comes to preparation for First Holy Communion, preparation takes place over two years. The emphasis is on seven different aspects. These are: 1. Gathering together. 2. Listening to the word of God. 3. Celebrating Jesus' love for us. 4. Giving thanks. 5. Celebrating God's forgiveness. 6. Sharing Jesus, the Bread of Life. 7. Going out in peace.

To be more specific, in the teacher's book for First Class, it is explained that:

Catechesis on the Eucharist is not confined to specific lessons on the Eucharist. Throughout the year, we try to develop attitudes in children that will help them to participate consciously in the celebration:
• An ability to work with symbol and take part in ritual
• A sense of coming together with others
• Listening to the word of God
• A sense of gratitude and thanksgiving
• A sense of the meaning of celebration
• Reflecting on the life, death and resurrection of Jesus Christ
• A desire to be a follower of Jesus

Term three of Alive-O 3 concentrates on four fundamental aspects of the Eucharist, each of which is central to the life of Jesus: shared story, shared meal, shared memory and shared living.[14]

To take just one of the four, shared meal, the teacher text reads as follows:

One the night before he died, Jesus shared the Last Supper. At the Last Supper, he took bread, blessed and broke it. He took wine, blessed and shared it. In this action he wove together his life of love and service, and his approaching death. What Jesus did at the Last Supper, he told his disciples to do in memory of him. When we come together to celebrate the Eucharist, we remember the Last Supper. The Risen Jesus is present in the consecrated bread and wine that we share in the Eucharist.[15]

The lesson plans for the section on shared meals include many different activities. For example, pupils are encouraged to create an album of photos or pictures of shared meals with the class, with each pupil explaining the significance of the picture they put in. They make banners saying 'Jesus is the bread of life' for the classroom. They listen to an account of the Last Supper and how the disciples probably felt. They learn a little verse:

Jesus is the bread of life,
We eat at Mass together,
Jesus gives his life for us,
Always and forever.

A prayer service to which parents are invited, which involves the sharing of bread or cake might raise some questions. It uses some of the words from the Mass.

Leader holds the cake of bread in his/her hands:

Blessed are you, Lord, God of all creation. Through your goodness we have this bread to offer, work of human hands. Bless this bread. May it make us strong. May it remind us always to share with those who are hungry.

All: Bless us, O God, as we sit together.
Bless the food we eat today.
Bless the hands that made the food,
Bless us, O God, Amen.

Teacher:

On the night before he died, Jesus blessed the bread and broke it and gave it to his disciples. Today as we cut/break our cake of bread, we give thanks to God.

There are some further prayers and then the teacher invites the children to come forward. He/she hands them each a piece of bread. Each child returns and breaks the bread with his parents/guardians. When everyone has a piece, everyone eats.

At the end they sing the hymn, 'Eat this bread'.

On one level, the catechetical value of showing that the Eucharist is a meal is obvious. On the other hand, it is very important that children would see clearly the difference between what they do in class and what the celebrant does at Mass. This clarification is not clearly made in the teacher's text. There is a similar ritual in Lesson Nine, using unleavened bread, but it is not so similar in structure to the Mass.

During the course of First class, if all the material is used, which presumes that the teacher will have a period of religion a day, the children will have been exposed to an impressive amount of scripture, meditation and actions geared to their age and ability. They will have been familiarised with the structure and responses of the Mass, and will have learnt many hymns. There are also prayers for before and after Communion. Many teachers spend a great deal of time and energy on the programme. However, as in any enterprise involving human beings, there will be variations in the quality of what is delivered. Given that many teachers are members of the post-Vatican Two generation profiled by Desmond O'Donnell, it is quite likely that they have the same ambivalent attitude to institutional religion as the young people he surveyed, which has obvious consequences for their role as catechists.

In the teacher's book of *Alive-O 4,* it is suggested that children be familiarised with the names of special objects within the church, such as the tabernacle, the ambo and so on. Many of the themes of the previous year are developed, but in greater depth. Another aim is added, that of helping children to develop a sense of God's presence in sign and sacrament. The instructions for the teachers on this aspect read:

> Throughout the lessons we lead the children to an awareness of the presence of Christ in the Eucharist. We help them to come to appreciate that when we celebrate the Eucharist we remember and make present in a special way the actions of Jesus at the Last Supper and on the cross. It is the Risen Jesus who is with us as we remember and it is the Risen Jesus whom we receive in the Eucharist.[16]

One very nice aspect of this year's work is that parents are asked to take part in a Celebration of Enrolment. In the ceremony, the parents and children are asked to renew their baptismal vows. It usually takes place in the parish church, and may be part of a vigil or Sunday Mass, depending on the parish. Parents and guardians are encouraged to support the child as he or she prepares for communion. From next year, all children will make their communion in Second Class. There is some repetition between the books because up until this year some children still made communion in First Class.

In Fourth Class, pupils look at the Mass as sacrifice. In Fifth Class, they look in greater depth at four aspects of presence: in the word, in the people gathered, in the celebrant and at the Real Presence, where Christ is present, body, blood, soul and divinity, under the appearances of bread and wine. In Sixth Class, they are introduced to the concepts of ritual and sacrament. This spiral curriculum has been controversial in the past, as many of us will remember being taught the concept of transubstantiation at six, though whether we understood it or not, is another question.

There are major difficulties around the actual celebration of the sacrament, including the whole culture, especially in poorer areas, of spending a fortune on the child's outfit, and of holding a party. However, if followed as prescribed, the programme has little to fault it and much to recommend it. Because it involves parents, it is quite a significant vehicle for catechesis for adults, too, and at least for the year leading up to Holy Communion, many parents resume going to Mass who had lapsed.

Second Level

It is amply documented that RE at second level suffered from being seen as a poor relation to examination subjects in many schools. It was a non-academic subject perceived as a 'doss class' by many pupils.[17] As a result, what religious knowledge pupils had gained at primary level seemed to evaporate by the end of the first term in First Year at second level. It reinforced for young people that religion is 'something for kids', that you concentrate on when you are making First Holy Communion and Confirmation. For many children, Confirmation is an exit cere-mony. Recently, in the Kildare diocese, I heard a priest celebrant at Confirmation asking the children to come to Mass, and to bring their families with them. This is a reverse of what one might hope for, that parents would bring their children to Mass.

Therefore, it is not surprising that the new examination syl-labus was greeted with open arms. Finally, academic respectabil-ity! While significant numbers of schools in the Republic have taken up the academic Junior Cert course, it is expected that far smaller numbers will implement the Leaving Cert course. The Irish Catholic Bishops welcomed the introduction of this syllabus, despite the fact that the Department of Education and Science guidelines clearly state that faith formation is not among its aims.

> The assessment of Religious Education at Junior and Leaving Certificate levels will be based on the objectives relating to knowledge, understanding, skills and attitudes within each section of the course. While students will draw on their own experience in an examination, their personal faith commitment and/or affiliation to a particular religious grouping will not be subject to assessment for national certification.[18]

The new religious education syllabus consists of six sections, five of which are compulsory. The area of sacrament is covered in Section E, the celebration of Faith.

> The overall aims of this section are:
> • To show how ritual and worship have always been part of the human response to life and to the mystery of God
> • To identify how communities of faith express their day-to-day concerns in various forms of ritual
> • To explore an experience of worship
> • And for Higher Level only: to explore the link between patterns of worship and mystery/ that which is of ultimate concern to individuals and communities.[19]

In part 4 of this section, sign and symbol, students are invited to:

> • Be aware of the place of sign and symbol in human life and religious traditions
> • Have an understanding of the power and meaning of religious symbols
> OR be familiar with the Christian understanding of sacrament and have a detailed understanding of the place of sacrament in two Christian denominations

The new examination syllabus permits the area of sacraments to be skirted entirely, in order to facilitate members of Christian or other traditions who do not subscribe to the concept. However, it is likely that Catholic schools will not take this option, and will deal with sacraments and Eucharist in some depth. However, they are under no statutory obligation to do so. If they choose to explore this section of the syllabus, it can provide a golden opportunity to examine, for example, what the differences are between the Church of Ireland's understanding of Communion and the Catholic understanding of it. It can be linked in to the history programme, which deals with the Reformation in some depth. There are many opportunities there, but again, little control over whether these opportunities are taken or not.

There is a sad fact that teachers tend to be very influenced by the textbooks which they use. In the beginning, around 2000, when this course was introduced, there were basically two options, the Veritas programme developed on behalf of the Irish Catholic Bishops, and *All about Faith*, written by Anne and Niall Boyle. *All about Faith* has an imprimatur from Bishop Michael Smith of Meath. It would be unfair to say that it does not include a faith perspective. For example, in one section, it provides compelling reasons for belief in the historical reality of the resurrection. However, in the main, it is an academic presentation of content, and it is up to the teacher to supply the faith dimension. The Eucharist is dealt with competently, but in two brief chapters.

The Veritas programme attempts to integrate a faith perspective with the academic requirements. The comments of Linda Quigley, the principal author of the texts, follow:

> In first year the students learn that 'When we come together to celebrate the Eucharist, the church is most visibly the Body of Christ, who is present in the world and especially in the Eucharist.' The students are encouraged to take a more mature look at the Sacraments of Initiation within the context of belonging to the Body of Christ (Section 1 – Community of Faith). They learn about the early Christian community and how 'They devoted themselves to the apostles' teaching and fellowship, to the breaking of bread and the prayers' – Acts 2.42 and of the transforming experience being a disciple of Jesus can be. (Section 2 – Community of Faith).

In Chapter 16 of *Community of Hope* (textbook) the students learn about the sacraments as sacred moments in the lives of members of the church, and specifically about the Eucharist. The main focus is to facilitate the students in deepening their understanding of the Eucharist as the most special way in which we celebrate God's presence in our lives. The book is full of examples and activities to encourage the students to respond to the call to discipleship. Eucharist in this context is like food for the journey – feeding our spirit and filling it with joy and hope. Through it we are united with our faith community and we are united with God. The link is made for them: 'Physical food makes us stronger and helps us to cope with the physical challenges of life. Spiritual food strengthens our spirit and helps us to face the challenge of being a Christian in the modern world.' We are encouraged to be counter-cultural because the peace and justice of Jesus Christ is present in us through the Eucharist. They also learn about thanksgiving, memorial and presence.[20]

This programme is specifically catechetical, attempting to make links between religion and life, school, home and parish. It deals in far greater depth than any other textbooks currently available, with Mass and Holy Communion. It also makes explicit links with what is learned in primary school. However, anecdotally, there is some evidence that because teachers are under pressure to complete a syllabus, many of the enriching activities, such as the prayer services which end each section, go by the wayside.

Therein lies the crux of the problem. Has the academic squeezed out the more creative aspects of teaching religion? It is not so bad if there are other elements within the school to take up the slack, such as a very active chaplaincy and pastoral care team who are committed to Catholic values. However, this is often not the case. Ironically, it is much more likely that there will be an active chaplain in a community school. The bishops issued excellent guidelines as to how to incorporate catechesis into the new syllabus, but they are likely to remain just guidelines in many schools.

There are now many other textbooks available. However, they are religious education texts, aimed at preparing students for an examination. The examination syllabus has a strong emphasis on world religions, and young people are often more interested in what is novel than in their own tradition. As a result, one parent said to me, 'They seem to speak about bits and pieces of Islam and Buddhism, but don't have a clue about their own religion.'

One popular text has a very sketchy introduction to the Catholic Eucharist. Each section ends with a section entitled 'Main points to remember'. Regarding Eucharist, it says:

> In Catholicism, the Eucharist is an example of a most important ritual and form of worship. Eucharist is a mystery beyond human understanding where the bread and wine are turned into the body and blood of Christ.[21]

Let's contrast that with what the Pope says in *EdE*. 'In the humble signs of bread and wine, changed into his body and blood, Christ walks beside us as our strength and our food for the journey, and he enables us to become, for everyone, witnesses of hope. If, in the presence of this mystery, reason experiences its limits, the heart, enlightened by the grace of the Holy Spirit, clearly sees the response that is demanded, and bows low in adoration and unbounded love.'[22]

Of course, this is an unfair comparison, as it is impossible to expect that any textbook could reproduce this kind of lyrical love.

At Senior Level, sacrament is covered in Section G, Worship, Prayer and Ritual. The aims of the Senior Cycle are very similar, down to the study of the meaning of sacrament in two Christian denominations, but they are explored in greater depth.

Final perspectives

A great deal of responsibility has been placed on schools to carry out catechesis. However, to return to the statement from RDECS:

> Catechesis takes place within a community living out its faith

at a level of space and time not available to a school; a whole lifetime.[23]

When the Veritas primary school programme was due for re-presentation, Martin Kennedy was asked to do some research on how the previous programme was working. Among his conclusions were the following three stark statements:

- The classroom is a place of positive religious discourse.
- The home is a space where there is little or no religious discourse or experience.
- The parish is a space of diminishing religious discourse and experience.

Given that he was speaking about primary schools, it is far from certain that one could conclude that the first is still true of secondary classrooms, that 'The classroom is a place of positive religious discourse' or that it has been for some time. This is in spite of the best efforts of teachers. It is no coincidence that Mater Dei graduates and other theology graduates often do not stay in teaching. The burnout rate is enormous. Part of that burnout is the breakdown between the triangle of home, school and parish. This obviously has had a great impact on the fact that so many teenagers and young people know so little about their faith, because they often leave it behind at primary school. Some of the people who are extremely critical of catechetical texts, particularly at primary level, have not taken into account the enormous cultural changes which have happened, and which mean that there is a need for a 'new evangelisation', which cannot be made the responsibility of the school alone. It is often forgotten that one of the primary sites for catechesis on the Eucharist is the celebration of the Eucharist itself. Young people attend Mass in declining numbers. Sadly, when they do attend Mass, they quite often do not find a celebration which includes them, or which gives them food for their journey. Instead, they are often treated to Masses where the Word is proclaimed indistinctly, where homilies are of indifferent quality, and there is little or no congregational singing or participation. The best classroom catechesis in the world cannot compensate for a lack of vibrant and prayerful liturgy at local level.

This poses enormous challenges for the church in Ireland. I am not sure if the enormity of the task has filtered through to those in authority just yet, or whether it has, and nobody has the heart to face up to it. Bishop Bill Murphy of Kerry said the faith could be lost in a generation. I believe he is right. This has obvious repercussions not only for catechesis of the Mass and Holy Communion, but for the foundations of belief in the Catholic faith.

O Sacred Feast
(O Sacrum Convivium)

Edward Holden

The challenge of setting a well-known text to music should inspire a composer to be original. As I saw it, my task was to compose a piece of music which would mirror the sacredness of each phrase of the text, whilst maintaining a unified musical structure. I did so by subdividing the main body of the text into individual phrases: the sense of each musical phrase conveys a spontaneous movement of awe and reverence. The part written for the organ, which is not a mere accompaniment, represents the eternity of heaven, with the phrases of the text representing the aspirations of the faithful. Thus the two become one, as happens at the celebration of the Eucharist where heaven and earth are united in the sacrifice of the altar.

The composition is a duet between organ and choir with two main themes passing from one to the other in a contrapuntal style. Following the seven bar introduction the two main themes are brought in simultaneously, one by the choir, the other by the organ. These themes pass from the one to the other, and are further developed each time they appear, either by means of adding notes to the music, or by shortening and changing the original musical idea. These quasi-developments can be interpreted as signifying the gift of God's grace bestowed on those who believe and trust in him, with the highest notes of the composition for both choir and organ occurring during the second statement of the phrase 'the mind is filled with grace'.

The concept of atonality (i.e. music written in no set key) seems appropriate to the composition of sacred music. Atonality seems to free the musical expression of heaven and heavenly themes from the latent restrictions imposed by writing in a fixed musical key. O Sacred Feast is written without the restriction of a

tonic key and recites around a note, 'C', with three phrases and
the Alleluia beginning on 'C'. The final chord of the composition
is the chord of 'C' major, the simplest and most uncomplicated
chord, signifying the glory of heaven in all its simplicity.

It is ultimately left to the listener to take from *O Sacred Feast*
what he or she will. Music says different things to different people;
it is those who perform it and listen to it who can best describe
how this composition *O Sacred Feast* affects them, and what it
means to them.

Commissioned for 'The Church and the Eucharist' Conference, May 2004

O Sacred Feast

(O Sacrum Convivium)

By Edward Holden
English Translation: John O' Keeffe
(April 2004)

2

3

of fu – ture glo – ry is given to__ us.

Al – le – lu – – ia!_____

Highlights from the Maynooth Exhibition

Penelope Woods

An exhibition was held in the Russell Library in conjunction with the conference. The Russell Library is home to the early-printed and manuscript collections of St Patrick's College, Maynooth. These form one of the finest theological collections in the country, with contemporary editions of European scholarship from the Renaissance onwards. Preeminently the collections reflect the history of the Irish Catholic Church and the spirituality of the Irish people.

The exhibition was divided into four sections: biblical texts; Office for the Feast of Corpus Christi; Irish catechisms, primers and liturgical supplements; and early illustrations.

BIBLICAL TEXTS

1. *Biblia Sacra Hebraice, Chaldaice, Graece, & Latine,* Antverpiae: Christoph. Plantinus excud., 1569-72. 8 vols.
There have been four Polyglot Bibles in the history of printing which have been denominated 'great'. In each, the several languages are presented in parallel, a typographical feat to be appreciated. The first Polyglot, the Complutensian, under the direction of Cardinal Archbishop Francisco Ximénez de Cisneros of Toledo, was printed in Alcalá de Henares (Complutum), between 1514 and 1517 and published following papal sanction, received in March 1520. The languages used are Hebrew, Chaldee, Greek and Latin.[1] The second, the Antwerp, was published between 1569 and 1572 by Christopher Plantin, the leading printer in that city. Plantin persuaded Philip II of Spain to underwrite the project, and the King agreed but insisted that the scholar Benito Arias Montano should supervise its publication. Surviving a shipwreck off the west coast of Ireland en route from Spain, Arias Montano arrived in Antwerp and worked tirelessly with Plantin and his team of scholars to produce eight monumental folio volumes. The first four comprise the Old Testament in Hebrew, with the Greek Septuagint, the Vulgate and Aramaic paraphrases. The New Testament, in volume five, has columns of Syriac with a literal translation in Latin, Greek, the Latin Vulgate and the Syriac in Hebrew characters. The remaining three volumes *repeat* the Hebrew and the Greek New Testament, this time with interlinear translations, word for word, followed by a weighty apparatus of dictionaries and grammars. Philip II ordered thirteen extra sets printed on vellum, each of which took 2,000 skins.[2] The great Paris Polyglot of 1629-45, initiated by Cardinal Jacques Davy du Perron, was published in nine tomes, and added Samaritan and Arabic.[3]

In the London Polyglot (1655-7), edited by Brian Walton, Bishop of Chester, Ethiopic and Persian were added to the complement.[4] The New Testament has five languages in parallel with a sixth for the gospels, and the texts used are the Latin Vulgate (following the Clementine text), Greek (following the Stephanus edition of 1550), Syriac (largely following Gabriel Sionita's edition which had appeared in the Paris Polyglot), Arabic (edited by Edmund Castell and Edward Pococke), Ethiopic (based on the 1549 edition and edited by the Irish Orientalist Dudley Loftus, with Castell); and Persian for the gospels of which the *editio princeps* had appeared only months earlier in an edition by Abraham Wheelocke of a 14th century manuscript belonging to Pococke. Each non-Roman script is accompanied by a Latin translation. There are two sets of this Polyglot in Maynooth, in company with over 2,000 other printed Bibles from 1482 to the present. Almost six hundred languages and dialects are represented. Editions in the vernacular range from the earliest edition of the Bible in Spanish (Basle, 1569), to St John's Gospel in Adi or Abor-Miri (Calcutta, 1923), spoken in the borders of Tibet and N.E. Assam; from the Gospels and the Psalter in Arabic (Rome, 1591; 1614), to the Epistles and Revelation in Babatana, a language of East Choiseul in the Solomon Islands in the Pacific ([Sydney], 1960).

2. The Holy Bible translated from the Latin Vulgate…, 6th edition, Dublin: printed and published by James Reilly, 1794.
This Dublin Bible of 1794 was the first Irish edition of the Vulgate in English to be printed in large, folio format. This was a visible mark of a changing Catholic consciousness in Ireland, a new sense of stature. The accompanying list of subscribers confirms it: 550 names from Dublin and several counties to the north, headed by Archbishop Richard O'Reilly of Armagh, and including seven other bishops, parish priests, Catholic gentry, merchants and even craftsmen, such as Patrick Conolly, a stucco-plasterer on South Cumberland Street. Though described as the sixth edition, this was only the third time the complete Vulgate had been printed in Ireland.[5] The first Irishman to undertake an English translation of the Vulgate was Cornelius Nary (1658-1738), Paris-educated and parish priest of St Michan's in Dublin. His translation of the New Testament was published in 1718.[6] No place of printing is given in the imprint, but the press corrector states that the translator was 'at a great distance' when the book was printed and the approbations and printer's signatures make Paris a possibility, without ruling out Dublin. Nary's translation was banned by Rome in 1722 for unorthodoxy.

The first publishing in Ireland of the complete Vulgate was in 1763-4: the translation of Bishop Richard Challoner (1691-1781), it comprised the second revision of his Old Testament and the fourth revision of his New Testament.[7] No place or printer is mentioned but Pat Lord and

Richard Fitzsimons of Dublin took the credit in a less conspicuous source.[8] Apart from a re-issue by Patrick Wogan in 1789 of a Liverpool-printed New Testament,[9] there was no further Irish edition until at the behest of John Carpenter, Archbishop of Dublin, Bernard MacMahon, priest of Hardwick Street Chapel, who had already published a *Missale Romanum* with an Irish Proper in 1777, published an extensive revision of Challoner's New Testament in 1783.[10] He went on to revise his New Testament further and to publish it with Challoner's Old Testament, just slightly revised, in 1791, in quarto, for the Archbishop of Dublin, John Thomas Troy OP.[11] Three years later it was brought out once more in this fine folio edition. Bernard MacMahon was also a noted scientist and drew up tide tables for Dublin Bay besides inventing the use of a great bell in the Bay which was rung by the rising water at high tide, and warned the ships at sea.

3. TISCHENDORF, Constantin (ed.): *Bibliorum Codex Sinaiticus Petropolitani*, Petropoli [Lipsiae, typis exscriptserunt Giesecke et Devrient], 1862. 4 vols.
This is a facsimile of the Greek text of the Bible (c. 4th century) which was discovered at the monastery of St Catherine on Mount Sinai in 1844. Constantin Tischendorf had visited libraries throughout Europe and the Near East in search of important biblical texts and had pre-pared careful editions of the most important of these. His most famous discovery was the *Codex Sinaiticus*. On his first visit to the monastery of St Catherine, he saw and was given, a few leaves of the Old Testament; on his third visit in 1859, he borrowed the entire manuscript and pre-sented it to the Tsar of Russia, Alexander II. The manuscript contained half the Old Testament and the complete New Testament. The 'dona-tion' was regularised in 1869 and was sold in 1933 to the British Museum for £100,000.[12] The manuscript was published in facsimile, by order of the Tsar, in 1862. Volume 4 contains the New Testament, here displayed. Dr Charles William Russell, President of Maynooth (1857-1880), petitioned the Tsar for a copy for the College Library, and we find him writing delightedly to Baron Philip von Brunnow, the Russian Ambassador in London, on 24 August 1865, to express his thanks and to say that he had just returned from vacation and found, in answer to the prayer 'que j'avais osé adresser' that the Codex had arrived.[13]

OFFICE FOR THE FEAST OF CORPUS CHRISTI

4. THOMAS AQUINAS, Saint : 'Officium de festo Corporis Christi' in *Opuscula Sancti Thome* … Impressum Venetiis mandato et expensis Octaviani Scoti …cura et ingenio Boneti Locatelli Bergomensis, ii Kal. Januarius, 1498.
Here amongst the shorter works, the *Opuscula*, of St Thomas Aquinas, is the Office that he wrote at Orvieto for the feast of Corpus Christi. The feast was instituted by Urban IV in 1264 and the Office (which includes

both proper Office and Mass) written at his request. By the Bull, *Transiturus de hoc mundo*, he then sought to extend its observance throughout Latin Christendom. This edition,[14] by Antonio Pizzamano, a Venetian Patrician, prefaced by his life of Aquinas, was first printed in 1490 by Hermann Lichtenstein in Venice and then eight years later by Octavianus Scotus.[15] In the fifteenth century, Venice ranked as one of the leading centres of printing, producing works of the finest quality. Octavianus Scotus, was perhaps the best-known of its publishers (Maurice O'Fihely or Mauritius de Portu (d. 1513), Franciscan Archbishop of Tuam, (1506-13), the first Irishman to write for the printing press, worked in close association with Octavianus Scotus as a scholar-corrector. Pizzamano dedicated the biography to Augustinus Barbadicus, the Doge of Venice. At the end of the biography he reproduces the bull of canonisation (1323). The book has a contemporary binding of blind-tooled panels on goatskin over wooden boards, and contains contemporary annotations. It came from the Irish College in Salamanca, which was founded in 1592; the College closed in 1951 and its archives, together with many of its books, came to Maynooth where they are now housed in the Russell Library. Here also is a Paris edition of the *Opuscula* of 1634 and an edition by Antonio Redetti, Bishop of Bergamo, published in that city in 1741.

IRISH CATECHISMS, PRIMERS AND LITURGICAL SUPPLEMENTS

5. O'KENNY, Nicholas Anthony: [*Officia Missarum tum in honorem Sanctorum Patronorum principalium Regni Hyberniae tum in honorem Novem Ordinum Coelestium Spirituum* Paris: [s.n.], 1734].
This is a rare volume of Irish liturgical supplements to the Mass in honour of Ireland's principal patronal saints, published by a Galway Dominican living in Paris. Nicholas Anthony O'Kenny, titular Abbot of Annaghdown, had left Ireland in 1714 and studied at the University of Paris where he was awarded a doctorate in Canon Law in February 1725, subsequently becoming Protonotary Apostolic and Chevalier de St Michel.[16] He saw himself as 'missionaire irlandois' and wrote instructive works, mostly in English, for 'the use of the three kingdoms'.[17] As *convertus* for the Royal College of Navarre he was also writing for the 'nouveaux convertis' in Paris, for there was great emphasis on bringing people back to the Catholic Faith, following the revocation of the Edict of Nantes in 1685. He later claimed to have converted three hundred to the Faith between 1716 and 1735.[18] In 1725, O'Kenny published two works, his *Gallway catechism* and *The Ordinary of the Holy Mass*,[19] and the approbations for each show that they were conceived as companion texts under the title *Le missionaire irlandois*, though this umbrella title was not used. The names of those who gave their approbation to both volumes reflect a close-knit intellectual Irish community in Paris.[20] In 1734 he published Masses for the patronal saints of France

and Ireland (unseen) and then it would seem, a separate publication of
the Irish Masses: the latter volume we have here in Maynooth, on display in the exhibition, though lacking its title-page.[21] No other copy has
been located. One of those who gave his approbation to this Irish volume was Richard Pierce, Bishop of Waterford (1696-1739), who had become suffragan to the Metropolitan Archbishop of Sens in 1701, and
who, according to his approbation had himself worked for several
years on producing a Missal and Breviary for the Diocese of Sens; the
information in his approbation is valuable, for neither the Missal nor
the Breviary accords Pierce that credit, or mentions his name.[22] In his
Officia Missarum, O'Kenny appends a most interesting list of churches
in Ireland at the time, most of them belonging to religious orders; he divides them into three groups: those dedicated to the Holy Trinity, those
to Our Lady and those to St Patrick. Unusually for an Irish Catholic
priest of the time, he had his own coat of arms and included an engraving of them in the text. His interest in the nine choirs of angels reflected
in the title, can also be seen in a Mass that he published in the following
year, *Messe en l'honneur des neuf choeurs d'anges et autres esprits célestes*.[23]
In the exhibition the *Officia Missarum* lay open at the Mass for St Mac
Nissi.

6. [LLOYD, Sylvester, OFM, Bishop of Killaloe]: *The Doway Catechism in
English and Irish. For the use of children and ignorant people*, Dublin: printed
for Ignatius Kelly, 1752.
Sylvester Louis Lloyd OFM (1680-1747), Bishop of Killaloe (1728-39),
and subsequently of Waterford and Lismore (1739-47), published two
catechisms. The first was an English translation of a highly popular catechism by François-Aimé Pouget, *Instructions générales en forme de
catéchisme ... imprimées par ordre de messire Charles Joachim Colbert, Evêque
de Montpellier* (Paris, 1702, revised 1707), known simply as the
Montpellier Catechism. Lloyd, said to be the son of a Protestant clergy-
man, began his career as a soldier in the army of William of Orange,
fighting in the Netherlands.[24] In 1697, he left the army and became a
Catholic. He joined the Hieronymite Order in Portugal in 1703 and then
spent nine years at Belem, near Lisbon. It was during this time that he
prepared his translation of Pouget's catechism, encouraged by Luke
Fagan, soon to become Bishop of Meath. He was ordained in 1711 and
joined the Franciscans the following year. The first edition of Lloyd's
catechism is reckoned to have appeared ca. 1711-12, though no copy of
it appears to have survived. There had been another English translation, made c. 1709 by an English priest, Thomas Hall (d. 1719), but this,
according to Lloyd, was 'stifled' and never published.[25] Pouget's catechism had been issued *'pour l'usage des anciens & des nouveaux catholiques
de son diocèse, & de tous ceux qui sont chargez de leur instruction; avec deux
catéchismes abrégez, à l'usage des enfans'.*[26] It was condemned by Rome in
1721 for its Jansenist tendencies. Lloyd quickly revised his translation.

He published the first part only, in 1722, describing it as having been carefully compared with the Spanish edition which had been approved by Rome.[27] There are no approbations, no dedication. In his address to the reader, Lloyd analyses the difficulty in translating catechisms 'above all other treatises': to endeavour to be true to the author's thinking, yet making it 'speak English so as to be understood by every capacity'. The only known copy of this is here in Maynooth. Part one was republished in full with parts two and three in 1723, in some 900 pages, with the approval of eleven Irish theologians for the first part. In 1725, despite all his efforts, Lloyd's translation was also banned.[28]

After he became Bishop of Killaloe in 1728, Lloyd spent the next four years travelling his diocese, confirming and preaching. Ten years later, in 1738, during a sojourn in Dublin, he prepared *The Doway catechism in English and Irish, for the use of children and ignorant people*. It was printed there for him by Henry Babe. Lloyd hesitated to put his name on the title-page, but we find a discreet attribution at the end 'By S. L. for the use of the clergy and people of Killaloe.' This was the first Catholic catechism published in Ireland, and only one copy is known to survive. The original Doway catechism, the work of Henry Turberville, appeared first in 1648.[29] and was based on that of Cardinal Robert Bellarmine. Lloyd's catechism was much simpler. The English text was taken almost entirely from the *Gallway catechism* of Nicholas O'Kenny, the Galway Dominican, printed in Paris in 1725.[30] O'Kenny, though, had different motives in writing his, for he intended it also for 'new Catholicks and such as are not as yet instructed in the Catholick religion'. Lloyd omits O'Kenny's scriptural readings for the *nouveaux convertis* and the prayers and ceremonies intended for use at their reception; he also makes some changes and additions of his own.

The Irish in Lloyd's catechism is a literal translation into Munster Irish, using roman typeface. James Gallagher, Bishop of Raphoe, had published his *Sixteen Irish sermons* only two years before Lloyd's catechism, in 1736.[31] In his preface, which is written in English, Gallagher explains his very pertinent reasons for using roman typeface: no Irish Catholic printer had Gaelic type and only one in ten readers could still read Gaelic script. Making a virtue of necessity, he said the roman script would be 'more familiar to the generality of our Irish clergy'. No doubt Lloyd's reasons were the same, but he took it one stage further and included a few instructions on pronouncing the Irish language, on the last two pages. Another edition of Lloyd's catechism (with the attribution still at the back but now in Latin) was printed in 1752, five years after Lloyd's death, by Ignatius Kelly, the leading Catholic printer in Dublin at the time. This rare edition is the one displayed.

7. THE PRIMER or Office of the B. Virgin Mary, to which are added a new improved version of the Church hymns and the remaining hymns of the Roman Breviary, Dublin: Coyne, [1810].

The first rendering in English of the post-Tridentine *Officium Beatae Mariae Virginis*, revised in 1571 by Pius V, appeared in Antwerp in 1599.[32] The first Primer that might be called Irish was that edited by Thomas Fitzsimon, of which the earliest recorded is an edition of 1669 printed at Rouen.[33] Addressing the 'pious reader', he writes how he has improved on the earlier Antwerp primers: the 'hymns are in a better verse'; and the book contains many 'sweet devotions which never were set forth in the Primer'. He signs it 'Thomas Fitzsimon, priest'. Besides the usual saints, the feasts of 'divers notable saints of England, Scotland, Ireland and Wales' are also included. Thomas Fitzsimon, Vicar-General of Kilmore (1666-75) has sometimes been credited with the work but his namesake, a priest from Drogheda, who in 1644 was Procurator of the German Nation at the University of Paris and rector of the Irish College, Rouen, might be another contender.[34]

The first known primer to be published in Ireland appeared in 1767.[35] It was possibly a collaboration between the bookseller, Richard Fitzsimons, and the printing firm of Thomas Meighan of London.[36] The calendar is certainly not distinctively Irish. Fitzsimons has an unusual and handsomely engraved title-page which states only that it is sold by himself; there is also a final leaf of advertisements promoting his publications, including an eight-penny life of St Joseph, which is no longer extant. The primer was substantial and expensive, costing 3s 3d. The copy in the National Library was most elegantly bound. A slim Cork primer of 1789 published by James Haly contains only the Office of the BVM, the Method of saying the Rosary and the Litany of Loretto.[37] It was most probably intended for the use of a Dominican confraternity. So also was another, printed by Richard Cross in Dublin in 1799, which similarly contained only the Office, the Devotion of the Rosary 'first revealed by the B. Virgin to St Dominick', and again the Litany of Loretto.[38]

This last edition 'being entirely disposed of' by 1803, a new edition, edited and revised by Bernard MacMahon of Hardwick Street Chapel was published that year, with a 'new calendar in which the Irish saints are inserted in their proper days'.[39] In 1810, the rising Catholic publisher Richard Coyne, published the edition in this exhibition, particularly notable for its 10-page list of Dublin subscribers, with their addresses. This was primarily a book for the laity, as no priests are listed as subscribers. The impetus may well have come from the Discalced Carmelites of Clarendon Street, whose chapel, begun in 1793 and only recently completed, was one of Dublin's largest at the time.[40] A number of subscribers lived in Clarendon street including John Maguire the engraver of the title-page image of the Blessed Virgin in glory.[41] Carmelite feasts including 'the Transverberation of the Heart of Our Holy Mother Saint Teresa' are included in the calendar. The feast days are studded with Irish saints and also include 'all the saints' of the Orders of Mount Carmel, St Augustine and St Francis. These subscribers were modest, pious Catholics, who largely lived on an axis between Clarendon Street on the south side of Dublin and Mary's Lane on the north. There were also addresses on St Stephen's Green and Dawson Street. None of the names are associated with the Catholic Convention of 1792-3.[42] None were titled or known to be of gentry families. None are mentioned in Henry Young's *Catholic Directory*, c. 1821 (the earliest extant) which lists the priests and officials in Catholic parishes, schools and institutions.[43] There are 295 subscribers, and what is most interesting, one third were women – an extraordinarily high proportion for that period. For the next one hundred years, Ireland took the lead in printing English-language primers. For the exhibition, the book lay open at the prayers recited before and after receiving the Blessed Sacrament, composed by St Thomas Aquinas and St Bonaventure.

EARLY ILLUSTRATIONS

8. *DAILY devotions, or the most profitable manner of hearing Mass, very necessary for all Roman Catholicks,* Dublin, printed in the year 1777.
Here we have a rare, tiny booklet of 72 pages, discovered at the back of a copy of *The poor man's manual and poesy of prayers; or the Key of Heaven* (Dublin, 1784). There are simple woodcuts on every alternate page, each depicting part of the Mass, with a prayer opposite, in large type, linking that part of the Mass with the different stages of the passion, twenty-nine illustrations in all. In these woodcuts, the scenes from the passion float as it were on a cloud, above the altar. The apparel and the interior with its tiled floor suggest an earlier period and a continental origin. The priest is bearded and there is a large cross on the back of his chasuble. Abbot Geoffrey Scott has discovered a fine Italian exemplar, *Devotissimo Esercizio per ascoltare con frutto la Santa Messa* (Firenze, 1761) containing the same images. The illustrations also occur in *The Devout manual* (Dublin, 1760), printed 'at the Cloysters', possibly by Bartholomew Corcoran whose business was on Inns Quay, near the Cloister. It is likely that there were other editions of the little booklet, which would have been intended for popular use, but this is the earliest Irish edition to survive. Two London editions are extant, published in 1722 and 1753; they too have the same woodcuts but in reverse and more finely cut. The use of illustration in eighteenth century Irish Catholic printing was very restrained, and was normally confined to a title-page or frontispiece, to catch the eye.

9. PICART, Bernard: *Cérémonies et coûtumes religieuses de tous les peuples du monde représentées par des figures dessinées de la main de Bernard Picart*, Amsterdam: J.F. Bernard, 1723-43. 8 vols in 9.

Volume two of this work lies open at an engraving which depicts a Mass inside a Catholic church in early eighteenth century France. The priest stands at the altar offering the sacred host and ciborium to the ladies and gentlemen kneeling before him: the women decorously dressed, with their heads covered, the men in skirted buff-coats and tie wigs. All those kneeling on the steps are holding close the large communion cloth as they receive the host.

In November 1720, Jean-Frédéric Bernard, a leading publisher in Amsterdam, had brought to public notice a very ambitious plan.[44] He proposed to publish, in French, an account of the customs and ceremonies of all the major religions of the world, which he optimistically expected to complete in four large folio volumes. Lavish illustrations in the form of copper engravings by Bernard Picart (1673-1733),[45] a leading French engraver, were to be the chief attraction. Picart was the son of Étienne Picart, also a painter and engraver, who had studied in Rome. The young Bernard, who was brought up in the Catholic faith, studied at the Académie Royale in Paris, and was a pupil of the well-known artist, Sébastien Leclerc. At the age of twenty three he left Paris, then moved back and forth between France and the Netherlands before finally settling in Amsterdam in 1711, at which point he became a Protestant. Throughout his life, he worked mostly on book illustration. The first two volumes of this work focus on the rites and ceremonies of the Catholic Church in the period following the Council of Trent. They provide a graphic portrayal of church and people in European city life in the early eighteenth century. The first edition of these two volumes appeared in 1723; Bernard brought out a second edition of them in 1739, with the text changed considerably. The work has been reprinted many times since.

10. VELAZQUEZ, Juan Antonio: *De Maria Immaculata Concepta*, Pinciae [Valladolid]: excudebat Barth. Portales, 1653.

The flamboyant title-page, engraved by the Spanish artist, Eugenio Orozco of Madrid, portrays Philip IV bearing the standard of Maria Immaculata, and being crowned with a wreath of laurels by an angel on either side. It is a wonderful example of Spanish book illustration. Juan Antonio Velazquez (1585-1669), from the Diocese of Avila, was born in Madrid and commenced his novitiate in the Society of Jesus in 1602 at Salamanca, later becoming Professor of Sacred Scripture there. At different stages of his career, he was rector of the Jesuit colleges of Monforte, Segovia, Medina and Valladolid, and Jesuit provincial of the province of Castile. Philip IV of Spain nominated him as consultor to the Congregation for the Defence of the Immaculate Conception. He died in Madrid in 1669.[46] Apart from commentaries on the scriptures, he wrote two other works on the Blessed Virgin.[47]

Notes

INTRODUCTION

1. The Planning Committee consisted of Rev Fr Raymond Moloney SJ; Rev Prof Maurice Hogan SSC; Rev Dr Michael Mullins, and Rev Prof James McEvoy, Director of the ICFC. Mr Stephen McGroggan acted throughout as secretary to the group and to the ICFC.

2. John Paul II, *Ecclesia de Eucharistia. Encyclical Letter on the Eucharist and the Church,* Catholic Truth Society, 2003. The abbreviation *EdE* will be employed throughout this book, with the exception of the Introduction and the Bibliography.

3. The model adopted for this book was that of conference acts supplemented by commissioned articles, as instanced in the work: *The Challenge of Truth: Reflections on 'Fides et Ratio',* James Mc Evoy (ed.), Dublin: Veritas, 2002, 272 pp.

4. *Instruction Redemptionis Sacramentum On Certain Matters to be Observed or to be Avoided Regarding the Most Holy Eucharist,* Congregation for Divine Worship and the Discipline of the Sacraments,Vatican City: Libreria Editrice Vaticana, 2004, 71 pp + Index.

5. John Paul II, *Apostolic Letter Mane Nobiscum Domine,* Dublin, Veritas, 2004.

6. The text published here of the lecture delivered at the Maynooth conference by Cardinal Danneels first appeard in *Liturgy in a Post-Modern World,* edited by Keith Pecklers SJ, and published by the Continuum International Publishing Group in 2003 (ISBN: 0826464122). It is reprinted by kind permission of the publishers.

7. Danneels's pastorals appear in both Dutch and French. The English version was prepared by Peter Forde from the French edition (*La nuit qu'il fut livré,* 'Paroles de vie', Pâques 1985), and tested for accuracy against the Dutch (*De Avond voor zijn Lijden en Dood,* 'Eeen woord bij Pasen 1985') by James McEvoy.

CHAPTER TWO

1. Joseph Cardinal Ratzinger, *The Spirit of the Liturgy,* San Francisco: Ignatius Press, 2000, p. 17.

2. The symbolism of the covenant, borrowed from social life, served to articulate the new kind of reciprocal relation between God and his people that was inaugurated at Sinai. Covenants were based on the fundamental values of law and cult. They were utilised from Mosaic times to structure the religious experience of the Israelites. The legal tradition beginning with the Decalogue embraced the religious, moral, social, economic and political spheres. This juridical aspect of the covenant was meant to foster and preserve a living relationship with Yahweh, the God of Israel, but only when it was interiorised. The process of

interiorisation was facilitated and expedited by active participation in
the liturgy as the public expression of the cult.

3. Cf. Roland de Vaux, *Studies in Old Testament Sacrifice*, Cardiff:
University of Wales Press, 1964; *Ancient Israel: Religious Institutions*, vol
2, New York: McGraw-Hill, 1965, pp. 415-456; Gary A. Anderson,
'Sacrifice and Sacrificial Offerings (OT),' in David N. Freedman (ed),
The Anchor Bible Dictionary, vol 5, New York: Doubleday, 1992, pp. 870-
886. For a useful summary, J. J. Castelot, Aelred Cody, 'Religious
Institutions in Israel,' in R. E. Brown et al., *The New Jerome Biblical
Commentary*, London: G. Chapman, 1990, pp. 1253-1283, especially pp.
1266-1275.

4. The Hebrew verb for sacrificing is *zabach*, to slaughter, and *mizbeach*,
the place of slaughter, the altar. It was at the altar that victims were
slaughtered, grains were burned, and blood and other liquids poured
out.

5. From the Hebrew verb *'alah*, to ascend. The smoke of the burning victim on the altar 'ascends' to God together with the sentiments of the offerer.

6. In Hebrew, *zebach shelamim*, *zebach* or *shelamim* alone. All these terms
are equivalent.

7. Eric Voegelin, *Order and History Volume I: Israel and Revelation*. The
Collected Works of Eric Voegelin, vol 14, edited with an Introduction
by Maurice P. Hogan, Columbia, MO: University of Missouri Press,
2001, p. 555.

8. Cf. Hans-Josef Klauck, 'Sacrifice and Sacrificial Offerings (NT),' *The
Anchor Bible Dictionary*, vol.5, pp. 870-886.

9. The Hebrew verb *zakar*, to remember and *zikkaron*, a remembrance,
include both recalling a past event and making it into a present experience through ritual participation.

10. Joseph Cardinal Ratzinger, *God Is Near Us*, San Francisco: Ignatius
Press, 2003, p. 38.

11. Martin Hengel, *The Atonement*, London: SCM Press, 1981, p. 73.

CHAPTER THREE

1. J. R. Donahue and D. J. Harrington, *The Gospel of Mark*, Sacra Pagina,
Collegeville, MN: Michael Glazier/The Liturgical Press, p. 400.

2. *ego eimi* is used in an absolute sense in Jn 8:24, 28, 58; 13:19; with understood predicate but absolute overtones in Jn 6:20; 18:5; in a participial
phrase with absolute overtones in Jn 4:26; with predicates that deal
with life and life-giving power in Jn 6:35, 51; 11:25; 14:6; 15:1, 5 and with
the related predicates of light and light of the world in Jn 8:12; 9:5.

3. In some texts Son, in others, Son of Man.

4. M. Hogan, *Seeking Jesus of Nazareth*, Dublin: Columba Press, 2001, p.
131.

5. Similarly, *remembering the Sabbath* is a call to share in the rest of the
Lord and the liberation from the burden of slavery.

6. Ex 29:38-46; *amnos* is used for lamb.

7. Lev 4:32ff, *probaton* is used for lamb.

8. 1 Pt 1:18f (JB).

9. Isa 53:7; The servant is designated *the chosen one* in the First and Third Songs of the Servant, Isa 42:1; 49:6f, empowered by the Spirit.

10. Cf. the Fourth Song of the Suffering Servant, Isa. 52:13–53:12. Scholars looking for an Aramaic background to the gospel have argued that underlying the idea of lamb in this context there may be the Aramaic word *talyâ*, (Hb *tâleh*) which can mean servant, child or lamb. Cf. W. H. Brownlee, 'Whence John?' in *John and Qumran*, J. H. Charlesworth (ed), p. 178. R. E. Brown argues against this on the grounds that the Hebrew equivalent *tâleh* is not used for the Isaian servant, but rather *'ebed,* the Aramaic equivalent of which is *'abda;* and there is no precedent for using *talyâ,* and *tâleh* is not translated as *amnos* in the LXX. However it can be argued that imagery is more fluid than vocabulary and cannot always be so closely tied down to an exact choice of words, particularly in translation.

11. Rev 5:8, 12f; 7:9f; 15:3; 22:1, 3 describe the Lamb enthroned and glorified, and Rev 13:8; 21:27 portray the Lamb as the judge who has the book of life, reflecting the judgement theme of the Johannine portrayal of the Son of Man.

12. Enoch 90:31; 89:52. In Revelation the term is the diminutive *arnion*, not *amnos* as in Jn 1:29, 36, but the concept is the same.

13. Rev 17:4 portrays the Lamb *(arnion)* as victorious in war.

14. Jer 11:19, *arnion* is used here for lamb in LXX, not *amnos* as in Jn 1:29, 36. The idea is the same.

15. After Ps 21 (22) this Ps 68 (69) is the most quoted psalm in the NT. Scholars see it as originally referring to the persecution of Jeremiah or of the Maccabees, or to the sufferings preceding the time of Ezra.

16. W. J. Harrington, *John, Spiritual Theologian, The Jesus of John*, Dublin: Columba Press, 1999, p. 34.

17. Mt 14:13-21; 15:32-39; Mk 6:35-44; 8:1-10; Lk 9:12-17.

18. Jn 6:2; cf. 2:23.

19. Luke's account stands alone among the six accounts in not having a sea crossing following the multiplication.

20. Cf. Mt 5:1ff; Mk 6:33f; Lk 9:12.

21. 2 Baruch 29:8 foretells a second feeding in the desert as the sign of the Messianic Age.

22. Num 11:1-3,13, 22 (JB).

23. The reference to barley bread conjures up the imagery of the Elijah-Elisha cycle with its promise of the return of Elijah, 2 Kings 4:42-44. The barley bread, cheaper than wheaten bread and so regarded as the bread of the poor, recalls the multiplication of the barley bread by Elisha, successor to Elijah: 'Give it to the people to eat', said Elisha to a man from Baal-Shalishah, 'they will eat and have some left over.' They ate and had some left over.

24. Mt 26:26; Mk14:22; Lk 22:17; 1 Cor 11:24.

25. Bread was not usually eaten on its own but would have some 'filling' as in a sandwich. *Opsarion*, a double diminutive, was used to describe such a filling. It literally means 'a small, little fish'. Combined with bread such a 'filling' is referred to as 'food' or, in the more general sense of the term, 'bread'. The 'fish' is not therefore left 'redundant' in the narrative.

26. *Didache* 9:3, 4.

27. Didache 9:4; 1 Clement 34:7; Ignatius, *Letter to Polycarp* 34:7.

28. Mt 8:23-27; 14:22-33; Mk 4:35-41; 6:45-52; Lk 8:22-25.

29. This epiphany reflects the biblical awareness of the divine presence in, and power over, creation, especially as manifested in the case of the angry sea.

30. The *egô eimi* statement of reassurance is inextricably linked to the words 'Do not be afraid'. This injunction not to be afraid is a recurring feature of Old Testament theophanies.

31. In the synoptic tradition the point is made explicitly that their fear results from their not having understood the real significance of the multiplication (Mk 6:52; Mt 16:5-12// Mk 8:14-21).

32. One reads in Exodus: 'I shall rain loaves from heaven on you' and 'This is the bread the Lord has given you to eat' (Ex 16:4, 15). The Psalmist says: 'He rained on them manna to eat and gave them the bread of heaven' (Ps 77/78:24). Wisdom of Solomon states: 'You fed your people with the nourishment of angels and you sent them from heaven bread that took no labour' (Wis 16:20).

33. Jn 6:32 f.; cf. Jn 6:27, 35, 39, 40, 44, 47, 48, 50, 51, 53-58. The Greek sentence emphasises 'from heaven' *(ek tou ouranou)* and 'true'*(alêthinon)*.

34. P. Borgen, *Bread from Heaven: An Exegetical Study in the Concept of Manna in the Gospel of John and the Writings of Philo*, p. 111f; cf. Malina, B. J., *The Palestinian Manna Tradition: The Manna Tradition in the Palestinian Targums and Its Relationship to the New Testament Writings*, 1968.

35. Neh 9:13, 15, 20; Wis 16:26; Gen Rab 70:5.

36. Ex 16; Nm 11; Ps 77 (78); Wis 16:20; Josephus *Antiquities*, III 1. 6. 30.

37. Philo, *De Mutatione Nominum*, 258-260.

38. This is similar to the statement in the defence he made after the healing of the invalid at Bethesda: 'Just as the Father possesses life in himself so has he granted that the Son possess life in himself' (Jn 5:26).

39. Mt 26:26-29; Mk:14:22-25; Lk:22:14-20; cf. 1 Cor 11:23-25.

40. Gen 9:4; Lev 3:17; Deut 12:23. Ezekiel, however, has a symbolic passage of a sacrificial banquet in which the people will eat the flesh of heroes and drink the blood of princes, a metaphor for a victory celebration.

41. The verb *gogguzein* signifies grumbling, whispering, displaying an attitude of smouldering discontent. It is used in the LXX for the discontent of the people in the desert. Jesus asks them if this teaching 'scandalises' them. The verb *skandalizein* means causing one to stumble, putting an obstacle in one's path.

42. *Sklêros* means hard, tough, unyielding. It is used in the compound noun *sklêrokardia*, 'hard of heart'.

43. Such disagreements may also explain the inclusion of the eucharistic teaching here in the broader context of *food for eternal life*, rather than in the traditional Last Supper context.

44. Jn 2:22 'after he was raised'; and 12:16 'after he was glorified'.

45. The narrative focuses on Peter and his objection. The salvific and cleansing nature of Jesus' action is particularly apt in his case in the light of Peter's forthcoming denials and his subsequent realisation of his need for cleansing and restoration. This will be well portrayed in his triple confession of love for Jesus and Jesus' confirmation of him in his shepherding role in Jn 21:15-19.

46. Paul develops a parallel theme in his 'dying and rising with Christ' which, like the footwashing, has been influential in the development of the Christian sacrament of baptism.

47. Jn 6:64; cf. Mt 26:20-25; Mk 14:17-21; Lk 22:21-23; Jn 13:21-30.

48. Preface of the Mass of the Sacred Heart.

49. Some commentators, particularly since the time of the Renaissance, have focused their attention on the description of the robe *(chitôn)*. In seeking its significance they have looked to the priestly garb described in Exodus as 'tunics of finely woven linen' and the High Priest's garb described as follows by Josephus Flavius: 'this garment consists not of two parts … but it is woven from a single length of thread'. Following this interpretation the robe symbolises the (High) Priesthood of Jesus, a Priesthood remaining intact after his death as he continues his High Priestly Prayer on behalf of his disciples initiated at the Last Supper.

50. *hoi men oun stratiôtai … heistékeisan de*

51. O. Treanor, *This is my Beloved Son, Aspects of the Passion*, London: DLT, 1997, p. 216.

52. R. E. Brown, *The Gospel According to John*, Vol. 2, London: G. Chapman, 1972, p. 923.

53. F. J. Moloney, op.cit., p. 504.

54. Ibid.

55. Arguments that *hyssopos*, hyssop, is a scribal alteration of *hyssos*, javelin, (as in the case of J. Camerarius in the 16th century), are weak, influenced by an overdependence on harmonisation with the synoptic tradition, failure to appreciate the Johannine symbolism, and supported by only one 11th century cursive manuscript.

56. Ex 12:22 f; cf. Heb 9:18-20 – sprinkling with hyssop to seal the covenant.

57. The idea of the head falling forward in death is communicated by the use of the past participle passive *inclinato* in the Latin translation *inclinato capite*, since Latin has no past participle active.

58. Scholars discuss whether the water will flow from Jesus' breast or the breast of the believer. It may be a typical Johannine double level of meaning. Taking the text in isolation in the context of the feast of

Tabernacles, both meanings are possible. In the broader context of the gospel, however, it seems more likely that 'from the breast of Jesus' is the primary meaning since life, revelation, and the promise of the Spirit come from him. Furthermore, the water comes from his side at the moment of glorification and the giving of the Spirit.

59. This specific statement of witness to the blood and water following on the handing over of the Spirit, forms an inclusion with the emphasis on the witness of the Baptist to the coming of the Spirit on Jesus at the beginning of the ministry.

60. Augustine, *Tractatus in Johannis Evangelium*, CXX 2; PL 35:1953.

61. F. J. Moloney, op.cit., p. 506.

62. W. J. Harrington, op. cit., p. 90.

63. The verb *helkuein* is used: Jn 6:43 *(helkusê)*; 12:32 *(helkusô)*; 21:6 *(helkusai)*; 21:11 *(heilkusen)*.

64. *schisma, mê schizômen, ouk eschisthê.*

CHAPTER FOUR

1. John Paul II, *EdE*, (2003), #16.

2. Ibid., #19.

3. Rev 3:20.

4. John Paul II, *Dives in Misericordia* (1980), #8.

5. John Paul II, *EdE*, #11, citing the Vatican Council II Constitution *Sacrosanctum Consilium*, #47: '… our Saviour instituted the Eucharist, Sacrifice of his body and blood, in order to perpetuate the sacrifice of the Cross throughout time, until he should return.'

6. John Paul II, *EdE*, #5.

7. 1 Enoch, in H.D.F. Sparks (ed.), *The Apocryphal Old Testament*, Oxford: Clarendon Press, pp. 211, 222.

8. Ibid., pp. 219, 214.

9. John Paul II, *Ecclesia de Eucharistia*, #18.

10. Bernard McGinn, 'John's Apocalypse and the Apocalyptic Mentality,' in Richard K. Emmerson, Bernard McGinn (eds), *The Apocalypse in the Middle Ages,* Ithaca and London: Cornell University Press, 1992, pp. 12-13.

11. John Paul II, *EdE*, #20.

12. Ibid., #57.

13. John Milbank, *Theology and Social Theory: Beyond Secular Reason*, Oxford: Blackwell, 1990, p. 207.

14. Frank Kermode, *The Sense of an Ending: Studies in the Theory of Fiction*, Oxford: Oxford University Press, 1966.

15. David Barr, 'The Apocalypse as a Symbolic Transformation of the World: A Literary Analysis,' *Interpretation* 38/1 (1984), pp. 39-50, pp. 44-45.

16. Hans Urs von Balthasar, *Theo-Drama: Theological Dramatic Theory. IV: The Action*, (Graham Harrison, ed.), San Francisco: Ignatius Press, 1994, p. 36.

17. Bruce Metzger, *The Canon of the New Testament: Its Origin, Development and Significance,* Oxford: Clarendon Press, 1987, pp. 198-199.
18. Hans von Campenhausen, *The Formation of the Christian Bible,* London: Adam and Charles Black, 1968, p. 241.
19. Jerome, *Commentarium in Isaiam* 18. prol., quoted in Bernard McGinn, 'John's Apocalypse and the Apocalyptic Mentality,' pp. 18-19.
20. Jerome, *Commentarium in Danielem,* quoted in Robert E. Lerner, 'The Medieval Return to the Thousand Year Sabbath,' in Emmerson and McGinn (eds), *The Apocalypse in the Middle Ages,* p. 51.
21. Augustine, *City of God,* Bk XX.7.
22. Ibid., Bk XX.9.
23. Augustine, *City of God,* Bk. XX.9.
24. Bernard McGinn, *The Calabrian Abbot: Joachim of Fiore in the History of Western Thought,* New York: Macmillan, 1985, pp. 64-65, citing Markus' *Saeculum* for the first point, and Gilles Quispel for 'demythologised eschatology.'
25. McGinn, *Calabrian Abbot,* pp. 64-65.
26. Augustine, *City of God,* Bk XX.9.
27. Ibid.
28. Bede, *Explanatio Apocalypsis,* 12.2-12.6.
29. Derk Visser, *Apocalypse as Utopian Expectation (800-1500): The Apocalypse Commentary of Berengaudus of Ferrières and the Relationship between Exegesis, Liturgy and Iconography,* Leiden: E. J. Brill, 1996, p. 61. As Visser explains, historians have yet to decide where to place Berengaudus between the 9th and 11th centuries.
30. Ibid., p. 59.
31. Jonathan Alexander, 'The Last Things: Representing the Unrepresentable: The Medieval Tradition,' in Frances Carey (ed.), *The Apocalypse and the Shape of Things to Come,* p. 60.
32. Visser, *Apocalypse as Utopian Expectation,* p. 104.
33. Bernard McGinn, *Visions of the End: Apocalyptic Traditions in the Middle Ages,* p. 36.
34. Robert E. Lerner, 'The Medieval Return to the Thousand Year Sabbath,' in Emmerson (ed.), *The Apocalypse in the Middle Ages,* p. 57.
35. McGinn, *Calabrian Abbot,* p. 110.
36. Norman Cohn, *The Pursuit of the Millennium,* London: Secker and Warburg, 1957, pp. 150, 99.
37. Robert E. Lerner, 'The Medieval Return to the Thousand Year Sabbath,' p. 57. My italics.
38. McGinn, *Calabrian Abbot,* pp. 21-22.
39. Ibid., pp. 109-110, quoting Marjorie Reeves, *The 'Figurae' Of Joachim of Fiore,* p. 182.
40. Cf. Robert E. Lerner, 'The Medieval Return to the Thousand Year Sabbath,' pp. 61-68.
41. Eugen Weber, *Apocalypses: Prophecies, Cults and Millennial Beliefs Through the Ages,* London: Hutchinson, 1999, pp. 58-60.

42. Bernard McGinn, 'John's Apocalypse and the Apocalyptic Mentality,' p. 19.

43. Voegelin notes his debt to von Balthasar's *Prometheus* (the published version of his massive PhD thesis), in *Science Politics and Gnosticism*, Chicago: Henry Regnery, 1968, p. v.

44. The title of one of Voegelin's early books, and a phrase often used by him thereafter: Erich Voegelin's *Political Religions* was printed in Austria 'in the spring of 1938 just in time to be confiscated by the invading Nazis.' See *Political Religions*, (T. J. Dinapoli & E. S. Easterly III trans.), New York: Edwin Mellen Press, 1986, p. xxxiii. Voegelin discusses the trajectory from the Apocalypse through Joachim to German National Socialism on pp. 42-45.

45. Voegelin, *Science, Politics and Gnosticism*, p. 105.

46. Bernard McGinn, *Calabrian Abbot*, p. 101, quoting Marjorie Reeves, 'The *Liber Figurarum* of Joachim of Fiore,' *Medieval and Renaissance Studies*, 11 (1950), p. 65.

47. John Paul II, *EdE*, #62.

48. Ibid., #8.

49. Cohn, *The Pursuit of the Millennium*, pp. 256-257.

50. Walter Klaassen, *Living at the End of the Ages: Apocalyptic Expectation in the Radical Reformation*, Lanham: University Press of America, 1992, p. 21.

51. Metzger, *The Canon of the New Testament*, pp. 241-244.

52. John Paul II, *EdE*, #59.

53. David Barr, 'The Apocalypse of John as Oral Enactment', *Interpretation* 40 (1986), pp. 243-256 (256).

54. John Paul II, *EdE*, #50.

55. 'The Community Rule' in Geza Vermes (ed), *The Dead Sea Scrolls in English*, London: Penguin, 1962, fourth edition, 1995, p. 87.

56. Jacques Ellul, *Apocalypse*, New York: Seabury Press, 1977.

57. Richard Bauckham, *The Theology of the Book of Revelation*, Cambridge: Cambridge University Press, 1993, p. 10.

58. Elisabeth Schüssler-Fiorenza, 'Composition and Structure of the Book of Revelation,' *Catholic Biblical Quarterly*, 39 (1977), pp. 344-66.

59. Paul Griffiths, *Olivier Messiaen and the Music of Time*, London: Faber and Faber, 1985, p. 29.

60. Ibid., p. 104.

61. Richard Bauckham, *The Theology of Revelation*, p. 10.

62. Hans Urs von Balthasar quoting Rilke's 'Archaic Torso of Apollo', in *Theo-Drama: Theological Dramatic Theory. II: The Dramatis Personae: Man in God*, (Graham Harrison trans.), San Francisco: Ignatius Press, 1990, p. 24.

63. Hans Urs Von Balthasar, *Theo-Logic. Theological Logical Theory. Volume I Truth of the World* (Adrian J. Walker trans.), San Francisco: Ignatius Press, 2000, p. 78.

64. John Paul II, *EdE*, #15.

CHAPTER FIVE

1. Augustine, *De civitate Dei*, 22, 17 (PL 41:779).

2. H. de Lubac, *The Splendour of the Church*, London: Sheed & Ward, 1956, p. 113.

3. H. de Lubac, 'Meditation on the Church', in J. H. Miller (ed), *Vatican II: An Interfaith Appraisal,* Notre Dame-London: Notre Dame University Press, 1966, pp. 258-66, at p. 263.

4. Vatican II, *Lumen gentium*, #3.

5. First used in H. de Lubac, *Corpus mysticum: L'Eucharistie et l'église au moyen âge,* Paris: Aubier, 1944, p. 103.

6. *The Splendour of the Church*, p. 92. The phrase was also invoked by the Holy Father in his Apostolic Letter, *Dominicae Coenae*, 4, AAS 72 (1980), p. 119.

7. On this method in general, see N. Ormerod, 'Quarrrels with the Method of Correlation', *Theological Studies* 57 (1996), pp. 709-19.

8. E.g. Andrew Furlong, *Trial for Heresy: A 21st Century Journey of Faith,* Winchester: O Books, 2003, pp. 141-45.

9. J. Zizioulas, 'The Mystery of the Church in Orthodox Tradition', *One In Christ* 24 (1988), pp. 294-303, especially pp. 299 f.

10. *Didascalia Apostolorum* 13, R. H. Connolly (ed), Oxford: Clarendon, 1929, p. 124.

11. De Lubac, *Catholicism*, p. viii.

12. Ibid., p. x.

13. H. U. von Balthasar, *Thérèse of Lisieux, The Story of a Mission*, London-New York: Sheed & Ward, 1953, p. 134.

14. Ibid., p. 169. Thérèse is also cited as a paradigm of this doctrine by Y. Congar, *The Mystery of the Church*, London: Chapman, 1960, pp. 30 and 37.

15. H. de Lubac, *The Church, Paradox and Mystery*, Shannon: Ecclesia, 1969, p. 99; *The Splendour of the Church*, p. 11.

16. Cited by E. Borgman, *Edward Schillebeeckx: A Theologian in His History*, London: Continuum, 2003, p. 137.

17. L. Bouyer, cited by de Lubac, *The Splendour of the Church*, p. 91.

18. Apostolic Constitution, *Indulgentiarum Doctrina*, #4, AAS 59 (1967), p. 9.

19. Cf. Augustine, *De civitate Dei* X, 3 (PL 41: 280), where he speaks of the sacrifices on the altar of our hearts. Cf. Vatican II, *Lumen gentium*, #10, cited *EdE*, #28.

20. Vatican II, *Sacrosanctum concilium*, #14.

21. Clement of Rome, *Ad Corinthios* 59-60; Aristides, *Apologia* 16; Hippolytus, *In Danielem* II, 4; Origen, *Contra Celsum*, VIII, 73-75; Clement of Alexandria, *Stromata* VII, 9 and 13, all cited by de Lubac, *The Splendour of the Church*, p. 96.

22. Encyclical, *Sollicitudo rei socialis*, #38; also *L'Osservatore Romano*, 4 December 1989.

23. *S.T.*, III, q. 56, a. 2.

24. Hilary of Poitiers, *Tractatus in Psalmum*, 125, 6 (CSEL 22.609, 19-20); Paschase, *In Lam. Jer.*, 2 (PL 120:1119A).

25. Cited by de Lubac without reference, *Catholicism*, p. 28.

26. *Corpus mysticum*, p. 19.

27. C. Giraudo, *Eucaristia per la Chiesa*, Rome: Gregorian University Press, 1989, p. 449.

28. *Splendour of the Church*, p. 24.

CHAPTER SIX

1. A convenient summary of New Testament teaching on the Eucharist can be found in X. Léon-Dufour, SJ, *Sharing the Eucharistic Bread. The Witness of the New Testament*, Translated from the French by M. J. O'Connell, New York/Mahwah: Paulist Press, 1987.

2. *The First Apology*, 66. Translation from T. Falls, *St Justin Martyr*, in *The Fathers of the Church*, Schopp, Defarri (eds), New York, 1949.

3. *On the Sacraments* Book 4. CSEL 73.46-65; translated in *The Fathers of the Church* 44.297-314.

4. T. Camelot, 'Réalisme et symbolisme dans la doctrine eucharistique de S. Augustin', *Revue des sciences philosophiques et théologiques* 31 (1947), pp. 394-410.

5. *Sermon Wolfenbüttel* 7, G. Morin (ed), *Miscellania Augustiniana* 1, Rome, 1930, 463; cf. also Sermon 227 in *Sources Chrétiennes* 116.234-242.

6. For a documented discussion of the theology of this period see E. J. Kilmartin SJ, *The Eucharist in the West: History and Theology*, R. J. Daly SJ (ed.), Collegeville: The Liturgical Press, 1998.

7. PL 30,281; see E. Schillebeeckx OP, *The Eucharist*, N. D. Smith (trans.), New York: Sheed and Ward, 1968, pp. 72-76.

8. Text in DS, #690.

9. Text in DS, #700.

10. Text in DS, #846.

11. DS, #1153.

12. DS, ##1256-1258.

13. *Concilii Tridentini Acta*, Görres-Gesellschaft (ed), Tomus 6, Pars 3, Vol. 1, pp.134-140; see E. Schillebeeckx, *The Eucharist*, p. 32, and n. 13.

14. The teaching of Trent on the sacrament of the Eucharist is in DS, ##1635-1661.

15. It is a tradition that is still dominant at the beginning of the 20th century, as can be seen in one of the most widely-used manuals of Catholic theology, Ad. Tanquerey's *Synopsis major Theologiae dogmaticae*: the first chapter of the treatise on the Eucharist is entitled 'On the mystery of the real presence'; this is followed by chapters 'On the sacrifice of the Mass' and 'On the sacrament of the Eucharist'.

CHAPTER SEVEN

1. Romano Guardini, *Before Mass* (Elinor Castendyk Briefs, trans.), London: Longmans, 1957, p. 154.

2. Romano Guardini, *The Lord* (Elinor Castendyk Briefs, trans.), London: Longmans,1954 , pp. 465-66.

3. Romano Guardini, *The Spirit of the Liturgy* (Ada Lane, trans.), London: Sheed & Ward, 1938, pp. 58-60.

4. Robert Sokolowski, *Eucharistic Presence. A Study in the Theology of Disclosure*, Washington: The Catholic University of America Press, 1994.

5. Cf. Sokolowski, *Eucharistic Presence*, p. 92. The Eucharist represents to us the most dramatic of events, the redemption of the world and of man, but Sokolowski and Guardini claim that the manner of the representation is not itself a dramatic one.

6. Josef Jungmann, S.J., *The Eucharistic Prayer*, p. 16, cited in Sokolowski, *Eucharistic Presence*, p. 19, n. 11 (italics mine).

7. Cf. Pierre-Marie Gy, 'The "We" of the Eucharistic Prayer', in *Theological Digest*, 41 (1994), p. 129.

8. Gregory Dix, *The Shape of the Liturgy,* London: 1945, p. 744, quoted in Aidan Nichols, *The Service of Glory*, Edinburgh: T & T Clark, 1997, p. 57.

9. Cf. Congregation for the Sacraments and Divine Worship, Decree on the *Ordo Dedicationis Ecclesiae et Altaris*, Rome: 29 May, 1977.

10. Ibid., IV 2, *Ordo dedicationis altaris*.

11. St Peter Chrysologus, *Sermons* 108 (PL 52, 500).

12. St Leo the Great, *Sermon* 4. 1-2 (PL 54, 149).

13. 'Graduation Masses – a Liturgist Responds' in *Intercom*, June,1999.

14. Peter McPartlan, 'The Eucharist as the Basis for Ecclesiology', *Antiphon* 6 (2001), pp. 12-19, p. 18.

15. Address, *l'Osservatore Romano,* 14 October, 1998.

16. *Christifideles Laici*, On the Vocation and Mission of the Laity, 1988, ##14-15.

17. Newman, Venerable J. H., 'Doing Glory to God in the Pursuits of the World,' in *Parochial and Plain Sermons*, London: Longmans, 1895, p. 468.

18. St Josemaría, Homily 'Christ's Death is the Christian's Life', 1960, in *Christ is Passing by*, Dublin: Veritas, 1974, p. 137

19. Gisbert Greshake enthused about *Lumen gentium*'s phrase that the common priesthood and the ministerial priesthood differ in essence and not in degree, for it spared us from the sterile discourse about whether the priest is 'more' than the layperson and permitted us to look, rather, at how they are ordered to one other (*Priestersein*, Freiburg: Herder,1982, pp. 73-75).

20. John Paul II, *Mulieris Dignitatem*, On the Dignity of Woman, 1987, #27. See also John Paul II, *Pastores Dabo vobis*, On the Formation of Priests, 1992, ##16, 17, 37; *The Catechism of the Catholic Church*, #1547.

21. Douglas Hyde, *Religious Songs of Connacht*, Volume 2, Shannon: Irish University Press, 1972, p. 257.

CHAPTER EIGHT

1. John Paul II, *Novo Millennio Ineunte* #4, London: Catholic Truth Society, 2001.

2. 'Subsequent to the Second Vatican Council, the Catholic image of priesthood, which had been defined by the Council of Trent and given fresh vigor as a result of renewed attention to the witness of Sacred Scripture at Vatican II, passed into a state of crisis. The large number of those who turned away from the priesthood and the great decrease in priestly vocations in many countries certainly cannot be explained solely on theological grounds. However, causes having their origin outside the Church would not have had such an impact unless the theological foundations of priestly ministry had reached a critical point for many priests and young people.' Joseph Ratzinger, 'Biblical Foundations of Priesthood', in *Origins*, 20:19 (1990), p. 310.

3. John Paul II, *EdE* #31, London: Catholic Truth Society, 2003.

4. The phrase *in persona Christi* is used in *EdE* ##28, 29 and 32.

5. For a full historical study see Bernard D. Marliangeas, *Clés pour une théologie du ministère: in persona Christi, in persona Ecclesiae*, Paris: Editions Beauchesne, 1978.

6. 2 Cor 2:10.

7. Aquinas cites the text of 2 Corinthians 2:10 on five occasions in the *Summa* and in these cases he interprets the text of St Paul in a very strong sense. See *Summa Theologiae* IIIa, q.22, a.4, c; Ia IIae, q.100, a.8, 2°; IIa IIae, q.88, a.12, c; IIIa, q.8, a.6, c; and III q.64, a.2, 3°.

8. Marliangeas, *Clés pour une théologie du ministère*, p. 55.

9. Ibid., p. 68.

10. Thomas Aquinas, *Summa Theologiae*, 1965, vol. 50: *The One Mediator.* IIIa q.22, a.4, c.

11. Thomas Aquinas, *Summa Theologiae*, vol. 58 (1965): *The Eucharistic Presence.* IIIa, 78, 1, c.

12. Thomas Aquinas, *Summa Theologiae*, vol. 59 (1975): *Holy Communion.* IIIa q.82, q.5, c.

13. Patrick McGoldrick, 'Orders, Sacrament of', in Peter Fink SJ (ed), *The New Dictionary of Sacramental Worship*, Dublin: Gill & Macmillan, 1990, p. 904.

14. David N. Power, OMI, 'Representing Christ in Community and Sacrament', in Donald J. Goergen (ed), *Being a Priest Today*, Collegeville, Minnesota: The Liturgical Press, 1992, p. 99.

15. McGoldrick, 'Orders, Sacrament of', p. 904.

16. Thomas Aquinas, *Summa Theologiae*, Vol. 59 (1975): *Holy Communion.* IIIa, 82, 6, c.

17. Thomas Aquinas, *Summa Theologiae*, Vol. 59 (1975): *Holy Communion.* III q. 82, a.7, 3um.

18. Fernand Van Steenberghen, 'The Priesthood according to Cardinal Mercier', in A. M. Charue (ed), *Priesthood and Celibacy*, Milan: Editrice Ancora, 1972, p. 189.

19. Aidan Nichols OP, *Holy Order: the Apostolic Ministry from the New Testament to the Second Vatican Council*, Dublin: Veritas, 1990, p. 126.

20. We see this in Pius X, *Haerent Animo* and in Pius XI, *Ad Catholici Sacerdotii*. The actual origin of the phrase '*sacerdos alter Christus*' in Christian theology is somewhat obscure. See the discussion provided by H. T. Henry, '*Sacerdos alter Christus*', *The Ecclesiastical Review*, 95 (1936), pp. 460-470.

21. Second Vatican Council, *Lumen Gentium*, ##10, 21 and 28. The Council also used other constructions which are quite close to the phrase *in persona Christi*. The phrase *nomine Christi* is used in *Lumen Gentium*, ## 25 and 27, and is also used in *Presbyterorum Ordinis*, # 2.

22. Second Vatican Council, *Lumen Gentium*, in Austin Flannery OP (ed), *Vatican Council II: the Conciliar and Post Conciliar Documents*, Dublin: Dominican Publications, 1988. Vol. 1. #10, p. 361.

23. Second Vatican Council, *Lumen Gentium*, # 21, pp. 372 & 374.

24. Second Vatican Council, *Lumen Gentium*, # 28, pp. 384 -385.

25. Second Vatican Council, *Sacrosanctum Concilium*, #33.

26. Second Vatican Council, *Presbyterorum Ordinis*, in Austin Flannery OP (ed), *Vatican Council II*, Vol. 1. #5, p. 872.

27. Second Vatican Council, *Presbyterorum Ordinis*, #2, p. 865.

28. Peter Fink SJ, 'The Priesthood of Jesus Christ in the Ministry and Life of the Ordained', in Robert Wister (ed), *Priests: Identity and Ministry*, Wilmington, Delaware: Michael Glazier, 1990, pp. 86-87.

29. John Paul II, *Pastores Dabo Vobis*, London: Catholic Truth Society, 1992, #15, p. 38.

30. Second Vatican Council, *Sacrosanctum Concilium*, #7. Subsequent statements from the Holy See again spelt out the various modalities of Christ's presence in the liturgy. See *Eucharisticum Mysterium*, #55 and *Mysterium Fidei*, #39.

31. Fink, 'The Priesthood of Jesus Christ …', p. 82.

32. Peter Fink SJ, *Worship: Praying the Sacraments*, Washington DC: The Pastoral Press, 1991, p. 128.

33. Fink, *Worship…*, p. 128.

34. John Paul II, *EdE*, #23.

35. Yves Congar, *I Believe in the Holy Spirit*, London: Geoffrey Chapman, 1983. Vol. III: The river of the water of life (Rev. 22:1) flows in the East and in the West, p. 234.

36. Second Vatican Council, *Presbyterorum Ordinis*, #2, p. 865.

37. *The Roman Pontifical*, 1978, p.213.

38. Patrick McGoldrick, 'The Holy Spirit and the Eucharist', *ITQ*, 50:1 (1983/1984), p. 48.

39. Second Vatican Council, *Presbyterorum Ordinis*, #1.

40. Second Vatican Council, *Lumen Gentium*, #28, p. 384.

41. Second Vatican Council, *Presbyterorum Ordinis*, #4, p. 868.

42. Second Vatican Council, *Presbyterorum Ordinis*, #2, p. 865.

43. John Paul II, *Pastores Dabo Vobis*, #15, p. 39.

44. Second Vatican Council, *Lumen Gentium*, #28, pp. 384 - 385.
45. Second Vatican Council, *Presbyterorum Ordinis*, #5, p. 871.
46. Second Vatican Council, *Presbyterorum Ordinis*, #5, p. 871.
47. John Paul II, *EdE* #31.
48. Lk 22:27.
49. Mk 10:43-45.
50. Eph 3:7.
51. Col 1:25.
52. Phil 1:1.
53. 1 Cor 9:19.
54. Aquinas himself quotes this text along with that of 2 Cor. 2:10 in *Summa Theologiae*, IIIa q.8, a.6, c.
55. 2 Cor 5:18-20.
56. Acts 6.
57. See Augustine, *Sermon* 272. 'You, however, are the Body of Christ and His members. If, therefore, you are the Body of Christ and His members, your mystery is presented at the table of the Lord: you receive your mystery. To that which you are, you answer: "Amen"; and by answering, you subscribe to it. For you hear: "The Body of Christ!" and you answer: "Amen!" Be a member of Christ's Body, so that your "Amen" may be the truth'.
58. John Paul II, *EdE*, #20.
59. The instruction, to 'know what you are doing, and imitate the mystery you celebrate', is also mentioned in the formal instruction which may be used prior to the laying on of hands and prayer of consecration in the ordination ceremony.
60. Ignatius of Antioch, *Letter to the Romans*, #4.
61. John Paul II, *Novo Millennio Ineunte*, #41, p. 38.
62. During 2002, at least 19 Catholic priests and 2 seminarians were murdered. Four of these were murdered while celebrating the Eucharist. Most of these murders took place in Latin America and Africa. See J. G. Orban de Lengyelfalva, *Violence against Christians in the Year 2002*, Netherlands: Aid to the Church in Need, 2003, pp. 245-246
63. Acts 20:35.
64. Phil 1:19.
65. John Paul II, *EdE*, #31, p. 27.

CHAPTER NINE

1. The English text of *EdE* being used is in *Origins*, vol. 32: no. 46, May 1, 2003.
2. The primary focus of the Council was to speak the faith with depth and so with a pastoral vigour. The theological depth of the conciliar texts has not been always realised. See Joseph Ratzinger, 'Die Ekklesiologie der Konstitution *Lumen gentium*,' in idem, *Weggemeinschaft des Glaubens*, Augsburg: Sankt Ulrich Verlag, 2002, pp. 107-150.
3. See Karl Rahner, *The Trinity*, translated by Joseph Donceel, New

York: Herder and Herder, 1970, p. 11. Hans Urs von Balthasar was of the same mind.

4. See Catherine Mawry LaCugna, *God for Us: The Trinity and Christian Life*, New York: HarperSanFrancisco, 1991; Patricia A. Fox, *God as Communion*, Collegeville, MN: The Liturgical Press, 2002.

5. St Augustine, *De Trinitate*, I, 1: PL, 42, 822.

6. N. Ciolo, *Teologia trinitaria, storia, metodo, prospettive*, Bologna: EDB, 1996, p. 198.

7. Bruno Forte, *La chiesa, icona della Trinità*, Brescia: Queriniana, 1984; idem, *La chiesa della Trinità. Saggio sul mistero della chiesa communione e missione*, Cinisello Balsamo: San Paolo, 1995.

8. *EdE* #34; see *Extraordinary Synod of Bishops Final Report 1985*, II.C.1: *L'Osservatore Romano*, Dec. 10, 1985.

9. See *SC*, ##51, 55, 59; *LG*, 3, 7, 11; *AG*, 9; *PO*, 4,6; *UR*, 2, 22; *AA*, 6; *DV*, 21. The text of Vatican II documents is Walter M. Abbott, SJ (ed.), *The Documents of Vatican II*, New York: Guild Press, 1966.

10. Second Vatican Council, *UR*, #2.

11. Texts of scripture are quoted from the *New Revised Standard Version*.

12. St Augustine, *Confessions*, X, 43.

13. Vatican II, *LG*, 4; see St Cyprian, *De oratione dominica*, 23: PL, 4, 553; St Augustine, *Sermo* 71, 20, 33: PL, 38, 463f; St John of Damascus, *Adversus Iconoclastes*, 12: PG, 96, 1358 D.

14. St Hilary of Poitiers, *De Trinitate*, VIII, 15-16, in PL, 10, 247-249 as translated in *The Divine Office*, vol. II, Dublin: Talbot, 1974, p. 565.

15. Ibid.

16. See Klaus Hemmerle, *Partire dall'unità*, Roma: Città Nuova, 1998, p. 55.

17. See Chiara Lubich, *La dottrina spirituale*, Milano: Mondadori, 2001, p. 173.

18. Henri de Lubac, *Corpus Mysticum. L'Eucharistie et l'Eglise au Moyen Age*, 2nd edition, Paris: Du Cerf, 1949.

19. Klaus Hemmerle, op. cit., pp.38-9.

20. *EdE*, #23.

21. St John Chrysostom, *Homilies on First Corinthians*, 24, 2: PG 61, 200. The footnote in the encyclical gives further references to the *Didache*, IX, 4: F. X. Funk, I, 22; St Cyprian, *Epistle LXIII*, 13: PL 4, 384.

22. St Augustine, *Confessions*, VII, 10: PL 32, 742.

23. Jerome Hamer, *L'Eglise est une communion*, Paris, 1962; F. Hauck, *koinonia* in ThWNT, IV, 804; Joseph Ratzinger, 'Communio: Eucharistie – Gemeinschaft – Sendung,' in *Weggemeinschaft des Glaubens*, Augsburg: Sankt Ulrich Verlag, 2002, pp. 53-78.

24. Plato, *Symposium* 188 b-c.

25. Joseph Ratzinger, op.cit., p. 66.

26. Walter Kasper, *Theology & Church*, New York: Crossroad, 1989, p. 154

27. Joseph Ratzinger, op. cit., p. 69.

28. Second Vatican Council, *LG*, #11; *AG*, #9.

29. Eric Voegelin, *Israel and Revelation, Order and History Volume One*. The Collected Works of Eric Voegelin, vol.14. Edited with Introduction by Maurice P. Hogan, Columbia, MO: University of Missouri Press, 2001, pp. 542-570.

30. 'I would like to rekindle this eucharistic "amazement" by the present encyclical letter, in continuity with the jubilee heritage which I have left to the church in the apostolic letter *Novo Millennio Ineunte* and its Marian crowning, *Rosarium Virginis Mariae*,' *EdE*, #6.

31. Pope John Paul, *Novo Millennio Ineunte*, #43.

32. St John Chrysostom, *Homilies on the Gospel of St Matthew*, 50:3: PG 58, 508; quoted in *EdE*, #20.

33. St Augustine, *In Joannem*, 65, 1-2: PL 35, 1808.

34. Ibid., 26, 6, 13: PL 35, 1613; quoted in *SC*, #47.

CHAPTER TEN

1. I have argued this in a number of papers and in my book *Language, World and God*, Dublin: Columba, 1996, Chapter Eight. A more advanced version will appear in the first volume of my, as yet unpublished, study *Incarnation and Transcendence*.

2. For more of this criticism of Heidegger, see my *Language and transcendence: A Study in the Philosophy of Martin Heidegger and Karl-Otto Apel*, Bern: Lang, 1994.

3. I do not mean to assert here that the 'ontological argument' for the existence of God actually works – it may or may not; but regardless of this, Anselm's 'definition' of God and what he deduces from it, nevertheless, constitutes a philosophical insight.

4. Indeed this seems to be a notion deployed by Hume in the *Dialogues Concerning Natural Religion*. Hume's point is that even if we do decide that the universe is the product of intelligence, we have no evidence that this intelligence still exists.

5. This is a very impacted version of the argument which I offer in *Language, World and God*, and in more developed form in *Incarnation and Transcendence*.

6. But things can exist without being God, just as things could be 'intelligent' without being John only if the intelligence that they have is an analogically diminished version of what John is.

7. One might play upon the word *imago* creatively: it means at once image and also, in insect biology, is the term for a creature which is immature and not yet all that it may be.

8. A discussion of whether this is our 'original' state or a consequence of original sin is beyond the scope of this essay.

CHAPTER ELEVEN

1. John Paul II, *Encyclical Letter Fides et Ratio: On the Relationship between Faith and Reason*, Boston, Mass.: Pauline Books and Media, 1998, #91.

2. See Georg Wilhelm Friedrich Hegel, *Lectures on the Philosophy of World History. Introduction: Reason in History*, trans. H. B. Nisbet, Cambridge: Cambridge University Press, 1975, pp. 25-43.

3. Ibid., p. 163.

4. See esp. Martin Heidegger, 'The Question Concerning Technology', in David Farrell Krell (ed.), *Basic Writings*, New York: Harper-Collins, 1993, pp. 311-41.

5. On the notion of 'destruction' in Heidegger, see *Being and Time*, (John Macquarrie and Edward Robinson trans.), New York: Harper-Collins, 1962, #6, pp. 41-49.

6. Genuine hearing requires listening, that is to say, careful attention to the source of sound – sound that is highly transient, unlike objects of vision. On Heidegger's critique of the philosophical root-metaphor of vision, see the brief remarks in my article, 'Heidegger's Transcendental History', *Journal of the History of Philosophy*, 40 (2002), pp. 501-23, esp. p. 510.

7. See Martin Heidegger, 'The End of Philosophy and the Task of Thinking', in *Basic Writings*, pp. 431-49, esp. p. 447.

8. This is the position Catherine Pickstock takes in *After Writing: On the Liturgical Consummation of Philosophy*, Oxford: Blackwell, 1998.

9. See John D. Caputo, *Heidegger and Aquinas: An Essay on Overcoming Metaphysics*, New York: Fordham University Press, 1982. Caputo formulates his conclusions on pp. 283-84.

10. On this point, the differences in emphasis between the French edition of *God without Being* and its English translation are well known. See esp. Jean-Luc Marion, *God without Being*, (Thomas A. Carlson trans.), Chicago and London: University of Chicago Press, 1992, pp. xxii-xxiv.

11. Werner Beierwaltes has been one of the foremost proponents of a dialogue between Neoplatonism and contemporary thought; see, for example, *Platonismus und Idealismus*, 2nd ed., Frankfurt am Main: Klostermann, 2004 and *Denken des Einen: Studien zur neuplatonischen Philosophie und ihrer Wirkungsgeschichte*, Frankfurt am Main: Klostermann, 1985.

12. Marion, *God without Being*, xix.

13. Marion, *Sur l'ontologie grise de Descartes: science cartésienne et savoir aristotélicien dans les 'Regulae'*, Paris: Vrin, 1975, (4th ed., 2000).

14. Marion, *Sur la théologie blanche de Descartes: analogie, création des vérités éternelles, fondement*, Paris: Presses universitaires de France, 1981, (rev. ed., 1991).

15. Marion, 'La splendeur de la contemplation eucharistique', *Résurrection*, 31 (1969), pp. 84–88.

16. Maxime Charles, *Guide de l'adoration eucharistique*, Paris: OEIL, 2002. For a recent monograph on Fr Charles, one may consult Samuel Pruvot,

Monseigneur Charles, aumônier à la Sorbonne, 1944–59, Paris: Éditions du Cerf, 2002.

17. Marion, *L'idole et la distance: cinq études,* Paris: Grasset, 1977 (3rd ed., Paris: Librarie générale française, 1991). English translation: *The Idol and Distance: Five Studies,* (Thomas A. Carlson trans.), New York: Fordham University Press, 2001.

18. Marion, *Dieu sans l'être,* Paris: Fayard, 1982 (2nd ed., Presses universitaires de France, 1991). For the English translation, see note 10 above.

19. Marion, *Prolégomènes à la charité,* Paris: Éditions de la Différence, 1986 (2nd ed., 1991). English translation: *Prolegomena to Charity*, (Stephen E. Lewis trans.), New York: Fordham University Press, 2002.

20. Marion, *Réduction et donation: recherches sur Husserl, Heidegger et la phénoménologie,* Paris: Presses universitaires de France, 1989. English translation: *Reduction and Givenness: Investigations of Husserl, Heidegger, and Phenomenology*, Thomas A. Carlson trans.), Evanston, Ill.: Northwestern University Press, 1998.

21. Marion, *Étant donné: essai d'une phénoménologie de la donation*, Paris: Presses universitaires de France, 1997 (2nd ed., 1998). English translation: *Being Given: Toward a Phenomenology of Givenness*, (Jeffrey L. Kosky trans.), Stanford, Cal.: Stanford University Press, 2002.

22. Marion, *Le phénomène érotique: six méditations,* Paris: Grasset, 2003.

23. For the concept of 'saturated phenomenon', see Marion, *De surcroît: études sur les phénomènes saturés,* Paris: Presses universitaires de France, 2001. English translation: *In Excess: Studies of Saturated Phenomena*, (Robyn Horner and Vincent Berraud trans.), New York: Fordham University Press, 2002.

24. Marion's publications on the theology of the Eucharist include the following titles: 'La splendeur de la contemplation eucharistique', *Résurrection*, 31 (1969), pp. 84-88; 'Présence et distance. Remarques sur l'implication réciproque de la contemplation eucharistique et de la présence réelle', *Résurrection*, 43-44 (1974), pp. 31–58; 'Le présent et le don', *Revue catholique internationale Communio* 2:6 (1977). The last article was revised for *Dieu sans l'être* (1982), in which it appeared as chapter 6 (pp. 225-58). In addition, *Dieu sans l'être* contains a chapter (no. 5) entitled, 'Du site eucharistique de la théologie' (pp. 197-222). Both chapters are of course included in the English translation of *Dieu sans l'être*. I have not seen 'La splendeur de la contemplation eucharistique', in *La politique de la mystique: hommage à Mgr. Maxime Charles*, Limoges: Éditions Criterion, 1984, pp. 17–28.

The later articles from this list often expand upon the argument of the earlier ones, although there are also some shifts of emphasis. For the purposes of the present essay, I shall attempt to distil a systematic theology of the Eucharist from Marion's publications on the subject. I shall not address the question of developments in Marion's thought.

My sincere thanks are due to Monsieur Georges Théry, of the journal *Résurrection*, for sending me photocopies of Professor Marion's articles.

25. Marion, *God without Being*, p. 164 (= *Dieu sans l'être*, pp. 229-30); translation amended.

26. Marion, 'Présence et distance', p. 31.

27. Cf. ibid., p. 50, n. 1.

28. In #15, the encyclical *Ecclesia de Eucharistia* quotes Paul VI, who used the expression, 'objective reality' to describe the real presence. It is crucial to interpret the term 'objective' correctly, that is, not according to the categories of modern epistemology.

29. For the following argument, see Marion, 'La splendeur', p. 86 and 'Présence et distance', pp. 38-39.

30. Marion uses this term in 'La splendeur', p. 86.

31. Marion, 'Présence et distance', p. 39: 'le don de soi va jusqu'à l'abandon de soi comme d'une chose'. I suspect that 'comme d'une chose' is a misprint and that the text should read 'comme une chose'. 'Présence et distance' contains an unusually large number of typographical errors, no doubt due to the semi-professional mode of publication of *Résurrection*.

32. On the topic of 'Transubstantiation as Mystery of Abandonment', see Marion, 'Présence et distance', pp. 34-41.

33. See Marion, 'Présence et distance', p. 44; *God without Being*, p. 169.

34. Marion, 'La splendeur', p. 86.

35. Marion, 'Présence et distance', p. 42.

36. Marion, 'La splendeur', p. 86.

37. Ibid., p. 88.

38. John Paul II, *Encyclical Letter Ecclesia de Eucharistia: On the Eucharist in Its Relationship to the Church*, Boston, Mass.: Pauline Books and Media, 2003, #15.

39. See Marion, 'La splendeur', p. 88: 'Le monde n'est séparé de Dieu que pour autant que notre regard ne réunit point encore en une seule évidence la présence et la "réalité" du Christ.'

40. Marion, *God without Being*, p. 14 (= *Dieu sans l'être*, p. 24).

41. Ibid., p. 11 (20).

42. Ibid., p. 17 (28).

43. Ibid., p. 171 (241).

44. Ibid., pp. 169–72 (239–42).

45. Ibid., pp. 170, 181 (239f., 256f.); trans. amended.

46. The literature on this topic is growing. The following volume may serve as a good introduction: *Flight of the Gods: Philosophical Perspectives on Negative Theology*, in Ilse N. Bulhof and Laurensten Kate (eds), New York: Fordham University Press, 2000.

47. Marion, *God without Being*, p. 171 (242).

48. See ibid., p. 229 n. 18. The topic of the Eucharist as memorial is developed more fully in 'Présence et distance', pp. 46-49.

49. Marion, *God without Being*, p. 173 (244).

50. Ibid., p. 172 (243f.); capitalisation adjusted. Marion uses the typographic convention of striking through the word 'God' in order to indicate a non-idolatrous conception of God.

51. John Paul II, *Encyclical Letter Ecclesia de Eucharistia*, #11, #15.

52. Marion, *God without Being*, p. 181 (256).

53. Ibid., p. 174 (246).

54. Marion, 'Présence et distance', p. 50.

55. See Marion, *God without Being*, chap. 4.

56. Ibid., p. 180 (256); trans. amended.

57. Marion does not discuss this ambiguity of the term *res*, on which one may read chap. 7 of my book, *Peter Lombard*, New York: Oxford University Press, 2004 (pp. 144-78). Marion's principal source on the premodern theology of the Eucharist is the work of Fr Henri de Lubac SJ, especially *Corpus mysticum: l'Eucharistie et l'Église au moyen âge. Étude historique*, 2nd ed., Paris: Aubier-Montaigne, 1949.

58. Marion, *God without Being*, p. 180 (255); trans. amended.

59. Ibid.

60. Marion, 'La splendeur', p. 88.

61. Marion, 'Présence et distance', p. 38.

62. Pickstock, *After Writing*, pp. 256 and 262, respectively.

63. Marion, *God without Being*, p. 145 (205).

64. Ibid., p. 171 (241).

65. Ibid., p. 143 (202).

66. Ibid., p. 153 (215).

67. Ibid., p. 158 (221). Italics in the original.

68. Ibid., p. 153 (215). Italics in the original.

69. Ibid., p. 157 (220); capitalisation adjusted. The theme concerning the impossibility of exhausting the infinity of meaning that the divine author has deposited in scripture appears in many Christian writers, from Pseudo-Dionysius and Augustine to John Scottus Eriugena.

70. I should like to thank Professor James McEvoy for discussing a previous version of this paper with me.

CHAPTER TWELVE

1. See the Vatican website at the Synod of Bishops entry.

2. Council of Trent, Session 13, Decree on the Sacrament of the Eucharist, 11 Oct 1551, in DZ, ##1635-1661.

3. Vatican Council II, Dogmatic Constitution on the Church, *Lumen Gentium*.

4. Ibid. and also the Explanatory note released with that document.

5. Council of Chalcedon, *Symbol*, 451, in DZ, ##300-303.

6. St Augustine, *Confessions*, 1, 1. (*Inquietum est cor nostrum donec requiescat in Te*).

7. The Roman Missal, Preface for the Feast of Corpus Christi.

8. Cf. Paul Poupard, 'Les idées dépressives du monde contemporain', in *Cultures and Faith* XI-4, pp. 280-291.

9. John Paul II, Encyclical, *Fides et Ratio*, #71.

10. M. P. Gallagher, *Clashing Symbols. An Introduction to Faith and Culture*, London: DLT, 1997, p. 38.

11. Vatican Council II, Pastoral Constitution on the Church in the Modern World, *Gaudium et Spes*, #53.

12. Paul VI, Apostolic Exhortation, *Evangelii Nuntiandi*, #20.

13. John Paul II, Letter to the Cardinal Secretary of State, establishing the Pontifical Council for Culture, 20 May, 1982, in *L'Osservatore Romano,* weekly edition in English, 28 June 1982, p. 7.

14. St Thomas Aquinas, *Summa Theologiae* III qu.60 art.3.

15. *Catechism of the Catholic Church*, #1362.

16. Paul Poupard, 'Eucaristia e cultura', in *L'Osservatore Romano*, 2 October 1999, p.10. Cf. P. Poupard, *Dio e la libertà. Una proposta per la cultura moderna,* Chapter VII, 'Eucaristia, fonte di nuova cultura per l'uomo di oggi', Città Nuova, 1991, pp. 106-122.

17. Cf. *Il Nuovo Areopago* X, 3-4: 'Cristianesimo e Cultura in Europa: Memoria, Coscienza, Progetto', *Atti del Simposio presinodale*, Imola: CSEO, 1991.

18. Pontifical Council for Culture, *Handing on the Faith at the Heart of Cultures, Novo Millenio Ineunte,* in *Cultures and Faith* X-2 (2002), pp. 138-139.

19. John Paul II, Encyclical, *Ecclesia de Eucharistia*, #20.

20. Ibid, #20.

21. E. Lévinas, *Time and the Other,* (Richard A. Cohen trans.), Pittsburgh: Duquesne University Press, 1987, p. 90. [originally published as 'Le temps et l'autre', in J. Wahl, *Le Choix, Le Monde, L'Existence,* Grenoble-Paris: Arthaud, 1947].

22. Ibid., p. 75.

23. Vatican Council II, Pastoral Constitution on the Church in the Modern World, *Gaudium et Spes*, #58.

24. Vatican Council II, Constitution on the Sacred Liturgy, *Sacrosanctum Concilium*, #47.

25. St Thomas Aquinas, *In Aristotelis* Posteriorum Analyticorum Libros I, 1.

26. Cf. Paul VI, Encyclical, *Populorum Progressio*, #42.

27. John Paul II, Speech to UNESCO, 2 June 1980.

28. B. Pascal, *Pensées*, 434.

29. Cf. Pontifical Council for Culture, *Towards a Pastoral Approach to Culture,* Vatican City: 1999.

30. John Paul II, Encyclical, *Fides et Ratio*, #70.

31. *EdE*, #1.

32. Cf. *EdE*, #6.

33. *EdE*, #62.

34. John Paul II, Post-Synodal Apostolic Exhortation, *Ecclesia in Africa*, #103.

35. John Paul II, Encyclical, *Fides et Ratio*, #70.

36. John Paul II, Letter to the Cardinal Secretary of State, 20 May, 1982.

37. *EdE*, #35.

38. J. H. Newman, *The Dream of Gerontius.*

CHAPTER FOURTEEN

1. *'Filius autem est Verbum, non qualecumque, sed spirans amorem'*: St Thomas Aquinas, *Summa Theologica*, I, Q. XLIII, Art. 5, ad 2.

2. 'Faith without Charity is dry, harsh, and sapless; it has nothing sweet, engaging, winning, soothing; but it was Charity which brought Christ down. Charity is but another name for the Comforter. It is eternal Charity which is the bond of all things in heaven and earth; it is Charity wherein the Father and the Son are one in the unity of the Spirit; by which the Angels in heaven are one, by which all Saints are one with God, by which the Church is one upon earth.' This is the final paragraph of Sermon 21 of the *Parochial and Plain Sermons*, Vol. 4, p. 318.

3. Elsewhere, the Holy Father had spoken of the church's responsibility in this regard: 'It is her duty to serve humanity in different ways, but one way in particular imposes a responsibility of a quite special kind: the *diakonia* of the truth. This mission on the one hand makes the believing community a partner in humanity's shared struggle to arrive at truth; and on the other hand it obliges the believing community to proclaim the certitudes arrived at, albeit with a sense that every truth attained is but a step towards that fullness of truth which will appear with the final Revelation of God: "For now we see in a mirror dimly, but then face to face. Now I know in part; the n I shall understand fully" (1 Cor 13:12).' John Paul II, *Fides et Ratio*, #2.

4. The Latin rendering of 'amazement' in the encyclical is, rather surprisingly, *stupor*, in quotation marks; the German version has *Staunen* and the French, *admiration*. It is beyond the scope of this paper to explore the various nuances of meaning in the different renderings.

5. 'The ordained ministry, which may never be reduced to its merely functional aspect since it belongs on the level of "being", enables the priest to act *in persona Christi* and culminates in the moment when he consecrates the bread and wine, repeating the actions and words of Jesus during the Last Supper. Before this extraordinary reality we find ourselves amazed and overwhelmed, so deep is the humility by which God "stoops" in order to unite himself with man! If we feel moved before the Christmas crib, when we contemplate the Incarnation of the Word, what must we feel before the altar where, by the poor hands of the priest, Christ makes his sacrifice present in time? We can only fall to our knees and silently adore this supreme mystery of faith' (Pope John Paul II, *Letter to Priests, Holy Thursday 2004*, #2).

6. The Holy Father continues: 'The Son of God became man in order to restore all creation, in one supreme act of praise, to the One who made it from nothing. He, the Eternal High Priest who by the blood of his cross entered the eternal sanctuary, thus gives back to the Creator and Father all creation redeemed. He does so through the priestly ministry of the church, to the glory of the Most Holy Trinity. Truly this is the *mysterium fidei* which is accomplished in the Eucharist: the world which came forth from the hands of God the Creator now returns to him redeemed by Christ' (#8).

7. St Thomas Aquinas, *Summa Theologica*, Ia IIae, q.41: Of Fear In Itself. Art. 4: Whether The Species Of Fear Is Suitably Assigned? Ad 5.

8. Margaret T. Monro, *Seeking for Trouble. Saints for Christian Civilization*, London: Longman Green, 1941, p. 193.

9. Walter Kerr, *The Decline of Pleasure in the West*, New York: Simon & Schuster, 1962, p.141: 'Pleasure is well-being itself; diversion is a temporary turning away from a lack of well-being. Pleasure is time ransomed; diversion is time passed. Pleasure changes a man; diversion changes what he is looking at, though not the quality of his looking. Whereas pleasure actively recharges, diversion keeps the battery running at an even purr.'

10. 'Because we have been sent into the world as a "people for life", our proclamation must also become a genuine celebration of the gospel of life. This celebration, with the evocative power of its gestures, symbols and rites, should become a precious and significant setting in which the beauty and grandeur of this gospel is handed on. "For this to happen, we need first of all to foster, in ourselves and in others, a contemplative outlook." Such an outlook arises from faith in the God of life, who has created every individual as a "wonder" (cf. Ps 139:14: "I give you thanks that I am fearfully, wonderfully made.") It is the outlook of those who see life in its deeper meaning, who grasp its utter gratuitousness, its beauty and its invitation to freedom and responsibility. It is the outlook of those who do not presume to take possession of reality but instead accept it as a gift, discovering in all things the reflection of the Creator and seeing in every person his living image (cf. Gen 1:27; Ps 8:5).' Pope John Paul II, *Evangelium Vitae,* Dublin: Veritas, 1995, #83.

11. 'Any reader of old poetry can see that brightness appealed to ancient and medieval man more than bigness, and more than it does to us. Medieval thinkers believed that the stars must be somehow superior to the Earth because they looked bright and it did not. Moderns think that the Galaxy ought to be more important than the Earth because it is bigger. Both states of mind can produce good poetry.' C. S. Lewis, *Miracles. A Preliminary Study,* London: HarperCollins, 1947, p. 85.

12. See the translation by Gerard Manley Hopkins in Kevin Mayhew, *Hymns Old and New*, #176. Thomas' identification with the prayer of the Penitent Thief (this is how Thomas names the thief on the right: it was his repentance that made him 'good') is expressed beautifully: *In cruce latebat sola Deitas, At hic simul et humanitas; Ambo tamen credens, atque confitens, Peto quod petivit latro poenitens.*

13. 'And all who heard it were amazed at what the shepherds told them' (Lk 2:18).

'And the child's father and mother were amazed at what was being said about him' (Lk 2:33).

'And all who heard him were amazed at his understanding and his answers' (Lk 2:47).

'When his parents saw him they were astonished …' (Lk 2:48).

'All spoke well of him and were amazed at the gracious words that came from his mouth. They said: Is not this Joseph's son?' (Lk 4:22), and yet 'when they heard this, all in the synagogue were filled with rage' (Lk 4:28).

'They were all amazed and kept saying to one another, "what kind of utterance is this: for with authority and power he commands the unclean spirits, and out they come!"' (Lk 4:36).

'Amazement (ekstasis) seized all of them, and they glorified God and were filled with awe, saying, "We have seen strange things today"' (Lk 5:26).

14. Cf. also Heb 11:16: 'God is not ashamed (confunditur, 'embarrassed' might also be a good translation) to be their God.'

15. 'Admonitions of Saint Francis of Assisi', I, 16, in Regis J. Armstrong, OFM Cap, J.A. Wayne Hellman, OFM Conv, William J. Short, OFM (eds), Francis of Assisi: Early Documents, New York, London, Manila, 1999, Vol. I, p. 129.

16. 'Letter to the Entire Order,' ibid., p. 118. See #26-29, p. 118 ff. Cf. Earlier Rule, Ch. XXIII, ibid., pp. 81-86.

17. See also Pope John Paul II, Redemptor hominis, Rome, 1979, #13.

18. 'In Christianity time has fundamental importance. Within the dimension of time the world was created: within it the history of salvation unfolds, finding its culmination in the "fullness of time" of the Incarnation, and its goal in the glorious return of the Son of God at the end of time.' John Paul II, Tertio millennio adveniente, Rome, 1994, #5.

19. See David Meconi SJ, "A Christian View of History", Catholic Faith, Chicago, March/April 2000.

20. Nicholas Harnan writes well of this: 'Our brokenness is what needs to be accepted. Unfortunately, this is what we tend to reject. Here the seeds of a corrosive self-hatred take root. This painful vulnerability is the characteristic feature of our humanity that most needs to be embraced in order to restore our human condition to a healed state.' Nicholas Harnan MSC, The Heart's Journey Home: A Quest for Wisdom, Notre Dame, Indiana: Ave Maria Press, 1992, p. 61.

21. Believe it or not, my edition of the Divine Office actually has the word 'property', instead of 'poverty' where this reading occurs, that is, Office of Readings, Monday, Week 17 of the Year, Volume III, p. 353.

22. 'Examine yourselves and only then eat of the bread and drink of the cup' (1 Cor 11:28).

23. There is, of course, a special link between John Paul II and Edith Stein. See Mette Lebech, 'Why does John Paul II refer to Edith Stein in Fides et Ratio?', in James McEvoy (ed), The Challenge of Truth, Dublin: Veritas Publication, 2002, pp.154-180.

24. Edith Stein, Sister Teresa Benedicta of the Cross, Discalced Carmelite, Finite and Eternal Being. An Attempt at an Ascent to the Meaning of Being, Washington, D.C.: ICS Publications, 2002, pp. 54,55. Later, reflecting on how the human soul is the form of the body, she ob-

serves: 'The "internal and innermost", however, means the "most spiritual", that which is farthest removed from matter, that which moves the soul in its innermost depth. If this strikes us as strange and wonderful, we shall find it even more awesome and "miraculous" when we discover that everything is built by the spirit.' pp.377-8.

25. Stein, *Finite and Eternal Being*, p. 504. The entire section, entitled 'The Vocation of the Soul to Eternal Life' (pp. 504-6) deserves careful reading. 'We have learned to know the innermost being of the soul as the "abode of God",' she writes. Her reflections indicate a familiarity with sacred scripture and a sense of wonder at God, who is 'the plenitude of love'. She concludes: 'love always bears the stamp of personal individuality. And this explains in turn why God may have chosen to create for himself a special abode in each human soul, so that the plenitude of divine love might find in the manifold of differently constituted souls a wider range for its self-communication.'

26. Pope John Paul II, Apostolic Letter issued *motu proprio* proclaiming Saint Bridget of Sweden, Saint Catherine of Siena and Saint Teresa Benedicta of the Cross co-patronesses of Europe, 1 October 1999, #3.

27. In his Letter to Priests, the Holy Father returns to this very theme: 'Jesus the High Priest continues personally to call new workers for his vineyard, but he wishes from the first to count on our active cooperation. Priests in love with the Eucharist are capable of communicating to children and young people that "Eucharistic amazement" which I have sought to rekindle with my Encyclical *Ecclesia de Eucharistia* (cf. No. 6). Generally these are the priests who lead them to the path of the priesthood, as the history of our own vocations might easily show' (Letter to Priests, Holy Thursday 2004, #5).

28. See Archbishop William Levada, 'Faith Seeking Understanding: The Catechism of the Catholic Church. 1. The Faith We Profess. Reflections on the First Pillar of the Catechism of the Catholic Church,' *Catholic International*, July 1995, p. 325.

29. *Catechism of the Catholic Church*, Dublin: Veritas, 1994, #113.

30. Privately published, *cum approbatione ecclesiastica*, Feldkirch, July 16th, 1984, p.15.

31. John Paul II, *The Theology of the Body. Human Love in the Divine Plan*, Boston: Pauline Books & Media, 1997, pp. 60-63.

32. St Francis De Sales, *The Love of God. A Treatise*, translated and introduced by Vincent Kerns, London: Orchard Books, Burns & Oates Ltd., 1962, p. 238.

33. See Placid Murray OSB, *The Graces of the Eucharist. Studies in the Postcommunions of the Missal*. Studies in Pastoral Liturgy, Maynooth: The Furrow Trust, 1961, pp. 117-131, especially p. 124, where he takes up an old postcommunion prayer: 'May the activity of the gift from heaven make itself master of us, Lord, in mind and body; may its influence forever forestall our impulse' (15th Sunday after Pentecost). He comments: 'Impulse then seems a happy rendering of *sensus*, and I suppose it could be further paraphrased as "our own sweet will". This con-

stant bubbling up within us of our own will, our own bent, our point of view, how often is it not in practice what holds us back in the spiritual life? It is this inner fold of the mind that we ask to have brought under the sway of the heavenly gift – *possideat*; and this not once or twice, not a whispered suggestion at the moment of Communion, but invariably, always, in all the circumstances of life, *jugiter*.'

34. Pope John Paul II, *Vita Consecrata*, #95.

35. Ibid., #38.

36. St Francis De Sales, *The Love of God*, Book 7, p. 286.

37. Ibid., p. 282.

38. Ibid., p. 287.

39. St Louis-Marie de Montfort, *Treatise on the True Devotion to the Blessed Virgin*, Athlone, Ireland: St Paul Publications, 1962, p. 184.

40. 'Are these feelings of fear and awe Christian feelings or not? I say this, then, which I think no one can reasonably dispute. They are the class of feelings which we should have – yes, have to an intense degree – if we literally had the sight of Almighty God; therefore they are the class of feelings which we shall have, if we realise his presence. In proportion as we believe that he is present, we shall have them; and not to have them, is not to realise, not to believe that he is present.' (John H. Newman, *Parochial and Plain Sermons* V, 2; quoted in the *Catechism of the Catholic Church*, #2144).

41. I once heard of a Cistercian monastery in the United States that invited a Buddhist monk to conduct their annual retreat. To the surprise of the monks he invited them to concentrate on one thing only during the entire retreat: how to make the sign of the cross!

42. Kathleen Norris, *Amazing Grace. A Vocabulary of Faith*, New York: Riverhead Books, 1998, p. 232.

CHAPTER FIFTEEN

1. Joseph Ratzinger, *Weggemeinschaft des Glaubens. Kirche als Communio*, Augsburg: Verlag Sankt Ulrich, 2002, pp. 68-73.

2. St Augustine, Sermon 227 in *Sant'Agostino, L'Eucaristia Corpo della Chiesa*, Vittorino Grossi (ed.), Rome: Borla, 2000, p. 90. In general, the fathers combine ontology and symbolism, and in that way reality and its radiance. See Henri de Lubac, *Corpus Mysticum. L'Eucaristie et l'Eglise au Moyen Age*, 2nd ed., Paris: du Cerf, 1949. St Thomas Aquinas describes the Eucharist as the *sacramentum unitatis* in Book IV of his *Commentary on the Sentences of Peter Lombard*, 12, 2, 1 and in the *Summa Theologica*, III, q.79, 1 and 5.

3. Blaise Pascal, *Pensées*, 434, ed. Brunschvicg.

4. St Thomas, *ST*, I, q. 80, 1c.

5. St Augustine, *Confessions*, I, 1. See Klaus Hemmerle, *Wie Glauben im Leben geht*, Munich: Verlag Neue Stadt, 1995, pp. 220-242.

6. Q. Moraschine & M. Pedrinazzi, *San Pietro Giuliano Eymard, apostolo dell'Eucaristia*, Rome, 1962, p. 5.

CHAPTER SIXTEEN

1. The church does not rule out the use of art from the past, on the contrary, the *Catechism of the Catholic Church* speaks of 'the promotion of sacred art, new and old, in all its forms' (*CCC*, #2503). The same article includes the statement that bishops should 'remove from the liturgy and from places of worship everything which is not in conformity with the truth of the faith and the authentic beauty of sacred art'.

2. It is interesting to compare Annunciation scenes from this period with artworks of the twentieth century in which the Trinity is not indicated in any way except perhaps by amorphous clouds of colour. See the collection called *Annunciation* published by Phaidon Press, 2000.

3. Fra Angelico's imagery may well have been influenced here by the well-known opening lines of Dante's *Divine Comedy:* 'Midway the path of life that men pursue / I found me in a darkling wood astray / for the direct way had been lost to view' (Dante: *Inferno,* Canto 1, lines 1-3).

4. This is used in several paintings to mark the transition point between the old and new covenants.

5. The palm tree is an ancient symbol of victory. Cf. Rev 7:9 and Jn 12:13.

6. John Drury, *Painting the Word,* New Haven: Yale University Press, in Association with National Gallery Publications Ltd, 1999, p.62.

CHAPTER SEVENTEEN

1. The second stanza reads: 'O thou, the wisest, mightiest, best / Our present food, our future rest / Come, make us each thy chosen guest / Co-heirs of thine and comrades blest / With saints whose dwelling is with thee'.

2. *'Futurae gloriae nobis pignus datur' (O Sacrum Convivium).*

3. *'Visus, tactus, gustus in te fallitur.'* The *Catechism of the Catholic Church* (#1381) quotes the first two verses of the same hymn and does so to the same effect; it makes reference to *Summa Theologiae* III, q.75, a.1.

4. *Summa Theologiae,* III, q. 83, a. 4c. Cf *Summa Theol.* III, q.73, a.3c: the Eucharist is 'the perfection of the spiritual life and the end to which all the sacraments tend' (quoted in the *Catechism,* #1374). A very useful summary of the eucharistic doctrine of St Thomas is to be found in Brian Davies, *The Thought of Thomas Aquinas,* Oxford, 1992, pp. 361-378.

5. 'You are the king of glory, O Christ, you are the everlasting Son of the Father'.

6. *The Life of Saint Thomas Aquinas.* Biographical Documents, transl. and ed. by Kennelm Foster OP, London / Baltimore, 1959, p. 37.

7. The first was the *Summa Aurea,* an exposition of the gospels drawn up with great scholarship in the form of an anthology of the fathers of the church, both Greek and Latin.

8. *The Life of Saint Thomas Aquinas,* ed. Foster; the extracts from Ptolemy regarding Aquinas cover pages 127-139. Cf. J.-P. Torrell OP, *Initiation à S. Thomas d'Aquin: sa personne et son oeuvre,* Paris, 1993, p.190 n. In what

follows I have drawn freely on this work (pp. 189-98: *'L'Office du Corpus Christi'*).

9. A. Duval, 'Tholomée de Lucques', in *Dictionnaire de Spiritualité*, v. XII, cols 268-9.

10. E.g. Torrell, op. cit. p. 190 and the references in the footnotes; J. A. Weisheipl OP, *Friar Thomas d'Aquino*, Oxford, 1975, p. 400 (n. 84); see p. 183.

11. For a recent collective work and study of St Julienne and the Feast see *Fête-Dieu* (1246-1996). 1. Actes du Colloque de Liège, 1996, A. Haquin (ed.); 2. *Vie de Sainte Julienne de Cornillon.* Édition critique par Jean-Pierre Delville, Louvain-La-Neuve, 1999. The following is a readable and informative monograph: Jean Cottiaux, *Sainte Julienne de Cornillon promotrice de la Fête-Dieu: son pays, son temps, son message*, Liège, 1991, 260 pp. Extracts from the Liège Office for Corpus Christi (*Animarum Cibus*) are printed in Latin and French on pp. 246-53

12. Cf. Saint Thomas d'Aquin, *Prières devant le Saint-Sacrement*, (D. Sureau trans.), Paris, 2002, p. 17.

13. Pierre-Marie Gy OP, 'Office liégois et office romain de la Fête-Dieu', in *Fête-Dieu*, vol. 1 (1996), p. 124.

14. Gy, 'Office liégois…, pp. 117-126.

15. 'Substance' and 'accidents' are Aristotelian terms indicating respectively a reality of a more or less independent kind, and a dependant reality falling into one of nine categories (e.g., quality, quantity, place or time).

16. *Summa Theologiae* III, q.75, a.1.

17. Alain Michel has written illuminatingly about Thomistic realism in its relationship to eucharistic doctrine: 'S'il élimine l'allégorie, Thomas garde la typologie, en insistant sur l'aspect historique qu'elle prend dans le grand projet du salut. Cela établit dans sa plénitude la notion *d'institutio*: pour la comprendre, il faut une philosophie qui donne tout son sens à la notion de causalité: c'est précisément ce qu'accomplit l'aristotélisme de Thomas'. The same author also comments, 'Nous croyons que la création poétique, chez S. Thomas d'Aquin, complète et traduit magnifiquement la création philosophique. De là, en même temps, l'originalité et l'universalité d'un langage qui peut s'accorder à la méditation la plus transcendante et à la plus humble prière'. A. Michel, *In Hymnis et Canticis: Culture et beauté dans l'hymnique chrétienne latine*, Louvain/Paris, 1976, pp. 223, 225.

18. F. J. E. Raby made a general appraisal of the poems, to the effect that 'The hymns and the sequence are admirable liturgical compositions; severity of form, economy of expression, scholastic exactness of doctrinal statement are joined to a metrical skill which owes as much to the genius of the poet as to a study of predecessors like Adam of St Victor'. See the work referred to in the following footnote, p. 405, and indeed the entire section devoted to St Thomas (pp. 402-13).

19. F. J. E. Raby, *A History of Christian-Latin Poetry From the Beginnings to the Close of the Middle Ages*, Oxford, 1953 (2nd ed.), p. 409.

20. 'Pange, lingua, gloriosi proelium certaminis,' *The Oxford Book of Medieval Latin Verse*, p. 74.

21. Raby, *A History* … p. 409. Compare his less-known but more focused short book, *The Poetry of the Eucharist*, (Alcuin Club Edition), London, 1957, 39 pp. (pp. 20-22).

22. The indeclinable noun *'phase'* came into Latin from a Hebrew word meaning passing. It signified (Ex 12:11) the passing of the angel sent to wipe out the first born of the Egyptians. From that it came to mean the celebration of the Passover (Num 9:2; cf. 2 Para 35:9, *'phase celebrare'*). At 2 Para 35:11 *'immolatum est phase'* means 'the lamb of Passover was sacrificed'.

23.   *'In figuris presignatur/Cum Isaac immolatur/Agnus paschae deputatur/Datur manna patribus.'*

24. Clare Asquith has speculated concerning parallels between *Lauda, Sion* and 'The Phoenix and the Turtle' of Shakespeare; see *Times Literary Supplement*, Good Friday, April 2003.

25. It is on the other hand difficult to find defenders of the prayer *Ave Verum Corpus* as a work of Aquinas's hand.

26. Raby, *History of Christian-Latin Poetry…*, p. 410.

27. See the Marietti edition of 1954, *Opuscula Theologica* II, pp. 285-89.

28. It would seem that Thomas underlined the effect of the Eucharist upon ecclesial unity in a way that his contemporaries were less given to do. For example, 1 Cor 10:16-17 is invoked in the Responses of Matins of the Office of Corpus Christi, and the three prayers of the Mass for the feast tend in the same direction. See Gy, 'Office liégois… ', pp. 123-24.

29. The translation used has been adapted from the reading in the Roman Breviary, which is a little shorter than what is printed here. Père Gy has published his definitive text of the first three Lessons at the close of his article in *Fête-Dieu*, vol. 1, 1999, pp. 244-5.

CHAPTER EIGHTEEN

1. Pope John Paul, *EdE* (2003).

2. Henri de Lubac, *The Splendour of the Church*, San Francisco: Ignatius, 1986, p.148.

3. World Council of Churches, *Baptism, Eucharist and Ministry*, Geneva: WCC, 1982 (Faith and Order Paper no. 111), 'Ministry', ##14, 11 and 17, respectively; cf. Vatican II, Dogmatic Constitution on the Church, *Lumen Gentium*, #10.

4. Ibid., 'Eucharist', #8.

5. Pope John Paul II, encyclical letter, *Ut Unum Sint* (1995), #58.

6. De Lubac, *Corpus Mysticum*, Paris: Aubier, 1949 (2nd ed.), p. 104. Cf. my book, *The Eucharist Makes the Church. Henri de Lubac and John Zizioulas in Dialogue,* Edinburgh: T & T Clark, 1993.

7. De Lubac, *The Splendour of the Church*, pp. 134, 152. The verb is translated on these two pages as 'produces' and 'realises', respectively, but is *'fait'* in de Lubac's original *Méditation sur l'Église* (1953), pp.113, 129; I

have also reproduced de Lubac's original italics. Cf. my book, *The Eucharist Makes the Church*, pp. xv, 75-120.

8. De Lubac, *Catholicism*, San Francisco: Ignatius, 1988 (French original, 1938), pp. 109-110.

9. Ibid., p. 53.

10. Joseph Ratzinger, *Principles of Catholic Theology*, San Francisco: Ignatius, 1987, p. 53, incorporating the final clause which, oddly, the translation omits from the original, *Theologische Prinzipienlehre*, Munich: Erich Wewel, 1982, p. 55.

11. Robert W. Jenson, 'The Church and the Sacraments', in Colin E. Gunton, *The Cambridge Companion to Christian Doctrine*, Cambridge University Press, 1997, p. 215.

12. Ibid., p. 216, quotation from K. Ware and C. Davey (eds.), *Anglican-Orthodox Dialogue: The Moscow Statement Agreed by the Anglican-Orthodox Joint Doctrinal Commission 1976 with Introductory and Supporting Material*, London: SPCK, 1977, p. 24.

13. Second Vatican Council, Dogmatic Constitution on the Church, *Lumen Gentium*, #11; cf. Constitution on the Sacred Liturgy, *Sacrosanctum Concilium*, #10. Quotations from the Council are taken from, Austin Flannery (ed), *Vatican Council II. The Conciliar and Post Conciliar Documents*, Dublin, Dominican Publications, 1975.

14. *Sacrosanctum Concilium*, #41 (amended translation).

15. World Council of Churches, *Baptism, Eucharist and Ministry*, 'Eucharist', #19.

16. *Lumen Gentium*, #2.

17. *Sacrosanctum Concilium*, #8.

18. Jenson, 'The Church and the Sacraments', p. 216.

19. John Zizioulas, 'The Mystery of the Church in Orthodox Tradition', *One in Christ* 24(1988), p. 301.

20. *Lumen Gentium*, #1.

21. *Catechism of the Catholic Church*, London: Geoffrey Chapman, 1992, #775, cf. ##760, 769.

22. Jenson, 'The Church and the Sacraments', p. 207.

23. De Lubac, *Catholicism*, pp. 110-111.

24. Cf. my book, *Sacrament of Salvation. An Introduction to Eucharistic Ecclesiology*, Edinburgh: T & T Clark, 1995 (reprinted in 2003 by Continuum, London), chapter one.

25. De Lubac, *Corpus Mysticum*, p. 269; cf. my book, *Sacrament of Salvation*, pp. 37-38.

26. Ibid., pp. 78-79; cf. my book, *The Eucharist Makes the Church*, pp. 76-77.

27. Cf. *Catechism of the Catholic Church*, #752.

28. Cf. ibid., #948.

29. Joint International Commission for Theological Dialogue between the Roman Catholic Church and the Orthodox Church, 'The Mystery of the Church and of the Eucharist in the Light of the Mystery of the Holy

Trinity' (1982). The statement may be found in P. McPartlan (ed.), *One in 2000? Towards Catholic-Orthodox Unity,* Slough: St Paul Publications, 1993, pp. 37-52.

30. 'The Mystery of the Church and of the Eucharist', I, 6.

31. Ibid., II, 1.

32. Ibid., III, 1.

33. Anglican-Roman Catholic International Commission, 'Eucharistic Doctrine' (1971), in *The Final Report*, London: CTS/SPCK, 1982, pp. 9-16; quotation from #6 of statement.

34. 'Introduction' to *The Final Report*, ##4, 6.

35. ARCIC 2, 'Church as Communion', London: Church House Publishing/Catholic Truth Society, 1991, #45.

36. *Baptism, Eucharist and Ministry*, 'Eucharist', #31.

37. Ibid., #18.

38. Cf. my article, 'The Catechism and Catholic-Orthodox Doialogue', *One in Christ* 30 (1994), pp. 229-244, here at p. 233.

39. 'The Mystery of the Church and of the Eucharist', I, 4a.

40. Ibid., I, 5c.

41. Ibid., I, 5d.

42. *Baptism, Eucharist and Ministry,* 'Eucharist', #14.

43. 'Eucharistic Doctrine', #10.

44. Ibid., #11.

45. *Baptism, Eucharist and Ministry*, 'Eucharist', #22.

46. 'The Mystery of the Church and of the Eucharist', I, 2.

47. Ibid., I, 4c.

48. Ibid., II, 1.

49. Ibid., II, 3.

50. Zizioulas, 'Preserving God's Creation', *King's Theological Review* 12 (1989), p. 3; cf. my book, *Sacrament of Salvation*, p. 123.

51. Cf. my article, 'Mastery or mystery? The Orthodox View of Nature', *Priests & People* 14 (2000), pp. 60-64.

CHAPTER NINETEEN

1. Desmond O'Donnell, 'Young Educated Adults: A Survey,' *Doctrine and Life,* 52: 1 (2000), p. 24.

2. Andrew M.Greeley and Conor Ward, 'Report on International Social Survey Programme', *Doctrine and Life,* (2000), p. 50.

3. David Tuohy and Penny Cairns, *Youth 2K, Threat or Promise to a Religious Culture?* Dublin: Marino Institute of Education, 2000, p. 51.

4. Ibid., p. 52.

5. Desmond O'Donnell, 'Young Educated Adults: A Survey', p. 9.

6. Sacred Congregation of the Clergy, *General Directory for Catechesis*, Rome, 1997. (*GDC*), #82.

7. John Paul II, encyclical letter, *Redemptoris Missio*, #33, AAS 83 (1991), p. 279.

8. *GDC*, #62.

9. Patrick M. Devitt, *Willingly to School – Religious Education as an Examination Subject,* Dublin: Veritas, 2000, p. 53.

10. Sacred Congregation for Catholic Education, *The Religious Dimension of Education in a Catholic School,* Rome: Vatican Press, 1988, (*RDECS*), #68.

11. *RDECS*, #22.

12. David Tuohy, *Youth 2K,* p. 199.

13. *GDC*, ##85, 86.

14. Irish Episcopal Commission on Catechetics, *Alive-O 3,* Teachers Book, Dublin:Veritas, 1998, pp. xviii-xix.

15. Ibid.

16. Irish Episcopal Commission on Catechetics, *Alive-O 4,* Teachers Book, Dublin: Veritas, 1998, p. xxii.

17. See, for example, Patrick M. Devitt, *Willingly to School,* p. 53; Ann Walsh, 'The Future of Religion at Post-Primary Level', in Hogan and Williams (eds), *The Future of Religion in Irish Education,* Dublin: Veritas, 1997, p. 64.

18. Department of Education and Science, *Junior Certificate Religious Education Syllabus,* p. 45

19. Ibid, p. 32.

20. Email correspondence with author.

21. ScholasTECH Media, *Religious Education, Junior Certificate, Year Two,* Wexford: n.d.

22. John Paul II, encyclical letter, *Ecclesia de Eucharistia,* Rome: Vatican Press, 2003, #62.

23. Sacred Congregation for Catholic Education, *The Religious Dimension of Education in a Catholic School,* Rome: Vatican Press, 1988, (*RDECS*), #68.

APPENDIX TWO

1. [Biblia polyglotta]. In Academia Complutensi: industria Arnaldi Guillelmi de Brocario, 1514-7. 6 vols; see T.H.Darlow and H.F. Moule, *Historical catalogue of the printed editions of Holy Scripture,* London: British and Foreign Bible Society, 1903-11. 4 vols; for all four polyglots see vol. ii, pp. 2-26, and variously for each language.

2. C. Clair, *Christopher Plantin,* London: Cassell, 1960, pp.57-86.

3. Biblia *1.Hebraica 2.Samaritana 3.Chaldaica 4.Graeca 5.Syriaca 6.Latina 7. Arabica,* Lutetiae Parisiorum: excudebat Antonius Vitré, 1629-45. 9 vols in 10.

4. *Biblia Sacra Polyglotta,* London: Thomas Roycroft, 1655-7, 6 vols.

5. H. Cotton, *Rhemes and Doway,* Oxford: University Press, 1855; invaluable is the ongoing bibliography [with locations] by Hugh Fenning OP: 'Dublin Imprints of Catholic Interest, 1701-39' in *Collectanea Hibernica,* 39-40 (1997-8), pp.106-54; for 1740-59, in *Coll. Hib.,* 41 (1999), pp. 65-116; for 1760-69, in *Coll. Hib.,* 42 (2000), pp. 85-119; for 1770-1782, in *Coll. Hib.,* 43 (2001), pp.161-208; 1783-9, in *Coll. Hib.,* 44-5 (2002-3), pp. 79-126;

there is evidence that the Catholic New Testament was first printed in Ireland in 1699, but was suppressed by the stationers of the Guild of St Luke, see J. W. Phillips, *Printing and Bookselling in Dublin, 1670-1800,* Dublin: Irish Academic Press, 1998, pp. 22-3.

6. [Cornelius Nary], *The New Testament of Our Lord and Saviour Jesus Christ, newly translated out of the Latin Vulgat. By C.N.C.F.P.D.* [s.l.], printed in the year, 1718; there was a corrected reprint in 1719; Nary is identified in the approbations; see also Patrick Fagan, *Dublin's Turbulent Priest: Cornelius Nary (1658-1738),* Dublin: Royal Irish Academy, 1991, pp. 79-99.

7. *The Holy Bible translated from the Latin Vulgat …,* [Dublin], printed in the year 1763-4; see Hugh Pope, *English Versions of the Bible,* rev. ed., St Louis: Herder, 1952, pp. 370-1.

8. R. Bowes, *Practical reflections for every day throughout the year,* [Dublin]: P. Lord and R. Fitzsimons, 1764, p.iv, *grazie,* Fr Fenning; not a re-issue of the 1749-50 *sine loco* edition which evidence suggests was not printed in Ireland.

9. *The New Testament of Jesus Christ … the sixth edition (the second in folio) adorned with cuts,* Liverpool: printed and sold by P. Wogan, 1789, printed in Liverpool, then imported by Wogan and re-issued with an additional engraved title-page and a list of Irish subscribers, see Fenning, 'Dublin Imprints' [note 5] and F. and J. Blom *et al, English Catholic Books, 1701-1800: a bibliography* [with locations], Aldershot: Scolar Press, 1996, no. 1955.

10. *The New Testament … with annotations … the fourth edition, newly revised and corrected …* Dublin: Daniel Graisberry for R. Cross and P. Wogan, 1783; see Pope, *English Versions* [note 7], pp. 372-8 and S. Ó Casaide, 'Bernard MacMahon, Priest and Scientist' in *Journal of the Co. Louth Archaeological Society,* ix, 4 (1940), pp. 267-79.

11. *The Holy Bible translated from the Latin Vulgat …* 5th ed. Dublin: H. Fitzpatrick for R. Cross, 1791, see *approbatio* on final leaf; with a subscription list, the New Testament was also issued separately.

12. F. L. Cross (ed), *Oxford Dictionary of the Christian Church,* third ed. by E. A. Livingstone, Oxford: University Press, 1997, p. 372.

13. Draft letter from Russell to von Brunnow, 24 Aug. 1865, Maynooth College Archives, Russell Papers, MCA 13/44/9.

14. Incunabula STC it00257000; Hain 1542.*

15. Not yet published in the Leonine edition.

16. L. W. B. Brockliss and P. Ferté, 'Prosopography of Irish clerics in the Universities of Paris and Toulouse, 1573-1792' in *Archivium Hibernicum,* lviii (2004), pp. 7-166, at p. 134, no. 1165.

17. N. A. O'Kenny, *The Gallway Catechism or Christ. Doctrin. Newly collected and augmented for the use of the three Kingdoms,* Paris: Langlois, 1725, p. 151 (microfilm in the National Library).

18. N. A. O'Kenny, *Sommaire de l'Isle des Saints, ou l'Almanach d'Irlande,* Paris: Gonichon, 1739, p. 87 *et seq.*

19. N. A. O'Kenny, *The Ordinary of the Holy Mass, or manual of choice*

prayers and other Christian devotions, newly corrected and amended, Paris: La Veuve de Hansy, 1725 (copy in the Bibliothèque Nationale).

20. Approbations for each were written by F. M. Williams and Michael Burke, Andrew O'Halloran, Theatine, Michael Flannery of Clonfert [MA, Paris, 1708], 'priest rector of Lauan', James Merrick of the Collège des Lombards and F. Lepy, a Doctor of the Sorbonne and Director of the *Maison des Nouveaux Convertis*.

21. *Missae Propriae sanctorum patronorum ac titularium Franciae et Hyberniae …*, Paris: G.C. Berton, 1734 (copy in the Bibliothèque Nationale).

22. O'Kenny, *Officia Missarum … Regni Hyberniae,* appendix, p. 7; P.C. Power, *Waterford and Lismore: A Compendious History of the United Dioceses,* Cork: University P., 1937, pp. 28-30; *Breviarum Metropolitanae,* Senonensis: A. Jannot, 1726; *Missale Senonense*, Senonis: C. A. Prussurot et A. Janot, 1715.

23. Printed Paris: Berton, 1735, also unseen; the unseen volumes are all in the Bibliothèque Nationale, and are currently receiving treatment for water damage.

24. P. Fagan, *An Irish Bishop in Penal Times: The Chequered Career of Sylvester Lloyd OFM, 1680-1747,* Dublin: Four Courts Press, 1993, p. 17.

25. Lloyd refers to Hall's translation in his address to the reader (p. iii) in his 1722 edition of Part One of Pouget: *General instructions by way of catechism … translated from the original French, and carefully compar'd with the Spanish approv'd translation. First Part. By S[ylvester] Ll[oyd]*, London: printed in the year, 1722; J.Gillow, *A Bibliographical History of the English Catholics,* London: Burns and Oates, 1885-95, 5 vols, ascribes to Thomas Hall, a manuscript translation of the Grenoble catechism, in 3 vols, 8vo.

26. From the title-page of the 1702 edition; these abridged catechisms were intended for teaching children who had been confirmed.

27. See n. 25.

28. Fagan, *An Irish Bishop,* pp 20-32 examines aspects of Lloyd's translation in some detail.

29. [Henry Turberville], *An abridgment of Christian Doctrine, with proofs of Scripture for points controverted. Catechistically explained by way of question and answer,* Doway: [s.n.], 1648.

30. Nicholas O'Kenny,*The Gallway catechism or Christ. Doctrin. Newly collected and augmented for the use of the three Kingdoms,* Paris: M. Langlois, 1725, see pp. 7-11.

31. [James Gallagher], *Sixteen Irish sermons in an easy and familiar stile, on useful and necessary subjects. In English characters; as being the more familiar to the generality of our Irish clergy. By J.G.D.D.,* Dublin: Henry Babe, 1736.

32. *The Primer … in Latin and English,* Antwerp: by Arthur Conings, 1599; for background, see J. M. Blom, *The Post-Tridentine English Primer,* [London]: Catholic Record Society,1982.

33. *The Primer more ample and in a new order containing the three Offices of the B. Virgin Mary in Latin and English, and al offices and devotions which*

were in former primers, Rouen : printed by David Maurry, 1669; note on additional saints at the end of the calendar; Sir James Ware, *The history of the writers of Ireland … continued down … by Walter Harris,* Dublin: Robert Bell; and John Fleming, 1764, p. 294 claims this was not the first edition; there was a later edition, c. 1729 described by Pádraig Ó Súilleabháin, 'Thomas Fitzsimons and the Primer of the Blessed Virgin Mary' in *Breifne*, iv, no. 13, pp. 92-3.

34. Fitzsimons of Kilmore had long links with Louvain and was in Ireland from 1663 onwards; in 1666 he was made Vicar-General of Kilmore and was *de facto* running the diocese, see Francis J. MacKiernan, 'Thomas Fitzsimons (1614-80)' in *Breifne*, ix, no. 37 (2001), pp. 313-35; on Fitzsimons of Drogheda, see Patrick Boyle, 'Irishmen in the University of Paris in the Seventeenth and Eighteenth Centuries' in *Irish Ecclesiastical Record*, xiv (1903), pp. 24-45, at p. 40.

35. *The Primer … with a new and approv'd version of the church hymns. To which are added the remaining hymns of the Roman Breviary,* Dublin: sold by Richd Fitzsimons, 1767; for locations of 18th century works, see Fenning, 'Dublin Imprints' [note 5] and F. Blom [*et al*], *English Catholic Books*, 1701-1800, Aldershot: Scholar Press, 1996.

36. Blom, *English Primer*, p. 72.

37. *The Primer, or Office of the Blessed Virgin Mary,* Cork: printed by James Haly, 1789.

38. *The Primer, or Office of the Blessed Virgin Mary,* Dublin: printed by R. Cross, 1799.

39. *The Primer, or Office of the B. Virgin Mary … with many useful additions and amendments,* Dublin: publish'd by Richard Cross, [1803]; see S. Ó Casaide, 'Bernard MacMahon' [footnote 10], pp. 267-79.

40. J. P. Rushe, *Carmel in Ireland,* Dublin: Sealy, Bryers and Walker, 1903, pp. 160-9.

41. *Wilson's Dublin Directory*, Dublin, 1810.

42. C. J. Woods,'The Personnel of the Catholic Convention, 1792-3' in *Archivium Hibernicum*, lvii (2003), pp. 26-76.

43. H. Young, *The Catholic Directory,* Dublin: printed and published by John Coyne, [c.1821]; Coyne describes himself as 'printer and bookseller to the General Confraternity of the Christian Doctrine'.

44. Vol. 1 (1739), p. 1.

45. A life of Picart and a catalogue of his work compiled by his widow were included in *B. Picart, Impostures innocentes, ou receuils d'estampes gravées dans le goût de différens maîtres célèbres … avec l'éloge de B. Picart, et le catalogue de ses ouvrages,* Amsterdam, 1734.; see also E. Bénézit, *Dictionnaire critique et documentaire des peintres, sculpteurs, dessinateurs et graveurs,* Nouvelle éd., Paris: Gründ, 1976, 10 vols, vol. 8; J. Turner (ed.), *The Dictionary of Art*, New York: Grove, 1996, 34 vols, vol. 24.

46. A. and A. de Backer, *Bibliothèque de la Compagnie de Jésus,* ed. Carlos Sommervogel, Louvain: Éditions de la Bibliothèque S.J., 1960, 12 vols, vol. 8, cols 542-6; *Dictionnaire de Théologie Catholique*, Paris: Letouzey,

1903-50, 15 vols, vol. 15 pt 2, col. 2613; quotes Roskovany, *B. V. Maria*, Budapest, 1873, p. 478: 'Opus eximium limata eruditione et mira erga mysterium pietate compositum'; H. Du Manoir, *Maria: études sur la Sainte Vierge*, Paris, 1949-64, 7 vols.

47. *De augustissimo eucharistiae mysterio sive de Maria forma Dei*, Vallisoletii, 1658; *De Maria advocata nostra adnotationes, et exempla*, Matriti, 1668 (copy at Maynooth).

Select Bibliography

The text of the Encyclical is available on the Vatican Website in English, French, German, Italian, Latin, Polish, Portuguese and Spanish: http://www.vatican.va/holy father/john paul ii/encyclicals. The document can be searched, and word frequency lists, concordances comprising every occurrence of a particular word used in the text, and statistics can be accessed.

John Paul II, *Ecclesia de Eucharistia. Encyclical Letter on the Eucharist and the Church,* London: Catholic Truth Society, 2003.

STUDIES

The Encyclical was published on 17 April, 2003. A series of commentaries was published in *L'Osservatore Romano* beginning in the English weekly edition n. 29, 16 July 2003, by writers including Cardinal José Saraiva Martins CMF, Albert Vanhoye SJ, Cardinal Avery Dulles SJ, Nello Cipriani OSA, Nicola Bux, Antonio Miralles, James J. Conn SJ, Cyril Vasil SJ, and Enrico dal Covolo SDB.

Ferraro, G., '"Ecclesia de Eucharistia": Aspetti della Lettera Enciclica di Giovanni Paulo,' *Ephemerides Liturgicae* 117 (2003), pp. 287-307.

Girando, C., SJ, 'Lo "stupore eucharistico": Spunti di riflessione a partire dall'enciclica "Ecclesia de Eucharistia",' *La Civiltà Cattolica* 155 (2004), pp. 142-155.

Pesch, O. H., 'Die Enzyklika "Ecclesia de Eucharistia": Gesichtspunkte zur Lektüre und Beurteilung,' *Stimmen der Zeit* 221:8 (2003), pp. 507-522.

Rigal, J., 'Une première approche de l'enclyique de Jean Paul II "L'Église vit de l'Eucharistie",' *Nouvelle Revue Theologique* 124 (2003), pp.287-307.

Schlabach, G., 'Eucharistic Theology for the Bridge,' *One in Christ* 39:2 (2004), pp.3-16.

THEOLOGY OF THE EUCHARIST

Catholic Bishops' Conferences of England & Wales, Ireland, Scotland, *One Bread One Body*. A Teaching Document on the Eucharist in the Life of the Church, and the Establishment of General Norms on Sacramental Sharing, London: CTS, Dublin: Veritas, 1998.

Guernsey, D. (ed.), *Adoration: Eucharistic Prayers throughout Church History*, San Francisco: Ignatius Press, 1999.

Kereszty, R. A. (ed.), *Rediscovering the Eucharist: Ecumenical Conversations*, New York: Paulist Press, 2003.

Kodell, J., *The Eucharist in the New Testament*, Collegeville, MN: The Liturgical Press, 1991.

LaVerdiere, E., *The Eucharist in the New Testament and the Early Church*, Collegeville, MN: The Liturgical Press, 1996.

McPartlan, P., *Sacrament of Salvation: An Introduction to Eucharistic Ecclesiology*, Edinburgh: T&T Clark, 1995.

Moloney, R., *The Eucharist*, London: Geoffrey Chapman, 1995.
— *Our Splendid Eucharist*, Dublin: Veritas, 2003.

Nash, T. J., *Worthy is the Lamb: The Biblical Roots of the Mass*, San Francisco: Ignatius Press, 2004.

Nichols, A., *The Holy Eucharist: From the New Testament to Pope John Paul II*, Dublin: Veritas, 1991.

O'Connor, J. T., *The Hidden Manna: A Theology of the Eucharist*, San Francisco: Ignatius Press, 1997.

Randolph, F., *Know Him in the Breaking of Bread: A Guide to the Mass*, San Francisco: Ignatius Press, 1998.

Ratzinger, J., *Called to Communion*, San Francisco: Ignatius Press, 1996.
— *The Spirit of the Liturgy*, San Francisco: Ignatius Press, 2000.
— *God is Near Us: The Eucharist, the Heart of Life*, San Francisco: Ignatius Press, 2003.

Vonier, A., *A Key to the Doctrine of the Eucharist*, San Francisco: Ignatius Press, 2004.

Wolf, M., *After Our Likeness: Church as the Image of the Trinity*, Grand Rapids: W.B. Eerdsmans, 1998.

PASTORAL

McKevitt, B., *The Eucharist: A Pocket Catechism,* Dublin: Alive Publications, 2004.

McPartlan, P., *Eucharist: The Body of Christ*, London: CTS, 2004.

Index of Scriptural References

Index of Names and Places

1. 'At the breaking of the Host'
Woodcuts from *Daily devotions or, the most
profitable manner of hearing Mass* (Dublin, 1777)
Russell Library, St Patrick's College, Maynooth

2. 'When the Priest puts part of the Host
into the Chalice'
Woodcuts from *Daily devotions or, the most profitable
manner of hearing Mass* (Dublin, 1777)
Russell Library, St Patrick's College, Maynooth

3. 'At the Agnus Dei'
Woodcuts from *Daily devotions or, the most profitable
manner of hearing Mass* (Dublin, 1777)
Russell Library, St Patrick's College, Maynooth

4. 'At the Communion'
Woodcuts from *Daily devotions or, the most profitable manner of hearing Mass* (Dublin, 1777)
Russell Library, St Patrick's College, Maynooth

Publications
of the Irish Centre for Faith and Culture (1999-200)

Eoin G. Cassidy, *A Faith Response to the Street Drug Culture. A Report Commissioned by the Irish Catholic Bishops' Drugs Initiative.* (Irish Centre for Faith and Culture), September 2000, 24pp.

Eoin G. Cassidy, ed., *Prosperity with a Purpose: What Purpose?*. Papers from the conference 'Economics, Values and the Common Good' organised by the Irish Centre for Faith and Culture, Veritas, Dublin, 2000, 140pp.
(This collective work, which includes lectures by Bishop Donal Murray and An Taoiseach, Bertie Ahern TD, was conceived as a series of reflections on *Prosperity with a Purpose. Christian Faith and Values in a Time of Rapid Economic Growth*. Pubished by the Irish Catholic Bishops' Conference, Veritas, Dublin, 1999).

Eoin G. Cassidy, Donal McKeown, John Morrow, eds., *Belfast: Faith in the City*, Veritas, Dublin, 2001, 151pp.

Eoin G Cassidy, ed., *Measuring Ireland: Discerning Values and Beliefs. Papers from the Symposium 'Measuring Society: Discerning Values and Beliefs—Religion, Culture and the Social Sciences', Organised by the Irish Centre for Faith and Culture,* Veritas, Dublin, 2002, 239pp.

James McEvoy, ed., *The Challenge of Truth. Reflections on Fides et Ratio*. Preface by Cardinal Cahal Daly, Veritas, Dublin, 2003, 272pp.